D0866681

MODERN DEMOCRACIES

THE MACMILLAN COMPANY
NEW YORK · BOSTON · CHICAGO · DALLAS
ATLANTA · SAN FRANCISCO

MACMILLAN & CO., Limited
LONDON · BOMBAY · CALCUTTA
MELBOURNE

THE MACMILLAN CO. OF CANADA, Ltd.
TORONTO

MODERN DEMOCRACIES

BY

JAMES BRYCE

(VISCOUNT BRYCE)

AUTHOR OF

"THE HOLY ROMAN EMPIRE," "THE AMERICAN COMMONWEALTH," ETC.

IN TWO VOLUMES

VOL. I

New York

THE MACMILLAN COMPANY

1924

PREFACE

MANY years ago, at a time when schemes of political reform were being copiously discussed in England, mostly on general principles, but also with references, usually vague and disconnected, to history and to events happening in other countries, it occurred to me that something might be done to provide a solid basis for argument and judgment by examining a certain number of popular governments in their actual working, comparing them with one another, and setting forth the various merits and defects which belonged to each. As I could not find that any such comparative study had been undertaken, I formed the idea of attempting it, and besides visiting Switzerland and other parts of Europe, betook myself to the United States and Canada, to Spanish America and Australia and New Zealand, in search of materials, completing these journeys shortly before the War of 1914 broke out. The undertaking proved longer and more toilsome than had been expected; and frequent interruptions due to the War have delayed the publication of the book until now, when in some countries conditions are no longer what they were when I studied them eight or ten years ago. This fact, however, though it needs to be mentioned, makes less difference than might be supposed, because the conditions that have existed in those countries, and especially in France, the United States, and Australia, from 1914 to 1920 have been so far abnormal that conclusions could not well be drawn from them, and it seems safer to go back to the earlier and more typical days. Neither is it necessary for the purpose here in view to bring the record of events in each country up to date; for it is not current politics but democracy as a form of government that I seek to describe. Events that happened ten years ago may be for this particular purpose just as instructive as if they were happening to-day.

The term Democracy has in recent years been loosely used to denote sometimes a state of society, sometimes a state of mind, sometimes a quality in manners. It has become encrusted with all sorts of associations attractive or repulsive, ethical or poetical, or even religious. But Democracy really means nothing more nor less than the rule of the whole people expressing their sovereign will by their votes. It shows different features in different countries, because the characters and habits of peoples are different; and these features are part of the history of each particular country. But it also shows some features which are everywhere similar, because due to the fact that supreme power rests with the voting multitude. It is of the Form of Government as a Form of Government — that is to say, of the features which democracies have in common — that this book treats, describing the phenomena as they appear in their daily working to an observer who is living in the midst of them and watching them, as one standing in a great factory sees the play and hears the clang of the machinery all around him. The actual facts are what I wish to describe, and it seems as if nothing could be simpler, for they are all around us. But the facts are obscured to most people by the half-assimilated ideas and sonorous or seductive phrases that fill the air; and few realize exactly what are the realities beneath the phrases. To those persons who, as politicians, or journalists, or otherwise, have been " inside politics," the realities of their own country are familiar, and this familiarity enables such experts to get a fair impression of the facts in other countries. But as regards large parts of every public that may be said which the cynical old statesman in Disraeli's novel *Contarini Fleming* said to his ardent son who wished to get away from words to ideas, " Few ideas are correct ones, and what are correct no one can ascertain; but with Words we govern men."

The book is not meant to propound theories. Novelties are not possible in a subject the literature of which began with Plato and Aristotle and has been enriched by thousands of pens since their day. What I desire is, not to impress upon my readers views of my own, but to supply them with facts, and (so far as I can) with explanations of facts on which they can reflect and from which they can draw their own conclusions.

I am not sufficiently enamoured of my own opinions to

seek to propagate them, and have sought to repress the pessimism of experience, for it is not really helpful by way of warning to the younger generation, whatever relief its expression may give to the reminiscent mind. The saddest memories of political life are of moments at which one had to stand by when golden opportunities were being lost, to see the wrong thing done when it would have been easy to do the right thing. But this observation was made by a Persian to a Greek at a dinner-party, the night before the battle of Plataea twenty-four centuries ago, and the world has nevertheless made some advances since then.

Though I have written the book chiefly from personal observations made in the countries visited, there are of course many treatises to which I should gladly have referred, were it not that the number to be cited would be so large as to perplex rather than help the reader who is not a specialist, while the specialist would not need them. My greatest difficulty has been that of compression. In order to keep the book within reasonable limits I have had to turn reluctantly away from many seductive by-paths, from history, from forms of political theory,— such as those of the conception of the State and the nature of Sovereignty,— from constitutional and legal questions, and above all from economic topics and those schemes of social reconstruction which have been coming to the front in nearly every country — matters which now excite the keenest interest and are the battleground of current politics. Though frequently compelled to mention such schemes I have abstained from any expressions of opinion, not merely for the sake of avoiding controversy, but because it seems to me, after a long life spent in study — and study means unlearning as well as learning — to be a student's first duty to retain an open mind upon subjects he has not found time to probe to the bottom. Even when one thinks a view unsound or a scheme unworkable, one must regard all honest efforts to improve this unsatisfactory world with a sympathy which recognizes how many things need to be changed, and how many doctrines once held irrefragable need to be modified in the light of supervenient facts. What we want to-day is a better comprehension by each side in economic controversies of the attitude and arguments of the other. Reconcilements are not always possible, but comprehension and appreciation should be possible.

The absorption of men's minds with ideas and schemes of social reconstruction has diverted attention from those problems of free government which occupied men's minds when the flood-tide of democracy was rising seventy or eighty years ago; and it has sometimes seemed to me in writing this book that it was being addressed rather to the last than to the present generation. That generation busied itself with institutions; this generation is bent rather upon the purposes which institutions may be made to serve. Nevertheless the study of institutions has not lost its importance. Let us think of the difference it would have made to Europe if the countries engaged in the Great War had in 1914 been all of them, as some of them were, oligarchies or autocracies; or if all of them had been, as some were, democracies. Or let us think of what may be the results within the next thirty years of setting up democracies in countries that have heretofore formed part of the Russian and Austro-Hungarian Monarchies; or (to take a still more startling case) of trying the experiment of popular government in India, in China, in Russia, in Egypt, in Persia, in the Philippine Islands. If any of the bold plans of social reconstruction now in the air are attempted in practice they will apply new tests to democratic principles and inevitably modify their working. There is still plenty of room for observation, plenty of facts to be observed and of thinking to be done. The materials are always growing. Every generalization now made is only provisional, and will have to be some day qualified: every book that is written will before long be out of date, except as a record of what were deemed to be salient phenomena at the time when it was written. Each of us who writes describes the progress mankind was making with its experiments in government as he saw them; each hands on the torch to his successor, and the succession is infinite, for the experiments are never completed.

It is, I hope, needless for me to disclaim any intention to serve any cause or party, for a man must have profited little by his experience of political life if he is not heartily glad to be rid of the reticences which a party system imposes and free to state with equal candour both sides of every

case. This is what I have tried to do; and where it has
been harder to obtain information on a controversial issue
from one side than from the other I have stated that to be so,
and gone no further in recording a conclusion than the
evidence seemed to warrant.

My cordial thanks are due to a few English friends whose
views and criticisms have aided me, and to many friends in
France and Switzerland, the United States and Canada,
Australia and New Zealand, who have been kind enough to
read through the proofs relating to the country to which
each of them respectively belongs and have favoured me with
their comments. The list of these friends is long, and their
names would carry weight; but as their comments were
given in confidence, and I alone am responsible for errors of
view and fact — errors which I cannot hope to have
avoided — I do not name these friends, contenting myself
with this most grateful acknowledgment of help without
which I should not have ventured into so wide a field.

                                        BRYCE.

Christmas Eve,
    1920.

BRYCE.

London,
1920.

CONTENTS

VOL. I

PART I

CONSIDERATIONS APPLICABLE TO DEMOCRATIC GOVERNMENT IN GENERAL

PART II

SOME DEMOCRACIES IN THEIR WORKING

FRANCE

END OF VOL. I

PART I
CONSIDERATIONS APPLICABLE TO DEMOCRATIC GOVERNMENT IN GENERAL

CHAPTER I

A CENTURY ago there was in the Old World only one tiny spot in which the working of democracy could be studied. A few of the ancient rural cantons of Switzerland had recovered their freedom after the fall of Napoleon, and were governing themselves as they had done from the earlier Middle Ages, but they were too small and their conditions too peculiar to furnish instruction to larger communities or throw much light on popular government in general. Nowhere else in Europe did the people rule. Britain enjoyed far wider freedom than any part of the European Continent, but her local as well as central government was still oligarchic. When the American Republic began its national life with the framing and adoption of the Federal Constitution in 1787–89, the only materials which history furnished to its founders were those which the republics of antiquity had provided, so it was to these materials that both those founders and the men of the first French Revolution constantly recurred for examples to be followed or avoided. Nobody since Plutarch had gathered the patterns of republican civic virtue which orators like Vergniaud had to invoke. Nobody since Aristotle had treated of constitutions on the lines Alexander Hamilton desired for his guidance.

With 1789 the world passed into a new phase, but the ten years that followed were for France years of revolution, in which democracy had no chance of approving its quality. It was only in the United States that popular governments could be profitably studied, and when Tocqueville studied them in 1827 they had scarcely begun to show some of their most characteristic features.

Within the hundred years that now lie behind us what changes have passed upon the world! Nearly all the monarchies of the Old World have been turned into democracies. The States of the American Union have grown from thirteen to forty-eight.   While twenty new republics have sprung up in the Western hemisphere, five new democracies have been developed out of colonies within the British dominions. There are now more than one hundred representative assemblies at work all over the earth legislating for self-governing communities; and the proceedings of nearly all of these are recorded in the press.   Thus the materials for a study of free governments have been and are accumulating so fast that the most diligent student cannot keep pace with the course of political evolution in more than a few out of these many countries.

A not less significant change has been the universal acceptance of democracy as the normal and natural form of government.   Seventy years ago, as those who are now old can well remember, the approaching rise of the masses to power was regarded by the educated classes of Europe as a menace to order and prosperity.   Then the word Democracy awakened dislike or fear.   Now it is a word of praise. Popular power is welcomed, extolled, worshipped.   The few whom it repels or alarms rarely avow their sentiments.   Men have almost ceased to study its phenomena because these now seem to have become part of the established order of things. The old question,— What is the best form of government? is almost obsolete because the centre of interest has been shifting.   It is not the nature of democracy, nor even the variety of the shapes it wears, that are to-day in debate, but rather the purposes to which it may be turned, the social and economic changes it may be used to effect; yet its universal acceptance is not a tribute to the smoothness of its working, for discontent is everywhere rife, while in some countries the revolutionary spirit is passing into forms heretofore undreamt of, one of which looms up as a terrifying spectre.   The time seems to have arrived when the actualities of democratic government, in its diverse forms, should be investigated, and when the conditions most favourable to its success should receive more attention than students, as distinguished from politicians, have been bestowing upon them.   Now that the abundant and ever-increasing data facilitate a critical study, it so happens that current events supply new reasons why such a study should be undertaken forthwith.   Some of these reasons deserve mention.

We have just seen four great empires in Europe — as well as a fifth in Asia — all ruled by ancient dynasties, crash to the ground, and we see efforts made to build up out of the ruins new States, each of which is enacting for itself a democratic constitution.

We see backward populations, to which the very conception of political freedom had been unknown, summoned to attempt the tremendous task of creating self-governing institutions. China, India, and Russia contain, taken together, one half or more the population of the globe, so the problem of providing free government for them is the largest problem statesmanship has ever had to solve.

The new functions that are being thrust upon governments in every civilized country, make it more than ever necessary that their machinery should be so constructed as to discharge these functions efficiently and in full accord with the popular wish.

And lastly, we see some of the more advanced peoples, dissatisfied with the forms of government which they have inherited from the past, now bent on experiments for making their own control more direct and effective. Since democracy, though assumed to be the only rightful kind of government, has, in its representative form, failed to fulfil the hopes of sixty years ago, new remedies are sought to cure the defects experience has revealed.

These are among the facts of our time which suggest that a comprehensive survey of popular governments as a whole may now have a value for practical politicians as well as an interest for scientific students. Any such survey must needs be imperfect,— indeed at best provisional — for the data are too vast to be collected, digested, and explained by any one man, or even by a group of men working on the same lines. Yet a sort of voyage of discovery among the materials most easily available, may serve to indicate the chief problems to be solved. It is on such a voyage that I ask the reader to accompany me in this book. Its aim is to present a general view of the phenomena hitherto observed in governments of a popular type, showing what are the principal forms that type has taken, the tendencies each form has developed, the progress achieved in creating institutional machinery, and, above all — for this is the ultimate test of excellence — what democracy has accomplished or failed to accomplish, as compared with other kinds of government, for the well-being of each people. Two methods of handling the subject present themselves. One, that which most of my predecessors in this field have adopted, is to describe in a systematic way the features of democratic government in general, using the facts of particular democracies only by way of illustrating the general principles expounded. This method, scientifically irreproachable, runs the risk of becoming dry or even dull, for the reader remains in the region of bloodless abstractions. The other method, commended by the examples of Montesquieu and Tocqueville, keeps him in closer touch with the actual concrete phenomena of human society, making it easier for him to follow reasonings and appreciate criticisms, because these are more closely associated in memory with the facts that suggest them. These considerations have led me, instead of attempting to present a systematic account of Democracy in its general features and principles, to select for treatment various countries in which democracy exists, describing the institutions of each in their theory and their practice, so as to show under what economic and social conditions each form works, and with what results for good or evil. These conditions so differentiate the working that no single democracy can be called typical. A certain number must be examined in order to determine what features they have in common. Only when this has been done can we distinguish that which in each of them is accidental from what seems essential, characteristic of the nature and normal tendencies of democracy as a particular form of government.

Six countries have been selected for treatment: two old European States, France and Switzerland; two newer States in the Western hemisphere, the American Union and Canada; and two in the Southern hemisphere, Australia and New Zealand. France has been the powerful protagonist of free government on the European Continent and has profoundly affected political thought, not only by her example but by a line of writers from the great names of Montesquieu and Rousseau down to Tocqueville, Taine, Boutmy, and others of our own time. In Switzerland there were seen the earliest beginnings of self-government among simple peasant

folk.   The rural communities of the Alpine cantons, appear-
ing in the thirteenth century like tiny flowers beside the
rills of melting snow, have expanded by many additions into
a Federal republic which is the unique example of a government both conservative and absolutely popular.   Among
the large democracies the United States is the oldest, and
contains many small democracies in its vast body.   Its Federal Constitution, the best constructed of all such instruments and that tested by the longest experience, has been
a pattern which many other republics have imitated.   Canada, Australia, and New Zealand, whose institutions have
been modelled on those of England, are the youngest of the
democracies, and the two latter of these have gone further
and faster than any others in extending the sphere of State
action into new fields.   To the comparatively full account
of these six, I have prefixed a shorter treatment of two
other groups.   The city republics of ancient Greece cannot
be omitted from any general survey.   Their brief but brilliant life furnished the earliest examples of what men can
achieve in the task of managing their affairs by popular assemblies, and the literature which records and criticizes their
efforts is one of the world's most precious possessions, destined to retain its value so long as civilized society exists.
The republics of what is called " Latin America," all of
them Spanish except Portuguese-speaking Brazil and French-
speaking Haiti, must also find a place, for they have a double
interest.   Their earlier history shows the results of planting
free representative institutions in a soil not fitted to receive
the seed of liberty, while the progress which some few of
them have been recently making towards settled order shows
also that with an improvement in economic and intellectual
conditions that seed may spring up and begin to flourish.
    Only one of the great modern democracies has been
omitted.   The United Kingdom, though in form a monarchy,
has a government in some respects more democratic than is
that of France, and the process by which it passed from an
oligarchy to a democracy through four constitutional changes
in 1832, 1868, 1885, and 1918 is full of instruction for the
historian.   But no citizen of Britain, and certainly no citizen who has himself taken a part in politics as a member,
during forty years, of legislatures and cabinets, can expect

to be credited with impartiality, however earnestly he may strive to be impartial. I have therefore been reluctantly obliged to leave this branch of the subject to some one, preferably some American or French scholar, who is not affected by a like disability.

These accounts of governments in the concrete constitute the centre and core of the book, and may, it is hoped, be serviceable to those who are interested in the practical rather than the theoretical aspects of politics. I have prefixed to them some introductory chapters analyzing the ideas or doctrines whereon popular governments rest, tracing the process by which they have grown, and indicating the conditions under which they are now worked; and have also called attention to certain generally operative factors which the reader must keep in sight while studying the features of the several communities examined. Such factors are the influences of education, of religion, of the newspaper press, of tradition, of party spirit and party organization, and of public opinion as a ruling force. These preliminary essays form Part I., and Part II. is occupied by the descriptions of the six actual modern democratic governments already enumerated. These descriptions do not enter into the details either of the constitutional mechanism or of the administrative organization of each country dealt with, but dwell upon those features only of its institutions, as seen in actual working, which belong to and illustrate their democratic character.

To these last-mentioned chapters which describe the working of actual democratic governments, past and present, there are subjoined, in Part III., other chapters classifying and comparing the phenomena which the examination of these governments reveals, and setting forth the main conclusions to which they point.

The book thus consists of three parts. Part I. contains preliminary observations applicable to popular governments in general. Part II. describes certain selected popular governments, giving an outline of their respective institutions and explaining how these institutions work in practice. Part III. summarizes and digests the facts set forth in Part II. and indicates certain conclusions which may be drawn from them as to the merits and defects of democratic institutions in general, the changes through which these institutions have been passing, the new problems that are beginning to emerge, and the possibility of other changes in the future.

Unlike to one another as are many of the phenomena which the governments to be described present, we shall find in them resemblances sufficient to enable us to draw certain inferences true of democratic governments in general. These inferences will help us to estimate the comparative merits of the various forms democracy has taken, and to approve some institutions as more likely than others to promote the common welfare.

There is a sense in which every conclusion reached regarding men in society may seem to be provisional, because though human nature has been always in many points the same, it has shown itself in other respects so variable that we cannot be sure it may not change in some which we have been wont to deem permanent. But since that possibility will be equally true a century hence, it does not dissuade us from doing the best we now can to reach conclusions sufficiently probable to make them applicable to existing problems. New as these problems seem, experience does more than speculation to help towards a solution.

Most of what has been written on democracy has been written with a bias, and much also with a view to some particular country assumed as typical, the facts there observed having been made the basis for conclusions favourable or unfavourable to popular governments in general. This remark does not apply to Aristotle, for he draws his conclusions from studying a large number of concrete instances, and though he passes judgment, he does so with cold detachment. Neither does it apply to Tocqueville who, while confining his study to one country, examines it in the temper of a philosopher and discriminates between phenomena peculiar to America, and those which he finds traceable to democratic sentiment or democratic institutions in general. The example of these illustrious forerunners prescribes to the modern student the method of enquiry he should apply. He must beware of assuming facts observed in the case of one or two or three popular governments to be present in others, must rid himself of all prejudices, must strive where he notes differences to discover their origin, and take no proposi-

tion to be generally true until he has traced it to a source
common to all the cases examined, that source lying in the
tendencies of human nature. But of this, and especially of
the comparative method of study, something will be said in
the chapter next following.

As the tendencies of human nature are the permanent basis
of study which gives to the subject called Political Science
whatever scientific quality it possesses, so the practical value
of that science consists in tracing and determining the relation of these tendencies to the institutions which men have
created for guiding their life in a community. Certain institutions have been found by experience to work better than
others; *i.e.* they give more scope to the wholesome tendencies, and curb the pernicious tendencies. Such institutions
have also a retroactive action upon those who live under
them. Helping men to goodwill, self-restraint, intelligent
co-operation, they form what we call a solid political character, temperate and law-abiding, preferring peaceful to violent means for the settlement of controversies. Where, on
the other hand, institutions have been ill-constructed, or too
frequently changed to exert this educative influence, men
make under them little progress towards a steady and har-
monious common life. To find the type of institutions best
calculated to help the better and repress the pernicious tendencies is the task of the philosophic enquirer, who lays the
foundations upon which the legislator builds. A people
through which good sense and self-control are widely diffused is itself the best philosopher and the best legislator, as
is seen in the history of Rome and in that of England. It
was to the sound judgment and practical quality in these
two peoples that the excellence of their respective constitutions and systems of law was due, not that in either people
wise men were exceptionally numerous, but that both were
able to recognize wisdom when they saw it, and willingly
followed the leaders who possessed it.

Taking politics (so far as it is a science) to be an experimental science, I have sought to make this book a record
of efforts made and results achieved. But it so happens
that at this very moment there are everywhere calls for new
departures in politics, the success or failure of which our

existing data do not enable us to predict, because the necessary experiments have not yet been tried.

The civilized peoples seem to be passing into an unpredicted phase of thought and life. Many voices are raised demanding a fundamental reconstruction of governments which shall enable them to undertake much that has been hitherto left to the action of individuals, while others propose an extinction of private property complete enough to make the community the only owner of lands and goods, and therewith the authority which shall prescribe to each of its members what work he shall do and what recompense he shall receive to satisfy his own needs. Here are issues of supreme and far-reaching importance. " How," it may be asked, " can any one write about democracy without treating of the new purposes which democracy is to be made to serve? Look at Germany and France, England and America. Look at Australia and New Zealand, where democratic institutions are being harnessed to the chariot of socialism in a constitutional way. Above all, look at Russia, shaken by an earthquake which has destroyed all the institutions it found existing." My answer to this question is that the attempts heretofore made in the direction of State Socialism or Communism have been too few and too short-lived to supply materials for forecasting the consequences of such changes as those now proposed. What history tells us of the relation which the permanent tendencies of human nature bear to political institutions, is not sufficient for guidance in this unexplored field of governmental action. We are driven to speculation and conjecture. Now the materials for conjecture will have to be drawn, not from a study of institutions which were framed with a view to other aims, but mainly from a study of human nature itself, *i.e.* from psychology and ethics as well as from economics. Being, however, here concerned with political institutions as they have been and as they now are, I am dispensed from entering the limitless region of ethical and economic speculation. We see long dim vistas stretching in many directions through the forest, but of none can we descry the end. Thus, even were I more competent than I feel myself to be, I should leave to psychologists and economists any examination of the theories and projects that belong to Collectivism or Socialism or Communism.[1]   A treatment of them would swell this book to twice or thrice its size, and would lead me into a sphere of enquiry where controversies burn with a fierce flame.

The ancient world, having tried many experiments in free government, relapsed wearily after their failure into an acceptance of monarchy and turned its mind quite away from political questions.   More than a thousand years elapsed before this long sleep was broken.   The modern world did not occupy itself seriously with the subject nor make any persistent efforts to win an ordered freedom till the sixteenth century.   Before us in the twentieth a vast and tempting field stands open, a field ever widening as new States arise and old States pass into new phases of life.   More workers are wanted in that field.   Regarding the psychology of men in politics, the behaviour of crowds, the forms in which ambition and greed appear, much that was said long ago by historians and moralists is familiar, and need not be now repeated.   But the working of institutions and laws, the forms in which they best secure liberty and order, and enable the people to find the men fit to be trusted with power — these need to be more fully investigated by a study of what has proved in practice to work well or ill.   It is Facts that are needed: Facts, Facts, Facts.   When facts have been supplied, each of us can try to reason from them.   The investigators who are called on to supply them may have their sense of the duty owed to truth quickened by knowing that their work, carefully and honestly done, without fear or favour, will be profitable to all free peoples, and most so to those who are now seeking to enlarge the functions of government.   The heavier are the duties thrown on the State, the greater is the need for providing it with the most efficient machinery through which the people can exercise their control.

[1] The subject is, however, touched upon in a chapter of Part III, for the sake of indicating the effects on political institutions which a system of State Socialism might produce.

CHAPTER II

THE contrast between the rapid progress made during the last two centuries in the study of external nature and the comparatively slow progress made in the determination of the laws or principles discoverable in the phenomena of human society is usually explained by the remark that in the former success was attained by discarding abstract notions and setting to work to observe facts, whereas in the latter men have continued to start from assumptions and run riot in speculations. As respects politics, this explanation, though it has some force, does not cover the whole case. The greatest minds that have occupied themselves with political enquiries have set out from the observation of such facts as were accessible to them, and have drawn from those facts their philosophical conclusions. Even Plato, the first thinker on the subject whose writings have reached us, and one whose power of abstract thinking has never been surpassed, formed his view of democracy from the phenomena of Athenian civic life as he saw them. His disciple Aristotle does the same, in a more precise and less imaginative way. So after him did Cicero, with a genuine interest, but no great creative power; so too did, after a long interval, Machiavelli and Montesquieu and Burke and others down to Tocqueville and Taine and Roscher.

The fundamental difference between the investigation of external nature and that of human affairs lies in the character of the facts to be observed. The phenomena with which the chemist or physicist deals — and this is for most purposes true of biological phenomena also — are, and so far as our imperfect knowledge goes, always have been, now and at all times, everywhere identical. Oxygen and sulphur behave in the same way in Europe and in Australia and in Sirius. But the phenomena of an election are not the same in Bern and in Buenos Aires, though we may call the thing

13

by the same name; nor were they the same in Bern two centuries ago, or in Buenos Aires twenty years ago, as they are now. The substances with which the chemist deals can be weighed and measured, the feelings and acts of men cannot. Experiments can be tried in physics over and over again till a conclusive result is reached, but that which we call an experiment in politics can never be repeated because the conditions can never be exactly reproduced, as Heraclitus says that one cannot step twice into the same river. Prediction in physics may be certain: in politics it can at best be no more than probable. If vagueness and doubt surround nearly every theory or doctrine in the field of politics, that happens not so much because political philosophers have been careless in ascertaining facts, but rather because they were apt to be unduly affected by the particular facts that were under their eyes. However widely and carefully the materials may be gathered, their character makes it impossible that politics should ever become a science in the sense in which mechanics or chemistry or botany is a science. Is there then no way of applying exact methods to the subject, and of reaching some more general and more positive conclusions than have yet secured acceptance? Are the materials to be studied, viz. the acts and thoughts of men, their habits and institutions, incapable of scientific treatment because too various and changeful?

The answer is that there is in the phenomena of human society one " Constant," one element or factor which is practically always the same, and therefore the basis of all the so-called " Social Sciences." This is Human Nature itself. All fairly normal men have like passions and desires. They are stirred by like motives, they think upon similar lines. When they have reached the stage of civilization in which arts and letters have developed, and political institutions have grown up, reason has become so far the guide of conduct that sequences in their action can be established and their behaviour under given conditions can to some extent be foretold. Human nature is that basic and ever-present element in the endless flux of social and political phenomena which enables general principles to be determined. And though the action of individual men may often be doubtful, the action of a hundred or a thousand men all subjected to the same influences at the same time may be much more predictable, because in a large number the idiosyncrasies of individuals are likely to be eliminated or evened out. Politics accordingly has its roots in Psychology, the study (in their actuality) of the mental habits and volitional proclivities of mankind. The knowledge it gives is the knowledge most needed in life, and our life is chiefly spent in acquiring it. But we are here concerned only with the political side of man, and have to. enquire how to study that particular department of his individual and collective life.

Two other differences between the Natural and the Human Sciences need only a word or two. The terms used in the latter lack the precision which belongs to those used in the former. They are not truly technical, for they do not always mean the same thing to all who use them. Such words as " aristocracy," " prerogative," " liberty," " oligarchy," " faction," " caucus," even " constitution " convey different meanings to different persons. The terms used in politics have, moreover, contracted associations, attractive or repellent, as the case may be, to different persons. They evoke feeling. An investigator occupied in the interpretation of history is exposed to emotional influences such as do not affect the enquirer in a laboratory. Nobody has either love or hatred for the hydrocarbons; nobody who. strikes. a rock with his hammer to ascertain whether it contains a particular fossil has anything but knowledge to gain by the discovery. The only chemical elements that have ever attracted love or inspired enthusiasm are gold and silver; nor is it chemists whom such enthusiasm has affected.

Human affairs, however, touch and move us in many ways, through our interest, through our associations of education, of political party, of religious belief, of philosophical doctrine. *Nihil humani nobis alienum.* We are so influenced, consciously or unconsciously, in our reading and thinking, by our likes and dislikes, that we look for the facts we desire to find and neglect or minimize those which are unwelcome. The facts are so abundant that it is always possible to find the former, and so obscure that it is no less easy to undervalue the latter.

If vigorous minds who have addressed themselves to the study of governments have, although they used the facts they saw, often differed in their conclusions and failed in their forecasts, this is because few subjects of study have suffered so much from prejudice, partisanship, and the habit of hasty inference from a few data. Even large-visioned and thoughtful men have not escaped one particular kind of prepossession. Such men are naturally the keenest in noting and condemning the faults of whatever system of government they happen to live under. Nearly every political philosopher has like Hobbes, Locke, and Burke written under the influence of the events of his own time. Philosophers who are also reformers are led by their ardour to overestimate the beneficial effects of a change, because they forget that the faults they denounce, being rooted in human weakness, may emerge afresh in other forms. Struck by the evils they see, they neglect those from which they have not suffered. One must always discount the sanguine radicalism of a thinker, who, like Mazzini, lived beneath the shadow of a despotism, and the conservatism, or austerity, of one who lived, like Plato, amidst the hustle and din of a democracy.

Human nature being accordingly a factor sufficiently constant to enable certain laws of its working to be ascertained, though with no such precision and no such power of prediction as is possible in the physical sciences, how is it to be studied?

The best way to get a genuine and exact first-hand knowledge of the data is to mix in practical politics. In such a country as France or the United States a capable man can, in a dozen years, acquire a comprehension of the realities of popular government ampler and more delicate than any which books supply. He learns the habits and propensities of the average citizen as a sailor learns the winds and currents of the ocean he has to navigate, what pleases or repels the voter, his illusions and his prejudices, the sort of personality that is fascinating, the sort of offence that is not forgiven, how confidence is won or lost, the kind of argument that tells on the better or the meaner spirits. Such a man forms, perhaps without knowing it, a body of maxims or rules by which he sails his craft, and steers, if he be a leader, the vessel of his party. Still ampler are the opportunities which the member of an Assembly has for studying his colleagues. This is the best kind of knowledge; though some

of it is profitable only for the particular country in which
it has been acquired, and might be misleading in another
country with a different national character and a different
set of ideas and catchwords. Many maxims fit for Paris
might be unfit for Philadelphia, but some might not. It is
the best kind because it is first-hand, but as its possessor seldom commits it to paper, and may indeed not be qualified
to do so, the historian or philosopher must go for his materials to such records as debates, pamphlets, the files of newspapers and magazines, doing his best to feel through words
the form and pressure of the facts. When he extends his
enquiry to other countries than his own, the abundance of
materials becomes bewildering, because few books have been
written which bring together the most important facts so as
to provide that information regarding the conditions of those
countries which he needs in order to use the materials aright.

These data, however, do not carry us the whole way
towards a comprehension of democratic government in general. The student must try to put life and blood into historical records by what he has learnt of political human nature in watching the movements of his own time. He must
think of the Past with the same keenness of interest as if it
were the Present, and of the Present with the same coolness
of reflection as if it were the Past. The English and the
Americans of the eighteenth century were different from the
men of to-day, so free government was a different thing in
their hands. There are, moreover, differences in place as
well as in time. Political habits and tendencies are not the
same thing in England as in France or in Switzerland, or
even in Australia. The field of observation must be enlarged to take in the phenomena of all the countries where
the people rule. The fundamentals of human nature, present everywhere, are in each country modified by the influences of race, of external conditions, such as climate and
the occupations that arise from the physical resources of the
country. Next come the historical antecedents which have
given, or withheld, experience in self-government, have
formed traditions of independence or submission, have created institutions which themselves in turn have moulded the
minds and shaped the ideals of the nations.

This mode of investigation is known as the Comparative

Method.   That which entitles it to be called scientific is that it reaches general conclusions by tracing similar results to similar causes, eliminating those disturbing influences which, present in one country and absent in another, make the results in the examined cases different in some points while similar in others.   When by this method of comparison the differences between the working of democratic government in one country and another have been noted, the local or special conditions, physical or racial or economic, will be examined so as to determine whether it is in them that the source of these differences is to be found.   If not in them, then we must turn to the institutions, and try to discover which of those that exist in popular governments have worked best.   All are so far similar in that they are meant to enable the people to rule, but some seek this end in one way, some in another, each having its merits, each its defects.   When allowance has been made for the different conditions under which each acts, it will be possible to pronounce, upon the balance of considerations, which form offers the best prospect of success.   After the differences between one popular government and another have been accounted for, the points of similarity which remain will be what one may call democratic human nature, viz. the normal or permanent habits and tendencies of citizens in a democracy and of a democratic community as a whole.   This is what we set out to discover.   The enquiry, if properly conducted, will have taught us what are the various aberrations from the ideally best to which popular government is by its very nature liable.

It is this method that I have sought to apply in investigating the phenomena each particular government shows, so as to indicate wherein they differ from or agree with those found in other governments.   Where the phenomena point to one and the same conclusion, we are on firm ground, and can claim to have discovered a principle fit to be applied. Firm ground is to be found in those permanent tendencies of mankind which we learn from history, i.e. from the record of observations made during many centuries in many peoples, living in diverse environments, physical and historical.   The tendencies themselves take slightly diverse forms in different races or peoples, and the strength of each relatively to the others varies. These diversities must be noted and allowed for; but enough identity remains to enable definite conclusions of general validity to be attained.

So expressed and considered in their application to practice, these conclusions have a real value, not only to the student but also to the statesman. Many an error might have been avoided had a body of sound maxims been present to the minds of constitution makers and statesmen; not that such maxims could be used as necessarily fit for the particular case, but that he who had them before him would be led to weigh considerations and beware of dangers which might otherwise have escaped him. Some one has said, There is nothing so useless as a general maxim. That is so only if you do not know how to use it. He who would use it well must always think of the instances on which it rests and of the instruction these may be made to yield. Its use is to call attention. It is not a prescription but a signpost, or perhaps a danger signal.

The conclusions obtained by these methods of investigation are less capable of direct application to practice than are those of the exact sciences. However true as general propositions, they are subject to many qualifications when applied to any given case, and must be expressed in guarded terms. The reader who may be disposed to complain of the qualified and tentative terms in which I shall be obliged to express the results which a study of the phenomena has suggested will, I hope, pardon me when he remembers that although it is well to be definite and positive in statement, it is still better to be accurate. I cannot hope to have always attained accuracy, but it is accuracy above everything else that I have aimed at.

CHAPTER III

THE DEFINITION OF DEMOCRACY

THE word Democracy has been used ever since the time of Herodotus [1] to denote that form of government in which the ruling power of a State is legally vested, not in any particular class or classes, but in the members of the community as a whole. This means, in communities which act by voting, that rule belongs to the majority, as no other method has been found for determining peaceably and legally what is to be deemed the will of a community which is not unanimous. Usage has made this the accepted sense of the term, and usage is the safest guide in the employment of words.

Democracy, as the rule of the Many, was by the Greeks opposed to Monarchy, which is the rule of One, and to Oligarchy, which is the rule of the Few, *i.e.* of a class privileged either by birth or by property. Thus it came to be taken as denoting in practice that form of government in which the poorer class, always the more numerous, did in fact rule; and the term *Demos* was often used to describe not the whole people but that particular class as distinguished from the wealthier and much smaller class. Moderns sometimes also use it thus to describe what we call " the masses " in contradistinction to " the classes." But it is better to employ the word as meaning neither more nor less than the Rule of the Majority, the " classes and masses " of the whole people being taken together.

So far there is little disagreement as to the sense of the word. But when we come to apply this, or indeed any broad and simple definition, to concrete cases, many questions arise. What is meant by the term " political community " ? Does it include all the inhabitants of a given area or those only who possess full civic rights, the so-called " qualified citizens "? Can a community such as South Carolina, or the Transvaal, in which the majority of the inhabitants, because not of the white race, are excluded from the electoral suffrage, be deemed a democracy in respect of its vesting political power in the majority of qualified citizens, the " qualified " being all or nearly all white? Is the name to be applied equally to Portugal and Belgium, in which women do not vote, and to Norway and Germany, in which they do? Could anybody deny it to France merely because she does not grant the suffrage to women? Or if the electoral suffrage, instead of being possessed by all the adult, or adult male, citizens, is restricted to those who can read and write, or to those who possess some amount of property, or pay some direct tax, however small, does that community thereby cease to be a democracy?

So again, what difference is made by such limitations on the power of the majority as a Constitution may impose? There are communities in which, though universal suffrage prevails, the power of the voters is fettered in its action by the rights reserved to a king or to a non-elective Upper House. Such was the German Empire, such was the Austrian Monarchy, such are some of the monarchies that still remain in Europe. Even in Britain and in Canada, a certain, though now very slender, measure of authority has been left to Second Chambers. In all the last mentioned cases must we not consider not only who possess the right of voting, but how far that right carries with it a full control of the machinery of government? Was Germany, for instance, a democracy in 1913 because the Reichstag was elected by manhood suffrage?

Another class of cases presents another difficulty. There are countries in which the Constitution has a popular quality in respect of its form, but in which the mass of the people do not in fact exercise the powers they possess on paper. This may be because they are too ignorant or too indifferent to vote, or because actual supremacy belongs to the man or group in control of the government through a control of the army. Such are most of the so-called republics of Central and South America. Such have been, at particular moments, some of the new kingdoms of South-Eastern Europe, where the bulk of the population has not yet learnt how to exercise the political rights which the Constitution gives. Bulgaria and Greece were nominally democratic in 1915, but the king of the former carried the people into the Great War, as the ally of Germany, against their wish, and the king of the latter would have succeeded in doing the same thing but for the fact that the Allied fleets had Athens under their guns.

All these things make a difference to the truly popular character of a government. It is the facts that matter, not the name. People used to confound — some persons in some countries still confound — a Republic with a Democracy, and suppose that a government in which one person is the titular and permanent head of the State cannot be a government by the people. It ought not to be necessary nowadays to point out that there are plenty of republics which are not democracies, and some monarchies, like those of Britain and Norway, which are. I might multiply instances, but it is not worth while. Why spend time on what is a question of words? No one has propounded a formula which will cover every case, because there are governments which are " on the line," too popular to be called oligarchies, and scarcely popular enough to be called democracies. But though we cannot define either Oligarchy or Democracy, we can usually know either the one or the other when we see it. Where the will of the whole people prevails in all important matters, even if it has some retarding influences to overcome, or is legally required to act for some purposes in some specially provided manner, that may be called a Democracy. In this book I use the word in its old and strict sense, as denoting a government in which the will of the majority of qualified citizens rules, taking the qualified citizens to constitute the great bulk of the inhabitants, say, roughly, at least three-fourths, so that the physical force of the citizens coincides (broadly speaking) with their voting power. Using this test, we may apply the name to the United Kingdom and the British self-governing Dominions,[1] to France, Italy, Portugal, Belgium, Holland, Denmark, Sweden, Norway, Greece, the United States, Argentina, and possibly Chile and Uruguay. Of some of the newer European States it is too

[1] Subject, as respects the Union of South Africa and its component States, to the remark made above regarding persons of colour.

soon to speak, and whatever we may call the republics of Central America and the Caribbean Sea, they are not democracies.

Although the words " democracy " and " democratic " denote nothing more than a particular form of government, they have, particularly in the United States, Canada, and Australia, acquired attractive associations of a social and indeed almost of a moral character. The adjective is used to describe a person of a simple and friendly spirit and genial manners, " a good mixer," one who, whatever his wealth or status, makes no assumption of superiority, and carefully keeps himself on the level of his poorer or less eminent neighbours. I have heard a monarch described as " a democratic king." [1] Democracy is supposed to be the product and the guardian both of Equality and of Liberty, being so consecrated by its relationship to both these precious possessions as to be almost above criticism. Historically no doubt the three have been intimately connected, yet they are separable in theory and have sometimes been separated in practice, as will appear from the two following chapters.

[1] I have read American writers who hold that the ownership of " public utilities " is what makes a community democratic.

CHAPTER IV

THE HISTORICAL EVOLUTION OF DEMOCRACY

THE facts and forces that have created Popular Government are partly of the Practical and partly of the Theoretic order. These two forces have frequently worked together; but whereas the action of the former has been almost continuous, it is only at a few epochs that abstract doctrines have exerted power. It is convenient to consider each order apart, so I propose in this chapter to pass in rapid survey the salient features of the historical process by which governments of the popular type have grown up. Some light may thus be thrown on the question whether the trend towards democracy, now widely visible, is a natural trend, due to a general law of social progress. If that is so, or in other words, if causes similar to these which have in many countries substituted the rule of the Many for the rule of the One or the Few are, because natural, likely to remain operative in the future, democracy may be expected to live on where it now exists and to spread to other countries also. If on the other hand these causes, or some of them, are local or transient, such an anticipation will be less warranted. This enquiry will lead us to note in each case whether the change which transferred power from the Few to the Many sprang from a desire to be rid of grievances attributed to misgovernment or was created by a theoretical belief that government belonged of right to the citizens as a whole. In the former alternative the popular interest might flag when the grievances had been removed, in the latter only when the results of democratic government had been disappointing.

When the curtain rises on that Eastern world in which civilization first appeared, kingship is found existing in all considerable states, and chieftainship in tribes not yet developed into states. This condition lasted on everywhere in Asia with no legal limitations on the monarch until Japan

framed her present Constitution in 1890. Selfish or sluggish rulers were accepted as part of the order of nature, and
when, now and then, under a strong despot like Saladin or
Akbar, there was better justice, or under a prudent despot
less risk of foreign invasion, these brighter intervals were
remembered as the peasant remembers an exceptionally good
harvest. The monarch was more or less restrained by custom and by the fear of provoking general discontent. Insurrections due to some special act of tyranny or some outrage
on religious feeling occasionally overthrow a sovereign or
even a dynasty, but no one thought of changing the form of
government, for in nothing is mankind less inventive and
more the slave of custom than in matters of social structure.
Large movements towards change were, moreover, difficult,
because each local community had little to do with others,
and those who were intellectually qualified to lead had seldom any other claim to leadership.

In early Europe there were no great monarchies like those
of Assyria or Egypt or Persia. Men were mostly organized
in tribes or clans, under chiefs, one of whom was pre-emi-
nent, and sometimes a large group of tribes formed a nation
under a king of ancient lineage (perhaps, like the Swedish
Ynglings, of supposed divine origin) whom the chiefs followed in war.

The Celtic peoples of Gaul and those of the British Isles,
as also the Celtiberians of Spain, were thus organized in
clans, with a king at the head of a clan group, such as the
king of the Picts in North-Eastern and the king of the Scots
in Western Caledonia. In Germany kingship based on
birth was modified by the habit of following in war leaders
of eminent valour,[1] and the freemen were, as in Homeric
Greece, accustomed to meet in public assembly to discuss
common affairs. It was only among the Greeks, Italians,
and Phoenicians that city life grew up, and the city organization usually began by being tribal. A few families pre-
dominated, while the heads of the older clans held power
over the meaner class of citizens, these being often strangers
who had gathered into the cities from outside.

From the king, for in most of these cities the government
seems to have been at first monarchical, power passed after

[1] Tacitus, *Germania*.

a while to the heads of the great families. Their arrogance and their oppression of the poorer citizens provoked risings, which in many places ended, after a period of turmoil and seditions, by overthrowing the oligarchy and vesting power in the bulk of the well-to-do citizens, and ultimately (in some cities) in all the free voters. The earlier steps towards democracy came not from any doctrine that the people have a right to rule, but from the feeling that an end must be put to lawless oppression by a privileged class.

Equality of laws (ἰσονομία) was in Greece the watchword of the revolutions, whether violent or peaceable, which brought about these reforms. Theoretic justifications of the rule of the multitude came later, when politicians sought to win favour by sweeping away the remains of aristocratic government and by filling the people with a sense of their own virtue and wisdom. The breaking down of the old oligarchy at Rome was due to the growth of a large population outside the old tribal system who were for a long time denied full equality of civil rights and subjected to harsh treatment which their incomplete political equality prevented them from restraining. These complaints, reinforced by other grievances relating to the stringent law of debt and to the management of the public land, led to a series of struggles, which ended in strengthening the popular element in the Roman Constitution. But Rome never became more than partially democratic, and theories regarding the natural rights of the citizen played no significant part in Roman history, the Italians having a less speculative turn of mind than the Greeks. Needless to say that the Rights of Man, as Man, were never heard of, for slavery, the slavery of men of the same colour as their masters and often of equal intelligence, was an accepted institution in all countries. Such development of popular or constitutional government as we see in the Hellenic and Italic peoples of antiquity was due to the pressure of actual grievances far more than to any theories regarding the nature of government and the claims of the people.

With the fall of the Roman republic the rule of the people came to an end in the ancient world. Local self-government went on for many generations in the cities, but in an oligarchic form, and it, too, ultimately died out. For nearly fifteen centuries, from the days of Augustus till the Turks captured Constantinople, there was never among the Romans in the Eastern Empire, civilized as they were, any more than there had been in the West till the imperial power ceased at Rome in the fifth century, a serious attempt either to restore free government, or even to devise a regular constitutional method for choosing the autocratic head of the State.

Few things in history are more remarkable than the total eclipse of all political thought and total abandonment of all efforts to improve political conditions in a highly educated and intelligent population such as were the inhabitants of the Western half of the Empire till the establishment there of barbarian kingdoms in the fifth and sixth centuries, and such as were the Helleno-Romans round the Ægean Sea till many centuries later. The subjects of the Eastern Roman Empire were interested in letters and learning, in law and in art, and above all, after the rise of Christianity, in religion. But though the political and historical literature of the classical ages had been preserved in Constantinople long after they had fallen out of knowledge in the West, nothing of a political kind was produced in the field of theory, nothing of a political kind attempted in the field of practice. Men were tired of politics. Free government had been tried, and had to all appearance failed. Despotic monarchies everywhere held the field. The few active minds cared for other things, or perhaps despaired. The masses were indifferent, and would not have listened. When a rising occurred it was because men desired good government, not self-government. Who can say that what has happened once may not happen again?

The progress of popular government in the modern world from its obscure Italian beginnings in the eleventh century A.D. may be referred to four causes:

The influence of religious ideas.

Discontent with royal or oligarchic misgovernment and consequent efforts at reform.

Social and political conditions favouring equality.

Abstract theory.

It would be impossible to sketch the operation of these

causes in all modern countries, so I confine myself to those few in which democracy has now gone furthest, treating each of these in the briefest way.

In England there are three marked stages in the advance from the old feudal monarchy, as it stood at the accession of the Tudor kings, to popular government. The first is marked by the struggle which began between king and Parliament under Charles I. and ended with the Revolution Settlement of 1688–89.

This was a struggle primarily against ecclesiastical oppression, secondarily against civil misgovernment, and in particular against the exercise of certain royal prerogatives deemed to infringe civil liberty, such as the claim of the king to levy taxes and issue executive ordinances without the consent of Parliament. The struggle, conducted in the name of the ancient rights of the subject, occupied more than half a century, and brought about not merely a recognition of these rights, but also an extension of them sufficient to make the House of Commons thenceforth the predominant power in the State. It was prompted by a spirit of resistance to actual oppressions rather than by any desire to assert the abstract right to self-government. Yet in the course of it questions of a theoretical nature did twice emerge.

Among the Puritans who formed the bulk of the parliamentary party in the Civil War, the Independents were the most consistent and most energetic element. In their view all Christians were, as Christians, free and equal, and therefore entitled to a voice in the affairs of a Christian State as well as of a Christian congregation. After the Restoration of 1660 this doctrine fell into the background. But at the end of the period (in 1689) John Locke, the most eminent English thinker of his time, published a treatise on Government, upholding the principles of the Whig party. As that book had its influence then and thereafter on the Whigs, so the seed of the Independents' doctrine, carried across the ocean, fell on congenial ground in the minds of the New England Puritans, and there sprang up, two generations later, in a plentiful harvest.

For a hundred years after the Revolution Settlement the English acquiesced in the political system then established.

It was an oligarchy of great landowners, qualified, however, by the still considerable influence of the Crown and also by the power which the people enjoyed of asserting their wishes in the election of members for the counties and for a few large towns. The smaller boroughs, from which came a large part of the House of Commons, were mostly owned by the oligarchs, and through them the oligarchy usually got its way. Towards the end of the eighteenth century the faults of this system, as well as that increase in the royal power which George the Third seemed to be effecting, began to create a demand for reform, but the outbreak of the French Revolution and the long war which followed interrupted all such schemes. Forty years later, when the horror inspired by the excesses of the Revolution had melted away, the call for reform was again heard, and was now the louder because there was much suffering and discontent among the labouring class in town and country. The grievances complained of were not so galling as those which had aroused the Puritans against Charles the First. But in times of enlightenment abuses are resented as grievances. Men of intellect and education saw more clearly than their fathers had done the defects in the laws of the country and the monstrous anomalies of the electoral system. Reinforced in its later stage by the excitement which the revolution that overthrew Charles X. in France had evoked, the movement grew fast, and triumphed in the Reform Act of 1832. The contest was almost bloodless. There were riots, but no civil war. The chief motive force behind the Whig leaders was the sense among the whole people that there were grave evils which could be cured only by a more truly representative House of Commons. But there was also a feeling, stronger than had been discernible since the seventeenth century, that the power possessed by the landowning class and by the rich in general belonged of right to the bulk of the nation.

The effect of the Act, which reduced the suffrage but left the great majority of the manual labourers still unenfranchised, was to transfer voting power to the middle classes and the upper section of the hand-workers, but the hold of the wealthy, both landowners and others, upon the offices of State, remained, though beginning by degrees to loosen. So things stood for thirty-five years.

The process of change by which Great Britain became a democracy was resumed in 1867 by an Act which lowered the electoral franchise in the boroughs, was continued in 1885 by another Act, which lowered it in counties also, and was ended by an Act of 1918 which enfranchised virtually the whole adult population, women as well as men. All these measures were accompanied by redistributions of seats which have now made representation almost exactly proportioned to population. Thus the United Kingdom has now universal suffrage, and in almost every constituency the labouring class compose the majority, usually a very large majority.

For none of these three Acts was there any strong popular demand. In 1866–67 a few more or less academic politicians advocated parliamentary reform on the ground that it would enable questions of social reform to be more promptly and boldly dealt with.[1] Others, led by two great orators, Mr. Bright and Mr. Gladstone, urged that the wider the basis of representation, the stronger would be the fabric of the Constitution and the more contented the people. But there was no real excitement, such as had forced the Act of 1832 upon a reluctant parliament, nor were there any violent demonstrations through the country such as had been common in the days of the Chartist agitation in 1840–48.[2] The young reformers of 1866, *quorum pars parva fui,* were rather disappointed at what seemed the apathy of the masses, and some of the Lancashire working-class leaders told me that they received only a feeble backing. The ex-

[1] Two volumes published in 1867 and entitled *Essays on Reform* and *Questions for a Reformed Parliament* by these academic writers make curious reading to-day.

[2] The overturning (in 1866) of the railings in Hyde Park in London by a crowd assembled to hold a reform meeting was made much of at the time in the British press and treated in the foreign press as the prelude to a revolution. But having been close to the railings when they fell, I can say that the fall was half an accident and the crowd was perfectly good-humoured and not at all excited. Led by a respectable old revising barrister, Mr. Edmond Beales, M. A., and composed chiefly of persons drawn by curiosity, it was so dense that its pressure on the railings, which were much lower and weaker than those which now enclose the park, made them give way, lifting as they sank the stone bases in which they were fixed. The front rank, who were squeezed against them, gleefully proceeded to shake them. Down they went, and the people jumped over them into the park amid general laughter.

planation of the ease with which the Bill of 1867 was carried is to be found partly in the cheery optimism of those days, when few people feared the results of change (for Socialism had not yet appeared), partly in the habit the two great parties were beginning to form of competing for popular favour by putting forth alluring political programmes. To advocate the extension of the suffrage was easy, to oppose it invidious as indicating distrust; and while the Liberal party thought it had something to gain by reform, the shrewd old leader of the Tory party saw he had little to lose. Neither perceived that in the long run both would suffer, for this result was not disclosed till the general election of 1905 brought into being a new Labour party, which drew voters away from both Liberals and Tories, and now threatens the working of the time-honoured two-party system.

The Acts of 1884–85, which extended the franchise to the agricultural labourers and miners in the counties and redistributed seats, passed even more easily, and ultimately by a compromise between the two parties. They were the logical consequence of the Act of 1867, and the fears formerly entertained by the richer classes had been removed by the electoral victory they won in 1874. The only heat that arose was when the House of Lords had threatened to defeat the extension of the suffrage by a side wind. The Act of 1918 was passed during the Great War by a Coalition Ministry with scarcely any opposition, and little noticed by the people, whose thoughts were concentrated on the battle-front. Never was a momentous change made so quietly.

Throughout this long march from feudal monarchy to extreme democracy which occupied three centuries, the masses of the people, whether peasants in the country or artisans in the towns, never (except in 1832) clamoured for political power. The ancient system was gradually broken down by the action of a part of the upper class aided by the bulk of the middle classes. The really active forces were, in the earlier stages of the march, the pressure of religious and civil tyranny which could be removed only by setting Parliament above the Crown, while in the later stages the operative causes were: First, the upward economic progress of the middle and humbler classes, which made it seem unfair to keep them in tutelage; secondly, the wish to root out the abuses incident to old-fashioned oligarchies and create a more efficient administration; and thirdly, the tendency of the two political parties to make political capital for themselves by proposals likely to attract both the unenfranchised masses and those who, sympathizing with the masses, thought they would be better cared for if they received full civic rights. Abstract principles, theories of political equality as prescribed by natural justice, played some part only at four epochs: during the Civil War; at the Revolution of 1688; during the years when the contagion of the French Revolutionary spirit of 1789 was active; and lastly, during the Chartist period, when there was much suffering and consequent discontent among the working class. That discontent had virtually subsided before the Act of 1867 and did not contribute to its passing. With the expanding manufacturing activity that set in from 1848 onwards, and before Socialism had made any converts, or any distinctive Labour· party had been thought of, the nation, complacent in the assurance of growing power, of commercial prosperity, and of the stability of its institutions, glided cheerfully down a smooth current, scarcely noting how fast the current ran, into a democratic system which, virtually unchecked by constitutional safeguards, now leaves its fortunes to the impulses of a single Chamber.

From Britain we may turn to trace the swifter growth of democracy in those branches of the English people which established themselves beyond the seas.

The North American colonies of England were settled by persons belonging (except to some extent in Virginia) to the middle and humbler classes, among whom there was at first little difference in wealth, and not very much in rank. Social and economic conditions creating social equality made political equality ultimately inevitable. The electoral suffrage was for a time restricted by property qualifications, but after the Revolution which severed the colonies from the British Crown, these restrictions were removed, slowly, but with little controversy, in all the States of the Union. By 1830 manhood suffrage had come to prevail (subject to some few exceptions) over the country. But while the Northern and Western States were democracies, the Southern States were, until slavery was extinguished, practically oligarchical, for in them there had grown up an aristocracy of slaveholding planters, who controlled the government, the landless whites following their lead. This condition of things disappeared after the Civil War, which broke up the aristocracy of large landholders, and now the Southern States are as purely democratic as the Northern. Yet one difference remains. In nearly all of these States the large majority of negroes are, despite the provisions of the Federal Constitution, excluded from the electoral franchise by various devices introduced into the State Constitutions.

As the United States were predestined to democracy by the conditions in which they began their career as an independent nation, so the swiftness and completeness with which the rule of the multitude was adopted were due to their antecedent history and to the circumstances of their separation from Britain. The principles of the English Puritans had formed the minds of the New Englanders. The practice of self-government in small areas had made the citizens accustomed to it in South as well as North. Independence had been proclaimed and the Revolutionary War waged in the name of abstract principles, and the doctrine of man's natural rights glorified. Over no other people of Teutonic stock has this doctrine exerted so great an influence.

The Australasian colonies, Australia, Tasmania, and New Zealand, have had a shorter and more placid career. In them even more markedly than in North America, the settlers came from the poorer and middle classes of Britain, carrying with them no distinctions of rank, and living on terms of social equality with one another. When the time came, in the middle of the nineteenth century, for granting representative institutions and responsible self-government, the British Parliament constructed these institutions on the British model as it then stood. Once established, however, the institutions showed themselves more democratic in their working than those of that model, because the English aristocratic traditions and the influence of landholders and rich men, then still potent in the mother country, were absent. Such property qualifications as at first limited the right of voting were soon swept away by the colonial legislatures.

Manhood suffrage was, after about forty years, followed by universal suffrage at the instance of some few women who asked for it. In neither case was there serious opposition, and therefore little need to invoke general principles against opposition. It seemed the obvious thing. People said, Why not? If the working men want it, if the women want it, let them have it.

Australia and New Zealand are the countries in which democracy has gone furthest in practice, and they are also those in which it has owed least to theoretic arguments. There were not (except as regarded land settlement) either grievances which it was needed to remove, or occasions for invoking abstract principles.

The history of Canada and that of South Africa have both of them been too chequered, and the racial conditions which affect their politics too complicated, to admit of being treated with the brevity needed in this chapter. So far as relates to the causes which created popular government, it may suffice to say that the circumstances of Canada (and to a less degree, those of South Africa) resembled those of Australia in respect of the general equality of wealth and education among the people, so it was natural that the British Parliament should there also reproduce by its grant of responsible government the self-governing institutions of the mother country. In Canada these have worked out in a sense somewhat more democratic than they were doing in Great Britain before 1918, but less so than in Australasia. In South Africa the existence of a large coloured population has prevented the grant of universal suffrage.

Returning to Europe, one may begin with the land in the mountain recesses of which the government of the people by the people first established itself, and from which the accents of liberty were heard in Continental Europe before England's example became known there.

> Two voices are there: one is of the Sea;
> One of the Mountains, each a mighty voice.

Early in the fourteenth century several small communities of peasants on the shores of the Lake of Luzern, owning their fields and enjoying in common the woods and pastures, rose in arms against the exactions of their feudal superior the Count of Hapsburg, who happened at the time to be also Emperor. Attempts made to subdue them were foiled by their valour and by the defensibility of the valleys in which they dwelt. Other Alpine communities followed their example, and were equally successful. None of them meant to disavow allegiance to the Empire, but merely to repel the insolence and tyranny of the feudal magnates, and maintain that local self-government which had been the ancient birthright of the freemen among many Teutonic lands, as in Frisia and in Norway. Presently they allied themselves with some of the neighbouring cities which had thrown off the supremacy of their ecclesiastical or secular lords. The cities were ruled by oligarchies; the rural cantons continued to govern themselves by the whole body of freemen meeting in the primary assembly which debated and determined matters of common interest and chose the officials who had to manage current business. In this federation democratic and oligarchic governments deliberated (through their delegates) and fought side by side. There was nothing surprising in such an alliance, for in old Switzerland Oligarchy and Democracy were Facts, untinged by Doctrines. Nobody had thought about general principles of government. The rural democracies of Uri, Schwytz, Unterwalden, and the Grey Leagues (Grisons) ruled the subject territories they had conquered on the Italian side of the Alps just as sternly as the oligarchies of Bern and Zürich did theirs: the interest both had in holding down their respective subjects being indeed one of the bonds that held the Confederates together.

The public meeting of freemen in the three Forest Cantons, as also in Zug, Glarus, and Appenzell, was a survival from times before feudalism, almost before history, when each tiny community, isolated from all others, managed its own affairs. So little did any theories of equality and liberty influence their minds that they were in fact the most conservative of all Swiss. They did not admit newcomers to share in their civic rights. They detested the French revolutionaries so late as 1848, and being strong Catholics, they strove against the liberalism of industrial cities like Zürich. One contribution, however, was made by them to those democratic theories which they disliked. The city republic of Geneva, not yet a member of the Confederation, gave birth in 1712 to J. J. Rousseau, and it seems probable that it was the political arrangements of the old rural cantons, directly governed by their own citizens, that suggested to him those doctrines which, announced in his *Contrat Social,* exercised an immense influence on men's minds in France and in North America at a time critical for both countries.

In 1796 the armies of revolutionary France shattered the Confederation, and out of the ruins there arose a shortlived Helvetic Republic, in which the inhabitants of the subject territories were admitted to civic rights. After many conflicts and changes, including a brief civil war in 1847, Switzerland became, by the Constitutions of 1848 and 1874, a democratic Federal State, all the twenty-two component members of which are also democracies.

It was only in the latest phases of Swiss political development that abstract theory played a conspicuous part. The ideas diffused by the French Revolution spread wide the faith in popular sovereignty now characteristic of the Swiss nation and have set their stamp upon the present form of its institutions. They were unheard of in the earlier days, when the Swiss fought against the South German princes and afterwards against Charles the Bold of Burgundy. In ancient Greece the democratic cities and the oligarchic cities stood generally in opposition to one another. There were exceptions, as when democratic Athens attacked the then democratic Syracuse; but as a rule similarity in the form of government was a ground for friendly relations. No tendency of this kind appeared among the Swiss. It deserves to be noted that in the Middle Ages monarchy was always assumed to be the normal, natural, and even divinely appointed form of government. Until by the Peace of Westphalia (1648), the independence of the Swiss Confederation was recognized, all republics both north and south of the Alps were vaguely deemed to be under the suzerainty, nominal as it had become, of the Romano-Germanic Emperor. In the middle of the thirteenth century the people of Iceland, the one republic then existing in the world, were urged by the envoys of the king of Norway to place themselves under his sovereignty on the ground (*inter alia*) that everywhere else in the world monarchy held the field.

Of France little need be said, because every one may be assumed to know the salient facts of her history since 1788. She is the capital instance of a nation in which abstract ideas have immense force, because in no other modern people are ideas so quickly irradiated by imagination and fired by emotion. Never did political theories attain such power and run so wild a course as in the years from 1789 to 1794. We are so startled by the fervour with which they were held, and the absurd applications made of them, as sometimes to attribute to them even more power than they really exerted over the course of events. The enthusiasts whom they spurred on, could not, great as· is the élan of enthusiasm, have destroyed the monarchy and the church with so little resistance had it not been for the existence of grievances which made the peasantry, except in parts of the West, welcome these sudden and sweeping changes. The oppressive exactions and odious privileges which exasperated the people, the contempt into which both the Court and the ecclesiastical system had fallen since the days of Louis XIV. and which was heightened by the weakness of the unlucky king, had struck away the natural supports upon which government usually rests, so that little effort was needed to overthrow the tottering fabric. It was not so much the doctrines of Liberty and Equality with which the Convention hall resounded as the wish of the masses to better their condition and the desire of all classes but one to be rid of galling social privileges. When these things· had been attained, the nation acquiesced for fourteen years in the rule of a military dictator, who gave them an efficient administration and as much prosperity as was compatible with heavy expenditure on war and a terrible toll of human lives. The later revolutions of 1830 and 1848 and 1870 were far less violent, not merely because the enthusiasms of 1789 had died out, but also from the absence of any such solid grievances as had existed under the *ancien régime*.

All three revolutions were the work of the capital rather than of the nation, and how little the nation as a whole had been permeated by the passion for political equality was shown by the very limited suffrage that prevailed under the reign of Louis Philippe, and of which it was rather the educated class than the excluded masses that complained, and by the long submission to the rule of Louis Napoleon, whose fall, when at last it came, came as the result of a foreign war. His government was costly and corrupt, but the country was prosperous, and the ordinary citizen, though he did not respect his rulers, had few hardships affecting his daily life to lay to their charge. It is nevertheless true that a theoretical preference of republicanism to other forms of government waxed strong in France, and has now, a generation having grown up under it, drawn to its support the conservative instincts of the people, while the Bonapartean Empire was associated with military misfortunes and the loss of territory. Since 1848, and still more so since 1870, the old watchwords of Liberty, Equality, Fraternity have been, if not superseded, yet overlaid by new doctrines involving new contests of principle. Liberty, *i.e.* popular representative self-government, is well established. Fraternity has become a mere phrase in the presence of a standing antagonism between the wage-earning class and the bourgeoisie. Social and political equality have been attained in so far as the former can be attained while great differences of wealth exist. The new doctrines and new issues are economic rather than political. They point to the extinction of private property, the enjoyment of which was placed by the men of 1789 among Natural Rights; and those who stop short of this at least suggest the absorption by the State of the means of production and distribution. The arguments advanced in support of these doctrines are rather economic than philosophical, and the controversy is carried on in the practical sphere, with the desire for Economic Equality as its motive force. In this sense it may be said that abstract doctrines of Human Rights figure less in the conflicts of to-day than in the generations that were fascinated by Rousseau and Tom Paine.

To this outline of the causes which have in some countries created popular government, a few sentences may be added as to the causes which in other countries retarded or arrested its growth. In Castile and Aragon, where in the later Middle Ages the prospects of free constitutional development seemed bright, the wars with the Moors and the power of the Church impressed on the national mind habits and tendencies which allowed the Crown to draw all power to itself. In Hungary the Turkish domination, followed by that of the Hapsburgs, strong by their other dominions, gave the ancient constitution little chance. In Poland foreign wars and internal dissensions weakened the country till it fell a prey to its neighbours. Of Holland and the Scandinavian kingdoms it would be impossible to speak without a historical disquisition, while the republics of Spanish America, in which the extinction a century ago of the arbitrary rule of a distant mother country raised high hopes for freedom, will be dealt with in a later chapter. But of modern Germany some few words must be said, because her recent history is instructive. Upon educated men in the German States, though less in Prussia than elsewhere, the principles of the French Revolution told powerfully. Unhappily, they were speedily followed by the armies first of the French Republic and then of Napoleon, so national patriotism was forced to support the sovereigns from whom it would otherwise have demanded constitutional freedom. When the War of Liberation was crowned with victory in 1814, the reformers expected a grant of political rights, but the sovereigns banded together in, or dependent upon, the Holy Alliance, refused all concessions. Frightened for a time by the revolutionary movements of 1848–49, they soon regained control. The desire for political liberty, a thing unknown for centuries, had not gone deep among the people, and the grievances they had to complain of were teasing rather than wounding, so the forces of reaction continued to prevail till the Prussian Liberals began that fight against Bismarck which from 1862 till 1865 seemed likely to establish the right of the legislature to financial control. But in 1864 the successful war against Denmark and in 1866 the successful war against Austria gave to the Crown and its audacious Minister an ascendancy which threw domestic issues into the background. In 1870 the tremendous victory over France, followed by the creation of national unity in the form of a German Empire, was taken as vindicating the policy of Bismarck, whose persistence in raising taxes without legislative sanction had given the Prussian army the military strength by which victory had been won. Though the Reichstag, a representative chamber for the Empire, was created in 1871 on the basis of universal suffrage, it failed to secure the control of the people over the executive. An assembly elected on a comparatively narrow franchise but with wide powers does more to make a government popular than one elected on a wider franchise with narrower powers. The cause of real constitutional freedom advanced no further in the Empire or in Prussia. The spirit of the old Liberalism withered, and when a strong opposition after a time grew up, it was a Socialistic opposition, whose aims were economic at least as much as political.

From 1814 to 1870 the German Liberals had striven for national unity and for a constitutional freedom like that of England. When the former had been attained, and its attainment, with the prestige of an unexampled triumph, had made Germany the greatest military power of the Old World, the interest in freedom declined. Commercial and industrial development became the supreme aim. The government, with its highly trained bureaucracy, helped the richer and middle classes towards prosperity in many ways, so they overlooked its defects in recognition of its services, and identified themselves with a system their fathers would have condemned. The Social Democratic party was less friendly. Its growth alarmed the Government. But it did not push opposition to extremes, believing material progress to be bound up with national strength and administrative activity. The professional classes, and especially the clergy, the teachers, and nearly all the men of science and learning, were devoted to a system under which science and learning were promoted and honoured. Moreover, the habit of obedience was in all classes deep-seated. Germany's strength depended on the army. A Prussian was a soldier first and a citizen afterwards. Patriotic ardour, the pride of nationality, loyalty to the dynasty under which the country had grown great, the passion for industrial development and commercial predominance — all these things combined to make the people as a whole acquiesce in the refusal of electoral reforms in Prussia and of that ultimate control of foreign policy and power of dismissing ministers that are enjoyed by every other people which counts itself free. The most educated and thoughtful part of the nation, from which many leaders of reform had come in earlier days, showed little wish to advance further in the path of constitutional freedom. This is the most illuminative instance of a movement towards democracy arrested in its course which modern times have furnished.

Of the Great War and the changes it has wrought in Germany the time has not yet come to speak.

The conclusion to which this brief summary seems to point is that while the movement which has in many countries transferred power from the Few to the Many has sprung partly from the pressure of actual grievances and partly from the abstract doctrine of Natural Rights, the latter has played a smaller part than its earlier apostles expected. Nowhere have the masses of the people shown a keen or abiding desire for political power. Looking back over the course of history, we moderns are surprised that our forefathers did not, so soon as they thought about government at all, perceive that few persons are fit to be trusted with irresponsible power, and that men know better than their rulers can be expected to know for them what their needs and wishes are. How came it that what are now taken as obvious truths were not recognized, or if recognized, were not forthwith put in practice? Why were ills long borne which an application of these now almost axiomatic principles would have removed?

I have tried in later chapters to suggest answers to these questions. Meantime, let us recognize that neither the conviction that power is better entrusted to the people than to a ruling One or Few, nor the desire of the average man to share in the government of his own community, has in fact been a strong force inducing political change. Popular government has been usually sought and won and valued not as a good thing in itself, but as a means of getting rid of tangible grievances or securing tangible benefits, and when those objects have been attained, the interest in it has generally tended to decline.

This does not mean that either in the English-speaking peoples or in France is democracy at present insecure. In the United Kingdom the practice of self-government has, especially since the Reform Act of 1832, become so deeply rooted as to have stood outside all controversy. The sovereignty of the people is assumed as the basis of government. The extensions of the suffrage made in 1867 and 1885 were desired by the middle classes who already enjoyed that franchise, as by the mass of working-men who did not, and were carried not so much for the sake of redressing social or economic grievances as because a restriction of the electoral franchise was itself deemed to be a grievance. Similarly in the United States and in the British self-governing colonies, the presumption that all citizens already enjoying equal civil rights should be voters was accepted with hardly any cavil. The masses, being generally educated, and feeling no deference to any other class, claimed the vote as obviously due to them; and there was no body to withstand the claim. In France, where the minds of men have been formed by the fifty years' practice of republican institutions, those institutions are now supported by the forces of conservative inertia on which monarchy formerly relied.

Nevertheless, although democracy has spread, and although no country that has tried it shows any signs of forsaking it, we are not yet entitled to hold with the men of 1789 that it is the natural and therefore in the long run the inevitable form of government. Much has happened since the rising sun of liberty dazzled the eyes of the States-General at Versailles. Popular government has not yet been proved to guarantee, always and everywhere, good government. If it be improbable, yet it is not unthinkable that as in many countries impatience with tangible evils substituted democracy for monarchy or oligarchy, a like impatience might some day reverse the process.

CHAPTER V

" WE hold these truths to be self-evident, that all men are created equal, that they are endowed by their Creator with certain inalienable Rights, that among these are Life, Liberty, and the pursuit of Happiness, that to secure these rights, Governments are instituted, deriving their just powers from the consent of the governed." (American Declaration of Independence, 1776.)

" Men are born and continue equal in respect of their rights.

" The end of political society is the preservation of the natural and imprescriptible rights of man. These Rights are liberty, property, security, and resistance to oppression.

" The principle of all Sovereignty resides essentially in the nation. No body, no individual, can exert any authority which is not expressly derived from it."

" All citizens have a right to concur personally, or through their representatives in making the law. Being equal in its eyes, then, they are all equally admissible to all dignities, posts, and public employments.

" No one ought to be molested on account of his opinions, even his religious opinions." (Declaration of the Rights of Man made by the National Assembly of France, August 1791.)

These two declarations, delivered authoritatively by two bodies of men at two moments of far-reaching historical importance, contain the fundamental dogmas, a sort of Apostles' Creed, of democracy. They are the truths on which it claims to rest, they embody the appeal it makes to human reason. Slightly varied in expression, their substance may be stated as follows.

Each man who comes into the world comes into it Free, with a mind to think for himself, a will to act for himself.

The subjection of one man to another except by his own free will is against Nature. All men are born Equal, with an equal right to the pursuit of happiness. That each man may secure this right and preserve his liberty as a member of a community, he must have an equal share in its government, that government being created and maintained by the consent of the community. Equality is the guarantee of independence.

These axioms, being delivered as self-evident truths, antecedent to and independent of experience, require no proof. They are propounded as parts of the universal Law of Nature, written on men's hearts, and therefore true always and everywhere.

While the Declarations of the Natural Rights of Man made at Philadelphia and at Paris were resounding through the world there were other thinkers who, like some Greek philosophers more than two thousand years before, were drawing from the actual experience of mankind arguments which furnished another set of foundations on which democracy might rest. Testing the value of a principle by its practical results, they propounded a number of propositions, some of which may be given as familiar examples.

Liberty is a good thing, because it develops the character of the individual, and conduces to the welfare of the community. When one man, or a few men, rule over others, some of the subjects are sure to resent control and rebel against it, troubling the general peace. No one is good enough to be trusted with unlimited power. Unless he be a saint — perhaps even if he be a saint — he is sure to abuse it.

Every man is the best judge of his own interest, and therefore best knows what sort of government and what laws will promote that interest. Hence those laws and that government will presumably be the best for a community as a whole which are desired by the largest number of its members.

Two men are presumably better able than one to judge what is for the common good. Three men are wiser still, and so on. Hence the larger the number of members of the community who have a right to give their opinion, the more likely to be correct (other things being equal) is the decision reached by the community.

Individual men may have selfish aims, possibly injurious to the community, but these will be restrained by the other members of the community whose personal aims will be different. Thus the self-regarding purposes of individuals will be eliminated, and the common aims which the bulk of the community desires to pursue will prevail.

As every man has some interest in the well-being of the community, a part at least of his own personal interest being bound up with it, every man will have a motive for bearing his share in its government, and he will seek to bear it, so far as his personal motives do not collide therewith.

Inequality, by arousing jealousy and envy, provokes discontent. Discontent disturbs the harmony of a community and induces strife. Hence equality in political rights, while it benefits the community by opening to talent the opportunity of rendering good service, tends also to peace and good order.

To sum up, government by the whole people best secures the two main objects of all Governments — Justice and Happiness, Justice, because no man or class or group will be strong enough to wrong others; Happiness, because each man, judging best what is for his own good, will have every chance of pursuing it. The principles of liberty and equality are justified by the results they yield.

From these propositions it follows that the admission on equal terms of the largest possible number of members of a community to share in its government on equal terms best promotes the satisfaction of all the members as individuals, and also the welfare of the community as a whole; and these being the chief ends for which government exists, a government of the people by themselves is commended by the experience of mankind.

Reflective minds in our day will find arguments of this type more profitable than the purely abstract doctrine of Natural Rights, a series of propositions called self-evident, incapable of proof or disproof, interpretable and applicable in whatever sense the believer may please to give them. But these transcendental axioms have in fact done more to commend democracy to mankind than any utilitarian arguments drawn from history, for they appeal to emotion at least as much as to reason. They are simpler and more direct.

Their very vagueness and the feeling that man is lifted to a higher plane, where Liberty and Equality are proclaimed as indefeasible rights, gave them a magic power. Rousseau fired a thousand for one whom Benthamism convinced.

Towards the end of the eighteenth century the spirit of reforming change was everywhere in the air. Reforms were long overdue, for the world had been full of tyranny, inequality, and injustice. But the rapacity and cruelty of the Middle Ages had been borne patiently, save at moments of exceptional excitement, because violence and the rule of force were then taken as part of the nature of things. In a quieter time, when ferocity had abated and knowledge had spread among the laity, setting free men's tongues and pens, injustices were more acutely resented, privileges of rank became odious, administrative abuses that had once passed unnoticed began to be felt as scandals. Then the spirit of reform suddenly kindled into a spirit of destruction. The doctrine of Natural Rights overthrew the respect for tradition, for it acted in the name of Justice, sparing neither birth nor wealth, and treating " vested rights " as vested wrongs. This was moreover the age of Illumination, when Authority, heretofore accustomed to enforce its decrees by persecution, had been dethroned that Reason might reign in its stead. Reason, accompanied and inspired by Justice, was expected to usher in a better world, with the sister angel Fraternity following in their train, because human nature itself would be renovated. Inequality and repression had engendered one set of vices in rulers and another in their subjects — selfishness and violence, hatred, perfidy, and revenge. Under good government — and in an age of reason little government would be needed — human nature, no longer corrupted by examples of successful wickedness, would return to the pristine virtues the Creator had meant to implant. With Liberty and Equality the naturally good instincts would spring up into the flower of rectitude, and bear the fruits of brotherly affection. Men would work for the community, rejoicing not merely in their own freedom, but because they desired the welfare of others also. These beliefs were the motive power which for a time made faith in democracy almost a religion. It was a finer spirit than that of later revolutionary extremists, by so much as Hope is better than Hatred, the dream of a moral regeneration more ennobling than the prospect of material advantage.

The blast of destruction which horrified Burke, whose insight perceived what havoc the uprooting of ancient habits and traditions must work, was to the ardent souls of those days a fresh breeze of morning, clearing away the foul vapours that had hung over an enslaved world. They desired to destroy only in order to rebuild upon an enduring foundation, finding that foundation in the imprescriptible Rights of Man. Wordsworth has described the enthusiasm of that time in memorable words: —

> Bliss was it in that dawn to be alive,
> But to be young was very Heaven! Oh times,
> When Reason seemed the most to assert her rights,
> A prime enchantress — to assist the work,
> Which then was going forward in her name!
> Not favoured spots alone, but the whole Earth,
> The beauty wore of promise — that which sets
> The budding rose above the rose full blown.
> What temper at the prospect did not wake
> To happiness unthought of?

To examine and criticize the doctrine of Natural Rights, round which an immense literature has grown up, would be impossible within the limits of this book, nor is such an examination needed, for I am here dealing with the phenomena of democracy, not with its theoretical basis. But it must be remembered that the conception of an Ideal Democracy which emerged in the eighteenth century has continued to affect politics not only on the speculative but on the practical side also. The view that natural justice prescribes this form of government continues to be reinforced by the belief that human nature, enlightened and controlled by Reason, may be expected so to improve under the influences of liberty and equality, peace and education, as to make that ideal a reality. An Ideal Democracy — the expression comes from Plato's remark that a pattern of the perfect State is perhaps stored up somewhere in heaven — may be taken to mean a community in which the sense of public duty and an altruistic spirit fill the minds and direct the wills of the large majority of the citizens, so that the Average Citizen stands on the level of him whom we sometimes meet and describe as the

Model Citizen. What then, expressed in the terms of our own day, would such a community be?

In it the average citizen will give close and constant attention to public affairs, recognizing that this is his interest as well as his duty. He will try to comprehend the main issues of policy, bringing to them an independent and impartial mind, which thinks first not of his own but of the general interest. If, owing to inevitable differences of opinion as to what are the measures needed for the general welfare, parties become inevitable, he will join one, and attend its meetings, but will repress the impulses of party spirit. Never failing to come to the polls, he will vote for his party candidate only if satisfied by his capacity and honesty. He will be ready to serve on a local Board or Council, and to be put forward as a candidate for the legislature (if satisfied of his own competence), because public service is recognized as a duty. With such citizens as electors, the legislature will be composed of upright and capable men, single-minded in their wish to serve the nation. Bribery in constituencies, corruption among public servants, will have disappeared. Leaders may not be always single-minded, nor assemblies always wise, nor administrators efficient, but all will be at any rate honest and zealous, so that an atmosphere of confidence and goodwill will prevail. Most of the causes that make for strife will be absent, for there will be no privileges, no advantages to excite jealousy. Office will be sought only because it gives opportunities for useful service. Power will be shared by all, and a career open to all alike. Even if the law does not — perhaps it cannot — prevent the accumulation of fortunes, these will be few and not inordinate, for public vigilance will close the illegitimate paths to wealth. All but the most depraved persons will obey and support the law, feeling it to be their own. There will be no excuse for violence, because the constitution will provide a remedy for every grievance. Equality will produce a sense of human solidarity, will refine manners, and increase brotherly kindness.

Some of the finest minds of Wordsworth's time, both in France and in England, hoped for the sort of community I have outlined. We hear less about it now, for democracy has arrived, and one hundred and thirty years have brought disappointments. New questions regarding the functions of the State have arisen dividing the votaries of democracy into different schools, one of which, denying the " natural right " to hold property proclaimed in 1789, conceives Nature to prescribe equality in property as well as in civic status. But though there is not much talk about Natural Rights, the influence of that old theory is still discernible. It gives strength to the movement for asserting popular sovereignty in the form of direct legislation by the people through the Initiative and Referendum, and their direct action in re-calling officials without a vote by the legislature or recourse to courts of law. It was a main factor in securing the exten-sion of the electoral suffrage to women. In England, the argument generally accepted in 1870 that fitness for the exer-cise of the suffrage should be a pre-condition to the grant of it was in 1918 tossed contemptuously on the dustheap of obsolete prejudices, because a new generation had come to regard the electoral franchise as a natural right. The same tendency appears in the readiness now shown to grant self-government to countries inhabited by races devoid of political experiences, such as the inhabitants of India and the Philip-pine Islands, and to sweep away the constitutional checks once deemed needful. If restrictions on the power of the people are deemed inconsistent with democracy, it is because democratic institutions are now deemed to carry with them, as a sort of gift of Nature, the capacity to use them well.

It was easy to idealize democracy when the destruction of despotism and privilege was the first and necessary step to a better world. Nowadays any one can smile or sigh over the faith and hope that inspired the successive revolutions that convulsed the European Continent in and after 1789. Any one can point out that men mistook the pernicious channels in which selfish propensities had been flowing for those pro-pensities themselves, which were sure to find new channels when the old had been destroyed. Yet the hopes of Words-worth's generation were less unwarranted than we are now apt to think them. People felt then, as we cannot so acutely feel to-day, how many evils had been wrought by a tyranny that spared neither souls nor bodies. It was natural to ex-pect not only the extinction of those abuses which the Revolu-tion did extinguish, first for France and thereafter for most West European countries, but something like a regeneration of humanity. Even in sober England, even in America which had never had much to suffer from misgovernment, there were great and good men who pardoned many of the excesses of the Revolution for the sake of the blessings that seemed likely to follow.

The abstract doctrines of the Revolutionary epoch and the visions of a better world that irradiated those doctrines, blurred as they have been in the lapse of years, have never ceased to recommend popular government to men of sanguine temper. But the Vision, the picture of an Ideal Democracy, a government upright and wise, beneficent and stable, as no government save that of the people for the people can be, has had greater power than the abstract doctrines, mighty as was their explosive force when they were first proclaimed. It is the conception of a happier life for all, coupled with a mystic faith in the People, that great multitude through whom speaks the Voice of the Almighty Power that makes for righteousness — it is this that constitutes the vital impulse of democracy. The country where the ideal democracy exists has not yet been discovered, but the faith in its existence has survived many disappointments, many disillusionments. Many more will follow, but them also the faith will survive. From time to time hope is revived by the appearance of a group of disinterested reformers, whose zeal rouses a nation to sweep away abuses and leaves things better than it found them. It is only sloth and torpor and the acquiescence in things known to be evil that are deadly. So we may hope that the Ideal will never cease to exert its power, but continue to stand as a beacon tower to one generation after another.

CHAPTER VI

LIBERTY

The late Lord Acton, most learned among the English-men of his generation, proposed to himself in his youth the writing of a History of Liberty from the earliest times to our own. The book remained unwritten not merely because the subject was vast, but also because his own learning was so wide and multifarious that he knew he would have been overcome by the temptation to endless digressions and profuse citations. Even the analysis of the conception of Liberty and the examination of the various meanings which the term has borne at different times and in different countries would need a treatise. No one seems to have undertaken the task. All that can be attempted here is to distinguish between some of the senses in which the word has been used and to indicate how they bear on one another.

Many questions arise. What is the relation between Liberty and Democracy? Does the former prescribe the latter? Does the latter guarantee the former? Is Liberty a Positive or a merely Negative conception? Is it an End in itself, or a means to an End greater than itself? But to explain the various senses which the word has borne let us look for a moment at the history of the conception.

The first struggles for Liberty were against arbitrary power and unjust laws. The ordinary Greek citizen of the sixth century B.C. was not free when oppressed by an oligarchy or a tyrant, who took his property or put him to death in defiance of old usage and common justice. To him Liberty meant equal laws for all — ἰσονομία — or what we should call a recognition of civil rights, securing exemption from the exercise of arbitrary power. The barons and prelates of England who extorted Magna Charta from the king complained of his tyrannical action contrary to the old customs

of the nation, and obtained from him a promise to abandon
these and to abide by the *Lex Terrae,* the ancient and general
customary law of the land.   So the conflict between the English Parliament and Charles the First arose over the acts of
royal power that transgressed common law and right, unjust
and unauthorized exactions and the extra legal action of the
Star Chamber, violating the long-established rights of the
subject to person and property.   By this time, however, a
new point of contention had emerged.   The subject, besides
suffering in person and property, was suffering also by being
forbidden the expression and dissemination of his particular
religious opinions and the right of worshipping God according to his own convictions.   In such cases the private civil
rights of the individual to life and property and the exercise
of religion were alleged to be infringed.   The struggle for
freedom was a struggle for the recognition of all these rights.
This was the original sense of the famous Whig watchword,
Civil and Religious Liberty.   The two were associated as
parts of the same thing, though Religious Liberty was more
difficult to define, for practices that seem to fall within the
sphere of religion may be injurious to public order or to
morality, and therefore fit to be forbidden.

In the course of this struggle the English combatants for
freedom realized, as had done their Greek and Roman predecessors, that they could not win and hold civil and religious
liberty so long as the constitution of the State left political
power in the hands of a monarch or of a class.   The rights
of the body of the people could not be safe till the people —
not necessarily the whole, but at least a considerable part of
the people — had an effective share in the government.
There was therefore a further conflict to secure Political
Liberty, *i.e.* a constitution restricting arbitrary power and
transferring supremacy from the Crown to the Nation.
Thenceforth, and for two centuries, the conception of Liberty covered not only private civil rights but public and political rights also; and especially the right of electing the representatives through whom the people were to exercise their
power.   Civil and Religious Liberty in the old sense receded
into the background, being assumed to have been secured,
while Political Liberty, being deemed to be still not complete
even in England, and not having been yet won in many other

countries, continued to occupy men's minds. Civil Liberty had originally been the aim and political liberty the road to it, but now Political Liberty was thought of as the cause and civil liberty as the consequence. So Liberty came to mean self-government. A " free people " was understood to be a people which rules itself, master of its own destinies both at home and wherever its power extends abroad.

Much later, and perhaps not fully till the nineteenth century, was it perceived that besides his private civil rights to person, property, and the exercise of religion, and besides also his political rights to share in the government of the State, there are other matters in which restrictions may be imposed on the individual which limit his action where restriction may be harmful, or is at any rate not obviously necessary. In the old struggle for Civil Rights the whole people, except the ruling man or class, usually stood together in demanding those rights.[1] Everybody therefore supposed that when Political Liberty had been secured, the rights of the citizen were safe under the aegis of self-government, which means in practice the rule of the majority. But it presently appeared that a majority is not the same thing as the whole people. Its ideas and wishes may be different from those of minorities within the people. As legislation is in its hands, it may pass laws imposing on a minority restrictions which bear hardly on them. Whether it does this from a wish to beat down their resistance, or in the belief that such restrictions make for the interest of the community as a whole, in either case it restricts the action of the individual, and that perhaps where restriction may be needless or mischievous. Thus a new conception arises, giving rise to new questions, viz. the conception of Individual Liberty, an exemption from control in respect of matters not falling within either the old and accepted category of private civil rights, nor within the category of political rights.

Thus we find four kinds of Liberty whose relations have to be determined:

Civil Liberty, the exemption from control of the citizen in respect of his person and property.

[1] Except of course where religious freedom was involved, for in such cases there was usually a section which supported persecution on behalf of its own faith.

Religious Liberty, exemption from control in the expression of religious opinions and the practice of worship.

Political Liberty, the participation of the citizen in the government of the community.

Individual Liberty, exemption from control in matters which do not so plainly affect the welfare of the whole community as to render control necessary.

These descriptions — they are not Definitions — are necessarily vague and general, for the conceptions of the matters that fall within each of the four terms aforesaid have varied and will continue to vary. Most vague, and indeed incapable of definition, are the matters that belong to the category of Rights of the Individual. Thinkers are not agreed as to what these rights are, yet none doubts their existence and their title to be protected. Each man has a presumptive right to enjoy that sort of natural exercise of free will which a bird has when it flits from bough to bough or soars singing into the sky. But when concrete examples begin to be adduced, what differences of view! Do laws forbidding the use of intoxicants, or the carrying of pistols, or limiting the hours during which a man may work, or suppressing lotteries, or punishing the advocacy of tyrannicide, or making vaccination compulsory, or fixing a minimum wage, or forbidding a gardener to groom his employer's horse, infringe either Individual Liberty or Civil Liberty in the old sense of the term? What is to be said of laws directed in some countries against certain religious orders, or of those which elsewhere forbid the intermarriage of white and coloured persons? These cannot be here discussed, but difficult as it is to find any line fixing the bounds of Individual Liberty, it is plain that the presumption is in favour of freedom, not only for the sake of securing to each man the maximum of harmless pleasures, but also in the interests of the community, for Individuality is precious, and the nation profits by the free play of its best minds and the unfettered development of its strongest characters. Individual Liberty, though it consists in exemption from control, has a Positive as well as a Negative side. It imports activity, it implies the spontaneous and pleasurable exercise of the powers of Willing and Doing.

What are the relations to one another of these several kinds of Liberty?

Civil Liberty may exist without Political Liberty, for a monarch or an oligarchy may find it well to recognize and respect it. But it was won by political struggles, and has in fact been seldom found where Political Liberty did not exist to guard it.

Conversely, the presence of Political Liberty practically involves that of Civil Liberty, at least in the old historical sense of that term, because in a self-governing people the majority are pretty certain to desire for each one among them the old and familiar securities for person and property, which are, however, in some free governments less ample than in English-speaking countries. This applies also to Religious Liberty. Yet it is easy to imagine a State in which an overwhelming majority of one persuasion, religious or anti-religious, would accord scant justice, or indulgence, to those who dissented from the dominant view.

As Individual Liberty consists in Exemption from Legal Control, so Political Liberty consists in participation in Legal Control. It is an Active Right. Between Individual Liberty and Political Liberty there is no necessary connection; each may exist without the other. An enlightened autocrat might think that discontent would be reduced if his subjects were given free scope for the indulgence of their tastes and fancies. But such rulers have been few. Monarchs have been surrounded by privileged aristocracies. An Absolute Government usually relies on its police, fears the free expression of opinion, is worked by a strong bureaucracy, naturally disposed to extend its action into the regulation of private life and the supersession of individual initiative. The individual has far better chances under constitutional government, for the spirit of democracy has generally fostered the sense of personal independence, and been a tolerant spirit, willing to let everybody seek his pleasure in his own way. Yet even popular government may care little for the " self-determination " or " self-realization " of the individual citizen.

It is hard to draw any line of demarcation between Civil Liberty and Individual Liberty. The distinction is rather historical than theoretical. Both consist in Exemption from Control, *i.e.* in the non-interference of State authority with the unfettered exercise of the citizens' will. But the conception of Civil Liberty was older than that of Individual Liberty. When men were fighting against oppression by kings or oligarchs, they assumed that there were certain restrictions to which every one must be subject by law, while there were certain other restrictions which must be abolished. It was against the latter, which nearly everybody felt to be oppressive, that they strove. Such were arbitrary arrests and general warrants and the power of the Executive over the Judiciary. What might be classed as being legitimate restrictions they did not stop to define, nor has anybody since succeeded in defining them, for the doctrines of thinkers as well as the notions of ordinary citizens have been different in different countries and have varied from time to time in the same country. Enough to say that although the conception of Individual Liberty may be made to include the exemptions our ancestors contended for in the seventeenth century, and though every kind of individual liberty may be called a Civil Liberty, there is this significant difference that the Civil liberties of those older days were extorted from arbitrary monarchs, whereas what we call Individual Liberty to-day has to be defended, when and so far as it needs defence, against the constitutional action of a self-governing community.

I pass by the cases in which a democratic nation has shown by its treatment of a subject country that it does not value the principles of liberty for their own sake — such cases as that of the Athenian democracy ruling over the outlying cities whom it called its allies, or that of some of the Swiss Cantons, in their rule over their subjects in the valleys south of the Alps. Nor need we stop to consider cases in which a compact majority of one colour denies equal rights to those of another colour who dwell in their midst, for these have special features that would need explanations out of place here. But it is worth while to note the tendencies which in many free countries have, in extending the scope of legislation and of the administrative interference of the State, encroached on the sphere in which individual will and action used to move unrestrained.

Our times have seen a growing desire to improve the conditions of the poorer classes, providing better houses and other health-giving conditions, fixing the hours of labour, raising wages, enacting compulsory methods for settling labour disputes. There is a wish to strike at the power of corporate wealth and monopolistic combinations by handing over large industries, or the means of transportation, or such sources of national wealth as coal and iron, to the State to be managed by it for the common benefit. There is also a passion for moral reform conspicuous in the effort to forbid the use of intoxicants. In these and other similar directions the power of the State seems to open the most direct way to the attainment of the aims desired. But every enlargement of the sphere of State action narrows the sphere left to the will of the individual, restricting in one way or another his natural freedom. So long as the people were ruled by a small class, they distrusted their rulers, and would have regarded administrative interference in many of the matters enumerated as a reduction of their liberty. But this jealousy of the State vanished when the masses obtained full control of the government. The administration is now their own: their impatience desires quick returns. "Why," they say, "should we fear government? Why not use it for our benefit? Why await the slow action of ameliorative forces when we can set the great machine to work at full speed?"

These tendencies have during the last half-century gained the upper hand, and have discredited, without refuting, the *laissez-faire* doctrine which had held the field of economic thought since the days of Adam Smith. They seem likely to keep the ground they have won. Regulative legislation may reduce the freedom of workmen and of employers, may take great departments of industry out of private hands, may impose new obligations and proscribe old forms of pleasure. A nation may, like the Prussian, submit to be forced into certain moulds in order to secure the military strength or industrial organization or commercial prosperity which a skilled administration and the use of public money can create.[1] Minorities may fare hardly at the hands of majori-

[1] A reaction against the extreme extension of State power has driven some philosophic minds into what is called Anarchism. Its principles, the attractiveness of which many of us have felt, do not solve the diffi-

ties apt to believe that numbers mean wisdom, and persuaded that if they choose to impose a restriction on themselves they are entitled to impose it upon others. Nevertheless, where the evident good of society is involved, individual preferences will be forced to give way on the ground that to arrest the will of a majority is to sacrifice their liberty, and so neglect the happiness of the greater number for that of the smaller. But, whatever the future may bring, the freedom of thought, speech, and writing do not seem at present threatened. The liberty of the press is a traditional principle in the popular mind; democratic habits foster the sense of personal independence and express themselves in the phrase "Live and Let Live."

Two tendencies run through the history of the Church as well as of the State, both having roots deep in human nature. In daily life we note the presence of what may be called the centripetal and centrifugal forces in human society, the working of one set of tendencies which make some men desire a close and constant association with others, and of other tendencies which make other men desire to stand apart and follow their own bent. Some men are happy with Nature and books and their own meditations, others need the stimulus of constant intercourse with their fellows. In the Church the social impulse consolidated the early Christian communities under the bishop, and created monastic orders abjuring the free life of the world to dwell together, while introspection and the feeling of the direct relation of the soul to God produced the anchorites of the fifth and sixth centuries, and that strenuous assertion of the rights of individual conscience which came from the English Puritans of the seventeenth. Without the one tendency, action would be disconnected and ineffective; without the other, thought would lose in variety and vigour; there would be less poetry and less philosophy. *Ubi spiritus Domini, ibi Libertas.* The world seems to have now entered an era in which the principles of associated action and of the dominance of the community are gaining strength. Though the Prussian doctrine of the State is un-

culty, for if anarchy means the withdrawal of legal control acting through State power, the door is opened to the rule of mere force, the force of the physically strong, in which the weak will go to the wall and individual liberty perish more completely than at the hands of the State.

welcome to English-speaking peoples, the policies it has suggested have been slowly, almost insensibly, supplanting the individualism of last century. The ideal of happiness may change from that of birds wantoning in the air to that of bees busy in carrying honey to the common hive. We perceive that the enthusiasm for liberty which fired men's hearts for a century or more from the beginning of the American Revolution down to our own time has now grown cool. The dithyrambic expression it found in the poets and orators of those days sounds strange and hollow in the ears of the present generation, bent on securing, with the least possible exertion, the material conditions of comfort and well-being.

Liberty may not have achieved all that was expected, yet it remains true that nothing is more vital to national progress than the spontaneous development of individual character, and that free play of intellect which is independent of current prejudice, examines everything by the light of reason and history, and fearlessly defends unpopular opinions. Independence of thought was formerly threatened by monarchs who feared the disaffection of their subjects. May it not again be threatened by other forms of intolerance, possible even in a popular government?

Room should be found in every country for men who, like the prophets in ancient Israel, have along with their wrath at the evils of their own time inspiring visions of a better future and the right to speak their minds. That love of freedom which will bear with opposition because it has faith in the victory of truth is none too common. Many of those who have the word on their lips are despots at heart. Those men in whom that love seemed to glow with the hottest flame may have had an almost excessive faith in its power for good, but if this be an infirmity, it is an infirmity of noble minds, which democracies ought to honour.[1]

Not less than any other form of government does democracy need to cherish Individual liberty. It is, like oxygen in the air, a life-giving spirit. Political liberty will have seen one of its fairest fruits wither on the bough if that spirit should decline.

---

[1] Mazzini and Gladstone were, among the famous Europeans of the last generation, the two who seemed to those who talked with them most possessed by this faith.

CHAPTER VII

EQUALITY

The conception of Equality needs to be here examined, for it has been the prime factor in the creation of democratic theory, and from misunderstandings of it have sprung half the errors which democratic practice has committed. Let us begin by distinguishing four different kinds of Equality.

A. Civil Equality consists in the possession by all the citizens of the same status in the sphere of private law. All have an equal right to be protected in respect of person and estate and family relations, and to appeal to the Courts of Law for such protection. Such equality was found in few countries two centuries ago, but is now (subject to trivial exceptions) the rule in all civilized communities.

B. Political Equality exists where all citizens — or at least all adult male citizens — have a like share in the government of the community, and are alike eligible to hold any post in its service, apart, of course, from provisions as to age or education or the taint of crime. Such equality now obtains in countries which have adopted manhood (or universal) suffrage.

C. Social Equality, a vaguer thing, exists where no formal distinctions are drawn by law or custom between different ranks or classes, such as, for instance, the right to enter places from which others are excluded, as the Romans reserved special seats in the amphitheatre for the senators and *Equites,* or as in Prussia certain persons only could be received at court (*Hoffähigkeit*). Sometimes the term is extended to denote the conditions of a society where nobody looks up to or looks down upon any one else in respect of birth or wealth, as is the case in Norway, and, broadly speaking, in Switzerland and the United States and the British self-governing Dominions.

These three kinds of Equality are familiar, and the two

former definable by law. To Social Equality we may presently return. There is, however, a fourth kind less easy to deal with.

D. Natural Equality is perhaps the best name to give to that similarity which exists, or seems to exist, at birth between all human beings born with the same five senses. Every human creature comes naked into the world possessing (if a normal creature) similar bodily organs and presumably similar mental capacities, desires, and passions. For some days or weeks little or no difference in these respects is perceptible between one child and another. All seem alike, all presumptively entitled to the same rights in this world and an equal prospect of happiness both in this world and the next, since all possess souls of the same value in the sight of God. It is this equality that the American Declaration of Independence means when it says that " All men are born free and equal "; it is this (applied to human beings when they have reached maturity) which the Greek orator Alcidamas meant when he said that God made no one a slave,[1] which St. Paul meant when he wrote, " In Christ there is neither Jew nor Greek, barbarian nor Scythian, bond nor free." Christianity, which first proclaimed the doctrine of Natural Equality, and did most to establish it, treated all who entered the Christian community as equals and brethren. Slavery lasted on in many parts of the world, even among Christians, but (except for a futile attempt made eighty years ago by a few slave-owners to argue that the negro was something less than a human being) the principle has not been denied for centuries past, and the right to liberty has been admitted among the primordial rights to which all men are entitled through the whole of life.

But as the infants grow, innate but previously undiscoverable differences are revealed. Some prove to be strong in body, forceful in will, industrious, intelligent. Some are feeble, timorous, slack, dull. When maturity is reached, some begin to render service to the community as workers or thinkers or inventors or soldiers. Others may become a burden to it, or prove fit only for occupations needing little strength or skill. Thus the supposed Natural Equality turns into an Inequality which is more evidently natural, because

---

[1] Ἐλευθέρους ἄφηκε πάντας θεός, οὐδένα δοῦλον ἡ φύσις πεποίηκεν.

due to the differences in the gifts which Nature has bestowed on some and denied to others. The fact that the progress of mankind in arts and sciences and letters and every form of thought has been due to the efforts of a comparatively small number of highly gifted minds rising out of the common mass speaks for itself. Natural Inequality has been and must continue to be one of the most patent and effective factors in human society. It furnished whatever theoretical justification the ancient world found for slavery; it was a basis used in argument by the slaveholders of North America and Brazil down to our own days, though the results of slavery, moral as well as economic, had long ago condemned that institution. To reconcile this Natural Inequality as a Fact with the principles of Natural Equality as a Doctrine is one of the chief problems which every government has to solve.

Does Natural Justice require Political Equality? Most Greek democrats held that it did, and that all citizens should have an equal right of voting and equal eligibility to office. In the modern world the sentiment of fraternity, mainly due to Christianity, has counted for more than any abstract theory. Whatever inequalities exist between men, the feeling remains that " one man is as good as another," or as Burns wrote, " a man's a man for a' that," in this sense at least, that the things men have in common are more important than the things in which they differ, and that the pleasure or pain of each (even if not measurable by the same standard) ought to be equally regarded. The association of Equality with Justice is strong, because every one feels that the chances of birth have given to some and refused to others a share of the external conditions of well-being which has no relation to intrinsic merit, so that the disparity ought not to be artificially increased. The sense of human sympathy appeals to the finer and gentler souls who desire to lift up those to whom fortune has been unkind, and it finds favour with that large majority of persons who have no special excellence that could entitle them to special treatment. Those who, agreeing with Aristotle's view that Justice is not absolute but relative to a man's capacities, so that each man's share in political functions should be proportioned to his virtue and his power of serving the State, have in modern

times argued that ignorance should disqualify for the suffrage, and that one who has not enough property to give him
a permanent interest in the country, or who contributes nothing in taxes, should not be placed on a level with the man of
education possessed of at least some taxable property.[1]

To this it was replied that the poor man has the same flesh
and blood as the rich. He has an interest in his country's
welfare, and suffers quite as much as the rich man by its
misfortunes. Even if he has little property, he has his labour, an indispensable contribution to the country's wealth.
He is liable to military service in time of war. If he is a
Roman Catholic, he receives the same sacraments as does the
rich, and his son may become a priest, dispenser of the means
of salvation. If he is a Protestant he is, at least in America
and Scotland and in the Nonconformist Churches of England, allowed his voice in the affairs of the congregation.
Why should he be debarred from bearing his part in the
civil government of the country?[2] If in these things Natural Equality is admitted, why not in politics? It is the
simplest rule, the expression of Natural Justice.

In the struggles over Political Equality, turning chiefly
on the extension of the electoral franchise, the equalitarian
view prevailed not so much because it was admitted in principle as in respect of the want of criteria that could be practically applied to determine a man's fitness to vote. Intelligence, knowledge, and a sense of civil duty were the three
qualities needed. But there were no means for testing these.
No line of discrimination could be drawn between those who
possess these merits and the rest of the community. No test
of fitness could be applied which would not admit many persons whom their neighbours knew to be personally bad citizens, and probably exclude many who were known to be
good. The possession of property was obviously no evidence
of merit. Many who disliked universal suffrage allowed
themselves to be driven to acquiesce in it for the sake of sim-

[1] In Belgium this notion induced a plan which, while bestowing votes
on all adult males, allotted what were called "supplementary votes"
to persons possessed of various property or educational qualifications.
This system was subsequently abolished.

[2] There were, of course, other arguments for extensions of the suffrage, such as the broadening of the basis of power and the securing
of more constant attention to grievances, but these need no notice here.

plicity. Thus it has come to be deemed the corner-stone of democracy. But though Natural Equality triumphed as a doctrine, Natural Inequality remained as a fact. To votaries of the doctrine it was, however, an unwelcome fact, which, since it could not be denied in the face of the evidence, they sought to ignore or minimize. Having decided that every man was fit to vote, they argued that as he was fit to vote upon policy he must be also fitted to execute policy. If one man is as good as another at the polls, one man is as good as another for office, or at least for all offices except the highest.[1]

The people having been recognized as competent to govern themselves, why scrutinize degrees of competence for elective posts? "The average man rules, and his authority is best delegated to one who best represents the mass, because himself an average man. To suggest that special knowledge and skill must be sought for in an official or a member of the legislature is to cast a slight on the citizens in general." This attitude was the easier to adopt because the bulk of the citizens were not sufficiently instructed to know the value of skill and knowledge. Popular leaders usually encourage the self-confidence of the multitude, and may carry their flattery so far as to disclaim their own attainments and dissimulate their own tastes, so as to make these seem to be just those of the average citizen, that type of simple untutored virtue which has come down to us from the fabled Golden Age of Hesiod. There have been times and countries in which this exaltation of the Common Man has been carried so far as to treat differences of capacity as negligible. The people is conceived of not as an aggregate of all sorts of different kinds of minds and characters, each kind the proper complement of the other, but as a number of individuals resembling one another like pebbles on the beach, their social unity based on their equality and guaranteed by their similarity. The doctrine of Equality, filling the people with a belief in their own

[1] At Athens almost all the officials, except the Generals, were chosen by lot, and in order still further to secure equality, chosen for short terms, so that many could enjoy office (see Chapter XVI.). A similar system was in force in Florence under the republic in the fifteenth century, though in practice it was so worked as frequently to vest the chief offices in the persons whom the ruling party preferred. In the United States the same tendency appears in the very slight regard had to personal fitness in choosing and running candidates for most elective posts.

competence, even for judgeships, was particularly strong in
new countries where the early colonists were nearly all occupied with the same tasks, developing a self-helpfulness
which could dispense with special knowledge.   But it has not
been confined to those countries.   Everybody remembers how
in the Terror of 1793 a plea that Lavoisier's life might be
spared was met by the remark " The Republic has no need of
chemists."   The Russian Communists of to-day appear to
take the " proletarian " handworker as the type, and propose
to reduce every one else to his level.   Nevertheless the progress of physical science, involving special training for the
purposes of production, and the enlarged sphere of governmental action, which increases the value of skill and knowledge, have been making the recognition of Natural Inequality
in the selection of administrative officials more and more inevitable.   A country which should fail to recognize this cannot but fall behind its competitors.

What then is the relation to one another of these different
kinds of Equality?

There has been a long conflict between the sentiment of
Natural Equality and the stubborn fact of Natural Inequality.   In the ancient world and the Middle Ages the latter had free course and prevailed.   With the progress of
civilization and the establishment of constitutional government the sentiment of Equality won its first victories in creating Civil Equality.   It overcame the selfishness and prejudice of ruling classes, and showed that Natural Inequality
is entirely compatible with the possession of equal private
rights by all subjects or citizens.   Its next struggle was for
Political Equality.   Here abstract theory and sentiment were
confronted by practical considerations, for the risks of conferring suffrage on masses of ill-informed persons, many of
them heretofore uninterested in public affairs, were un-
deniable.   Were those who were for any reason — and there
were many different reasons in different cases — palpably
inferior in the capacity for self-government to be entrusted
with a power they might, because unfit, use to their own
detriment as well as to that of the whole community?   Abstract theory has, however, generally prevailed, though in
one remarkable case Natural Inequality avenged itself, for
the suffrage granted after the American Civil War to the

recently emancipated negroes has now been virtually withdrawn. It had embittered the whites; it had not helped the coloured people.

The sentiment of Natural Equality, strengthened by the attainment of Political Equality, has done much to promote Social Equality. That kind of Equality can, no doubt, exist under a despot who allows no voting rights to his subjects, and may stand all the stronger if they are all alike powerless.[1] Yet it is hard in any government except a democracy, and not too easy even there, to prevent the rise of families or corporations accumulating wealth, and, through wealth, gaining power. Legislation has, in sweeping away class distinctions in the civil and political spheres, left social relations untouched. Law indeed could not, except perhaps under a fullblown Communist régime, prevent citizens from choosing their friends among those whose habits and tastes are like their own. Even in Norway and Switzerland, and still more in the United States, social sets continue to exist which are more or less exclusive, and the admission to which men, and still more women, are found to desire. The value of Social Equality — and how great that value is appears when we compare our century with the eighteenth — depends upon its spontaneity. It does much to smooth the working of democratic institutions. The economic antagonism of classes, dangerous in free governments, is less acute when there is no social scorn on the one side and no social resentment on the other.

Last of all we come to Economic Equality, *i.e.* the attempt to expunge all differences in wealth by allotting to every man and woman an equal share in worldly goods. Here arises the sharpest conflict between the principle or sentiment of Natural Equality and the fact of Natural Inequality. It is argued that Natural Justice, in prescribing Equality, requires the State to establish a true and thoroughgoing Equality by redressing the injustices of fortune — taking from those who have too much to supply the needs of

---

[1] A sort of Social Equality has always existed in Musulman countries, because all Musulmans are, as True Believers, gathered into a religious community which, despising the members of other faiths, recognizes an internal brotherhood. This sentiment has given civil equality, but done little or nothing for political equality, no Muslim country having so far succeeded in working constitutional government.

those who have too little, and providing that in future all shall share alike in the products of labour. Wealth, produced by the toil of the Many, must not be allowed to accumulate in the hands of the Few. The establishment of Political Equality has not, as was fondly hoped, secured general contentment and the peace of the community, but has rather accentuated the contrast between two sections of those citizens who, alike in the possession of voting power, are alike in little else. Of what use is that political power which the masses have won if it does not enable them to benefit their condition by State action, carried, if necessary, even to the extinction of private property?

To this it was answered that Economic Equality, no new conception, has always been nothing more than a conception, a vision unrealizable in fact. Something like it may have existed among primitive savages whose only goods were a deerskin and a weapon, but as life became more civilized by the invention of new means to provide for new wants, so much the more did intelligence, strength, persistent industry, and self-control enable their possessor to acquire and retain more than his less gifted fellows. By these qualities the arts of life advanced, enabling greater comfort to be secured for all. If all property were divided up on one New Year's Day, the next would see some men rich and some poor. To ignore differences in productive capacity would be not to follow Nature but to fly in her face.

With this controversy we are not here concerned, for Democracy — which is merely a form of government, not a consideration of the purposes to which government may be turned — has nothing to do with Economic Equality, which might exist under any form of government, and might possibly work more smoothly under some other form. The people in the exercise of their sovereignty might try to establish community of property, as they might try to establish a particular form of religion or the use of a particular language, but their rule would in either case be neither more nor less a Democracy. Political Equality can exist either along with or apart from Equality in property.

Equality has in this chapter been considered only with regard to civilized communities in which a government more or less popular exists. Other considerations arise in coun-

tries where white men rule over, or are in close and permanent contact with, races of a different colour. How far can
the principles which seem fit for the former set of cases be
applied to such facts as are presented by Louisiana, or South
Africa, or the Philippine Isles? On this subject some observations will be found in a later chapter.[1]

Nearly a century ago Tocqueville remarked that the love
of Equality was stronger than the love of Liberty, so that
he could imagine a nation which had enjoyed both parting
less reluctantly with the latter than with the former. Nothing has happened since his day to contradict, and some things
to support, this view. Although the belief in Equality as an
abstract principle is weaker in men's minds to-day, the passion for Equality in practice remains strong in France and
the United States, and has spread to Australia and New
Zealand. It may continue so far as our eye can reach into
the future, for nothing is nearer to a man than the sense of
his personal importance.[2] Yet we must remember that this
was not always so. The feeling of reverence, the disposition
to look up and to obey, is also rooted deep in human nature.
It appeals not only to that indolence or lack of initiative
which disposes men to follow rather than to think or act for
themselves, but also to imagination, as when any striking
figure appears, rising high above them, or when associations
have gathered round ancient and famous families, like those
of Rome even in the later days of the republic. There was
a time when men nourished their self-esteem, as did the de-
pendants of a great house in mediaeval England, as in later
times the soldiers of some great warrior have been known to
do, on an identification of their efforts and hopes with the
glory and fortunes of those who led them. Improbable as
is the recurrence of the conditions which, down to the eighteenth century, and in some countries even later, not only
secured respect and deference for what was then called the
Upper Class, but inspired romantic devotion to a legitimate
sovereign, however personally unworthy, it remains true that
what men once have felt they may come to feel again. The

[1] See chapter " Democracy and the Backward Races " in Part III.
[2] An American who, having fallen on evil days, was obliged to hire
himself as day labourer to a negro employer is reported to have stipu-
lated that the employer should always address him as " Boss."

instinct of personal independence, vehement in days when there were many injuries to resent and many abuses to destroy, may wane under new conditions, and come to count for less in the political life of nations than it does to-day in the English-speaking world.

CHAPTER VIII

DEMOCRACY AND EDUCATION

In 1868, when Britain was taking its first long step towards Universal Suffrage, Robert Lowe, who had been the most powerful opponent of that step, said in Parliament, " Educate your masters." Two years later the first English Act establishing public elementary schools was passed. Thenceforth the maxim that the voter must have instruction fitting him to use his power became a commonplace; and the advocates of democracy passed unconsciously, by a natural if not a logical transition, from the proposition that education is a necessary preparation for the discharge of civic functions to the proposition that it is a sufficient preparation. Modern democratic theory rests on two doctrines as its two sustaining pillars: that the gift of the suffrage creates the will to use it, and that the gift of knowledge creates the capacity to use the suffrage aright. From this it is commonly assumed to follow that the more educated a democracy is, the better will its government be. This view, being hopeful, was and is popular. It derived strength from the fact that all the despotic governments of sixty years ago, and some of them down to our own day, were either indifferent or hostile to the spread of education among their subjects, because they feared that knowledge and intelligence would create a wish for freedom,[1] and remembered that such old movements of revolt as Wat Tyler's rising in 1381 and the Peasants' War in Germany in 1522, had failed largely because the discontented subjects did not know how to combine.

To determine the relation between popular government and education, let us begin by asking what Education means in its relation to citizenship. In the England of 1868 ele-

---

[1] Even the Venetian rulers of Dalmatia in the eighteenth century kept their Slav subjects ignorant so that they might be less able to assert themselves.

mentary education included little more than reading, writing, and arithmetic, for that was practically all that the large majority of schools for the people attempted. The conception has now widened, as schools have improved and as school life has been lengthened. Most primary schools in every English-speaking country now include in their curriculum some grammar, history, and geography, often also a little physical science. Yet when we talk of popular education it is still the ability to read and write that is uppermost in our minds, and the standard by which a nation's education is judged is that of Illiteracy. Wherever any law fixes an educational qualification for the suffrage, that is the test applied. Thus we naturally slip into the belief that the power to read is a true measure of fitness, importing a much higher level of intelligence and knowledge than the illiterate possess.

In modern civilized countries, where schools abound, ignorance of letters is *prima facie* evidence of a backwardness which puts a man at a disadvantage, not only for rising in the world, but for exercising civic rights, since in such countries nearly all knowledge comes, not by talk, but from the printed page. The voter who cannot read a newspaper or the election address of a candidate is ill-equipped for voting. But the real question is not whether illiteracy disqualifies, but to what extent literacy qualifies. How far does the ability to read and write go towards civic competence? Because it is the only test practically available, we assume it to be an adequate test. Is it really so? Some of us remember among the English rustics of sixty years ago shrewd men unable to read, but with plenty of mother wit, and by their strong sense and solid judgment quite as well qualified to vote as are their grandchildren to-day who read a newspaper and revel in the cinema. The first people who ever worked popular government, working it by machinery more complicated than ours, had no printed page to learn from. Athenian voters who sat all through a scorching summer day listening to the tragedies of Euripides, and Syracusan voters who gave good treatment to those of their Athenian captives who could recite passages from those tragedies, whereof Syracuse possessed no copies, were better fitted for civic functions than most of the voters in modern democracies. These Greek voters learnt their politics not from the printed, and few even from any written page, but by listening to accomplished orators and by talking to one another. Talking has this advantage over reading, that in it the mind is less passive. It is thinking that matters, not reading, and by Thinking I mean the power of getting at Facts and arguing consecutively from them. In conversation there is a clash of wits, and to that some mental exertion must go. The Athenian voters, chatting as they walked away in groups from the Assembly, talked over the speeches. They had been made to feel that there were two sides to every question, and they argued these with one another. Socrates, or some eager youth who had been listening to Protagoras or Gorgias, overtook them on the way, and started fresh points for discussion. This was political education. But in these days of ours reading has become a substitute for thinking. The man who reads only the newspaper of his own party, and reads its political intelligence in a medley of other stuff, narratives of crimes and descriptions of football matches, need not know that there is more than one side to a question, and seldom asks if there is one, nor what is the evidence for what the paper tells him. The printed page, because it seems to represent some unknown power, is believed more readily than what he hears in talk. He takes from it statements, perhaps groundless, perhaps invented, which he would not take from one of his fellows in the workshop or the counting-house. Moreover the Tree of Knowledge is the Tree of the Knowledge of Evil as well as of Good. On the printed page Truth has no better chance than Falsehood, except with those who read widely and have the capacity of discernment. A party organ, suppressing some facts, misrepresenting others, is the worst of all guides, because it can by incessantly reiterating untruth produce a greater impression than any man or body of men, save only ecclesiastics clothed with a spiritual authority, could produce before printing was invented. A modern voter so guided by his party newspapers is no better off than his grandfather who eighty years ago voted at the bidding of his landlord or his employer or (in Ireland) of his priest. The grandfather at least knew whom he was following, while the grandson, who reads only what is printed on one side of a controversy, may be the victim of selfish interests who own the organs which his simplicity assumes to express public opinion or to have the public good at heart. So a democracy that has been taught only to read, and not also to reflect and judge, will not be the better for the ability to read. That impulse to hasty and ill-considered action which was the besetting danger of ruling assemblies swayed by orators, will reappear in the impression simultaneously produced through the press on masses of men all over a large country.

These considerations have a significance for European democracies only so far as they suggest the need for carrying education in politics much further than most of them have yet carried it. But in countries hitherto ruled by absolute monarchs, like China or Russia, or by a foreign power, like India or the Philippine Isles, countries in which the experiment of representative government is now about to be tried, those who try the experiment will do well to enquire what the prospect is that ability to read will carry with it the ability to participate in government. Will elementary schools started among the Filipinos qualify them for the independence promised after some twenty years of further tutelage? Will the now illiterate inhabitants of British India be better fitted to cast their votes, whenever the suffrage may be extended to them, by being enabled to read, far more widely than now, newspapers published in their vernaculars? In Russia, a nearer and more urgent case, where the experiment of press freedom would have been instructive, it was not tried, for the censorship exercised by the Czardom was promptly re-established in a more stringent form by the Bolshevists who suppressed all newspapers but their own. No one doubts that in all these countries the sooner elementary education is provided the better: but how soon will it begin to tell for good in politics?

Here is one set of reasons to shake the faith that reading and the habit of reading are enough to make men good citizens of a democracy. Now let us hear another set of sceptics who bid us go from the children that leave a village school at thirteen to the " upper " or educated classes, and enquire from an observation of their minds and conduct whether political capacity increases in proportion to knowledge. There are those who ask whether experience has shown that education helps men to political wisdom. " If it does "— so they argue —" we should find that when in some political dispute the majority of the so-called educated classes have been found on one side, and the bulk of the less educated on the other, the judgments and forecasts of the more educated were usually approved by the result. But has this in fact happened? Has not the untutored instinct of the masses been frequently vindicated by the event against the pretensions of the class which thinks itself superior? Take English history during the nineteenth century, and mark in how many cases the working men gave their sympathy to causes which 'Society' frowned upon, and which subsequent events proved to have deserved that sympathy. What outworn prejudices, what foolish prophecies, what wild counsels may be heard from the lips of the rich! What ridiculous calumnies against political opponents have been greedily swallowed in the fashionable circles of Paris and London! What narrow views have been expressed even by brilliant writers and accomplished teachers or divines! High attainments in some branch of science or learning are compatible with crass ignorance and obstinate perversity where practical issues are involved. Heraclitus said long ago, 'Much knowledge does not teach wisdom.' [1] Have not associations of working men been more often right in their political judgment of measures than college common rooms and military clubs? The instincts of the multitude are as likely to be right as the theories of the learned."

These two sets of criticisms seem worth stating, for extravagant estimates of the benefits to be expected from the diffusion of education need to be corrected by a little reflection on the hard facts of the case. But they do not affect the general proposition that knowledge is better than ignorance. The elementary school may do little to qualify four children out of five for his duty as a voter. But the fifth child, the child with an active mind, has gained much, and it is he who will influence others. The rich man, or the highly trained man of science, may be — and often is — a purblind politician, but that is the result of partisanship or class prejudice, not of knowledge, without which partisanship and class selfishness would be even commoner than they are.

And now we may return to ask, with moderated hopes,

---

[1] Πολυμαθίη νόον οὐ διδάσκει.

What can education do in the way of making good citizens?

Philosophers, and among them some of the greatest, have dwelt much upon and expected much from the formation of political habits by instruction and training. Plato, the earliest whose thoughts on the subject have come down to us, and indeed Greek thinkers generally, had an ethical as well as a political aim, wishing the State to elevate and maintain at a high standard the character of its members for the preservation of internal peace as well as for strength in war. Their favourite example of what training could do was drawn from Sparta, though they saw the hard narrowness of the character it produced. The idea, which in the Middle Ages had been lost except in so far as it was left in the keeping of the Church, was frequently revived by modern theorists while ignored by practical men, till in our own days the example of Japan reawakened a sense of what may be accomplished by the persistent inculcation of certain beliefs, and showed how the long-cherished traditions of a nation may make its members prefer death to any deviation from the accepted code of personal honour and national duty. Still more recently in another country the diffusion of a militaristic spirit and the wide acceptance of theories which place the State above morality — theories proceeding from a few forcible teachers and writers and seconded by the success which had attended their application in war — have exemplified the power of a system of doctrines when glorified by the small ruling class and accepted by nearly all of the more cultivated classes of a great nation. These results are in both instances attributable at least as much to Tradition and Authority as to school instruction, the former repeating through life the maxims delivered in early years. If we can imagine a free people to have all but unanimously agreed on certain principles of faith and practice, and to require every school to teach them, as Rousseau thought that his State should have a civic religion with a civic creed to be enforced, on pain of expulsion, upon those who did not believe it, such a people might succeed in establishing a political orthodoxy which would stand for centuries, just as the Inquisition established a theological orthodoxy in Spain which lasted from the days of Ferdinand and Isabella till Napoleon's invasion. Each generation growing up in the same unquestioned belief would impose unquestioning acceptance on the next. In our day, when every belief is everywhere contested, and intercourse between nations is unprecedentedly active, this may seem impossible, but an Ice Age may await the mind of man, as ice ages have from time to time descended upon his dwelling-place.

Assuming, as may safely be assumed (for it is done with success in Switzerland) that some service can be rendered by instilling in early years an interest in civic functions and a knowledge of their nature,[1] let us ask what sort of instruction is possible: (a) in the Elementary Schools; (b) in the Secondary Schools; and (c) in the Universities?

(a) In schools where pupils remain till about fourteen years of age everything depends on the teacher. To most boys of thirteen, such terms as constitutions, ministries, parliaments, borough councils and voting qualifications are mere abstractions, meaning nothing, because the things which the names denote are outside the boy's knowledge. Text-books are of little use except in furnishing a syllabus which will help the teacher in his efforts to explain in familiar language, and by constant illustrations, what government does mean. To do even this successfully implies a skill not always found. Most teachers need to be taught how they should teach such a subject.

(b) In Secondary Schools and evening Classes for older pupils more may be done. As the school curriculum includes history, the origin of representative institutions may be explained, and the course of their development in countries like Britain and the United States may be outlined. Attention may be called to passing events, such as elections, which show how institutions are actually worked. Even the elements of economics may be added, such as the principle of the division of labour, the nature of money as a medium of exchange, and the arguments for and against Free Trade. The difficulty which inevitably recurs, that of dealing with

---

[1] "Civisme" is taught in the Swiss schools, the book most used being the *Manuel de Droit Civique* of the late M. Numa Droz, famous among the Presidents of the Confederation for his calm wisdom. In most of the American States the subject is regularly taught, with special reference to the Federal Constitution, and something, though not much, has been done in the same direction in Great Britain. In France the teacher in the public elementary schools is a mainstay of the Republican party, relied upon to combat the influence of the parish priest.

matters which have little reality or " content " to one who has not yet come into contact with them in actual life, can be reduced, if not surmounted, by a conversational treatment enlivened by constant illustrations.

(c) When we come to the Universities a wider field opens. Here there are students of high intelligence, some of whom will in after life be leaders, helping to form and guide public opinion. As they already possess a knowledge of the concrete facts of politics, they can use books and can follow abstract reasonings. They discuss the questions of the hour with one another. The living voice of the teacher who can treat of large principles and answer questions out of his stores of knowledge, can warn against the fallacies that lurk in words, can explain the value of critical methods, and, above all, can try to form the open and truth-loving mind, is of inestimable value. In times when class strife is threatened there is a special need for thinkers and speakers able to rise above class interests and class prejudices. Men can best acquire wide and impartial views in the years of youth, before they become entangled in party affiliations or business connections. The place fittest to form such views is a place dedicated to the higher learning and to the pursuit of truth. Universities render a real service to popular government by giving to men whose gifts fit them for leadership that power of distinguishing the essential from the accidental and of being the master instead of the servant of formulas which it is the business of philosophy to form, and that comprehension of what the Past has bequeathed to us by which history helps us to envisage the Present with a view to the Future.

Lest it be supposed that in dwelling on the value of highly educated leaders I am forgetting the qualities needed among the mass of the citizens, let me say a word about the country in which that mass had shown itself most competent. What have been the causes of the success of democracy in Switzerland? Not merely the high level of intelligence among the people and the attention paid to the teaching of civic duty, but the traditional sense of that duty in all classes and, even more distinctly, the long practice in local self-government. Knowledge and practice have gone hand in hand. Swiss conditions cannot be reproduced elsewhere, but the example indicates the direction which the efforts of other democracies may take.   The New England States of the North American Union, till they were half submerged by a flood of foreign immigrants, taught the same moral.   Trained by local self-government to recognize their duty to their small communities, the citizens interested themselves in the business of the State and acquired familiarity with its needs by constant discussion among themselves, reading the speeches and watching the doings of their leaders.   Not many were competent to judge the merits of the larger questions of policy debated in the National legislature.   But they learnt to know and judge men.   They saw that there are always two sides to a question.   They knew what they were about when they went to the polls.   Valuing honesty and courage, they were not the prey of demagogues.   It is because such conditions as those of Switzerland and early Massachusetts cannot be secured in large modern cities that it becomes all the more necessary to try what systematic teaching can do to make up for the want of constant local practice.

The conclusions which this chapter is meant to suggest may be summed up as follows:

Though the education of the citizens is indispensable to a democratic government, the extent to which a merely elementary instruction fits them to work such a government has been overestimated.   Reading is merely a gate leading into the field of knowledge.   Or we may call it an implement which the hand can use for evil, or for good, or leave unused.

Knowledge is one only among the things which go to the making of a good citizen.   Public spirit and honesty are even more needful.

If the practical test of civic capacity in individuals or classes be found in voting for the best men and supporting the best measures, i.e. the measures which ultimate results approve, the masses may be found to have in some countries acquitted themselves as well as what are called the educated classes.

Attainments in learning and science do little to make men wise in politics.   Some eminent scientific men have been in this respect no wiser than their undergraduate pupils. There have been countries in which the chiefs of public services and the professors in Universities were prominent in the advocacy of policies which proved disastrous.

The habit of local self-government is the best training for democratic government in a nation. Practice is needed to vivify knowledge.

The diffusion of education among backward races such as the Filipinos or the African Bantu tribes, or even among the ignorant sections of civilized peoples, such as the Russian peasantry, or the Chinese, or the Indian ryots, will not, desirable as it is, necessarily qualify them to work a democratic government, and may even make it more difficult to work in its earlier stages.

These conclusions (if well founded) may damp hopes, but must not discourage action. Instruction must be provided, in civilized and uncivilized countries, and the more of it the better, for every man must have his chance of turning to the best account whatever capacity Nature has given him, and of enjoying all the pleasure the exercise of his faculties can afford. This will doubtless work out for good in political as well as in other fields of effort. The seed of education will ultimately yield a harvest in the field of politics, though the grain may be slow in ripening.

CHAPTER IX

DEMOCRACY AND RELIGION

WHOEVER tries to describe popular government as it is now and has been in the past, cannot pass over in silence the strongest of all the forces by which governments have been affected. The influence of religion springs from the deepest sources in man's nature. It is always present. It tells upon the multitude even more than it does upon the ruling, or the most educated, class. When roused, it can overpower considerations of personal interest, and triumph over the fear of death itself.

A history of the relations of the spiritual power to the secular during the last eighteen centuries would distinguish two things, essentially different, but apt to be confused in thought because generally intertwined in fact. One is Religion, *i.e.* the religious sentiment as it exists in the mind, disposing those who think and feel alike about man's relation to the Unseen Powers to the recognition of a special tie of sympathy, but not taking concrete form in association for any purpose save that of common worship. The other is Ecclesiasticism, that is to say, some form of religious doctrine solidified in institutions and practices, and especially in the organization in one body of those who hold the same faith, in order that they may not only worship together but act together. This action may be for various purposes, some of which are connected with the secular life, though helping to subserve the spiritual life also. Ecclesiasticism has appeared in divers forms. A caste system, such as existed in ancient Egypt and still exists in India, is one.[1] Another is a religious order, such as those which have been so powerful in the Roman Church. But the most important form is that we call a

---

[1] There are Dervish fraternities among the Muslims, and organized sects such as the Senussi of North-East Africa have sometimes risen to importance.

Church, a body of persons organized and disciplined as a community, on the basis of a common belief, whose officials constitute a government obeyed within the community and able to make itself felt by those without.

Infinitely varying have been the relations between the Church and the State, nor has any really satisfactory solution of the difficulties created by their rival claims been ever discovered. Wherever contractual relations or questions of property are involved, there is contact and there may be conflict. We are here concerned only with one small branch of this vast subject, viz. the force which religions or churches have exerted either in aiding and developing and colouring, or in condemning and opposing, the democratic spirit in general or any particular democratic governments.

In the ancient world religions did not embody themselves in churches, though there were priests and sometimes priestly castes, and the priest could be a potent figure. A profound difference between that ancient world and ours lay in the fact that in it all religions were mutually compatible, so that a polytheist, while primarily bound to worship the gods of his own country, might worship those of other countries also. All alike were deemed able to help their worshippers and defend against its enemies the nation that worshipped them, thus requiring its devotion. The first people that claimed exclusive reality and wide-stretching power for its own Deity was Israel, though no particular time can be fixed as that when it attained to the conception of Jehovah as the one and only true God. The first rulers who tried to enforce by persecution conformity to their own religious usages were the Sassanid kings of Persia, who, being fire-worshippers, forbade their Christian subjects, and doubtless other non-Zoroastrian subjects also, either to bury or to burn the bodies of the dead, these modes of interment being to them a desecration of Fire or of Earth. The first form of worship prescribed by law and enforced by penalties was the worship of the Roman Emperor, or rather of his " Genius " or protecting spirit. Having begun as a voluntary manifestation of loyal devotion to the reigning sovereign, this worship became general in the Eastern provinces, and was used as a test to be applied to persons suspected of being Christians, whenever the emperor, or some local governor, chose to put in force the

laws which forbade Christianity as an " illicit superstition." [1]
Impartial between religious beliefs, the Emperors feared the
Christians partly because they were a secret society, partly
because, "looking to another kingdom, that is, a heavenly,"
they stood apart from the general body of Rome's subjects.
They did not, however, even when persecuted, attempt to
resist or overthrow the temporal sovereign, continuing to protest their civil loyalty to him who was, albeit a pagan, the
Power ordained of God.

The ancient polytheisms need not further concern us,
though religious passion often played a part in Greek politics;
and a few sentences may suffice for the faiths which bear the
names of Buddha (Sakyamuni) and Mohammed, since in no
people professing either has the rule of the people ever been
established.   Buddhism is compatible with any form of government, and though it has (contrary to its essential principles), given rise to wars, it has not favoured any particular
form.   In Tibet it developed a strong hierarchy, and became
practically a State as well as a Church, presenting singular
resemblances to the Catholic hierarchy as it stood in the days
of Popes Gregory VII. and Innocent III.   Islam, specially interesting to the lawyer as Buddhism is to the student
of philosophy, is a State no less than a Church.   The Sacred
Law (like that of the Pentateuch) regulates civil relations
as well as those we should call religious; and ancient Muslim
custom assumes a Commander of the Faithful, or Khalif, a
leader, not a sacred person, nor invested with spiritual authority, but entitled to respect and to some undefined and un-
definable measure of obedience as the successor of the Prophet,
so long as he himself observes the Faith and enforces the
Sacred Law.[2]   All who hold that faith are equal in civil
rights, and in a sense socially equal.   Political rights are a
different matter, but there seems to be nothing (unless it be

---

[1] The interdiction of human sacrifices among the Celts of Gaul was
due not to hostility to Druidical beliefs but to motives of humanity.

[2] The word means "successor or representative."   According to the
old orthodox doctrine, the Khalif must belong to the tribe of the Koreish,
and must be in control of the sacred cities, Mecca and Medina.   Since
the fall of the Abbasside Khalifate at Bagdad, the office possessed
scarcely any political importance till Abdul Hamid II., whose predecessor Selim I. had obtained it from the helpless Fatimite Khalif of
Egypt, began to employ it as a means of increasing his influence outside Turkey.

the conception of the Khalifate) to prevent Muslims from trying the experiment of a republic.

We return to Christianity as the religion which, claiming to be universal, necessarily addressed itself to the conversion of all mankind, though at first only by methods of pacific persuasion.   When it became the official religion of the Roman world it received the support of the State, and recognized the authority of the Emperor, by whom the first six great General Councils were convoked.   It had of course nothing to do with approving or disapproving any form of government, nor was popular government so much as dreamt of.

After a thousand years there came in the eleventh century that great controversy between the secular and the spiritual power in which modern political thought had its beginnings. The Emperors Henry IV., Henry V., and Frederick I. in Italy and Germany, and the Kings of England, William the Conqueror, his two sons and his great-grandson Henry II. found their authority disputed by the Popes from Gregory VII. onwards.   The question at issue was not one of popular rights, but between two kinds of monarchy, the ecclesiastical power and the civil power, the former claiming an authority higher, because exercised over the immortal soul and so reaching forward into the future state, whereas the power of the temporal monarch was only over the body and ended with this life.   The Popes claimed, and sometimes put in force, the right to absolve subjects from allegiance to heretical or schismatic or disobedient sovereigns.   Archbishops, like the pious and gentle Anselm and the haughty Thomas of Canterbury, both received the halo of sainthood for defending the spiritual against the secular power.   In this controversy, although the kings and most of the feudal nobility stood on one side while most of the Italian republics stood on the other, maintaining, with the blessing of the Pope, their rights of practical self-government, no distinctively democratic principles were involved, yet the institution of the priesthood was an assertion of human equality, for every ordained priest was, as a duly commissioned minister of God, the equal of any temporal potentate, and in one respect his superior, since able to dispense sacraments necessary to salvation.   As the rule of celibacy saved the priesthood from becoming a hereditary caste, it was not, like the hereditary priestly and warrior castes in Egypt and India, an oligarchic institution; and less than ever so after the creation in the thirteenth century of the two great mendicant Orders, Dominicans and Franciscans, which sprang from and had great power with the masses of the people.

When in the sixteenth century the Reformers claimed for all Christians freedom of opinion and worship, the revolt became one against both temporal and spiritual monarchy. " Call no man master," neither the king nor the Pope, nor even the whole Church, speaking through a General Council. To meet this protest against authority, and to prop up kingship, the doctrine of Divine Right was invented, partly as a device for transferring to the secular monarch that sort of headship of a National Church which Henry VIII. assumed in England, partly by thinkers who, feeling the need for some sanction to civil authority, argued that whoever is allowed by God to rule *de facto* should, at least after a time, be recognized as ruling *de jure*. This theory, challenged both by the Jesuits, who asserted the right of subjects to overthrow or kill heretical princes condemned by the Pope, and by those Protestants who carried to their logical development the principles of the Reformation, became at last ridiculous. Its dying echoes were heard in the coronation speeches of William I. of Prussia and his unfortunate grandson.

Calvin, the most constructive mind among the Reformers, set himself to replace the Papal and hierarchical system by erecting in Geneva a theocratic scheme of government in close alliance with the State. Each Christian community was to elect its ministers and elders, who were to rule through a Consistory, exercising certain powers in civil matters. His disciples developed this into a frame of representative church government, the locally elected ministers and elders choosing others to represent them in larger governing assemblies. This system, which spread to, and has maintained itself in Presbyterian churches all over the world, became a political force in England and still more effectively in Scotland. It was, however, republican rather than democratic, nor was Calvin himself disposed to trust the multitude.[1]

[1] Calvin observed that it was a vain thing to dispute as to the best form of political institutions; circumstances must determine that. His own preference was for a well-tempered liberty under a wise oligarchy. I quote from Hasbach, p. 2 and note.

The first proclamation of democratic theories in modern countries, if we omit occasional outbursts in the Italian cities and in Germany during the Reformation excitements, the most notable among which was that of the Westphalian Anabaptists, came with the Independents (themselves partly influenced by Anabaptist notions) during the English Civil War. How the ideas of the English Puritans were carried to New England, how they were developed among the American insurgents at the time of the Revolutionary War, how from America they affected the French mind, already stirred by the writings of Rousseau, all these things are too familiar to need description. Christianity itself, however, either in its Roman or its Protestant form, was never involved. That anti-religious, or at least anti-Christian, character which has marked revolutionary movements on the European Continent is due to the enmity felt towards highly secularized State Churches as a part of the established political order which had become odious. Men remembered the persecutions they had prompted, and contrasted the lives of not a few prelates, holders of richly endowed offices, with the precepts they were supposed to teach. The intellectual reawakening and moral reformation of the Roman Church in France have not removed this antagonism, because that Church was long the supporter of monarchy and still exerts a power outside the State which advanced Republicans denounce as Clericalism. The same thing has happened in Italy and Spain, in Spanish and Portuguese America, and to some slight extent even in some Protestant countries. Everywhere in proportion as the Church, more or less completely secularized, was despotic and persecuting, just in that proportion was dislike of it more bitter. Spanish and Italian anarchists show a specially ferocious hostility to Catholicism as well as to the established order of society. Identifying Christianity with capitalism, the Russian and German disciples of Karl Marx display a similarly aggressive antagonism, while in France the alliance between the Roman Church and Louis Napoleon served to exacerbate the old anti-clerical sentiment of the Republicans. In English-speaking countries there has been no such hostility. Democrats and Socialists are there no less and no more Christians than other citizens. The associations, at one time or another, of Christian Churches with monarchies or oligarchies or popular republics have been due to what some have called "the accidents of history," to external causes rather than to essential principles, and they need not affect our view of the true relations, whatever these may be, between forms of faith and forms of government.

As in our own time, however, parties have arisen which call themselves Christian Socialists, while some who do not use that name have argued that Socialism is a legitimate development from the teaching of the Gospels, it is worth while to examine whether any such connection exists.

If the aims of Socialism and Communism be defined as being the establishment of a greater equality of economic conditions and the extinction of suffering due to poverty, these are ends which Christianity also seeks. But the means by which it would attain these ends are different from those which any political party has advocated. The renunciation or abolition of private property is not inculcated in the New Testament, although some of the first believers, in the passionate exaltation of their new sense of brotherhood, had all things in common.[1] Communist politicians propose to carry out their programmes (whatever form these may take) by law, *i.e.* by the compulsive power of the State using physical force. The Gospel contemplates quite other means of bettering human society. It appeals to the sympathy and conscience of the individual, bidding him love his neighbour as himself, and, since he is bound to rejoice in his neighbour's happiness equally with his own, to treat his neighbour, not as a competitor, but as a partner or a brother, giving to him freely all he needs. In a Christian society regulated by these principles there would be no need for the various organs of State action, for an army, or a navy, or courts of law, or police, nor would there be any State relief of poverty, because relief would already have been voluntarily effected by private benevolence. Under the conditions of such a society the State would in fact be superfluous, except as an organization for devising and carrying out a variety of purposes beneficial to all, such as the construction of public works and the preservation of public health. It need hardly be added, for this follows from what has been said already, that there is nothing in the New Testament to require a Christian to be or not

[1] Acts of the Apostles, iv. 32.

to be a political Socialist, nothing either to dissuade or to recommend the use of State power to effect social or economic reforms. If it is sought to effect those reforms by legal compulsion methods, that is a matter for the State which has its own means and methods.

Some have complained that in the Gospel precepts for the conduct of life there is no reference to public or civic duties, unless it be in the saying "Render unto Caesar the things that are Caesar's." But the answer or explanation seems to be, not only that any such precepts would have been inapplicable (if indeed intelligible) to men living in the political conditions of those to whom the Gospel was first preached, but also that they would have been superfluous. Had Christianity been put in practice, forms of government would have mattered little.

But Christianity never has been put in practice. Even that precept which it might have seemed comparatively easy to observe — the avoidance of war between Christians — was entirely disregarded. Whatever was the original meaning of the saying "I am come to send not peace but a sword," one of those many dicta in the Gospels whose true sense remains doubtful, the prophecy was fatally fulfilled, for many wars have sprung from religion, and wars have been as frequent between so-called Christian States as ever they were between those heathen States which Augustine held to be the offspring of sin.

This brief survey may suffice to show that the relation of the Christian Church or Churches to the State has varied from people to people and from age to age according to local circumstances and transitory issues. Many were the attempts from time to time to represent Christianity as the natural bulwark of some set of political doctrines, or to draw the Church into an alliance with the party that professed them. Monarchy and Democracy alternately, or both at the same moment, made bids for ecclesiastical support. Theologians or statesmen appealed to the Bible as favouring the views they propounded. Monarchists and democrats could equally well do so, for there were plenty of texts for both to cite. In England High Churchmen like Laud and Sheldon maintained the divine right of kings by quoting the passages in the book of Samuel which refer to Saul the king of Israel as the Lord's anointed, but the Puritans and the Jesuits alike could counter them by references to the deposition of Saul by the prophet acting under the direction of Jehovah.   Every one can find in the Christian Scriptures what he seeks, because those books are not, like the Koran, the product of any one mind or time but of eight centuries, and record not only events and the words of men, but also the emergence and growth of ideas and beliefs slowly developed in the long life of a people which has contributed more than any other to the religious thought of mankind.   The habit of trying to apply to current politics isolated dicta meant for other conditions has now passed away.   No party resorts to an arsenal which provides weapons equally available for all.

But though, as we have seen, none of the great religions has any natural or necessary affinity to any particular form of government, there are still ways in which religion, or an ecclesiastical body, can affect the course of political events.   Such an organization can unite with and intensify racial or national or party passion.   When strong enough to command the obedience of its own members, it can strengthen by its alliance a secular government or a political party.   A glance at the world of to-day shows that although ecclesiastical influences on politics are slighter than formerly, they still exist.[1] In Russia the Orthodox Church of the East may, though she failed to stem the Bolshevik tide in 1917, prove to have retained part of that power over the peasantry and the middle class which seemed immense ten years ago.   In Canada, Australia, and Ireland, in Belgium and Holland and Switzerland, the support of Roman bishops and priests counts for something in elections.   In France the Church is the pillar of the conservative Right; in Germany it has furnished the foundation of a considerable political party.   It is in English-speaking countries only that the Roman Church has frankly embraced democratic principles, declaring that she has no complaint against popular government, and confining her action to educational questions.

What, then, is the relation to democracy of the fundamental ideas of the Gospel ?   Four ideas are of special significance.

[1] In Japan an attempt was recently made to revive, as against foreign influences, the declining power of Buddhist worship.   In India there are agitators who appeal to Muslim sentiment or Hindu sentiment for the purposes of their political propaganda.

The worth of the individual man is enhanced as a being to whom the Creator has given an immortal soul, and who is the object of His continuing care.

In that Creator's sight the souls of all His human creatures are of like worth. All alike need redemption and are to be redeemed. " In Christ there is neither barbarian nor Scythian, bond nor free."

Supremely valuable is the inner life of the soul in its relation to the Deity. " The kingdom of Heaven is within you."

It is the duty of all God's creatures to love one another, and form thereby a brotherhood of worshippers.

The first of these ideas implies spiritual liberty, the obligation to obey God (who speaks directly to the believer's heart) rather than man. It is freedom of conscience.

The second implies human equality, in respect not of intellectual or moral capacity but of ultimate worth in the eyes of the Creator, and it points to the equal " right of all men to life, liberty, and the pursuit of happiness."

The third idea, expressed in those precepts which bid the Christian to live, with a pure heart, in close communion with God, and the fourth which implies the creation of a Christian community, cannot but affect a man's attitude to life in the world, and may influence it in one of two ways. Absorption in the inner life may tend to individualism, engendering a Quietism or isolated mysticism. On the other hand, the idea of a Christian brotherhood of worship points to the value of the collective life and may dispose men to submission in matters of faith and a merging of their own wills in the will of the community.

Either of these principles, taken alone, may be pushed to an extreme. He who regards the welfare of his own soul may neglect his social and political duties, may passively endure tyranny, or may withdraw, like the early Christian hermits, into the desert. On the other hand, the gathering of the individual worshippers into a community which almost inevitably passes into an organization, may build up a hierarchy which will sacrifice liberty to orthodoxy and become a worldly power. Each of these tendencies was pushed very far, and each has exposed Christianity to censure. Voltaire attacked it as an aggressive and persecuting force, inimical to freedom, yet also a troublesome rival to well-ordered civil government.   Rousseau attacked it as an anti-social influence which, in detaching men from the life of this world and turning their hopes to another, made them neglectful of civic duty. The one thought it dangerous as a stimulant, the other as a narcotic.

If we regard the essential quality of Christianity rather than the errors and corruptions which led men to neglect or pervert its teachings, if we fix our minds not so much on its direct action upon events in history as upon the ideas it contained which affected the course of events, we shall find its influence to have been operative in two respects chiefly.   It implanted the conception of a spiritual freedom prepared when necessary to defy physical force.   The sentence, " We must obey God rather than men," [1] went echoing down the ages, strengthening the heart of many a man accused for his opinions.   It created a sentiment of equality between men — all alike sinful beings, yet also all worth saving from the power of sin — which restrained the degrading idolatry of power which had existed under Asiatic despotisms.   The greatest king was a sinner no less than the humblest subject, and might, as a sinner, be resisted and, if the need arose, deposed.   These ideas, which from time to time broke through the crust of monarchical tradition in the Middle Ages, became potent factors among the Protestants in the sixteenth and seventeenth centuries, wherever monarchs stood opposed to the principles of the Reformers.

In the political as in the moral sphere the fundamental ideas of the Gospel have effected much, yet how much less than was expected by those who first felt their purifying and vitalizing power.   That power sank lowest just when it had secular authority most fully at its disposal.   The more the Church identified itself with the world, the further did it depart from its own best self.   The Church expected or professed to Christianize the world, but in effect the world secularized the Church.   The Kingdom of Heaven became an Ecclesiastical State.   Such victories as Christian principles have from time to time won in the unending strife of good and evil have been won by their inherent moral force, never through earthly weapons.   Neither Voltaire nor Rousseau saw that the belief in " life and immortality brought to light

[1] Acts of the Apostles, v. 29.

through the Gospel " may vivify a man's higher impulses and give a new worth and force to all the work he can do under the sun.

The teachings of the Gospel live and move and have their being in a plane of their own. The values they reveal and exalt are values for the soul, not to be measured by earthly standards. Their influence is not institutional but spiritual. It has nothing to do with governments, but looks forward to a society in which law and compulsion will have been replaced by goodwill and the sense of human brotherhood. However remote the prospect that such a society can be established on earth, the principles which that teaching inculcates are sufficient to guide conduct in every walk of life. He who does justice and loves mercy and seeks the good of others no less than his own will bring the right spirit to his public as well as his own private duties. If ever that spirit pervades a whole nation, it will be a Christian nation as none has ever yet been.

CHAPTER X

THE PRESS IN A DEMOCRACY

It is the newspaper press that has made democracy possible in large countries. The political thinkers of antiquity assumed that a community of self-governing citizens could not be larger than one voice could reach, because only by the voice could discussion be carried on: and they might have added that only where the bulk of the citizens dwell near one another can they obtain by word of mouth the knowledge of political events that is needed to make discussion intelligent and profitable. Within the last hundred years the development of the press has enabled news to be diffused and public discussion to be conducted over wide areas; and still more recently the electric telegraph has enabled news and the opinions of men regarding it to be so quickly spread over a vast and populous country that all the citizens can receive both news and comments thereon at practically the same moment, so that arguments or appeals addressed to the people work simultaneously upon their minds almost as effectively as did the voice of the orator in the popular assembly.

Even before this immense change had arrived, it had been recognized in all free countries that the function of diffusing news and arguments must be, in normal times, open to all persons, so that every man may publish what he pleases, subject to whatever liability law may impose in respect of the misuse of this power. From the days of Milton, whose *Areopagitica* was the first great statement of the case for unlicensed printing, the friends of popular government have treated the freedom of the press as indispensable to its proper working, so much so that it has figured in nearly all the written constitutions of modern free States. The faith in popular government rested upon the old dictum: "Let the people have the truth and freedom to discuss it, and all will go well" (*Fortis semper veritas* [1]). A free press — so it was

[1] "Truth abideth and is strong for ever: she liveth and conquereth for evermore" (I Esdras iv. 38).

assumed — may be relied on to supply true facts because false facts will soon be discovered and discredited. Competition among those who know that the people desire the truth will enable truth to be discerned from falsehood. Free discussion will sift all statements. All arguments will be heard and canvassed. The people will know how to choose the sound and reject the unsound. They may be for a time misled, but general freedom will work out better than any kind of restraint. In free countries no one now impeaches the principle, whether or not he expects from it all it seems to promise. The liberty of the press remains an Ark of the Covenant in every democracy.

To this let it be added that the press was earning the favour it received. During many years in which one country after another was striving to extort full self-government from monarchs or oligarchies the press was one of the strongest forces on the popular side. It exposed oppression and corruption; it arraigned an arbitrary executive, denouncing its selfish or blundering policies; it helped the friends of liberty to rouse the masses. It won popular confidence and sympathy, because it embodied and focussed the power of public opinion. Without it the victory of opinion over the armed force of governments could not have been won.

A time, however, arrived when difficulties and dangers previously unforeseen came to light. It was perceived that the power of addressing large masses of men could be used in many ways and for many purposes. Two or three of these may be mentioned as illustrations.

The old monarchies had possessed their official organs which set forth the facts — or falsehoods — to which it was desired to give currency, but these organs were generally discredited by their official character. Bismarck, if he did not invent, was the first who practised extensively and efficiently the practice of suborning newspapers not supposed to be connected with the government to propagate the statements and views he sought to foist upon the people. His so-called "Reptile Press" proved an effective engine for strengthening his position, and set an example followed in other countries. This method involved no restriction of press freedom, but the well-spring of truth was poisoned at its source.

In countries long attached to the principles of liberty such

as the United States and England some violent journalists
were found advocating the assassination of rulers or statesmen. Could this be permitted? Did the existence of a
political motive justify incitement to murder? This question was answered in the United States by the conviction and
punishment, nearly forty years ago, of Johann Most, a German anarchist. The murder, in 1901, of President Mc-
Kinley, by a Polish anarchist, probably under the influence
of literature suggesting the removal of the heads of States,
gave further actuality to this issue. In a country which
provides constitutional means for the redress of grievances,
political assassination is an offence against democracy, and
cannot plead the arguments used to justify tyrannicide in
lands ruled by tyrants. Will democracy allow itself to be
stabbed in the back?

In a different quarter another problem arose which showed
how hard it is to apply, irrespective of special conditions,
principles previously assumed to be of universal validity.
British administrators in India were agreed, whatever their
school of thought, in holding it unsafe to allow the same
liberty to newspapers published in the native languages as
might be allowed to all newspapers in Europe or North
America. The absence of restrictions would enable unscrupulous persons not only to disturb public order by false
statements, hard to track and refute, and by pernicious incitements addressed to ignorant minds, but also to extort
money from individuals by methods of blackmailing, a device peculiarly hurtful in a country where women are secluded. The ordinary penal law could not be effectively
used to prevent these evils. Thus a people like the English,
heartily democratic in sentiment, found itself unable to apply to the vernacular Indian press its own cherished maxims.
Cases like these — and others might be added — show that
unlimited publicity, the life-blood of free government, may
have its dangers, just as explosives, useful for mining and
tunnelling, have been turned to the purposes of violent crime.

Other things have happened in our time to shake the complacent optimism which the growth of a cheap press had inspired. With the growth of population in industrial centres,
with the diffusion among all classes of the habit of reading,
with the need for information on many new topics of inter-

est, newspapers began to be far more widely read, and as their circulation increased, so did the size of their daily and weekly issues, and the volume of their non-political matter. So also did the pecuniary returns which, if successful, they brought in to their proprietors. They became lucrative business undertakings. Moreover, as most of their readers now belonged to a class with less education and less curiosity for what may be called the higher kinds of knowledge, and with more curiosity for the lower kinds, such as reports of sporting contests, fatal accidents, and above all, accounts of crimes and matrimonial troubles, there appeared in some countries newspapers of a new type which throve by the support of this uninstructed, uncritical, and unfastidious mass of readers. Such papers, free from that restraint which the public opinion of the more educated class had hitherto imposed, could play down to the tastes of the crowd and inflame its passions or prejudices by invectives directed against other classes or against foreign nations, or by allegations and incitements the falsity of which few of its readers were qualified to discover. Since many in this less educated social stratum read newspapers of this type and no others, currency could be given with impunity to misrepresentations and fallacies which there was no means of exposing, however deceptive the colour they gave to the questions before the nation.

The rise of these journals, inauspicious in their moral as in their political influence, has led observers to note a change which has been passing on the press as a whole. But first let us distinguish two aspects a newspaper wears, two functions it discharges.

In one aspect it is a commercial undertaking. It sells news to those who wish to buy news. It sells space in its columns to those advertisers who desire means for bringing their wares (or offered services) to the notice of the public. So far its aims and purposes are simple, straightforward, unexceptionable. It is a trading concern, directed to the making of pecuniary profits.

Its other aspect is that of a guide and adviser, seeking to form the opinion and influence the action of the public. It comments on current events; it advocates or opposes certain views or politics, professing to be in such advocacies animated by public spirit and a disinterested wish to serve the whole community. This spirit may, and often does, prompt the proprietor's or the editor's action. But the real though of course unavowed motive may be selfish and even sordid, perhaps the desire to make gain for the proprietor or his friends out of some undertaking which the State can help or discourage, perhaps a pecuniary inducement offered by persons needing the help of the press. It is of course impossible for the public to know in any given case what may be the motives that lie behind the action of the newspaper; and in most cases its professions of disinterested patriotism are taken at their face value. The same confiding spirit which makes the average reader believe the news which he reads in the paper makes him assume that the views and arguments which accompany the news are also, even though they may be partisan, at least honestly partisan. Thus, that commercial character which a newspaper has in its first-mentioned aspect of a seller of news and of advertising space, and which is innocuous in that aspect, because understood by everybody, may be secretly present and potent in affecting its performance of the function of commenting on events and advocating policies. Premising this significant distinction between the two aspects a newspaper wears, we may return to consider the course of recent developments in political journalism.

The leading organs of the press have been, and are still, in free countries, the one great and indispensable medium for the diffusion of information and opinion on political topics. The daily paper reports events and the views, spoken and written, of prominent men regarding events, and it does this with a perfection of machinery and a display of executive talent that are among the most conspicuous achievements of our time. As already observed, it generally adds to its accounts of events happening and words spoken its own comments, intended to influence the minds of its readers in favour of the political views which it professes and which are, presumably, those of the proprietors and the editorial staff. This is partisanship, but when, as usually happens, the partisanship is known to the reader, it can be allowed for and discounted. So long as there is no suppression or perversion of truth no harm is done. The attitude is (subject to two differences to be hereafter noted) substantially the same as that of a public speaker advocating on a platform the cause of his party. Neither from him nor from the newspaper can impartiality be expected. We are satisfied if each is fairly honest, neither distorting facts nor misrepresenting the position of opponents.

If every newspaper did its best to ascertain and to tell the truth, the whole truth and nothing but the truth, and gave equal opportunities for the expression of all views, leaving the public to judge between those views, newspapers would be, so far as politics are concerned, an almost unmixed good. Everything that can be done would have been done to enable the formation of a sound and sober public opinion, and though the people would sometimes err they would have only themselves to blame. This virtue is not to be looked for in such a world as the present. To demand it would be what theologians call a Counsel of Perfection. The people are pretty well served when a party paper reports events and speeches with fairness to both sides. Such a paper consults its own interests in doing so, for it is respected, and is more likely to be read, by members of the other party. The paper has, moreover, a sort of responsibility to its own party, which regards it as an asset, the value of whose advocacy is reduced if it becomes intemperately reckless, or descends to personal abuse, for that may produce a reaction beneficial to the person assailed, who might relish attacks as a tribute to his importance. It is not invective that damages an antagonist but the bringing up against him of his own errors in word or deed. Sensible men, a minority no doubt, but a minority which influences the rank and file, form their own opinion from the facts little affected by newspaper praise or dispraise.

Till past the middle of last century a newspaper occupying itself with political affairs — and it is only with these that we are here concerned — was primarily a party organ, in close touch with party leaders. The editor was often an independent and forceful personality, who took his own line, perhaps trying to hold an Olympian position in which he could bestow censure or praise on one or other party at his pleasure.[1] But in either case it was as an organ and leader

[1] As instances may be mentioned Horace Greeley (in his better moments) and Edwin L. Godkin in America, Edward Sterling and John T. Delane in England, Emile Girardin in France.

of public opinion that the paper stood out to the world. It was, of course, also a commercial undertaking which had to pay its way and earn a profit; and the wish to earn a profit might influence its political attitude. But the advocacy of political doctrines and the function of giving the public the means of judging for itself by a copious supply of news purported to be its first aim.

Latterly, however, the newspaper has developed another side. Though it still claims to stand as the purveyor of truth and the disinterested counsellor of the people, it is now primarily a business concern, an undertaking conducted for profit like any other. The proprietor has begun to dwarf the editor. The latter has been a man of letters with a pride in his gifts, and usually with a set of opinions which he seeks to propagate. The proprietor is a man of business, and though he may desire power as well as money, profit comes before political opinions. The editor and his staff may be animated by the purest public spirit and may believe all they write, but the proprietor must make money by extending his circulation and (through the circulation) the more considerable returns from advertisements. When the function of purveying truthful news and tendering sound advice seems to conflict with that of increasing the paper's circulation, the obvious way of attaining the latter aim is by taking the line most likely to please the buyers. Noting the direction in which public opinion is moving, the paper will follow, perhaps exaggerate and intensify, the feeling of the moment, or, still more adroitly, it will anticipate the feeling it sees just arising. Another form of gainful activity occurs when the paper's help is desired by a class or a group of persons who have some private interests to promote. They may induce it to advocate legislation from which they expect some benefit, perhaps a protective duty, or a railroad project. Or they may wish to work up a boom in the stock market or to influence the action of Government in some foreign or colonial question out of which money may be made. A financial group may acquire a number of journals, and while working them for profit may also use its power to promote other business enterprises, and to further the ambitions of political leaders. In cases of this kind, where the attitude of the paper is determined not by honest conviction but by an un-

disclosed motive, the public, ignorant of the secret inducement, is misled. It is only in some few countries where the
tone of journalism has declined with that of public life in
general that these evils have become serious. But the risk
is always present.

Another perversion of press power appears when a group
of politicians, or perhaps a single person, works a paper, or
even a number of papers, for their or his political advancement. In a country where service in the legislature, or eloquence on the stump, is not the only door open to high political office, an ambitious man may seek to win influence and
votes by addressing the electorate through his journal or
journals just as a politician would do by platform speeches.
In such instances it may be thought that the journal's influence is lessened when the facts are known, because intelligent
readers understand and discount the motives for its proprietor's action. Yet this may not happen. If the paper
commands a host of readers by the attractiveness of its non-
political matter, the support it gives to the political group, or
to the man, still continues to tell on their minds; and it must
be remembered that the great majority of these readers are
neither well informed nor intelligent enough to realize the
nature of the game that is being played.

Where a journal, from whatever motives, desires to influence opinion and votes in a particular direction, it has two
methods available. One is that of argument. It will advocate or oppose a policy, will extol, or disparage or even calum-
niate, a party chief, after the manner of party speakers on
the platform. Experience has shown that, where party government exists, such advocacy is inevitable and is, within reasonable limits, the best way of bringing out the issues involved and rousing the attention of the citizens. This
method, if it abstains from falsification and calumny, is fair
and above-board. Sensitive men may suffer more than they
would if attacked by a public speaker, because to him they
can reply directly, calling him to account for misrepresentation more easily than they can an anonymous journalist.
Yet no great harm is done. In political warfare hard knocks
must be expected.

The other method is more crafty and more effective.
Since it is Facts that count for most in the formation of

opinion, the newspaper which desires its views to prevail will
try to make out its case by facts.   Sometimes it may assume
facts: *i.e.* it will put forward a theory of the motives or intentions of a person or a group of politicians, and presently
treat that theory as an accepted reality, proceeding to ground
charges upon it.   Sometimes it may even invent facts — *i.e.*
it will catch up (possibly itself set agoing) a rumour, and
then proceed to refer to the rumour as a fact, give it prominence, hammer it into the public mind by repeated blows.
This method needs to be prudently applied, for the alleged
fact may be disproved, and if this happens frequently, the
paper's credit will suffer.   A safer and more telling device
than either argument or misrepresentation is found in the
Selection of facts.   In every controversy there are plenty of
facts fit to be adduced on both sides.   If a paper skilfully
and systematically selects for publication all the facts that
point to one conclusion, and suppresses or mentions curtly
and scantily all the facts that bear the other way, it cannot
be charged with direct falsehood, though it practically falsi-
fies the case by withholding from its readers the means of
forming a just judgment.   The suppression of the truth is
more insidious than the suggestion of the false.   This Negative misrepresentation is as easy and more prudent than
Positive, because detection and conviction are more difficult.
Partisan speakers as well as journals slip into it more or less
unconsciously, but it is far more effective, and usually more
deliberate, in the hands of the journal, and has been employed on a great scale, especially in matters of foreign policy.   Before the outbreak of the war between the United
States and Spain in 1898 the newspapers of the former country were deluged with matter putting the conduct of Spain in
Cuba — conduct doubtless open to grave censure — in the
worst light and letting little or nothing appear on her behalf.
A more remarkable case was seen a year later, when the bulk
of the British press [1] stated and exaggerated what case there
was against the Transvaal Government, while ignoring the
facts which made in favour of that republic, with the result

[1] There were, however, some conspicuous exceptions.   In one of these
an important newspaper incurred much unpopularity and lost heavily,
but it held on, and when the South African War was over regained
more than it had lost.

that the British public never had the data necessary for forming a fair judgment.

These instances, to which others might be added, illustrate the fact that press exaggerations or misrepresentations are especially mischievous in questions arising with foreign countries. Where the controversy is domestic, the citizens know more about it, and the activity of the opposing parties may be relied on to bring out the facts and provide answers to mendacious statements and fallacious arguments. This may not happen where a foreign country is concerned, whose case no political party nor any newspaper need feel bound (except from purely conscientious motives) to state and argue. To do so is usually unpopular, and will be stigmatized as unpatriotic. Here, accordingly, the policy of suppressing or misrepresenting what may be said on behalf of the foreign case commends itself to the journal which thinks first of its own business interests. Newspapers have in all countries done much to create ill feeling and bring war nearer. In each country they say the worst they can of the other country, and these reproaches, copied by the newspapers of the other, intensify distrust and enmity. All this is done not, as sometimes alleged, because newspapers gain by wars, for that is not always the case, since their expenditure also increases, but because it is easier and more profitable to take the path of least resistance. The average man's patriotism, or at least his passion, is aroused. It is comforting to be told that the merits are all on his side; nor can there ever be too many reasons for hating the foreigner.

Arts of this nature have long been used by public speakers. The newspaper is only an orator addressing a reader instead of a hearer. It lacks the personal charm, the gift of attracting enthusiasm and inspiring attachment, which the great orator possesses. But in other respects its power is greater than his. It addresses many audiences at once. It is indispensable, because it gives a mass of non-political news which most people want for business purposes, and the rest from curiosity. For the multitude who follow public affairs with an interest not strong enough to draw them to public meetings or make them read the reports of proceedings in a legislature, it is the only source of political instruction, perhaps almost their only reading of any kind. It can go on reiterating its arguments, or setting forth the same set of facts intended to suggest or enforce those arguments, day by day and week by week.

The last fifty or sixty years have seen an evident increase in the power of the great newspapers. As the number of their readers, as well as the habit of reading, has grown, and as their range has expanded, for they supply news from all over the world and treat many new subjects, which only specialists can handle, so also their revenue and their expenditure have increased. Since they require a larger capital than formerly, the stronger papers have grown, and the weaker have withered away, while few new rivals have appeared, because to establish a daily journal is a costly and risky enterprise. Thus, in the great cities of nearly every country, the number of leading papers is now comparatively small, but each wields a greater power than formerly. This is not due to any finer quality in their articles, for the writing is no more brilliant than formerly — in some countries it seems to have declined. The " leading articles," moreover, count for less than does the news and what may be called the " attitude " of the great journal, with the prestige it derives from the vast scale of its operation, addressing myriads at the same moment, in the same words, with the same air of confidence. The feeling that so many people read it and believe in it raises the presumption that if they do read it, it is because they believe. Seeing in it a force that cannot be ignored, each accepts its views because each thinks that others are accepting. It speaks *ex cathedra* with a pontifical authority which imposes deference. Goldwin Smith said fifty years ago that he remembered an article in which a great British newspaper claimed that it discharged in the modern world the functions of the mediaeval Church.

Prestige is heightened by mystery. Scarcely any of those who read what the paper tells them know who has written what they read, or what sources of information he possesses, or what intellectual weight. The voice seems to issue from a sort of superman, and has a hypnotic power of compelling assent. An elderly clubman who has been behind the scenes may remark to his friend over their coffee: " After all, these thundering articles are written by a fellow with the arrogance of inexperience, who knows much less about the matter than you and I do, a young fellow scribbling in a dingy room up three pair of stairs." But to the tens of thousands in and all round the city the thunder seems to come from the sky above. It is like the voice of a great multitude. And in truth the paper does represent much more than the scribe in the dingy room, for a great journal has traditional authority as well as large capital behind it, and its policy may be the product of the combined action of a number of shrewd minds, watching the ebbs and flows of opinion, studying how to please the vast electorate, or how to terrify the men in office. Behind the argumentative advocacy, in itself a small matter, is the power of manipulating news, and of reporting what the proprietors wish to be known and ignoring what they wish to keep out of sight. Strange is the fascination of the printed page. Men who would give little credence to a tale told them by a neighbour, or even written to them by a friend, believe what the newspaper tells them merely because they see it in print. In one country where newspaper inaccuracy is taken as matter of course, the same man who says, " You know the papers are full of lies," will forthwith repeat some charge against a politician on the faith of a paragraph, believing, because he saw it in the newspaper, that there must be something in it.

There are countries in which one source of a journal's power consists in its relations, real or supposed, with the ministry of the day, or with those great financial interests which are believed, not without reason, to exert an influence more permanent than that of officials, since they do not come and go with a popular vote. Ministers, and also prominent politicians not in office, have frequently used, and been helped by, newspapers, repaying them sometimes by private intelligence, sometimes, as in the United States, by the bestowal of foreign missions, sometimes, as in England, by titular honours.[1] Not to speak of Germany under Bismarck, Katkoff rendered great services to the Russian Government in the 'seventies, and some English politicians have owed much to the incessant efforts of their press friends, while in Aus-

[1] Cases have even occurred in which the Ministry (or a Minister), in one country has, in the course of a controversy with a foreign Power, endeavoured to win domestic support for itself or frighten the foreign Power by secretly directing attacks upon the latter through the press.

tralia there have been times when a powerful paper could make or unmake a Prime Minister.

A more important element in the growing ascendancy of the press may be found in the fact that in most countries it depends less than it did two generations ago on the favour of what is called " Society " and the educated classes. The political and literary sides of its action had then a significance which has declined with the increasing importance of its commercial aspects. It is less amenable to the critical judgment of what are called the " men of culture," because it relies on the vast mass of persons who buy it merely for news or for business purposes, and who advertise in it for the latter. To the majority of such persons its political attitude is indifferent; and this makes the political news it publishes, and the interpretations of that news it supplies, a more efficient means of propaganda. Secure in its hold upon the business community and the multitude of readers who are glad to have their thinking done for them, it need not regard criticisms proceeding from the austere or fastidious few.

Those whose recollections go back half a century seem agreed that the power of journalism, as compared with that of the most eminent individual statesmen, has in nearly every free country been growing. Let us compare the opportunities of influence which were open to such men as Peel or Gladstone, Calhoun or Seward or Grover Cleveland, with those which their successors to-day enjoy, and estimate the advantages the journal possesses when engaged in a conflict with the statesman.

To-day the statesman, even if he be a brilliant speaker whose speeches are invariably reported, has a far smaller audience than the newspaper, because it is read steadily from day to day, and he only occasionally. He may have a personal charm which the paper lacks. He may be an orator on whose lips the crowd hangs. He may, like Theodore Roosevelt, be a figure throbbing with life, who becomes the hero, almost the personal friend, of a multitude who admire his force and love his breezy ways. But the aggressive quality which is indispensable to prominence makes enemies, and exposes him to a fire of criticism and misrepresentation. He cannot be always contradicting misstatements and repelling charges; nor be sure that his denials will reach those who have read the charges. He can grapple with and throw a personal foe, but in a conflict with the impersonal newspaper it will always have the last word. It can persistently take for granted statements which require proof until the reader believes they have been proved. It can incessantly repeat the same argument or the same accusation, and can do this incidentally, as well as in a set way, so as to influence that host of readers who are too listless to enquire into the truth of assertions or insinuations sandwiched in between the news about markets or sport. Tactics like these will win against all but those strongest antagonists who have already by intellectual force and moral dignity secured the confidence of the people. Iteration is like the ceaseless stream of bullets from a machine-gun. It is the deadliest engine of war in the press armoury.

The power of the newspaper, one of the most remarkable novelties of the modern world, has two peculiar features. It has no element of Compulsion and no element of Responsibility. Whoever exposes himself to its influence does so of his own free will. He need not buy the paper, nor read it, nor believe it. If he takes it for his guide, that is his own doing. The newspaper, as it has no legal duty, is subject to no responsibility, beyond that which the law affixes to indefensible attacks on private character or incitements to illegal conduct. It is an old maxim that power and responsibility should go together, and that no man is good enough to be trusted with power for the employment of which he need give no account. Here, however, we have power which can be used without anything except conscience to restrict or guide its use. A journal is not liable, civilly or criminally, for propagating untruth or suppressing truth unless damage to a particular individual or harm to the State can be proved.

This is the case with politicians also, as with all who speak in public, but they, being individuals, have something to lose by speaking untruth or perverting truth. They can be denounced, and deprived of whatever respect or influence they may have enjoyed. To penalize a newspaper for like conduct is so difficult as to be often scarcely possible. The paper is an impersonal entity. Its writers are unknown: its editor, and even its proprietors, may be known to comparatively few.

Proof of a deliberate purpose to mislead will not necessarily affect its circulation or reduce its influence upon masses of men who know little and care less about such offences.   Except in the most glaring cases, it can with impunity misuse its power.   The proprietor, or the editor to whom his proprietor gives a free hand, may be patriotic and well-intentioned, but the power either wields is not accompanied by responsibility.

These things being what they are, it may seem surprising that the influence of the press should not, in English-speaking countries, have been more abused than has in fact been the case.   How far it is now abused, either there or elsewhere, is a subject which cannot be here dealt with, for the facts, differing in different countries, are everywhere hard to ascertain.   It is enough to indicate how liable to abuse power so irresponsible must be, and how salutary the traditions which have, in the countries just referred to, maintained, among the leading journals, a creditable standard of courtesy and a fair, if not perfect, standard of honour.   The vigilance of public opinion, the strenuous competition which exists between the able men who fill the higher posts, and their pride in their profession, have helped to guard these traditions.

In the chapters of Part II. which deal with the six democracies there selected for description, I have attempted to estimate the authority actually exerted in each by its press. That authority seems to be stronger in Great Britain — possibly also in the British self-governing Dominions — than in the United States; but it must be remembered that in a very large country there are so many journals, each relying on the circulation it holds in its own territory, that no such general predominance can be won as a very few may possess in a small country.   In England, and even in Scotland, politicians, and especially candidates for Parliament, a class prone to the habit of nervously " tapping the weather-glass," are apt to exaggerate the political importance of the press.   There have been General Elections at which the balance of journalistic strength was heavily on the side which suffered a crushing defeat at the polls.   A member may hold his seat for many years against the hostility of all the local papers.   If he is personally liked and trusted, their attacks produce a reaction in his favour.   But in a large country, and even in a city like New York, full of ignorant voters, persistent denigration may destroy a politician.   A calumny once launched cannot be overtaken.   Attack is easier than defence: and the resources of misrepresentation are infinite.[1]

A journal which addresses itself specially to one particular section of a nation, be it a racial, or religious, or industrial section, needed as it may be for some purposes, can be dangerous if it presents to that section a purely partisan set of facts and opinions, exaggerating whatever grievances the section has, and intensifying its sense of separation from and antagonism to other parts of the nation.   Those belonging to such a section who read other newspapers also will not be seriously affected, but where they see only their own class organ, and take its statements for truth, an irritable fanaticism on behalf of sectional ideas and class aims may be engendered.   This is an instance of the general principle that the best remedy against whatever dangers the dominance of the press involves is to be found in the free and full competition of independent newspapers.   It is the predominance in one particular area or among the members of one particular class, of a single paper, or of several controlled by the same person or group and working for the same ends, that threatens the formation of a fair and enlightened public opinion.   The tyranny of monopoly is even worse in opinion than in commerce.   Suppose a capitalistic combination to acquire a large number of newspapers, placing them under the direction of one capable mind and forceful will, and using their enormous resources to drive rivals out of the field.   The papers would be able to supply the fullest and latest news in every department of journalism, and to purchase the service of the ablest pens.   With their vast circulation, they could, by presenting facts of one colour and tendency and suppressing or discolouring all news of an opposite tendency, succeed in impressing, if not on the majority yet on a large percentage of the voters, whatever opinion they desired.   The weaker kind of politician would succumb to them.   Ministries would fear

---

[1] Among them the cartoon representing a public man in the commission of offences he has never committed is one specially difficult to deal with.   When this is done at an election, the result desired may be attained before the calumny can be refuted, and there are countries in which the law of libel gives no sufficient protection.

to offend them.   Foreign countries would soon begin to recognize their supremacy.   If the capital needed to finance such an enterprise and the powerful brain needed to direct it were to be united, what might not happen in a country not too large for such an enterprise?   The contingency is improbable, but those who know what centralization and combination have in all branches of business been able to effect will hardly deem it impossible.   How could the dictatorship of such a syndicated press be resisted?   The remedy proposed for industrial monopolies is nationalization, but here nationalization would aggravate the evil, making the State itself the tyrant.   Recourse might be needed to drastic legislation of a kind not yet tried.

The coincidences of opportunity with a supreme talent for using opportunity mark the turning points of history. Alexander of Macedon having received from nature extraordinary gifts, inherited a well-trained army and saw before him a divided Greece and an effete Persian empire waiting to be conquered.   Had he been born earlier or later, the whole course of events might have been different.   The career of Napoleon points the same moral.   There have doubtless been many other men of genius who might have equally affected the fortunes of the world had like opportunities come to them.[1]

What has been said as to the influence the press can exert on the working of popular government through its power of forming opinion may be summed up in a few propositions.

Universal suffrage has immensely increased the proportion

[1] A parallel, perhaps not too fanciful, may be drawn between such cases and those of famous thinkers whose creative gift, continuing to work long after them, was evoked, or turned into the needed channel, by the circumstances of their own time.   St. Paul coming at a moment when a new religious teaching had to be diffused over the world, St. Augustine when the fall of Rome made it necessary to create a theological view of history to replace the reverence for the Empire that was breaking in pieces, Thomas of Aquinum meeting the call of the moment for a philosophic systematization of Christian doctrine, Kant stirred to his constructive work by the scepticism of Hume, may be cited as instances of this.   Whenever such minds had come into the world they would probably have done memorable work, but the stimulus of the moment would have been wanting, and the state of the world might have prevented their gifts from having full effect.   Conversely there are cases to be noted in which, when a great opportunity arrives, no genius appears capable of turning it to account.

of electors who derive their political views chiefly or wholly
from newspapers.

The causes which enable newspapers well managed, and
commanding large capital, to drive weaker papers out of the
field, have in all countries reduced the number of influential
journals, and left power in comparatively few hands.

The influence upon opinion exercised by a great newspaper
as compared with a prominent statesman or even with the debates in legislative bodies, has grown.

Newspapers have become more and more commercial undertakings, devoted primarily to their business interests.

The temptations to use the influence of a newspaper for
the promotion of pecuniary interests, whether of its proprietors or of others, have also increased.   Newspapers have become one of the most available instruments by which the
Money Power can make itself felt in politics.

The power of the press is a practically irresponsible power,
for the only thing it need fear (apart from libel suits) is the
reduction of circulation, and the great majority of its readers,
interested only in business and sport, know little of and care
little for the political errors or tergiversations it may commit.

Press power is wielded more effectively through the manipulation and suppression of news than by the avowed advocacy
of any political views.   It is more dangerous in the sphere
of foreign than in that of domestic policy, and is one of the
chief hindrances to international goodwill.

Democratic government rests upon and requires the exercise of a well-informed and sensible opinion by the great
bulk of the citizens.   Where the materials for the formation
of such an opinion are so artfully supplied as to prevent the
citizens from judging fairly the merits of a question, opinion
is artificially made instead of being let grow in a natural way,
and a wrong is done to democracy.

No one will suppose that an indication of the dangers
which misuse of the power of the press may bring implies
any disparagement of the invaluable services it renders in
modern free countries.   Without it, as already observed,
there could be no democracy in areas larger than were the
city communities of the ancient world.   The newspaper enables statesmen to reach the whole people by their words, and

keeps legislatures and executive officials under the eyes of the
people.   Itself irresponsible, it enforces responsibility upon
all who bear a part in public work.   It is because the press
alone can do and is doing so much salutary and necessary
work that attention needs to be called to any causes which
might, by shaking public confidence in it, impair its useful-
ness to the community.

CHAPTER XI

POLITICAL parties are far older than democracy. They have existed in nearly all countries and under all forms of government, though less in monarchies than in oligarchies, in the latter of which they have been particularly frequent and fierce. The Guelfs and Ghibellines, after having for a time divided Germany, divided the feudal nobility and the cities of northern and middle Italy for three centuries.

In popular governments, however, parties have a wider extension if not a more strenuous life, for where every citizen has a vote, with the duty to use it at elections, each of the parties which strive for mastery must try to bring the largest possible number of voters into its ranks, organize them locally, appeal to them by the spoken and printed word, bring them up to the poll. Ballots having replaced bullets in political strife, every voter is supposed to belong to one of the partisan hosts and to render more or less obedience to its leaders. He has, moreover, at least in theory, something to gain from its victory, because each party promises legislation of the kind he is supposed to desire, whereas most men who called themselves Guelfs and Ghibellines fought merely out of an attachment, usually hereditary, to a party name, and probably also to the cause of some particular leader, as in Mexico to-day if the member of a band is asked to what he belongs, he answers, " To my chief " (*mi jefe*).

Many have been the origins whence in time past parties have sprung. Religious or ecclesiastical differences have given birth to them, as in England and Scotland in the seventeenth century, or racial divisions, or loyalty to a dynasty, as in the case of the Stuarts in England after James II.'s expulsion, and the Bourbons in France after 1848. Even attachment to a particular leader who has gathered followers round him may keep them together long after he has passed away. In the republic of Uruguay there were, sixty years ago, two prominent generals, each with a band of adherents. These Reds and Whites still divide the country. A party may in its first beginnings be built on any foundation — wood or stubble as well as rock — for it is not the origin that matters so much as the forces which, once created, a party can enlist. However, in more recent days, and especially in countries enjoying representative government, the normal source is found in the emergence of some type of political doctrine or some specific practical issue which divides the citizens, some taking one side, some another.

Though the professed reason for the existence of a party is the promotion of a particular set of doctrines and ideas, it has a concrete side as well as a set of abstract doctrines. It is abstract in so far as it represents the adhesion of many minds to the same opinions. It is concrete as consisting of a number of men who act together in respect of their holding, or professing to hold, such opinions. But being a living organism, it develops in ways not limited by its theory or its professions, and is affected by the constantly changing circumstances amid which it moves and to which it must adapt itself.

Whatever its origin, every party lives and thrives by the concurrent action of four tendencies or forces, which may be described as those of Sympathy, Imitation, Competition and Pugnacity. Even if intellectual conviction had much to do with its creation, emotion has more to do with its vitality and combative power. Men enjoy combat for its own sake, loving to outstrip others and carry their flag to victory. The same sort of passion as moves the crowd watching a boat race between Oxford and Cambridge or a football match between Yale and Harvard, is the steam which works the great English and American parties. Nothing holds men so close together as the presence of antagonists strong enough to be worth defeating, and not so strong as to be invincible. This is why a party can retain its continuity while forgetting or changing its doctrines and seeing its old leaders disappear. New members and new leaders, as they come in, imbibe the spirit and are permeated by the traditions which the party has formed. It is pleasant to tread in the steps of those who have gone before and associate one's self with their fame.

Life becomes more interesting when each talks to each of how the opposite party must be outgeneralled, and more exciting when the day of an electoral contest arrives. Though a certain set of views may have been the old basis of a party, and be still inscribed on its banner, the views count for less than do the fighting traditions, the attachment to its name, the inextinguishable pleasure in working together, even if the object sought be little more than the maintenance of the organization itself. In England, sixty years ago, few indeed of the crowds that at an election flaunted their blue or yellow colours could have explained why they were Blues or Yellows. They had always been Blues or Yellows; probably their fathers were. It was irrational, but it expressed a sentiment of loyalty to a cause. If the bulk were not fighting for principles, they were fighting unselfishly for something outside themselves, expecting from victory nothing but the pleasure of victory.[1]

It was in English-speaking countries that party first became a force in free political life. Whigs and Tories in England date from the days of Charles II., parties in America from the presidential election of 1796. In the former case party appeared first in Parliament. In the latter it appeared simultaneously in Congress and in the people at large. The influence and working of a party system need to be considered separately in each of these two fields. Let us begin with the people.

In countries which enjoy representative government parties have two main functions, the promotion by argument of their principles and the carrying of elections. These provide constant occupation, and success in either contributes to success in the other. The business of winning elections involves the choice of candidates. In every election area, the local members of the party must agree upon a candidate for whom their united vote will be cast. While constituencies were small, because electoral districts were small and the suffrage was

[1] I knew a Scottish constituency in which a party had from personal dissensions become cleft into two sections where there was no political difference between the sections, but each held together and, during a long series of years, tried to carry a candidate of its own merely because each desired to be the ruling force in the town.

This used to happen in the Italian republics of the Middle Ages, the personal rivalries of leaders becoming the basis for factions.

restricted by a property qualification, men either put themselves forward as candidates, or induced a small group of influential electors to nominate them. A person of local prominence as landowner in a county or merchant in a borough was known to many of the electors, and accepted on the score of his position or personal abilities or popularity. This still happens in parts of France and of Switzerland, and formerly happened in America. But when constituencies became large and the feeling of democratic equality pervaded all classes, the principle of popular sovereignty required the choice of a party candidate to be made by those of the electors who belonged to the party. So local party Committees grew up, and local party meetings were convoked to select the candidate. This custom was, many years later, adopted in England where, however, the Central Office (*i.e.* the national party managers) may tactfully suggest to the local association the name of a particular aspirant. Without some party authority recognized as entitled to recommend a candidate, the voting strength of the party might be dispersed among competing party candidates, many electors not knowing for whom they ought to vote. In large constituencies, guidance is essential,[1] so when in the United States it is desired to put forward as candidates for city offices better men than those whom the party organization is nominating, a Citizens' Committee or Good Government Organization, formed for the occasion, issues a list of candidates whom a bevy of respected inhabitants join in recommending.

Another branch of political work formerly left to private initiative has now become recognized as incumbent on a party. It is the conduct of elections and the defraying, where the candidate is a poor man, of part at least of the expenses of a contest, expenses which have grown with the increased size

[1] When in 1897 the whole of London was divided into ten boroughs, each with an elected Council, few residents in a borough had any means of judging the merits of the candidates offering themselves for election. The nominators were not known to the vast majority of the voters, and as the elections were not fought on party lines one could not, even if one had wished to do so, vote for a man as a Tory or a Liberal. I remember at such an election (in a borough of 300,000 inhabitants) to have scanned the lists of candidates, and found no clue to guide my choice till in one I discovered the name of a learned Homeric scholar. For him I promptly voted, and, assuming that a man of his distinction would choose his company well, voted for most of those on the list in which his name appeared.

of constituencies due to universal suffrage. Every party has now funds available for helping candidates, a practice liable to be abused, yet unavoidable, for without help capable men might be excluded, and the candidate with the longest purse would have an unfair advantage.

Another and not less important function of a party is that of holding together the members of a representative assembly who profess the political opinions for which the party stands, so as to concentrate their efforts on the advocacy of its principles and the attainment of its ends. This is especially needed in countries living under what is called Parliamentary Government, where the Executive is virtually chosen and dismissible by the majority of the legislature. Under such a system the majority, called the Party in Power, carries on the government of the country through some of its leaders, the executive ministers, whom it keeps in office so long as they retain its confidence. Such a scheme cannot work without some sort of discipline to keep the members of the majority solid, reminding them of their responsibility to their supporters in the constituencies. From Great Britain, which has been governed in this way for about two centuries, this scheme spread to such countries as Canada, Australia, France, Belgium, Holland and the three Scandinavian kingdoms, in all of which a " Party in Power " carries on the government, while the rest of the legislature constitute the Opposition or Oppositions.

In other countries, such as the United States, the majority in the legislature, though it controls legislation, does not choose the Executive, that function being reserved to the people voting at the polls; so that the expression " Party in Power " describes the party which holds the Executive. But this difference reduces but little the need for party organization and discipline in the legislative chambers. In both cases the party must hold together in order to pursue its purposes. In both the motive and regulative force that keeps them united together, consists in the common wish to give effect to their doctrines by legislation, and in both, moreover, the party leaders have a prospect of winning authority, distinction, and emoluments, the rank and file of the party sharing, when their turn comes, in getting or securing for their friends whatever patronage may be going. Thus the im-

pulse to hold together is strong: thus a party may maintain
unity and vigour even if it has ceased to care for the principles for whose sake it professes to exist.

This system, under which the fortunes of a nation are entrusted to one set of persons who represent the majority, possibly only a bare majority, of the voters, has been much censured, especially by theorists unfamiliar with the actual working of representative institutions. Why, it is urged, should
administrative officers, most of whose work has nothing to do
with their party opinions, be they Whig or Tory in England,
Republican or Democratic in America, be taken entirely from
those who profess one set of political views and belong to one
organization? The man with the fullest knowledge of foreign relations, or the man who best understands educational
problems, may belong to the minority. Why should his abilities be lost to the public service? Why make so many public
questions controversial that need not be so? What is the
sense of setting up one group of men, A, B, C and D, to introduce legislation and handle administrative problems, and
of setting up a second set, W, X, Y, Z, to harass and trip up
the former, opposing their proposals and hampering their
executive action? Yet this is understood to be, under the
British system, the especial business of a parliamentary opposition, for the men who compose it find a motive for their
attacks in the hope of turning their antagonists out of office
to install themselves therein. Thus a parliament becomes a
battlefield, and its deliberations a perpetual struggle of the
Ins and the Outs, in which the interests of the country are
forgotten.

Other charges brought against the party system may be enumerated, because they indicate dangers which threaten the
working of democratic government.

It is alleged to encourage hollowness and insincerity. The
two great American parties have been compared to empty
bottles, into which any liquor might be poured, so long as the
labels were retained. Party divides not only the legislature
but the nation into hostile camps, and presents it to foreign
states as so divided. It substitutes passion and bitterness
for a common patriotism, prejudices men's minds, makes each
side suspect the proposals of the other, prevents a fair consideration of each issue upon its merits, enslaves representa-

tives and discourages independent thought in the party as a whole, because the " solidity " or " regularity " which casts a straight ballot is enforced as the first of duties. It prompts each party to make promises and put forward plans whose aim is not to benefit the country but to attract popular support. When one party plays this game, the other party has to follow suit with another and, if possible, more attractive programme.

Another perversion is the extension of national party issues to local elections, with which they have, as a rule, nothing to do. To run a candidate for a county or city office in an American state, or for a county or borough council in England, as a Republican or Democrat, as a Tory or Liberal, diverts attention from the personal merits of the candidates to their party affiliations, obscures the local issues of policy by putting loyalty to the national party into the foreground, and tends to divide the members of a deliberative local authority into sections drawn together by their political affinities, so that these affinities determine their action in questions purely local.

A further dereliction from principle is found in countries where posts in the public service are reserved for persons who belong to the dominant party. This practice, known as the Spoils System, though reduced of late years, is not yet extinct in the United States, nor France, Canada, and Australia. In Britain, where it was formerly general, it can be still discovered in odd corners, such as some legal, and more rarely, some educational, posts. Here, however, it is only a secondary force, sometimes giving one candidate a slight advantage over another, but seldom installing an incompetent man. Retained as a means of rewarding supporters, it is excused on the ground that as the other side have practised it, " our fellows must have their chance." Neither party desires to run ahead of the other in the practice of austere virtue.

Lastly, party spirit is accused of debasing the moral standards, because it judges every question from the standpoint of party interest. It acclaims a successful leader as a hero and secures forgiveness for his faults. If the leaders of a party in power embark in an unwise foreign policy, or if some ardent spirits among the Opposition resort to questionable methods of resistance to what they think unjust, the voice of temperate criticism within the party is overborne, because party spirit either blinds men to the truth or fears to admit errors which the other party will use against it.[1] Even if the heads of a party organization are discovered to have been using their power for selfish — perhaps for sordid — purposes, the party tries to shield them from exposure; and it may accept the tainted aid of rich men seeking their own private gains. In one way or another, the sentiment of party solidarity supersedes the duty which the citizen owes to the State, and becomes a weapon in the hands of an unscrupulous chief who can lead the party to victory. Party spirit will always be an instrument on which personal ambition can play. In the republics of antiquity a party might help its leader to make himself a Tyrant because it hated the other faction more than it loved freedom. Similar phenomena were seen in mediaeval Italy, and their pale reflex has been sometimes visible in modern states.

That these are among the dangers to which the system of party government exposes a State is practically admitted by each party when it is denouncing the action of a rival party. They describe those rivals as actuated by the " spirit of faction." They exhort the wiser and more moderate members to shake off that spirit, rid themselves of prejudice, and consider all proposals, even those of opponents, with an open mind, while in the same breath they exhort their own followers to close their ranks and go to the polls cherishing the traditions of their party, grateful for its services, mindful that it emancipated the slave or bestowed old-age pensions upon working men. They must sometimes wish that it was possible for them to address their own followers in one tongue, and their opponents in another, each uncomprehended by the

---

[1] Thus in 1899–1901 many persons in England who disapproved the South African War kept silence, because they belonged to the party which had led the country into what they thought a needless conflict, and in 1903 many who disapproved what was called the policy of " passive resistance " to the levying of a local tax, part of whose proceeds went to support denominational schools, abstained from expressing their disapproval of that policy, though they privately admitted that those prominent men in their own party who had advised it were setting a dangerous precedent. One expects this from the more ignorant or thoughtless members of a party, but in both these and other similar cases the same phenomenon was visible among the " wise and good " also.

other, as shepherds in the Scottish Highlands are said to shout their orders to one dog in English and to another in Gaelic.

History is full of the mischiefs wrought by party spirit. Yet there is another side to the matter. If parties cause some evils, they avert or mitigate others.

To begin with, parties are inevitable. No free large country has been without them. No one has shown how representative government could be worked without them. They bring order out of the chaos of a multitude of voters. If in such vast populations as those of the United States, France, or England, there were no party organizations, by whom would public opinion be roused and educated and directed to certain specific purposes? Each party, no doubt, tries to present its own side of the case for or against any doctrine or proposal, but the public cannot help learning something about the other side also, for even party spirit cannot separate the nation into water-tight compartments; and the most artful or prejudiced party spell-binder or newspaper has to recognize the existence of the arguments he is trying to refute. Thus Party strife is a sort of education for those willing to receive instruction, and something soaks through even into the less interested or thoughtful electors. The parties keep a nation's mind alive, as the rise and fall of the sweeping tide freshens the water of long ocean inlets. Discussion within each party, culminating before elections in the adoption of a platform, brings certain issues to the front, defines them, expresses them in formulas which, even if tricky or delusive, fix men's minds on certain points, concentrating attention and inviting criticism. So few people think seriously and steadily upon any subject outside the range of their own business interests that public opinion might be vague and ineffective if the party searchlight were not constantly turned on. And it may be added that the power of the press to influence the average voter by one-sided statements of fact, incessantly repeated, would be still greater than it is were there not party organizations whose business it is to secure a hearing for their own views.

Of nominations and elections I have already spoken. But a vast deal of preparatory work is needed beyond that which the State does when it makes up a register of voters and pro-

vides machinery for taking the votes.   Who is to do this?
Who is to get literature to the voters, stir them out of their
apathy, arrange public meetings, remind the citizens of their
duty to vote?   Only a permanent party.   Temporary organizations formed to promote a particular cause, such as were
(in England) the Anti-Corn Law League of 1838 and the
Eastern Question Association of 1876, may effect much for
the time being, but die out when the crisis has passed; and
it becomes increasingly difficult and costly to find means for
reaching the enormous voting masses of our time.

Political philosophers have been wont to deplore the existence of party in legislative assemblies and to accuse it of
leading to dishonesty.   They observe that, in the words of
the comic opera, a member who has " always voted at his
party's call " cannot but be demoralized.   But if there were
no party voting, and everybody gave his vote in accordance
with his own perhaps crude and ill-informed opinions, Parliamentary government of the English type could not go on.
Ministers would not know from hour to hour whether they
could count on carrying some provision of a Bill apparently
trifling, but the loss of which would destroy its coherency,
many of those who would have supported it might be absent,
while others might give an unconsidered vote.   Perpetual uncertainty and the weakness of the Executive which uncertainty involves would be a greater public evil than the subordination to his party of a member's personal view in minor
matters.   Where he has a strong conviction, he must of course
obey it, even at the risk of turning out a ministry, but when,
dismissing any thought of his own personal interest, he honestly applies the general principle that party government requires some subordination of individual views, his conscience
will not suffer.[1]

Party discipline in a legislature imposes a needed check
on self-seeking and on the greater mischief of corruption.

[1] Cases of conscience do no doubt arise, and are sometimes perplex-
ing, but twenty-seven years' experience in the British House of Commons have led me to believe that they are less frequent than one would,
looking at the matter *a priori*, have expected them to be.   Old members
have often told me that they had more often regretted votes given
against their party under what they thought a sense of duty than those
which they had, though with some doubt, given to support it.   I have
discussed the limits of party obligation in a little volume entitled **Hindrances to Good Citizenship**, published in 1909.

The absence of discipline, far from helping conscience to have free scope, may result in leaving the field open for selfish ambitions. Some years ago a group of strong men who had practically controlled the party majority in the United States Senate was broken up, and party discipline vanished. Ingenuous persons expected an improvement. But the first result was that a few pushing men came to the front, each playing for popularity, and things fell into confusion, the legislative machine working in so irregular and unpredictable a fashion that a call soon came for the restoration of discipline. In every governing body there must be some responsibility, some persons on whom blame can be fixed if bad advice be given and bad results follow. How a ruling body can suffer by the want of permanent parties was illustrated by the Athenian Assembly, a crowd of citizens largely guided by brilliant speakers holding no office, owning no allegiance to any party, each using his talents for his own advancement. When the multitude had been misled by such an orator there was nobody to be blamed except the orator, and his discredit was only a passing incident, for which he might have had secret compensation in a corrupt payment. An organized party with recognized leaders has a character to lose or to gain; and this applies to an Opposition as well as to a Ministerialist party, for every minority hopes to be some day a majority. In Great Britain during the war of 1914–19 party warfare was suspended, and two successive Coalition Ministries formed, so that for a time there was no regular Opposition to keep the Ministry up to the mark, inasmuch as those party chiefs who stood outside were unwilling to be charged with embarrassing their former opponents. The result was that a number of members, who, like the Athenian orators, were not sufficiently important to feel the bridle of responsibility, carried on, each for himself, a sort of guerilla warfare, which had not force enough to impose an effective check on ministerial errors. An administration formed by a coalition of parties is usually weak, not merely because the combination is unstable, but because men whose professed principles differ are likely to be entangled in inconsistencies or driven to unsatisfactory compromises. So a well-compacted party in Opposition which stands on its own feet, having had power before and hoping to have power again, is steadied by the fact that it has a character to lose. Inspiring confidence because it is known to be responsible, it can follow a definite policy and expect a loyal obedience.

In countries where the few large parties of former times have dissolved into small groups, no one of which is large enough to command a majority of the legislature, and in few of which is there any party discipline, other inconveniences are added. The leaders of a large and strong party have an opinion of their followers to regard, as well as the public opinion of the nation outside. That opinion within the party keeps them straight, for if they are seen to be playing for their own hand the party ceases to be trusted. Where there are small groups, each becomes a focus of intrigue, in which personal ambitions have scope. The groups make bargains with one another and by their combinations, perhaps secretly and suddenly formed, successive ministries may be overturned, with injury to the progress of legislation and to the continuity of national policy. Since there must be parties, the fewer and stronger they are, the better.

Must there then always be parties? No one has yet shown how such governments could get on without them.[1] Statesmen of exceptional force, such as Peel, Disraeli, Gladstone, while fully aware of their faults most clearly recognized their value. One can imagine a small community in which the citizens know one another so well that they select men for legislative and executive posts on the score of personal merit, and where the legislators are of a virtue so pure that they debate every question with a sole regard to truth and to the advantage of the State. If any such community has existed, its records have not been preserved for our instruction. One can also imagine that in some far distant future when all experiments have been tried, and nations, weary of politics, wish to settle down to a quiet life, a plan may be devised by which each small community, trusting its local concerns to its most honest and capable men, shall empower them to choose others who will go to some centre where they can deliberate

[1] Political philosophers have incessantly denounced parties, but none seems to have shown how they can either be prevented from arising or eliminated when they exist. I could never extract from Mr. Goldwin Smith, with all his mastery of history and political acumen, any answer to the question how representative government could be carried on without them.

on matters of common concern with other such delegates, party being eliminated, because the questions out of which the old parties arose have become obsolete. But the wings of fancy do not support our flight in a thin air so far above the surface of this planet.

We have so far been considering political parties of the old type, co-extensive with the nation and trying to draw adherents from all sections and classes within it. There are, however, three other kinds of party which ought to be noticed, and which may be either within or outside of a large non-sectional political party covering the whole country.

One of these is an ecclesiastical or anti-ecclesiastical organization. Where the interests of a religious body are supposed to need advocacy or protection, or where, on the other hand, a Church is deemed to be unduly powerful in political affairs, an organization may be formed either to defend it in the former case or to resist it in the latter.[1] There are in France and Belgium Catholic or so-called " Clerical " parties. Examples have been seen in the United States, where an apprehension that the Roman Catholic Church was acquiring undue power gave birth to the " Know Nothings " in 1853, and long afterwards created what was almost an Anti-Catholic party, under the title of American Protective Association (A. P. A.). Both rose suddenly into prominence, but died out after a few years. The chief instance of an organization acting as an anti-ecclesiastical force, all the stronger for being secret, is to be found in the Freemasons of Continental Europe. This society with its branches exists in England and the United States for purposes purely social and charitable, but the Masonic Lodges have in France and Italy an ardently anti-clerical, even indeed anti-Christian, colour. They are believed to exert an influence before which candidates and deputies quail.

The second class has grown out of the Trade or Labour Unions which sprang up during last century among the industrial populations of Europe, North America, and Australasia. Formed originally for the purpose of mutual chari-

---

[1] Neither the Primrose League in England nor the Carbonari of Italy can properly be referred to this category. The latter is now virtually extinct. As to the former, see in the *Démocratie et Partis politiques* of Mr. Ostrogorski, p. 250 of French edition of 1912, an instructive treatment of the whole subject.

table help, they became effective in planning and carrying on strikes, and thereafter, realizing the voting power which an extended suffrage had given them, passed into the field of political action. Out of them and the congresses which they hold there have arisen in many countries what are called Labour Parties, putting forward programmes of legislation intended to benefit the wage-earning class, and to throw more of the burden of taxation upon the wealthier part of the community. Such platforms, while commanding sympathy from those among the richer who think that the wage-earners have not yet received a sufficient share in what their toil produces, make their most direct appeal to the labouring class itself and draw most of their strength from the prospect they open of improving its material condition. Though extending over the whole country, they are in so far contrasted with the older parties that they create a cleavage in the nation which is not, as formerly, vertical, but horizontal, having a social as well as a political character. In England the Whig and Tory parties were each of them composed of persons of all degrees of rank and wealth, poor as well as rich. In both the ruling section belonged to the richer class, and was apt to legislate in its own interest, but between the two sections there was no social antagonism. So also in the United States, both the Republican and the Democratic party have been composed, in almost equal proportions, of the poorer and the richer citizens. Now, however, there is a tendency for the community to be divided, as the Greek republics were already in Plato's time, into a party of the poor and a party of the rich, a state of things unfavourable to the formation of a truly national opinion and to some extent to national unity in general.

A third species is the Local or Racial party, familiar examples of which are furnished by the Nationalists and the Sinn Feiners of Ireland and the Regionalists of Catalonia, and were furnished in the Austrian Reichsrath before 1914 by the Polish and Czech parties. These, like the ecclesiastical organizations, are apt to suffer by undue preoccupation with their own particular aims and tenets. But what they lose in this way they may gain in the power of purchasing, by the solid vote they can deliver, the help of one or other of the great national parties.

Other new parties which have appeared in recent years are those called Socialist or Communist. They are not, strictly speaking, class parties, for although they have many aims in common with the Labour parties, they base themselves not on proposals for the benefit of the working class as such, but upon theoretic systems of economic doctrine which are held by many persons in all classes. Their emergence, coupled with that of Labour parties, has had the effect of drawing away from each of the old established parties many of its adherents. This has brought these old parties nearer together, for those who dislike the new doctrines or scent danger in the new proposals, begin to find the familiar differences between the old parties less important than is the coincidence of their opposition to the new parties.[1] In some cases accordingly the old parties have been fused into one; in others they have agreed to make common cause at elections with one another. Questions relating to the distribution of political power having been everywhere largely disposed of, the dividing lines between parties tend to be economic. The result has been to accentuate class sentiment, making a sharper division than previously existed between the richer and more conservative element in every country and that which is poorer and more disposed to experimental legislation.

This, however, has been compatible with a tendency for the large parties to split up into smaller sections. There are shades in Conservatism, and even more shades in Radicalism and in Socialism, for the activity of thought and the disappearance of respect for authority multiply new doctrines, helping them to spread fast. Such a tendency makes for definiteness and sincerity in the views of each section or group, but it increases the difficulty of working the machinery of government. This difficulty is in some countries aggravated by the rise of parties founded in the interests of a particular set of producers, such as is the Farmers' party in Canada, and the party of Peasants (*i.e.* small land-owning agriculturists and pastoralists) in Switzerland.

Two other features characteristic of party in democratic countries deserve mention. The increase in the number of voting citizens and the disappearance of those distinctions of

[1] See the Chapters on Australia in Part II., *post*.

social rank which made the rich landowner the obvious leader in a rural district, as was the rich merchant in a city, have made organization more needful. Those parties which have behind them either an ecclesiastical or a labour organization are in this respect stronger than parties with no religious or class basis. The latter are therefore obliged to find funds to conduct propaganda and to pay their agents. The smaller parties, or the groups which appear in representative assemblies, suffer from want of funds, having few adherents over the country at large, nor are they aided by contributions from capitalists, though the latter readily support a strong party capable of serving their commercial or financial interests. Poverty shortens the life of many groups or drives them to fusion, for "Publicity," *i.e.* the advertising, in a direct or indirect form, now deemed essential to success, is so costly that money tends to become the sinews of politics as well as of war.

In every party — and this is especially true of the United States and Britain — one may distinguish three sets of men. There are the national leaders, eminent persons who associate their own fortunes with those of the party and desire by it to obtain office and power. There is the mass of moderate men who have a general sympathy with the party aims, and have been accustomed to vote with it. The third class are zealots and care more for the principles or aims of the party than for its immediate victory. These are the men who do unpaid work in the constituencies and keep the local party machinery going. They summon the meetings of associations, and generally carry their resolutions in the local meetings of the party which are attended by its more ardent members. Their enthusiasm, often coupled with inexperience, makes them eager to go full steam ahead, and their activity often enables them to commit the party, at its larger gatherings, to a policy more extreme than is pleasing to the bulk of the members. The more prudent chiefs sometimes try to slow down the pace, but are not always able to do so in time, so it may befall that the party is officially pledged to proposals in advance not only of public opinion generally but even of the average opinion of its own members. The result is that the moderate members drop away, and may possibly drift into the opposite camp. This phenomenon is of course more frequent in the parties of movement than in those of resistance, but even in the latter the formally declared attitude of a party may not truly represent its general sentiment, for the moderate men, because less keenly interested, usually take least part in the deliberations at which the attitude of the party is proclaimed and its course determined. Thus party spirit often appears to be hotter, and party antagonisms more pronounced, than is really the case, for in a large nation the mass of the electors take their politics more coolly than is realized by those who derive their impressions from newspaper reports of party meetings.

The power of Party Organization and the power of Party spirit are of course very different things, and not necessarily found together. If either should assume undue proportions, what remedies can be found for checking the undue power of an organization over its own members, and what can be done to soften the antagonisms which party spirit creates in a nation, disturbing its internal concord and weakening it in its relations with foreign powers?

Law can do little or nothing. Though many countries have tried to repress by penal legislation factions from which the ruling power apprehended danger, only two seem to have attempted to regulate them. Czarist Russia in the earlier days of the Duma allowed certain parties to apply for and obtain legalization. Many States in the American Union have created administrative Boards on which provision is made for the representation of both the great political parties, and nearly all have passed laws for regulating the nomination of party candidates by the members of the parties or by the voters at large. The rather disappointing results of these expedients are described in later chapters.[1]

Party spirit as a Force working for good or evil in public life is a matter which must be left to the citizens themselves. Upon them it must depend whether it is reasonable and temperate or violent and bitter. It is no greater a danger in democracies than elsewhere. So, too, experience seems to show that it is only the members of a party who can control the action of organizations and can keep them from being either perverted by astute party managers for their own selfish purposes, or used by honest extremists to launch pro-

[1] See Chapters on the United States in Part II., *post.*

posals which the party as a whole does not approve. The more a party lives by the principles for which it stands, the more it subordinates its own aims to the strength and unity of the whole people, and the more it is guided by men who can recognize whatever may be sound in the views of their opponents and prevent opposition from passing into enmity, the better will it serve the common interests of its country.

CHAPTER XII

LOCAL SELF-GOVERNMENT

The beginnings of popular government were in small areas, rural communities and tiny cities, each with only a few hundreds or possibly thousands of free inhabitants. The earliest form it took was that of an assembly in which all the freemen met to discuss their common affairs, and in which, although the heads of the chief families exerted much influence, the mind and voice of the people could make itself felt. Such assemblies marked the emergence of men from barbarism into something approaching a settled and ordered society. In many places these communities lay within a monarchy, in others (as in Iceland) they were independent, but everywhere they accustomed the people to cherish a free spirit and learn to co-operate for common aims. First among these was joint defence against a neighbouring and hostile community. A second, important for the prevention of internal strife, was the settlement, by some kind of judicial method, of disputes between the members, frequently arising from the demand of compensation for the killing of some one whose kinsfolk were bound by custom to avenge his death, such blood-money being awarded by the assembly, or the elders, to the kin, who thereupon desisted from revenge.[1] A third was the disposal and management of land belonging to the local community (whether forest or pasture) not allotted in severalty to the members, or of arable land in which there were usually rights assigned to each individual, even if only for a limited period and subject to re-allotment when the period has expired. This was frequent among peoples of South Slavonic stock.

[1] Cf. *Iliad*, Book ix. 1. 628 and xviii. 498, with which compare the laws of the West Saxon King Ine; and many references in the Icelandic Sagas (see the author's *Studies in History and Jurisprudence*, Essay on Primitive Iceland). The custom of blood revenge, which is as old as the Pentateuch, is still alive in Albania and among the Pathans. Only recently did it vanish from Corsica, and it long remained among the peasantry of Ireland.

129

K

It existed till quite recently in the Russian Mir, and still exists in many parts of India.

This self-governing assembly, though there are some races (such as the Celtic) in which we find little or no trace of it, was widely diffused, though its power or influence was greater in some countries than in others. A familiar example may be found in the Agora of Homeric Greece, in the Comitia of Rome, in the meeting of the People (Folk Mot) of the Angles and Saxons in England, in the Thing of the Norsemen in Norway and Iceland. That it is an institution not confined to any one stock of mankind appears from its presence among the Bantu races of South Africa, where it maintains a vigorous life in the Pitso of the Basutos and Bechuanas.[1]

In the process of time nations were formed by the expansion of these small communities, or by their fusion, or by their absorption into larger units. The other functions of the assembly were either assumed by the whole nation (as was defence) or transferred to special authorities. In the ancient Greek and Italic republics regular courts were set up. In most parts of Europe judicial functions passed to the feudal landowners, and ultimately, first in England and later in Scotland, to the king. Thus popular self-government came to lose what may be called its political (including its military) and its judicial side. But it usually retained the right of managing whatever land belonged to the community; and in some countries functions connected with the parish church, while afterwards other matters of local welfare came under its care. The only country in which the small autonomous unit of the thirteenth century held its ground as a political unit was Switzerland, and particularly those Alpine valleys in which Swiss freedom had its origin. In a few cantons the Landesgemeinde or primary assembly of the whole canton continues to meet to-day.[2] In England the Parish, originally similar to the Commune of continental Europe as an ecclesiastical unit and land-holding body, had retained a feeble life, but for ecclesiastical purposes only, until it received a re-grant of limited civil functions by a statute of 1894,

[1] An account of the Pitso may be found in the author's *Impressions of South Africa*.
[2] See Chapters on Switzerland in Part II., *post*.

while beyond the Atlantic the self-government of small areas
had a new birth among the English who settled in the States
of Massachusetts, Rhode Island, New Hampshire, and Connecticut. The Town (rural as well as urban) became a
strong organism, drawing life not only from the English traditions which the colonists brought with them, but also from
the daily needs of a people dispersed in small groups over
a wild country, who had to help one another in many ways,
and defend themselves against native tribes. Thus the old
Teutonic form of self-government has continued to flourish
and to spread out over all the northern States of the American
Union.[1]

The small communities here described may be called the
tiny fountain-heads of democracy, rising among the rocks,
sometimes lost altogether in their course, sometimes running
underground to reappear at last in fuller volume. They
suffice to show that popular government is not a new thing
in the world, but was in many countries the earliest expression of man's political instincts. It was a real misfortune
for England — and the remark applies in a certain sense
to Germany also — that while local self-government did maintain itself in the county and borough it should in both have
largely lost the popular character which once belonged to it,
as it was a misfortune for Ireland and for France that this
natural creation of political intelligence should not have developed there. Many things that went wrong in those four
countries from the end of the sixteenth century onwards
might have fared better under institutions like those of Switzerland or the Northern United States.

Of the part to be assigned to Local Government in a modern democracy, of its relations to the Central Government,
and of the forms in which it works best, I propose to speak
in a later chapter, following upon those which describe the
working of democracy in six modern countries. Here, however, a few words may be said as to the general service which
self-government in small areas renders in forming the qualities needed by the citizen of a free country. It creates
among the citizens a sense of their common interest in common affairs, and of their individual as well as common duty

---

[1] See Chapters on United States, Part II., *post.* The word "Town"
includes a rural as well as an urban area.

to take care that those affairs are efficiently and honestly administered. If it is the business of a local authority to mend the roads, to clean out the village well or provide a new pump, to see that there is a place where straying beasts may be kept till the owner reclaims them, to fix the number of cattle each villager may turn out on the common pasture, to give each his share of timber cut in the common woodland, every villager has an interest in seeing that these things are properly attended to. Laziness and the selfishness which is indifferent to whatever does not immediately affect a man's interests is the fault which most afflicts democratic communities. Whoever learns to be public-spirited, active and upright in the affairs of the village has learnt the first lesson of the duty incumbent on a citizen of a great country, just as, conversely, "he that is unfaithful in the least is unfaithful also in much." The same principle applies to a city. In it the elector can seldom judge from his own observation how things are being managed. But he can watch through the newspapers or by what he hears from competent sources whether the mayor and councillors and their officials are doing their work, and whether they are above suspicion of making illicit gains, and whether the taxpayer is getting full value for what he is required to contribute. So when the election comes he has the means of discovering the candidates with the best record and can cast his vote accordingly.

Secondly: Local institutions train men not only to work for others but also to work effectively with others. They develop common sense, reasonableness, judgment, sociability. Those who have to bring their minds together learn the need for concession and compromise. A man has the opportunity of showing what is in him, and commending himself to his fellow-citizens. Two useful habits are formed, that of recognizing the worth of knowledge and tact in public affairs and that of judging men by performance rather than by professions or promises.

Criticisms are often passed on the narrowness of mind and the spirit of parsimony which are visible in rural local authorities and those who elect them. These defects are, however, a natural product of the conditions of local life. The narrowness would be there in any case, and would affect the elector if he were voting for a national representative, but there would be less of that shrewdness which the practice of local government forms. Such faults must be borne with for the sake of the more important benefits which self-government produces. The main thing is that everybody, peasant and workman as well as shopkeeper and farmer, should join in a common public activity, and feel that he has in his own neighbourhood a sphere in which he can exercise his own judgment and do something for the community. Seeing the working, on a small scale, of the principle of responsibility to the public for powers conferred by them, he is better fitted to understand its application in affairs of larger scope.

These good results have been sometimes wanting in municipal governments, especially in Transatlantic cities where the rapid growth of enormous populations has created abnormal conditions, making it impossible for the citizens to have such a knowledge of one another as is needed to secure a wise choice of councils or administrative officials. Of these I shall speak elsewhere. Meanwhile it is enough to observe that the countries in which democratic government has most attracted the interest of the people and drawn talent from their ranks have been Switzerland and the United States, especially those northern and western States in which rural local government has been most developed. These examples justify the maxim that the best school of democracy, and the best guarantee for its success, is the practice of local self-government.

CHAPTER XIII

Moribus antiquis stat res Romana virisque

W<small>HAT</small> Habit is to an individual during the brief term of his existence here, Traditions are to a nation whose life extends over hundreds or thousands of years. In them dwells the moral continuity of its existence. They link each generation to those that have gone before and sum up its collective memories. To understand their action upon the nation, let us begin by considering how habit affects the individual.

Habit, that is to say, the tendency of each man to go on thinking and acting upon the same general lines, is due not only to hereditary predispositions rooted in a race or in a family, but also to certain fundamental ideas which each person either forms for himself or has received from instruction, or from the example of others who have influenced him in that formative period of life when the mind and character are still comparatively fluid. Once such ideas have been solidified, they constitute, for nearly all persons, the permanent basis of conduct and the standard by which they judge both themselves and others. Most men are indolent, prone to follow the line of least resistance in thinking as well as in acting, so they find it easier to apply the maxims already in their minds than to think out afresh on each occasion every serious question. That would make life too burdensome. Here habit helps; for where it is so strong that there is no need felt for turning the mind on to examine the question, judgment and action in minor matters become almost automatic. A man's disposition to imitate others, or to repeat himself, has its source in physiological facts, certain in their action though obscure in their causes, which I cannot attempt to deal with here.

134

Psychologists since Aristotle have dwelt on the supreme importance of habit as the basis of moral action. Once settled, it is the most constant factor, especially in those persons, everywhere the majority, to whom independent thinking is an effort for which they have neither taste nor talent. Under its power, action becomes instinctive. Parents, teachers, the public opinion of the school, stamp certain notions and rules of conduct on the soft metal of a young mind, and when the metal has hardened they are not readily effaced. For one who can think out a doubtful ethical question, there are ten who can remember what they were taught to believe. If men are from childhood accustomed to regard certain conduct as honourable, because approved by the general sentiment of their fellows, they do not ask why that should be so, but promptly judge themselves and others by the standards they have accepted. If, on the contrary, they either have not imbibed, or have not made for themselves, such standards, they yield to the desire or passion of the moment, or are deterred from obeying it only by a fear of the consequences. So when one generation after another of a people has grown up valuing certain virtues and believing that the welfare of the nation depends on their maintenance, when it respects those who are faithful to virtue, and reveres the memory of those heroes of the past in whom virtue shone forth with peculiar lustre, the virtues and the memories become a part of the people's heritage, and are cherished as an ancient family prizes the shield and sword which a forefather carried in battle. In one of the finer and more impressionable spirits, the glory of national heroes becomes a living force, part of himself, inspiring him as he reads its history. He is proud of belonging to such a stock. He feels a sense of duty to it. He asks himself what made the nation great, and finds the source of greatness in what are deemed its characteristic virtues.

Something similar is observable on a small scale in a profession, or in any body, such as a college, with a long corporate life behind it. Its members feel a measure of pride in belonging to such a body. The mantle of old distinction falls upon them, and helps to maintain a high standard of conduct. It is of course only persons of superior intelligence and some historic knowledge in whom any such sentiments are strong, but it is usually such men who lead the nation in action, or instruct it by their words, or set in public life an example which the average man respects. Thus there is formed in the people a standard by which statesmen are tested, an ideal created to which they must live up, if they are to receive the people's confidence. Truthfulness, honour, unselfishness, courage are enshrined as parts of that ideal. In a democracy where the sentiment of equality has gone so far as to make men unwilling to recognize the authority of the wise or defer to the counsels of experience, references to what their ancestors felt or did may still command respect. And while the nation's own self-esteem willingly appropriates such virtues as its own, those who aspire to leadership feel that they must try to possess or seem to possess them. If they are high-minded, their good intentions are strengthened; if of common clay, they must at least pay homage to the ideal by not falling too far below it. Nobody wants to be compared to " the fause Menteith " [1] or to those whom history has branded as unworthy, such as the timorous pontiff who made " the great refusal." [2] Thus the ideals of public conduct, and the recollections of those in whom the ideals were exemplified, become the traditions of a nation, deemed by it to be a part of its national character, most familiar and powerful when embodied in famous persons who are the shining lights of its history.

The best instances of the influence of such ideals and traditions are to be found in the histories of more or less popularly governed countries, and especially of Rome, of England, of Switzerland, and of the United States.

In Rome the virtue most honoured was that of devotion to the State. Decius giving himself to death in order to secure victory over the Samnites, the legendary Curtius leaping into the gulf, Regulus returning to a cruel death at Carthage rather than advise the Senate to sanction an unfavourable peace, even Manlius Torquatus condemning his own son to death in order that military discipline might be maintained, were real or imagined examples held up for imitation to the Roman youth, and for a long time serving to inspire it. Patriotism possessed the mind of the Swiss before it had laid

---

[1] The person who betrayed William Wallace to the English.

[2] Dante, *Inferno*, canto III. v. 60. The reference is supposed to be to Pope Celestine V.

hold on any other people in mediaeval Europe. The memory of those three confederates of Grutli who led the revolt against the oppressions of the Count of Hapsburg, and of Arnold von Winkelried sacrificing himself in Decian fashion to win the fight at Sempach, have sunk into the heart of every Swiss. They helped to form the sentiment of dauntless loyalty in the Swiss Guards who perished at the Tuileries in 1792, fighting not even for their own country, but in defence of the monarch with whom they had taken service. And in Switzerland patriotism has been turned into a peaceful channel in creating a sense of the civic duty which every man owes to his canton. Nowhere in the world has this sense been so strong, or done so much to make men take an interest in domestic politics and bring so much intelligence to bear upon it. It shows us a tradition embodied in a habit of daily life.

In England whose national independence was never threatened from the Norman Conquest until the time when Bonaparte was encamped at Boulogne, the growth of national traditions was more gradual and less definitely connected with particular historical cases. Nevertheless there were incidents from the days of Magna Charta down to the revolution of 1688 which created in the more educated classes a steady attachment to liberty as well as to law, law being regarded not merely as the enforcement of order but as the safeguard of liberty. Whatever unconstitutional acts might be done by any king or minister, no one in either English party ventured, after the fall of the Stuarts, to disparage liberty as a fundamental principle.

Taken in their widest sense Traditions include all the influences which the Past of a nation exerts upon its Present, in forming its thoughts and accustoming its will to act upon certain fixed lines. The traditions of valour are, of course, those most generally cherished in every country, because every one understands and honours courage. In mediaeval Spain, however, the crusading character of the wars waged against the Moors for four centuries formed not only a love of battle but also a religious intolerance which is not yet extinct. Its strength is shown by the violence of the anti-clerical recoil among Spanish anarchists. The victorious campaigns of Frederick the Great which made Prussia a nation, created also that spirit of militarism and that supremacy of military ideals which a series of successful wars brought to their highest development a century after his time. In Japan the religious devotion to a dynasty whose origin is lost in the mist of fable combined with the personal devotion of the feudal retainer to his lord to produce that chivalric self-forgetting loyalty to State and Nation which has made the Japanese warrior feel it a privilege to offer up his life in the national cause.[1] Nowhere does this sort of loyalty seem to have equally pervaded all classes of a people.

Besides these traditions of honour and dignity in conduct there are also certain ideas or principles of policy which have so often been recognized by a nation, and applied in the management of its affairs, that they have become a part of its mental equipment. Some of these ideas have been embodied in its institutions, and by them the institutions have stood. Some are associated with events in national history which approved their soundness. In the United States, for instance, the dogmas contained in the Declaration of Independence and the view of policy known as the Monroe Doctrine, the theory of the sovereignty of the people and the necessity of separating the executive, legislative, and judicial powers, have by general consent become axiomatic. Abiding foundations of policy glide into other principles which have come to so inhere in national consciousness as to seem parts of national character. Such, for the English, are the respect for law as law, the feeling that every citizen is bound to come forward in its support, the confidence in the Courts which administer it — a confidence not felt in the seventeenth century, because then not yet deserved. Such in France is the passion for equality, still more recent, and a deference to executive authority greater than Englishmen or Americans feel, together with a passionate attachment to the soil of France which has replaced the old feudal attachment to the person of the sovereign.

Among traditions, those which approve and maintain principles and habits of political action have been due to the people itself, guided by wise leaders, while those which have

[1] The famous story of the forty-seven Ronins who died for their chief is familiar to every Japanese. The temple at Tokyo where their figures are reverently shown has become almost a place of pilgrimage.

a moral character and secure respect for public virtue, are generally due to the influence and example of some famous man who so impressed his contemporaries as to become a model for later generations. The classic instance comes from the United States. Its people had the singular good fortune to find in the beginning of their national life a hero whose character became a tradition for them of all that was highest and purest in statesmanship. George Washington set a standard of courage, calmness, dignity, and uprightness by which every public man's conduct was to be tried. Seventy years later the tradition of unselfish patriotism, as well as of firmness and of faith in the power of freedom was, so to speak, reconsecrated by Abraham Lincoln. Two such lives (the former of which had much to do with inspiring the latter) have been an asset of incomparable value to the people among whom they were lived. When the War of Secession had ended and the dawn of reconciliation began after a time to appear, Northern as well as Southern men found in the memory of Washington a bond of reunion, for it was a memory cherished and honoured by both alike.

Habits can be bad as well as good, though when found in a people they are commonly attributed not so much to historical causes as to the inherent depravity of mankind, allowed to indulge itself unchecked, and infecting one generation after another, because there was neither legal penalty nor public disapproval to restrain it. An offence that is familiar and goes unpunished is deemed venial and excites no surprise. Corruption and malversation were common in the Greek republics, even among brilliant leaders. They were common in the later days of Rome among ambitious politicians, who were wont to bribe the voters, or the jurors before whom they were prosecuted, with money extorted from the provincial subjects of the republic. The laws were stringent, but the offenders frequently escaped. Among the statesmen of Italy, and indeed of Europe generally, in the fifteenth and sixteenth century there was little honour. Machiavelli was no worse than others in his means, and better than most in his aims. In Russia, under the Tsars, corruption was the rule among officials, civil and military. In China it successfully overcame, a few years ago, the nascent virtue of many among the young enthusiasts who had proclaimed a republic. In

England bribery was rife in Parliament under Walpole and in parliamentary constituencies till the middle of last century. It was, for the briber, a matter of jest, not of social stigma, the habit being an old one. So in tropical America there are some republics in which the ruling faction has for many a year "made the elections," and many in which a President is expected to enrich himself, and leaves a good name if he has shot comparatively few of his opponents.[1]

Traditions are built up slowly but crumble quickly, just as it takes longer to form in an individual the virtue that will resist temptation than it takes to break down what had seemed to be a settled habit. Seldom can he who has once succumbed to strong inducements be thereafter trusted to stand firm.[2]

Various have been the causes that have weakened or destroyed old traditions. Sometimes the quality of a population is changed; it may be, as happened in Rome, by the impoverishment of the bulk of the old citizen stock and the increase in the number of freedmen; it may be by the influx of a crowd of immigrants, ignorant of the history of their new country, irresponsive to sentiments which the old inhabitants have cherished. The English stock to which the farmers and artisans of Massachusetts and Connecticut belonged has now become a minority in these States.

There are times when under the pressure of some grave national crisis, such as a foreign or even perhaps a civil war, a nation resigns some of its liberties into the hands of the Executive, or adopts new methods of government calculated to strengthen its position in the world. If the period of suspension of liberties be short and the attachment of the people to their old institutions exceptionally strong, no harm may be done. This proved to be the case after the American War of Secession, when constitutional government was restored uninjured. But there is always a risk that the stream may not return to its old channel. After a great war a nation is never, for better or worse, what it was before. Sometimes the waves of internal discord run so high that the tradi-

---

[1] The Irish tradition of "voting agin the Government" was formed in the first half of last century, and was not without its justification.

[2] *Nec vera virtus, quum semel excidit,*
　　Curat reponi deterioribus.

So Horace (*Odes*, iii. 5).

tion of devotion to common national interests is forgotten in
the strife of religions or of classes. Sometimes the intellectual development of a people has sapped the foundations
of its beliefs without replacing them by new conceptions of
duty fit to stand the strain of new conditions. The most familiar instance is that of the Greek republics in the age of
Socrates when the teachings of some eminent Sophists, pul-
verizing the simple belief in gods who punished perjury and
bad faith, were representing justice as merely the advantage
of the stronger. Here the traditions first affected were religious and ethical, but an old system of beliefs and habits
hangs together; when the religious part of it is smitten, other
parts feel the shock. Traditions last longest in peoples who
live amid simple conditions and whose minds are slow and
steady rather than swift. The Roman spirit was more conservative than that of the highly susceptible Greeks, as the
English have been less prone to change than have the nimbler-
minded French. No tradition lasts for ever, not even in
China. When it shows signs of decay, the best chance of
saving it lies in reinforcing an ancient sentimental reverence
by considerations drawn from reason and experience. These
are supplied by history, the teaching of which in schools and
universities might in most countries do more than it has yet
done to fill the people's mind with memories of what is
finest in its history and to dwell upon the worth of experience
as a guide in politics.

The traditions of virtue shown in political life are not
so well remembered by all classes of any people as are those
of warlike valour or disinterested patriotism, because they
appeal less to the imagination, and are more apt to be associated with those who have been the leaders of parties rather
than of the nation. Nelson and Garibaldi are names more
popular than Hampden, Mazzini, or Kossuth. Even in
Switzerland there are few outstanding civil figures — and
hardly any known outside its own borders — to whom traditions are attached. Appealing to reason rather than to emotion, they are less promising themes for rhetoric. But the
greatest statesmen have rendered services greater than any
rendered by arms, except indeed where the war was for national independence. The traditional love of liberty, the traditional sense of duty to the community, be it great or small,

the traditional respect for law and wish to secure reforms by constitutional rather than by violent means — these were the habits engrained in the mind and will of Englishmen and Swiss which have helped each people to build up its free institutions from rude beginnings, and have enabled those institutions to continue their beneficent work. Those traditions carried across the sea rendered the same service in America. When similar institutions, however skilfully devised, are set down among those who, like the peoples of tropical America, have no such traditions, the institutions work imperfectly or do not work at all, because men have not that common basis of mutual understandings, that reciprocal willingness to effect a compromise, that accepted standard of public honour, that wish to respect certain conventions and keep within certain limits, which long habit has formed in the minds of Englishmen or Americans or Switzers.

CHAPTER XIV

THE PEOPLE

THE Sovereignty of the People is the basis and the watchword of democracy. It is a faith and a dogma to which in our time every frame of government has to conform, and by conformity to which every institution is tested. We shall have, in the course of our examination of the working of many forms of government, to observe in what ways doctrine is applied to practice, and how far each of the methods of applying it gives good results. It is therefore worth while to begin by enquiring what that sovereignty imports, and who are those that exercise it?

What is the People? The word has always had a fascination. It appeals to the imagination by suggesting something vast and all-embracing, impersonal and intangible. We are in the midst of a multitude and a part of it, and yet we do not know its thoughts and cannot forecast its action, even as we stand on the solid earth and cannot tell when it will be shaken by an earthquake; or as we dwell under and constantly watch the sky yet can seldom say when tempests will arise and lightnings flash forth, or as we live in the midst of the vibrating ether and have no sense-perceptions of its presence. There seems to be something about the mind and will of the People so far transcending human comprehension as to have a sort of divine quality, because it is a force not only unpredictable but irresistible. It has the sacredness of an oracle. The old saying, *Vox populi, vox Dei,* was meant to convey that when the People speaks, it speaks by that will of the Higher Powers which men cannot explain but are forced to obey.

This kind of feeling seems grounded, consciously or unconsciously, on an assumption that the People cannot go wrong. Wisdom must dwell in it because it includes all the wisdom there is in the nation, and Justice must dwell in it because it includes all there is of justice; and Justice must be present even more certainly than wisdom, because the injustice and selfishness of individuals and groups, each of which has its own conflicting interests, will be swallowed up in the justice which is the common interest of all. Moreover, man is naturally prone to worship Power. That is an impulse that underlies all religion. To-day the people are the ultimate source of Power. Their will, be it wise or unwise, must prevail. Just as an individual man is carried away by the passion that sways a vast crowd filled by one emotion and purpose, so when that purpose is universalized to embrace the nation of which he and all the others in the crowd are a trifling part, he realizes the insignificance of each and the grandeur of all. He is awed by something mystical in the conception. That which was once the divine Right of the king has become the overriding Majesty of the People.

Passing from these abstractions, let us see what in various concrete cases the term People has been taken to mean, and what questions have arisen as to the persons or classes included under it. Does it in any given country cover, or ought it to cover, the whole population or only those who are legally " citizens," *i.e.* entitled to share in the government by expressing their mind and will on public questions ? In the ancient world the right of governing went with the obligation to fight. That obligation fell upon all free adult males, so that the army meant in practice the voters, and the voters (subject to exceptions hardly worth noting) meant the army. Duty and power went together. This view would not be accepted now either in countries which have extended the suffrage to women, or by those persons who deny that there should be any general obligation to serve the country in arms. Are resident aliens part of the people, or ought they to be deemed such, at least so far as to have a right to be after a time admitted to citizenship ? Even if they are not permitted to vote how far are their wishes to be regarded ? [1]

---

[1] It might be argued that those aliens who are taxed ought to be represented. The question is usually unimportant, but there is one European country (Switzerland) in which aliens constitute 15 per cent of the population; and the exclusion of foreigners from the suffrage in the Transvaal was the chief grievance out of which the South African War arose in 1899.

If there is any distinct section of a nation few of whose members concern themselves with public affairs, is it to be deemed a part of the people for political purposes? If most of the members of such a section have no political opinions, can they be said to share in Popular Sovereignty, whether or no they vote, for if they do, they vote as others bid them? This question was much discussed in England and America before women were admitted to the suffrage; and in France it is still under discussion. Where a racially distinct body of unwilling subjects is included within a State, as were the Poles in the German Empire before 1919, or the German-speaking Tyrolese in the Italian kingdom since 1919, are they to be reckoned as part of the people? Where a race, confessedly backward, remains socially distinct from the rest of the population, is it to be counted as a part of the people, or if some few of its members are admitted to share in power as voters, does that imply that the whole body shall be so counted? This point is raised by the position of the Kafirs in the Union of South Africa, of the Chinese in Australasia, of the negroes in the Southern States of America. They are so sharply differentiated from their white neighbours by the fact that their chief interest is not in the general welfare of the country but in obtaining for themselves an equal status and the effective protection of the law that their wishes and hopes do not move on the same plane. When a white orator in Louisiana talks of " our people " he is thinking of whites only; but if he is speaking in Ohio, are negroes included? [1]

Further questions arise when we consider how the people has to express its will. This, formerly done by a shout of the assembled freemen, now takes the form of voting. In voting, as normally in fighting, that oldest method of settling differences, numbers prevail. The majority is taken to speak for the whole. This need not be the majority of the whole nation, for the votes may be taken in some artificial divisions, as in the Roman Republic it was in " centuries " or in

[1] There is a constantly recurring fallacy which makes men unconsciously think of the majority as if it were the whole. When we talk or " the American people," we forget the many millions of non-Americanized immigrants; when we talk of " the English people " we forget the non-English elements in Britain; when we talk of " the Irish people " we forget the inhabitants of Ulster; when we talk of " the people of Ulster " we forget that large section which is politically and religiously out of sympathy with the majority.

" tribes," and as it is in the American Republic (at a presidential election) by States. Whatever be the mode, the greater number must, in any ordered State, prevail, and the lesser must submit. But although the legal authority goes with the majority, does the moral authority of the people go with it? What presumption is there that the majority, especially if it be small, is right? Is there likely to be any more wisdom in the Yeas than in the Nays? If it be true that most men are governed by emotion, and few men by reason, a cynic might argue that the presumption was the other way. Can one say that because the people are always right a decision reached by a majority of five in a body of five hundred will be right? In the General Councils of the mediaeval Church it was asked whether when a point of doctrine had to be decided by a vote, infallibility dwelt in the odd man, and whether, if so, it would not have been quite as easy, and much more impressive, for Divine Providence to arrange that the majority should be larger.

The cynic already referred to goes a step farther, and asks what ground there is for the trust reposed in the justice and wisdom of the People. " Why should they be less liable to error than monarchs or oligarchies? What is there in a nation of twenty or forty or one hundred millions of men, women, and children except so many individual human beings? Whence does there come into this mass any more wisdom or goodness than exists in these individuals, a large number of whom we all know to have little knowledge and less wisdom? The collective wisdom of the People is but the sum of their individual wisdoms, its excellence the sum of their excellences. A thing does not become different because you call it by a collective name. The Germans, a philosophical race, no doubt talk of the State as not only grander but also wiser than the individuals who compose the State, but that may be because their government took pains to gather as much trained wisdom as possible into the service of the State, so that the bureaucracy became a treasure-house of knowledge and experience beyond what any individuals can command. The State, they argued, is wiser than its component parts, because those who administer it are the refined quintessence distilled from all the sources of individual wisdom. Democratic nations do not attempt thus to concentrate knowledge and skill in a body of State servants; they put their faith in the individuals who come to the polling-booth. It is not true, as is alleged, that the selfishnesses of many individuals cancel one another, so as to produce a general unselfishness; rather may it be said that the selfish aims of men and sections of men are the materials with which the crafty politician plays, turning them to his own ends, giving to each section favours pernicious to the whole community.

" Every crowd poses as the people, and affects to speak in its name. The larger the crowd, the less is it guided by reason and the more by its emotions. The First Crusade was determined by a gathering at Clermont in Auvergne, when the mighty multitude is said to have shouted ' Deus id Vult.' But no one had weighed the difficulties of the enterprise, and sixty thousand of those who were the first to start perished long before they had approached the goal of pilgrimage. Have we not all seen how often the people err in their choice of representatives and how often their representatives err in their decisions on matters of policy ? They admit their errors by frequently reversing those decisions.

" The people generally mean well. But what is the people for practical purposes when it comes to vote ? Many, in some countries one half, and at some elections even more, abstain. How many of the thousands or tens of thousands who come to the polling-booths have any real acquaintance with the issues they are to decide, or with the qualities and the records of the candidates from among whom they are to choose their representatives and officials ? How many, on the other hand, are voting merely because some one has brought them and told them that A, or B, is their man ? Could the minds of most be examined, we should find that the vote cast did not express their individual wills, but rather the will of a group of leaders and wire-pullers who have put out the ' party ticket.' A decision no doubt there must be, and this may be the only way of getting it. But why bow down and worship the judgment of the people unless they are to be deemed to act, like a General Council of the Church, under Divine guidance ? Is this the meaning of *vox populi, vox Dei?* "

Some of the questions raised by the critics whose views I

have stated will be found, when we proceed to consider the practical working of popular government, to have been answered by the nations that have adopted that government, each for itself in its own way. But it is worth while to consider the causes which have given power to that faith in the people which has been for several generations a potent and pervasive force in politics.

It began as a combative and reforming force, a protest against monarchical government and class government. Men who saw the evil wrought by the overbearing arrogance of a ruling class saw the remedy in the transfer of authority to the whole body of a nation. Exclusive or even predominant power was a temptation to selfishness. Power shared by all would be honestly exercised for the benefit of all.

In the course of efforts to get rid of class rule, the contrast drawn between the enfranchised classes and the unenfranchised mass outside made men think of the latter as " the people," giving the word a significance almost equivalent to what it is now the fashion to call the " proletariate." This was the more natural because that part of the nation was the more numerous part. To it the more enthusiastic reformer attributed those virtues in which the rich had been found wanting. It was believed that by sinking a deep shaft into the humbler strata of society the springs might be tapped of a simple honesty and sense of justice which would renovate politics. The association of poverty with simplicity and of luxury with corruption is an old one. In the Golden Age there was no wretchedness because there were no rich. Virgil, who talks of the city crowd as an *ignobile vulgus,* tells us that when Justice quitted the earth her last footprints were among the tillers of the soil. The latest echo of the old sentiment is found in the pastoral poetry of the eighteenth century. Yet those who thus idealized the hand-workers and thought first of them when they talked of " the people," did not mean to represent them as a class which should predominate and be deemed, because it was the largest, entitled to be the exponent of the national will. Rather was it thought that the intermingling in political action of all classes would give unity and strength to the nation as one body, because each would make its own contribution. Harmony would give solidity. When men were thinking not of class interests but of the national welfare, there would be less discord. Classes are naturally selfish; the People cannot be, for it is the welfare of all that they must desire. The generation in which these ideas sprang up and prevailed were influenced by abstract ideas and optimistic theories. As their experience extended only to cases in which a small privileged class had abused its authority to the prejudice of the whole community, it did not occur to them that a single class which constituted a majority of the whole might be possessed by a similar self-regarding spirit. They would indeed have grieved to think that this could happen, for they hoped to be rid of classes altogether, popular rule being to them the antithesis to class rule.

With these conceptions there went a belief in him whom they called the " common man," or, as we should say, the average man. He is taken to be the man of broad common sense, mixing on equal terms with his neighbours, forming a fair unprejudiced judgment on every question, not viewy or pedantic like the man of learning, nor arrogant, like the man of wealth, but seeing things in a practical, businesslike, and withal kindly, spirit, pursuing happiness in his own way, and willing that every one else should do so. Such average men make the bulk of the people, and are pretty sure to go right, because the publicity secured to the expression of opinion by speech and in print will supply them with ample materials for judging what is best for all.

The experiences of recent years have dimmed the hope that class antagonisms would disappear under the rule of the People as a whole, and that the admission of all to a share in power would make every element of a nation rely on constitutional methods for curing whatever evils legislation can cure. Faith in the people was meant to be faith in the whole people, and must suffer when a people is distracted by class war. Yet whatever cynical critics may say, there remains a large measure of truth in that faith as it inspired the poets and philosophers of democracy a century ago. Where rights and duties are shared by all, there is full opportunity for ideas to make their way, for arguments to be heard, for projects to be considered. The unrestricted interchange of thought works for good. In the intermixture and collision of views a breadth of result is attained. Truth and wisdom have their chance, and truth, in an intelligent people, has a better chance than error. That Average Man to whom we recur when we talk of the People is in most countries neither captivated by theories nor swept off his feet by passion. If he does not, as some have fancied, become by the grant of citizenship fit for the functions of citizenship, he is usually raised to a higher level by the sense of a duty thrown on him, and has a sense of justice and fairness sometimes wanting in members of a privileged class. He may have limited knowledge and no initiative, yet be able to form, especially if he has a chance of seeing them at close quarters, a shrewd judgment of men. His instincts are generally sound, nor is he insensible to high ideals when presented to him in a form which makes them plain to him. What he lacks in knowledge he often makes up for by a sympathetic comprehension of the attitude of his fellow-men. Thus there is a sense in which the People are wiser than the wisest person or group. Abraham Lincoln, whom no one ever surpassed in knowing how to deal with men, summarized the results of his observation in the famous sentence, " You can fool all the people some of the time and some of the people all the time, but you can't fool all the people all the time."

If this dictum of the great President seems severe in its recognition of the risk that the people may hastily commit a fatal error, it is none the less a tribute to their open-mindedness, to the value of an abounding variety of views and of free criticism, to the probability that with due consideration things will go well. Where the people rule, you cannot stifle independent views. You cannot presume on the ignorance of the people, nor on the appearance of apathy they may show, nor on the power party organization may acquire over them. If you can get at the people — for that is the difficulty — things will usually go well. But the people must have time.

CHAPTER XV

ALL power springs from the People. This axiom accepted, the question follows: How is the People to exercise its power? By what means shall its mind and will be delivered? The answer given in all constitutional countries is, By Voting, *i.e.* or, as J. R. Lowell said, by counting heads instead of breaking them. Voting, an invention of the ancient Greek and Italian republics, has been adopted in all civilized States, whether, as in Switzerland and in many States of the North American Union, it is used to express directly the people's judgment upon a proposition submitted by Initiative or by Referendum, or is applied to the choice of persons to represent the people in an assembly, or to act on their behalf as officials.[1]

But voting, though everywhere practised, has nowhere given complete satisfaction. The faults charged on it as a method of applying the popular will to self-government may be summarized as follows.

The purposes of the people cannot be adequately expressed through persons chosen to represent them, for these persons may innocently misconceive or dishonestly misrepresent the wishes of the people, nor can any instructions given by the people remove this danger. Moreover, any election of representatives is an imperfect expression of the views on public policy of the voters, because it turns largely on the personal merits of the candidates, not on the doctrines they profess.

[1] The oldest method of ascertaining the wishes of the assembled people was by a calling for a shout of " Yea " or " Nay." This custom continued at parliamentary elections in England till the Hustings were abolished by the Ballot Act of 1872, and it still survives in both Houses of the British Parliament, the Speaker calling for the " Ayes " and " Noes," and ordering a division only when one or the other section challenges his statement that the " Ayes " or " Noes " (as the case may be) " have it." In the House of Lords the words used are " Contents " and " Not Contents," in the Convocation of the University of Oxford " Placet " and " Non placet."

There may, moreover, be among the voters many who, having no mind of their own to express, give their vote at the bidding or under the influence of other persons. Some may have been intimidated or bribed. Some take no interest in the matter and, in default of personal knowledge, merely obey their party organization. Thus what purports to be the will of the people is largely a factitious product, not really their will.

In voting, every vote has the same effective value. One man may have conscience, knowledge, experience, judgment. Another may lack all these, yet his vote counts for just as much in the choice of a representative or the decision of a momentous issue. The wisest and the most foolish are put on the same level. Opinions are counted, not weighed.

Is there any answer to these criticisms or remedy for these alleged evils?

The first criticism is accepted as valid by that large body of opinion which, advocating direct popular voting on as many questions as possible, seeks to have the Initiative and Referendum methods adopted wherever constitutional government exists. Others, emphasizing the risk that representatives may fail to give effect to the people's wish, desire to make the mandate delivered at an election imperative and precise, and to give the people a power of recalling a representative whose action they disapprove.

The second evil has been in many countries reduced by laws against bribery and intimidation, but where these tangible offences are absent, no remedy seems possible, for how can any one know how far a voter has a mind of his own, or is merely an instrument in other hands? He may not himself know.

The third objection taken goes down to the root difficulty of democratic government, and has been made the ground of the severest arraignments of the People as a Ruling Power. An attempt was made in some of the ancient republics to give proportionately greater weight in voting, not indeed to virtue and wisdom, but to property and (implicitly) to education, by dividing the citizens into classes or sections, and allotting to each a single collective vote, determined by the majority within the section. The richer sort were placed in several of such sections and the poorer in others, each of these latter containing a larger number of voters than the sections of the richer citizens. Thus the votes of the richer sections balanced those of the poorer, *i.e.* the voting power of numbers was balanced by the power of voting wealth. Similarly, by the constitution of Belgium persons possessing certain property or educational qualifications were formerly given three or two votes each, the ordinary citizen having only one. This Belgian plan has now been abolished; and is not likely to be tried elsewhere. It was proposed in England many years ago, but then rejected on the ground, *inter alia,* that the rich had various means of exerting influence which other classes did not possess.[1] Whatever objections may be taken to a method which gives an equal voice to the wisest and most public-spirited citizen and to the ignorant criminal just released from gaol, no one has yet suggested any criterion by which the quality of voters should be tested and more weight allowed to the votes of the fittest. Equal suffrage as well as Universal Suffrage has apparently to be accepted for better or worse.

Is there then no other way in which the people can express their mind and exert their power? Can any means be found of supplying that which elections fail to give? Is the judgment delivered by polling, *i.e.* the counting of heads, the same thing as public opinion? Polling is the only explicit and palpable mode yet devised of expressing the people's will. But does a judgment so delivered necessarily convey the opinion of the thoughtful element among those who vote, and may not that opinion be able to exert a moral authority at times when no legal opportunity is provided for the delivery of a judgment at the polls?

What is Public Opinion? The term is commonly used to denote the aggregate of the views men hold regarding matters that affect or interest the community. Thus understood, it is a congeries of all sorts of discrepant notions, beliefs, fancies, prejudices, aspirations. It is confused, incoherent, amorphous, varying from day to day and week to week. But in the midst of this diversity and confusion every question as

[1] I do not forget, but cannot find space for an adequate discussion of, the other objections taken to a representative system which ignores minorities. Much light may be expected from the many experiments that are now being tried in various forms of Proportional Representation.

it rises into importance is subjected to a process of consolidation and clarification until there emerge and take definite shape certain views, or sets of interconnected views, each held and advocated in common by bodies of citizens. It is to the power exerted by any such view, or set of views, when held by an apparent majority of citizens, that we refer when we talk of Public Opinion as approving or disapproving a certain doctrine or proposal, and thereby becoming a guiding or ruling power. Or we may think of the Opinion of a whole nation as made up of different currents of sentiment, each embodying or supporting a view or a doctrine or a practical proposal. Some currents develop more strength than others, because they have behind them larger numbers or more intensity of conviction; and when one is evidently the strongest, it begins to be called Public Opinion *par excellence,* being taken to embody the views supposed to be held by the bulk of the people. Difficult as it often is to determine the relative strength of the different streams of opinion — one cannot measure their strength as electric power is measured by volts — every one admits that when one stream is distinctly stronger than any other, *i.e.* when it would evidently prevail if the people were called upon to vote, it ought to be obeyed. Till there is a voting, its power, being open to doubt, has no legal claim to obedience. But impalpable though it may be, no sensible man disputes that power, and such governing authorities as ministries and legislatures are obliged to take account of it and shape their course accordingly. In this sense, therefore, the People are always ruling, because their will is recognized as supreme whenever it is known, and though it is formally and legally expressed only by the process of counting votes, it is frequently known for practical purposes without that process.

What I am trying to convey may be illustrated from phenomena perceived by any one who sits in a deliberative assembly such as the British House of Commons. In that body, which is a sort of microcosm of the nation, the opinion of the House, as pronounced in a division and recorded in the division lists, is not the same as that opinion gathered from the private talks which members have with one another. Many propositions which are carried on a division would be rejected if the members were free to express by their votes exactly what they think. Their judgment, formed after hearing all that can be said on both sides, is frequently different from, and sounder than, that which they deliver by their votes. The members are not to blame for this. It is incident to their position. They are required, not only by the pledges they have given to their constituents, but by the system of party government which could not be worked if every one was to vote exactly as he thought, to give votes not consistent with their personal views. Everybody knows this, and a ministry often feels it so strongly that it drops a proposal which it could carry if it put full pressure on the party loyalty of its adherents. The case of a nation differs from the case of a parliament, because the voters are not bound by pledges or by allegiance. They have only their own consciences to obey. But the cases are in this respect similar, that opinion as declared by voting may differ widely from that which would be elicited by interrogating privately (were it possible to do this on a large scale) those citizens who have what can be called an opinion: and the latter opinion so elicited would be more likely to be right than the former.

How is the drift of Public Opinion to be ascertained? That is the problem which most occupies and perplexes politicians. They usually go for light to the press, but the press, though an indispensable, is not a safe guide, since the circulation of a journal does not necessarily measure the prevalence of the views it advocates. Newspaper accounts given of what men are thinking may be coloured and misleading, for every organ tends to exaggerate the support its views command. Neither are public meetings a sure index, for in populous centres almost any energetic group can fill a large hall with its adherents. Stray elections arising from the death or retirement of a legislator or (in the States of the North American Union) of an elected official, are much relied on, yet the result is often due rather to local circumstances than to a general movement of political feeling. There is, moreover, such a thing as an artificially created and factitious opinion. The art of propaganda has been much studied in our time, and has attained a development which enables its practitioners by skilfully and sedulously supplying false or one-sided statements of fact to beguile and mislead those who have not the means or the time to ascertain the facts for themselves.   Against all these sources of error the observer must be on his guard.

The best way in which the tendencies at work in any community can be discovered and estimated is by moving freely about among all sorts and conditions of men and noting how they are affected by the news or the arguments brought from day to day to their knowledge.   In every neighbourhood there are unbiassed persons with good opportunities for observing, and plenty of skill in " sizing up " the attitude and proclivities of their fellow-citizens.   Such men are invaluable guides.   Talk is the best way of reaching the truth, because in talk one gets directly at the facts, whereas reading gives not so much the facts as what the writer believes, or wishes to have others believe.   Whoever, having himself a considerable experience of politics, takes the trouble to investigate in this way will seldom go astray.   There is a *flair* which long practice and " sympathetic touch " bestow. The trained observer learns how to profit by small indications, as an old seaman discerns, sooner than the landsman, the signs of coming storm.

There have doubtless been some remarkable instances in which English party managers anticipated success at a general election and encountered defeat.   But these instances, like that of the prophets who bade Ahab go up against Ramoth Gilead, are explained by the propensity of party agents to find what they set out to seek, and to prophesy smooth things when it is anywise possible to do so.

How does public opinion grow, and how can the real volume and strength a view possesses be distinguished from those artificial and delusive appearances which politicians are obliged to present as true, each party wishing to pose before the public as the majority?

Three classes of persons have to do with the making of public opinion.   There are the men who seriously occupy themselves with public affairs, whether professionally, as members of legislatures or journalists or otherwise actively engaged in politics, or as private persons who care enough for their duty as citizens to give constant attention to what passes in the political world.   These persons are, taken all together, an exceedingly small percentage of the voting citizens.   It is they, however, who practically make opinion.

They know the facts, they think out and marshall and set forth, by word or pen, the arguments meant to influence the public.

The second class consists of those who, though comparatively passive, take an interest in politics. They listen and read, giving an amount of attention proportioned to the magnitude of any particular issue placed before them, or to the special interest it may have for them. They form a judgment upon the facts and arguments presented to them. Their judgment corrects and modifies the views of the first class, and thus they are, though not the originators, yet largely the moulders of opinion, giving to a doctrine or a proposition the shape it has to take if it is to succeed. Most of them belong to a party but are not so hotly partisan as to be unable to consider fairly both sides of a case. In countries accustomed to constitutional government, and when not swept off their feet by excitement, such men have the qualities of a good juryman and deliver a sensible verdict. What they think and feel is the opinion of the nation as a whole. It is Public Opinion.

The third class includes all that large residue of the citizens which is indifferent to public affairs, reading little and thinking less about them. So far as it has any opinion, it adopts that which prevails in the place where it lives, or in the social class or industrial milieu to which it belongs. Men of this type will now and then be attracted by a personality, and follow him irrespective of his politics, because some of his qualities, not always his better qualities, appeal to certain tastes of their own. Though they neither make opinion as thinkers nor help to mould it as critics, they swell its volume, and form, in some countries, a considerable proportion of those whom a party can enrol as loyal supporters, all the more sure to be loyal because they do not reflect, but are content to repeat current phrases. The proportion of this class to the total adult population varies in different countries, but is everywhere larger than is commonly supposed. It has been much increased in countries which have adopted universal suffrage. Smallest in Switzerland, it is small also in Scotland and Norway and New Zealand, and would be small in the United States but for the presence of eleven millions of negroes and some millions of recent immigrants.

Among the conditions requisite for the formation of a wise and tolerant public opinion the intelligence of the people and the amount of interest which the average citizen takes in public affairs are the most important.   Another is the extent to which agreement exists upon certain fundamental political doctrines.   In the United States everybody is attached to the republican form of government: everybody assumes the complete separation of Church and State and the exclusion of ecclesiasticism from politics.   In France, on the other hand, the chasm between Roman Catholics and the opponents of Christianity is deep; and there are still many who desire some form of government which, whether or not monarchical in name, shall be monarchical in substance.   In Canada and South Africa differences of race prevent the existence of a homogeneous public sentiment, for they may tend to make men judge a proposal not so much by its value for the community as by its probable effect on their own section.   So if social classes are unfriendly, suspicion is rife, and agreement becomes difficult even on questions, such as those of foreign policy, which scarcely affect domestic interests.[1]   Where marked incompatibilities of thinking or of feeling, whatever their source, breed distrust, that useful process of gradual assimilation and half-conscious compromise by which one general dominant opinion is formed out of the contact and mixture of many views works imperfectly.   A truly national patriotism stills domestic discords at moments of danger, and helps to keep some questions above party even in quiet times. But such a patriotism needs to be strengthened and enlarged in each country by a better understanding among the citizens of one another's characters and aims, and a better sense of what each class or section gains by the others' prosperity, than most nations possess.

Now let us, returning to the point whence this discussion started, compare that influence upon the conduct of public affairs which is called, somewhat loosely, the Rule of Public Opinion, with the direct control exerted by the citizens when they vote either on a question submitted (Referendum) or

[1] As to the influence of Public Opinion on international policy see Chapter on Democracy and Foreign Policy in Part III., *post*.   It need hardly be said that Public Opinion cannot, and much less can Voting, pass judgment on details in legislation.   Its action, both in that sphere and in foreign policy, deals with broad principles only.

for a candidate.   The action of Opinion is continuous, that of Voting occasional, and in the intervals between the elections of legislative bodies changes may take place materially affecting the views of the voters.   In France, where the duration of a Chamber is four years, in England where it is five, they cannot be assumed to be of the same mind after two years.   At elections it is for a candidate that votes are given, and as his personality or his local influence may count for more than his principles, the choice of one man against another is an imperfect way of expressing the mind of a constituency.   In countries which (like Britain and the British self-governing Dominions) allow a ministry to fix the date for a general election, a moment may be seized when the people are stirred by some temporary emotion which prevents a considered and temperate expression of their will.   Such a " snap election " may misrepresent their more deliberate mind.

The result of an election may be determined by the action of an insignificant knot of voters specially interested in a question of slight importance.   Anti-vaccinationists, or a few dozens of government employees demanding higher wages, have thus turned elections in English boroughs where parties were of nearly equal strength.   The result seemed to give a victory to one political party, but the real victory was that of the little knot and more pliable candidate, with the result that the rest of the electors were debarred from delivering the judgment of the constituency on national issues.

Note also that in elections the spirit of party or of class, and the combative ardour which such a spirit inspires, cloud the minds of many voters, making them think of party triumph rather than either of a candidate's merits or of his principles.   A large percentage of the votes are given with little reference to the main issues involved.   It is the business of the managers to " froth up " party feeling and make excitement do the work of reason.[1]

In all the points just enumerated Public Opinion, when and in so far as it can be elicited, is an organ or method through which the People can exert their power more elastic

[1] The observations here made regarding voting at public elections or on questions submitted by Referendum or Initiative are equally applicable to votings in party gatherings or at the meetings of ecclesiastical or labour organizations.

and less pervertible than is the method of voting. It is always operative: its action changes as the facts of the case change and keeps pace with them. It sets the larger and the smaller issues in their true perspective. It reduces petty "fads" or selfish groups to insignificance. It relies, not on organization and party drill, but on the good sense and fairness of the citizens as a whole. It expresses what is more or less thought and felt in all the parties by their more temperate and unbiassed members. It is a counterpoise to the power of mere numbers. At a poll one vote is as good as another, the ignorant and unreflecting counting for as much as the well-informed and wise, but in the formation of opinion knowledge and thought tell. The clash and conflict of argument bring out the strength and weakness of every case, and that which is sound tends to prevail. Let the cynics say what they will, Man is not an irrational animal. Truth usually wins in the long run, though the obsessions of self-interest or prejudice or ignorance may long delay its victory. The turbid fluid is slowly clarified as the mud sinks to the bottom, and the liquid is drawn off pure from the top of the vessel. Voting, though indispensable as a means of determining the view of the majority, is a mechanical operation, necessarily surrounded with legal forms, while in the formation and expression of opinion the essential spirit of democracy rises above the machinery and the trammels which machinery imposes and finds a means of applying its force more flexible, more delicate, more conciliatory and persuasive than is a decision given by the counting of votes.

Voting, I repeat, is indispensable, for it is positive, giving an incontrovertible result. But voting is serviceable just in proportion as it has been preceded and prepared by the action of public opinion. The discussion which forms opinion by securing the due expression of each view or set of views so that the sounder may prevail enables the citizens who wish to find the truth and follow it to deliver a considered vote. It is an educative process constantly in progress. In the intervals between elections it imposes some check on the vehemence of party spirit and the recklessness or want of scruple of party leaders, and restrains the disposition of party government to abuse its power. When a ministry or legislature feels the tide of opinion beginning to run against some of their pur-

poses they pause.   Many a plan has been abandoned without any formal declaration of popular disapproval because
disapproval was felt to be in the air.   This is not to say that
the current of opinion for the time being dominant is always
right, any more than that the people voting at the polls are
always right.   The people may err, in whichever way its will
may be expressed, but error is more probable at moments,
such as elections, when the passion of strife is hottest.   It
may be suggested that when the citizen is called to deliver
his vote he will be impressed by the seriousness of the occasion and have a specially strong sense of his responsibility.
But those who know what is the atmosphere elections gen-
erate, and how many persons vote under the influence of misrepresentations contrived to mislead them at the last moment
when any correction will come too late, how many pledges
are recklessly given, and how hard it is afterwards to escape
from the pledge, will have no implicit faith in an election
as an expression of genuine popular will, still less of popular
thought.

As the excellence of public opinion — its good sense, its
tolerance, its pervasive activity — is the real test of a nation's fitness for self-government, so the power it exerts,
being constantly felt as the supreme arbiter irrespective of
electoral machinery, is the best guarantee for the smooth and
successful working of popular government, and the best safeguard against revolutionary violence.

What does a nation need to secure that excellence and to
enable Opinion to exert its power as supreme ?   Besides the
conditions already enumerated, the things to be chiefly desired
are :

The presence in the nation of many vigorous minds, constructive and critical, constantly occupied in the public discussion of the current problems of statesmanship.   These are
the minds already referred to as constituting that first and
relatively small class which makes Opinion.

The preponderance in the rest of the nation of men of the
second, as compared with men of the third, of the three
classes aforesaid, *i.e.* persons whose sense of civic duty makes
them give steady attention to public affairs, and who bring
to their consideration a fair judgment and an insight into
character which, unseduced by the demagogue, respects up-

rightness and capacity in the leader who has given proof of these qualities.

In countries like France, the United States, and Britain, men of the first class are never wanting. But a nation needs something more than the intellectual guidance which such men can give. Among them there must also be leaders of a firmness which will face opprobrium and defend causes for the moment unpopular. The chief defect of public opinion is its tendency in times of excitement to overbear opposition and silence the voices it does not wish to hear. Courage is the highest and perhaps the rarest quality among politicians. It is specially needed in democratic countries.

PART II

SOME DEMOCRACIES IN THEIR WORKING

CHAPTER XVI

THE REPUBLICS OF ANTIQUITY

THOUGH it is the newer forms of democracy that are the subject of this book, some account must be given of popular government in the ancient world, where that government appeared in its earliest and simplest form, for though the constitutional arrangements were often complicated, the principles stand out sharp and clear. In the history of the Greek commonwealths we discover many traits of character which recur in the modern world. It is instructive to study in their free play, when mankind was making its first political experiments among economic and social conditions diverse from ours, those tendencies inherent in human nature which are the groundwork of scientific history.

There is also another reason why the ancient republics should still interest the student. Democracy is a new thing in the modern world. More than nineteen centuries have passed since it died out on the coasts of the Mediterranean. During all those centuries down to the days of our great-grandfathers, those who thought or wrote about it had to go back to classical antiquity for example and for instruction, since the only descriptions of its actual working they could use were provided by ancient writers. Among those writers there were two of such outstanding power and range of mind that they formed the views of all who came after them till the eighteenth century saw a new series of experiments in free government begin. To Plato and Aristotle, and to the historians of Greece and Rome, often misunderstood and sometimes misrepresented, may be traced nearly all the doctrines that have been propounded regarding the respective merits and defects of divers forms of government. Their writings have become a part of the subject itself.

Only in three countries of the ancient world did men reach the stage of a settled and constitutional political life, and of these three only one need occupy us here. There were the Phoenicians of Carthage, there were some peoples in Italy, and there were the Greeks, whose small self-governing city communities scattered themselves out from continental Hellas along the coasts of the great inland sea as far as Trebizond and Kertch in the east, Monaco and Marseilles in the west.

Moderns have been apt to say: " What light can these little city states give to us who frame our systems for vast countries? Athens and Syracuse in the height of their power had fewer citizens than a single English or French constituency counts to-day. The voters who at Rome chose a Fabius or a Julius to be Consul were sometimes fewer than those who fill the hall of a nominating Convention at Chicago." But the difference in scale and in other things, too, are not so remarkable as the similarities. As the problems of good government were essentially the same, so were the motives and the temptations. The gifts by which power is won and the faults by which it is lost are as discernible in the careers of Greek and Roman statesmen as in those which engage our curiosity to-day. On the small stage of an ancient city republic both figures and tendencies stand out more boldly, the personalities are less conventional, the action moves faster, and it is often more dramatic.

Of Carthage I have not space to speak, and the data we possess are scanty. It was an oligarchy rather than a democracy, in its earlier course singularly stable, for Aristotle tells us it never had a revolution. Neither was the Roman Constitution democratic, though it had a popular element in the assemblies which chose the magistrates and passed laws. It is the Greek democracies that best deserve attention. Before coming to their governments, let us note some of the points in which the conditions of their political life differed from those of modern times.

That social stratum which has been in the modern world the poorest and least educated lay altogether below the level of civic rights. Slavery did in one sense make democratic institutions more workable, because the class on whom hardship first fell had no political power, because the menace of its revolt sometimes prevented the free citizens from pushing their quarrels to extremity, and because every freeman, having as large or an even larger class below him than he had above him, acquired a certain sense of independence and personal dignity. Though servitude was less harsh among the Greeks than at Rome, it everywhere disposed men to cruelty and a disregard of human life. Unscrupulous adventurers could recruit among the slaves a force for revolutionary purposes, or might degrade citizenship by the admission of an ignorant and dangerous element.

The small size of a Greek republic, the territory of which seldom extended beyond a few dozens of square miles round the city, and the number of free citizens, usually less than ten and seldom exceeding thirty thousand, made it easy to bring within the hearing of one voice a majority of all who were entitled to vote in the popular Assembly, and enabled everybody to form his opinions on the personal qualities of those who aspired to leadership or to office.[1] But it increased the power of personal attraction, intensified hatreds and antagonisms, furnished opportunities for conspiracies or secret combinations formed by a few families or a group of ambitious politicians.[2]

Representative government was unknown, superfluous where the whole body of citizens could meet in one spot to discuss public affairs. It does not seem to have entered the thoughts of any among the philosophers or constitution framers.[3] This deprived the ruling power in a State of such benefits as may be expected from the deliberations of a parliament whose members their fellow-citizens have chosen as best fitted by their abilities and character to give counsel, but on the other hand it raised the capacity, as well as the familiarity with public business, of the average citizen, raised it indeed to a higher point than it has ever attained elsewhere, except perhaps in Switzerland.

[1] Aristotle in his *Politics*, where the best kind of constitution for a republic is fully discussed, contemplates a city which is not too large for one man's voice to be heard by the whole assembly (*Pol.* Bk. vii. ch. 4).

[2] A striking picture of the fierce hatreds which internal strife aroused in these city republics is given by Thucydides in the chapters of Book III., Chapters 70–85 of his *History*, which describe the seditions at Corcyra.

[3] The nearest approach to representation made in the ancient world seems to have been in the assembly of delegates from the chief cities of the Roman province of Asia under the Roman Empire; but it met for religious or ceremonial not for political purposes.

The citizens of these republics were originally, and most of them continued to be, cultivators of the city's territory, and many of their internal troubles arose over the distribution and enjoyment of land. Some, like Marseilles and Byzantium, were commercial: a few, like Miletus, derived wealth from the making or dyeing of woollen stuffs. But they were, taken all in all, less industrial in the character of their population than the cities of mediaeval Italy and Germany; and industries (apart from mines) were seldom worked by large-scale producers employing many hands. The organization of the citizens into orders or sections was accordingly not by trades or guilds, as in most parts of modern Europe, but either by tribes, based on real or supposed kinship, or else locally connected in respect of the district where they dwelt. Religion played a great part. As the city had its common gods whom it took for its protectors, and as every family worshipped the ghosts of its ancestors, so also tribes, and often local divisions also, had local or peculiar deities or semi-divine heroes whom it honoured at local shrines.[1]

The citizens were organized on a military as well as a civil basis, for war service was obligatory. The cavalry, the heavy-armed infantry, and the light troops often constituted different classes for political purposes, the two former enjoying a privileged political position, and furnishing their own equipments according to their wealth. An interesting parallel may be found in the arrangements of the two Dutch Republics of South Africa, where the military officers (such as field cornets) also discharged political functions.

That which seems the most conspicuous contrast between these communities and modern European States, viz. the absence of newspapers and of the use of the printing-press for political purposes, did not make quite so much difference as might be supposed, for in small communities news spreads fast, and the inaccuracy to which it is exposed in spreading was hardly greater than the divergence between " happenings " and the newspaper reports of them observable in some modern countries, where nevertheless the average reader

[1] A brilliant, if possibly exaggerated, description and estimate of the influence of religion on civic organization and politics will be found in the well-known book of Fustel de Coulanges, *La Cité Antique*.

continues to fancy that a statement is true because he has
seen it in print.   The Greeks, enjoying their open-air and
leisurely life, spent much of their time in talking, as do
their descendants even unto this day.   News was never
wanting.

Abstract principles affected politics less than they have
done in most modern democracies.   Those who owned slaves
could not very well have talked of the Rights of Man, for
though the Americans of the South did so talk before the
Civil War, reading the Declaration of Independence publicly
on every Fourth of July, their difficulty was reduced by the
fact that the bondmen were of a different colour, whereas
among the ancients the slave might well be of as light a tint
as his master, and possibly superior in natural intelligence.[1]
The one abstract principle which did lead to strife and induce revolutions was the passion for political equality.   Free
citizens of a gifted race, prone to vanity, and valuing themselves all the more because they saw slaves beneath them,
would not, when society had passed from its earlier stages
into conditions comparatively orderly and peaceful, submit
to the rule of a few persons who, while richer or better born,
were neither wiser nor morally better than themselves, and
dwelt as their neighbours in the same city.   Political equality seemed to be prescribed by justice, for though Aristotle
is at great pains to explain that justice must be measured
with reference to the difference in the capacities of the individual, and in the value of what service each citizen can
render, so that Proportionate Justice will assign larger functions, not indeed to the Rich, but to the Wise and Good, this
was a doctrine then as now unwelcome to the average man.
Moreover, Greek oligarchs always abused their power, so
there were sure to be practical as well as theoretic grounds
for attacking them.

In all or nearly all the Greek states the first form of government was a monarchy or chieftainship, but, as we learn
from the Homeric poems, it was a monarchy tempered by
public opinion, which found expression in the public assembly (of the city or tribe) convoked by a chieftain and in prac-

[1] The Athenian prisoners enslaved after their defeat at Syracuse improved their lot by reciting passages from Euripides to their owners,
who had heard of the poet's fame, but had never seen his dramas acted.

tice guided by the leading men, but in which any freeman
might speak his mind.[1]

After a time kingship either died out, being replaced by
elected magistracies, or was greatly reduced in authority,
though sometimes (for religious reasons) continued in name.
Power passed, in most cities, to the heads of the chief families, who were also the rich and the lenders of money.   Their
rule, sometimes respecting forms prescribed by old custom,
sometimes based on force only, became more or less odious
according as it was more or less harsh, but everywhere demands arose for a definition by law of the powers of magistrates and for the admission of the bulk of the citizens to the
public offices and the councils.   This was the beginning of
democracy.   In many cities the transition took place through
the stage of a so-called Timocracy, in which only the richer
sort held the offices and enjoyed a greater voting power than
the rest of the citizens.   Without attempting to trace in detail the process of evolution, which in Athens lasted for more
than a century, it will suffice to describe the features of a
normal full-blown democracy such as was that of Athens from
the reforms of Cleisthenes (508 B.C.) till the days of Demosthenes, when the combined forces of Athens and Thebes were
overthrown by the Macedonian Philip (338 B.C.) on the fatal
field of Chaeroneia.

All these democratic republics had what we should call a
Constitution.   But this was not a Rigid Constitution (such
as that of the United States or Switzerland), but merely a
mass of laws, which could be altered by the people when and
as they pleased.   Constitutional law was constantly altered,
not only, as was natural, during the process of evolution from
an oligarchy to democracy, sometimes with intervals of tyranny, but also when the occurrence of a sedition had made
new guarantees for liberty necessary.   Athens had lived
under eleven constitutions from the time of Draco (624
B.C.) to the settlement of 404 B.C.   Aristotle collected and
described in a treatise an immense number of constitutions,
only one of which, that of Athens, is known to us in its
minuter details.

[1] As to this institution of the Assembly of all freemen, which appears
in Switzerland as the Landesgemeinde, see Chapter XII p. 130, *ante*.

The laws of these States covered the whole of civic life, every little city commonwealth being for political purposes an independent nation, making war and peace, maintaining its own army and navy, frequently at war with its neighbour cities. None (except possibly Athens) had a population of more than thirty or forty thousand free citizens, and few more than five thousand. Imagine such towns as Dover, Canterbury, and Maidstone in England, or such cities of the second or third rank as Salem, Concord, and Pittsfield, in Massachusetts, each one standing alone in a world full of other equally independent communities, if you wish to form an idea of what ancient republics were. In England all municipalities have practically the same form of municipal government. In the United States there is more, yet not very great, variety. In the Hellenic cities the variety was infinite, and the changes in the same city were frequent. There was seldom any distinction between what we should call National government and Local government, because the whole republic was usually smaller than most of our local administrative divisions in England or America. All offices were in fact national as well as municipal.

Confining ourselves to the democracies, let us note their characteristics. The salient feature was the vesting of supreme power for all purposes in the whole body of the citizens. That body was at once a Parliament and a Government, an Executive, Legislature, and Judiciary in one. It did much executive work, because it settled many important current questions by its vote. Not only did it choose the generals and other magistrates, it also instructed the generals, listened to envoys from other States, declared war, concluded peace, ratified treaties, ordered public ceremonials, civil or religious, received public accounts. It was the Legislature, passing Laws intended to be permanent, and Decrees prescribing the main issues of State policy from one meeting to another, and imposing taxes or burdens either generally or on some particular class of rich men. It, or a part of it, formed also the Judiciary, for the citizens acting as one body or divided into sections which may be described as gigantic juries, heard and determined nearly all cases, both civil and criminal, while the Assembly as a whole could,

and sometimes did, even if irregularly, pass without any trial
sentences of death or fine or exile upon those officials whose
action had displeased it.

How did this system work in each of the three branches
of government? I take Athens as the best example, for we
know more about it than about any other republic, but, as already observed, there was no one general form of republican
government.

As respects executive business, there were magistrates, civil
and military, the former chosen almost wholly by lot, the
latter by the vote of Assembly, for even these ardent equali-
tarians felt that skill and experience are essential in war.
Whereas in other offices no man could serve more than once —
even in the Council only twice — generals were often re-
elected, Pericles fifteen times, Phocion forty-five. Terms of
office were short, none exceeding a year. The chief civil officials, the nine archons, were chosen by lot for a year, but
the post carried little distinction and gave little scope for
ambition. Far more important were the generals, elected
yearly, ten together, each to be a sort of check on his colleagues. Sometimes an important command was given to
one specially, but more frequently they exercised their functions jointly. They, or some of them, not only led in the
field, but brought questions of foreign policy before the
Assembly, and, since charged with military preparations,
had war finance also to deal with. Whoever showed high
capacity and won confidence became a leading man in the
city.

For legislative purposes there was a Council which was
meant to prepare work for, and to some extent guide, the
Assembly.[1] It consisted of five hundred members, fifty being taken by lot from each of the ten tribes. No one under

[1] See *Polity of the Athenians* (now generally accepted as a work of
Aristotle), where (chapters 43–46) the functions of the Council and the
duties of these and other official persons are described. This treatise,
discovered in an Egyptian papyrus, and published by Sir F. Kenyon
in 1891, is the only part of Aristotle's treatise (or treatises) on the
Greek constitutions which has been preserved to us. Parts of it are
wanting, or undecipherable, in the MS. The outline I have given in
the text describes the system generally. To set forth the variations
between the earlier and the later arrangements would involve a much
fuller treatment.

[2] Eighteen was the age which qualified a man to sit in the Assembly.

the age of thirty [2] was eligible, no one could serve in it more than twice. Each tribal group of fifty was placed in charge for the term of thirty-five days (one-tenth of a year), called a Prytany, and was responsible for the arrangement of the business that had to come before the Assembly during its term. This Council appointed, again by lot, a president (ἐπιστάτης) whose office lasted for twenty-four hours only, and who could not be reappointed. This president took, again by lot, nine other persons (πρόεδροι) out of the nine other tribes who were not then presiding, and from these nine took, once more by lot, one to be chairman. These nine then received the programme (πρόγραμμα) of business to be dealt with by the Assembly, and provided for the orderly conduct of business in that body, proposing the questions to be dealt with (including the elections of the magistrates chosen by vote), taking the votes, supervising the proceedings generally, but leaving to the Assembly all matters of policy. These ingenious arrangements were devised not only to respect the principle of equality, but also to prevent any one tribe from having things too much its own way, even during its thirty-five-day term. Yet the function of arranging and directing the course of business, though it gave importance to the annual appointment of the Council, carried less power than that which the Speaker enjoyed till recently in the American Congress, or that which the " Steering Committee " now exerts there; and much less than the Cabinet exerts in the British House of Commons. The Council nowise interfered with the freedom of the Assembly to discuss and (if it pleased) to decide a question raised by any ordinary private citizen.

The power of the Assembly was complete and absolute. As Aristotle remarks, it did what it pleased.[1] Its action embraced every department of State work, and was uncontrolled. There was no King, no President of the Republic, to interpose his veto, no Second Chamber to amend or reject a bill, no constitutional limitations fettering the Assembly's action, save one (not always respected) which is peculiar enough to be worth describing.

Holding the doctrine that political sovereignty, complete and final, rested not with the citizens but with the laws of

1 *Polity of the Athenians*, ch. 41.

the city, embodying the settled mind and will of the people, the Greeks drew a distinction between Laws (Νόμοι), containing general rules of permanent operation and Decrees (ψηφίσματα),[1] passed for a particular occasion or purpose. Now at Athens the Laws were liable to be amended once at least in every year on the proposal either of any private citizen or of a body officially charged with the duty of revision (Thesmothetai). When on the proposal either of the Thesmothetai or of a citizen, a resolution to amend was accepted by the Assembly, a body of citizens called Nomothetai, and constituting a Legislative Commission, was appointed by lot to preside over the process of amendment. The Commission discussed and voted on the amendments submitted, thus giving to the Laws their revised form, which lasted till another process of amendment was put through. This may be called Constitutional Legislation in the strict sense of the term. It was passed at a special time and by a sort of special Committee, though a huge one, sometimes of as many as one thousand citizens, taken by lot. Now in order to protect the Laws from being infringed by the Assembly, that is to say, to protect the citizens against their own hasty or ignorant action, a check was contrived. Whoever brought forward and carried in the Assembly any Decree or proposition which transgressed any Law in form or in substance, might be prosecuted by any citizen for his wrongful act in misleading the Assembly into an illegality. If the prosecution succeeded, the culprit was fined, or possibly even put to death, and the decree of the Assembly (if still operative) was annulled; but if a year had elapsed from the date of the illegality, no penalty was inflicted. This was called the Indictment for Illegality (γραφὴ παρανόμων), and served to deter the orators who guided the Assembly from reckless proposals infringing the formal safeguards; though often enough the threat was insufficient, and resolutions were passed which had worked their mischief before their illegality had been established. The same kind of indictment was employed where some one had proposed to amend a Law without following the formalities prescribed for that purpose. In this way the

---

[1] A somewhat similar distinction is drawn in France and Switzerland between *Lois* and *Arrêtés* (*Beschlüsse*), though the Greek νόμος corresponds in a sense to a French *loi constitutionelle*.

Constitution (as we should say), was deemed to be guarded, and that by a sort of judicial proceeding, the people being too jealous of their power to permit any presiding official to arrest their action as illegal, or to entrust to any authority but their own (acting in a judicial capacity) the duty of afterwards declaring it to have been illegal.

Though we know far less than we should like to know of the way debates were conducted in the Assembly, a few things stand out clearly.[1] There were no regularly organized parties. Any citizen could speak, but much of the debating fell to the practised orators whom the people knew and were apt to follow. The rule that every proposition ought to come through the Council was not strictly observed, and as those proposals which were brought from the Council could also be added to or varied, the Assembly's hands were practically free. There was little disorder, though sometimes much excitement, for the audience, which might number more thousands than any hall in London or Washington could well accommodate, and met in the open air (at Athens usually in the early morning), was so well accustomed to the exercise of its functions that we must think of it not as a mob or a mass meeting but rather as a House of Commons or Congress raised to seven or ten times the number of those legislatures. Four regular meetings were held in each Prytany period of thirty-five days, notice being usually given five days beforehand; and special meetings could be summoned in an emergency, sometimes by a trumpet-call. For some few purposes a quorum of 6000 was prescribed. Every one who attended received a sort of ticket or token, on presenting which at the proper office he was (in later days) paid his small attendance fee, payment having been introduced in the fourth century, long after the time of Pericles. Order was kept by the Scythian archers, public slaves or servants acting under the directions of the presidents.[2] We hear of no rules of closure, but large popular assemblies have speedier and more drastic means of curtailing debate. Attendance was chiefly given by those who dwelt in the city, or in the port of Piraeus,

[1] For a vivacious description of what the Assembly may have been like, see the bright and suggestive book of Mr. A. E. Zimmern, *The Greek Commonwealth*, pp. 163-7.

[2] There was also a corps of 1600 free citizen archers maintained at Athens and paid as a city guard.

and seldom exceeded 5000 out of a possible total of 30,000 to 35,000 adult male citizens. Voting was usually by the holding up of hands, but sometimes by pebbles dropped into urns for the Ayes and the Noes.

Besides passing decrees and carrying on the executive work already described, the Assembly acted also as a Court of Justice to hear an impeachment (εἰσαγγελία) of persons charged with political offences, and could inflict on those whom it condemned fines, or exile, or death, all this without the formalities of a judicial proceeding.[1]

There were, however, many details of current business which it could not deal with. These were left to the Council, formed as already described. It was a sort of Committee of the Assembly, as the British Cabinet is a sort of Committee of Parliament. But it was chosen by lot, and thus represented not the ripest wisdom and experience of the Assembly, but its average intelligence, consisting not of leaders, but of rank and file, with no preference for men of ability and influence. It sat in public, and was approachable by every citizen. Besides preparing business to be brought before the Assembly, it exerted a general supervision over the state administration as a whole, and particularly over finance, doing this mainly by committees or commissions appointed from itself for special purposes. Meeting daily, the Council was the constantly working organ of state life, by which the other numerous administrative Boards were kept in touch with one another, so that nothing should be omitted through the default of any one of them. Responsibility for neglect or misfeasance was strictly enforced, even when the error was one of judgment only, not of evil purpose. The Athenians thought they made up for their laxity in some respects by their stringency in others. The Assembly might break its own rules, but that made it none the less harsh towards others who did the like. Greek governments were often unjust and sometimes cruel.

Oddest of all, to modern eyes, of the features of Athenian democracy was the machinery provided for judicial business,

[1] The Assembly sat judicially also where another kind of charge was brought by what was called a προβολή, condemnation in which did not carry therewith a penalty, but might be followed by a prosecution in the courts.

and the use made of it for political purposes. The citizens were organized for judicial work in a body called the Heliaea, which consisted of all who offered themselves to take the judicial oath. Its normal number is given as 6000; that being the number chosen annually for the purposes by the Demes ($\delta\tilde{\eta}\mu o\iota$), local circumscriptions which exercised a sort of self-government in local affairs. Probably no more than 6000 could be found willing to serve, at least in the Demes with an agricultural population living some way from the city. Though the Heliaea might sit as a whole, it usually acted by sections, of which there were ten. They were called Dikasteries, and their members Dikasts, names which I use because the words " juries " and " jurors " would inevitably convey to modern readers the notion of small bodies, whereas these sections were very large.[1] The normal number seems to have been 500, but it was often smaller, perhaps 250 or 200. The lot determined who should sit in each section. To some one of the Dikasteries every case, civil or criminal, was referred. Plaintiff and defendant, accuser and accused, pleaded their cases in person, though they often read aloud the speeches which had been prepared for them by professional advocates. Sometimes a party to a cause was allowed to have the aid of a friend who would follow him and support his cause. The Dikasts were judges of every issue, for the presiding magistrate had no right either to state the law or to sum up on the facts. All was left to the crowd of Dikasts who, being a crowd, were impressionable, quickly excited by appeals to their feelings or prejudices, easily beguiled by plausible misrepresentations.[2] In such conditions, the law came off ill, and the pleader's skill was chiefly directed to handling, or mishandling, the facts. From the vote of the majority of the Dikastery there was no appeal. It not only delivered the verdict but fixed the penalty.

[1] The great size of the courts was due not only to the idea that the people ought to rule, but probably also to the fear that smaller tribunals would be bribed. The *judicia* at Rome, despite their large numbers, often were.

[2] The speeches of the Athenian orators which have come down to us furnish abundant illustrations. These speeches were of course hardly ever, if ever, reported as delivered, but were written out before or afterwards, and possibly used as political pamphlets, as were some of the famous orations of Cicero, *e. g.* the speech for Milo and the Second Philippic (*divina Philippica*), neither of which was actually delivered.

Seriously as these defects injured the course of justice in private suits, they were even more pernicious in their political results. There were not, as in modern countries, regular public prosecutors. Any citizen could indict another for an alleged offence against the State, and that not merely when an official was charged with negligence or other breach of duty, or corruption, or when any person was arraigned for a treasonable plot, or for having led the Assembly into a breach of the Laws or given it bad advice which it had followed. To prosecute became an obvious means not only of injuring a political opponent but of winning distinction for the accuser, and of levying blackmail by the threat of legal proceedings. A class of informers called Sycophants sprang up who made prosecutions their trade, and deterred many good citizens from coming forward to serve the public. Thus the battles of politics were fought out in the law courts almost as often as in the Assembly, the former being scarcely more impartial or circumspect than was the latter. Not only politicians, but almost every wealthy citizen who was worth worrying or harrying lived in perpetual disquiet.[1] He might be at any moment accused of some offence which could not be disproved without labour and anxiety, so it was probably cheaper to buy off the Sycophant than to fight him before the Dikastery. The system was often denounced, but it stood, partly because it was deemed to guarantee the safety of the State both against the predominance of any one man and against secret conspiracies, but also because the Dikasts found occupation and drew emolument from this incessant political as well as private litigation. Their pay, three obols a day, was scanty, but living was cheap, and the work light, suited to elderly men who liked to sun themselves in the city listening to well-turned rhetoric. A citizen drawing pay on most days for his judicial duties, and for his presence in the Assembly at least once a fortnight, had a chance of further pay for some other among the numerous lot-awarded offices, could attend some theatrical performance for which the means of paying were provided him, and received a share, small as it might be, from the silver mines or other source of public

[1] The rich were also heavily taxed, but in spite of everything there were always rich men. It is wonderful how much the richer class can bear and still be rich. We shall find this in Australia also.

revenue.   The fear of losing these " stakes in the country "
was sufficient — so we are told — to make the orators use the
argument that if heavy fines were not imposed on rich de-
fendants so as to replenish the coffers of the State, there
would not be enough left to pay the jury fees and Assembly
fees of the citizens.

Who worked this machinery of government, legislative and
administrative and judicial ?   Not a Cabinet, for there was
none.   Not party organizations, for there were no organized
parties, but only tendencies which disposed this or that section
of the voters to adhere generally to one type of view or follow some particular politician who had gained popularity.
One can hardly talk even of political leaders, for though there
were always prominent men who figured in debate, these
could not count on any assured following among the voters.
So far as there was any one centre of authority, it existed in
the Assembly, a crowd of four, five, or six thousand persons,
not always the same men, for the country dwellers came irregularly, and the more ignorant and irresponsible seaport
folk and small tradespeople were apt to give more frequent
attendance than did the richer class, who had their private
affairs to look after.   This grew in course of time as the
number of poor citizens increased ; and complaints were made
that the quality of the Assembly was declining, though it did
not sink so low as did that of the Comitia in the last century
of the Republic at Rome.   The Assembly never, however,
became a mob, for it knew how to listen, and those who addressed it were commonly either orators with whom it was
familiar, or some few generals whose services or character
had won its confidence.   Usually it was led by the orators,
practised rhetoricians, most of whom held no office, and who
devoted themselves to politics, some from ambition, some
from public spirit, some in the hope of turning their influence to personal gain.   Nowhere perhaps has the power
of eloquence been so great as it was in these republics, where
the ruling Assembly was full of bright and alert minds,
equally susceptible to ingenious arguments and to emotional
appeals, with every passion intensified by the contagion of
numbers.   It was the orators that practically held sway, and
that an irresponsible sway, for as they had not the measures
like the executive of a modern country, to carry out, they

recommended, any blame for the failure of those measures would fall on others. They were Demagogues in the original sense of the word, for they "led the people." Among the leaders there were great men like Themistocles and Pericles and Demosthenes, honest men like Aristides and Nicias and Phocion, who commanded respect by their talents or character. But many, especially in later days, were demagogues in the sense the word came to acquire, unscrupulous politicians, flattering and cajoling the people for their own selfish ends. Having power, they were often tempted by those who wished to get some benefit from the people. When tempted, they mostly fell. To take a bribe was hardly deemed an offence, unless it was given as payment for treason to the city's interests.

To a modern eye the strangest part of all this strange frame of government was the plan of leaving to chance the selection of nearly all officials except those generals for whom military skill was indispensable. Yet the use made of the Lot, as well as the other arrangements described, was deemed to be imposed by the supreme need of averting oligarchy, and still worse, Tyranny, the disease always threatening Greek republics, as it destroyed sixteen centuries later the republics of mediaeval Italy.[1] The vesting of public functions in large Boards instead of in individual officials was meant to make each member a check upon his colleagues. The short terms of office tended to prevent corrupt men from forming secret schemes for robbing the public funds. Thus power was brief as well as limited. The throwing open to every citizen of the right to prosecute officials made the way of transgressors hard, for it turned every ambitious rival into a detective. The Lot itself not only gave each man, however obscure, his chance of office, making him feel his equality with the richest, but threw difficulties in the way of treasonable plots, for those who had to exercise political power together were not, as in modern popular governments, party associates or social intimates, with common aims in view.

[1] See as to the use of the Lot the interesting little book of Mr. J. W. Headlam, *Election by Lot at Athens*, with which compare the concise *Handbook of Greek Constitutional History* of A. H. J. Greenidge, a scholar too soon lost to learning. The Lot is to Aristotle a characteristically democratic institution. It was used in the Italian republics, notably in Florence in the fifteenth century.

By all these devices, and also by Ostracism, the power of voting into exile, without any specific charge, a politician whom it was desired to keep away from the city, the Athenians sought to prevent any man from rising markedly above others in influence or power, and if this could not be quite prevented, to reduce his opportunities for doing mischief.   And, on the whole, the devices succeeded.   It was defeats in war that brought the first democracy to an end.   After its re-establishment in 403 B.C. Athens never regained the commanding position she had held in the days of Pericles as the head of a confederacy of subject allies.   But though her government was thereafter perhaps less efficient and certainly more offensive to the rich, its democratic character was not seriously endangered during the eighty years that followed down to the melancholy day when Macedonian troops were placed in the port-fortress of Munychia to overawe the people.

Athens lacked, and so did most of her sister republics, some features found in modern free governments.   There was no proper judicial establishment, no regular civil service, no permanent military establishment (despite the frequent wars), no organized political parties, little interest in or importance attached to elections to office, and an imperfect constitutional check on the action of the ruling legislature.   Executive power was comminuted and distributed among a large number of Boards, each consisting of many persons and restricted to a few special functions.   Such a government could hardly have been worked save by a wonderfully keen and active-minded people, whose courage and resourcefulness largely compensated for their instability and deficient respect for authority.   They held their ground well against their neighbour and often hostile republics, whose weaknesses were like their own.   Had no other foes appeared, the Republics of Hellas might have provided the world with still more to admire, and still more to take warning from.   What would the democracy of Athens have become had its quality been tested by another two centuries of life?   Would ingenuity and patriotism have discovered remedies for the evils which Aristotle noted?   Or would the intensification of that antagonism of Rich and Poor which was already visible in the later days of Plato have led to revolution and the establishment of an oligarchy or even of a tyranny. Unhappily the drama was never played out. After the first three acts, in the first of which Solon, in the second Pericles, and in the third Phocion and Demosthenes played the leading parts, the curtain suddenly fell. The military monarchy of Macedonia, reared by the craft of Philip, and thereafter wielded by the resistless force of Alexander, cut short the free life of Athens. Democracy virtually ended when (in 323 B.C.) Antipater reduced the number of citizens and planted a garrison to control them. Free governments, more or less democratic, remained in some other cities, notably in those of the Achaean League, till they succumbed to Rome. But at Athens, though she continued to be the most famous seat of instruction in philosophy till Justinian closed her schools in A.D. 529, the day of great statesmen, great poets, and great philosophers was gone for ever.

The defects of the Greek Republics have been dwelt upon by a host of writers, who found material for their strictures in the accounts given by the two finest philosophic minds of the ancient world, both of whom lived in Athens and described its democracy in treatises which were the earliest and remain among the most precious contributions ever made to political thought. The judgments of Plato are more severe than those of his great disciple, because he tries what he saw by the standard of that Ideal Polity which he imagines to be stored up somewhere in the heavens, never to become actual on earth till the day comes when philosophers are kings or kings are philosophers,— a day of which not even the dawn is yet discernible. Aristotle applies a standard drawn from the facts of his own time, and he finds Athens rather above than below the average of excellence which its republics presented. The kind of government he sketches as being the best attainable under existing Greek conditions is founded on his observations of the institutions which were working well in various cities, including Carthage (he had unfortunately no data from Rome), and shows that he wished to blend some features of an aristocratic with others of a democratic type.[1]

---

[1] He wished to have magistrates chosen from persons possessing a property qualification, not so high as to exclude the majority of the citizens, to let offices be unpaid, to strengthen the power of the middle class by taking steps to reduce the inequality of fortunes, and to have the legal tribunals filled by competent citizens. He prefers elections by

Both philosophers should of course be compared with the contemporary references to the working of democracy to be found in Thucydides and Xenophon and the Attic orators, nor should the plays of Aristophanes, albeit caricatures, be omitted. From all these sources we get a vivid picture of public life in the most keen-witted, versatile, and inventive community the world has ever seen, men whose achievements in art and literature are models for all time. The Athenians had no doubt the defects of their qualities. But what qualities!

A farewell glance at the salient features of their public life shows us a whole people always busy, or supposed to be busy, directing and administering their State in the Assembly, in the Council and its Committees, in the law Courts, in the various other bodies, Thesmothetai, Nomothetai, and the numerous smaller Boards. Most citizens had at some time or other filled some office, and everybody was paid, even for attending the Assembly. But the Athenians were also fond of talking and fond of amusement. The ideal of a steady and strenuous co-operation of all citizens in the daily duties of government was far from being attained in practice. State work was compatible with laziness.[1] The average man loved oratory and was readily moved by it, was clever enough to enjoy its brilliance and not quite wary enough to discount its artifices. Its sway was tempered only by bribery and by the fear of a prosecution for having misled the people.

Gathered in their Assembly the citizens were hasty and variable, easily swept off their feet by passion, unable to pursue a fixed foreign policy, unless they found a Pericles or a Phocion whom they had grown to trust as both sagacious and incorruptible. Impatient of restraints, even such restraints as they had by law imposed upon themselves, they ruled as a despot rules, exemplifying the maxim that no one is good enough to be trusted with absolute power. Demos, says Aristotle, is the sole sovereign, Demos becomes a Tyrant.

the citizens in tribes rather than by the whole people, and so may be cited as favouring *scrutin d'arrondissement* as against *scrutin de liste* " ward elections " as opposed to the " general ticket " of American cities (see chapters on France and on the U.S.A., *post*).

[1] "Ἀργοὶ καὶ λάλοι . . . ἀνειμένη καὶ μαλακὴ πολιτεία, says Aristotle, in whose time the sense of civic duty was probably lower than it had been in the days of Pericles.

The spirit of independence, the love of equality, and the dread of an ambitious usurper made them trust their magistrates with so little power that in many branches of administration there was no permanent control, no fixed policy, no means of throwing responsibility on any one for the neglect to take action when needed or to provide precautions against impending danger. But when roused they could put forth efforts worthy of heroes, manning their fleets with splendid celerity and throwing their hearts into combat.

In their relations with other States they showed that deficient respect for the rights of others, and for liberty as a principle, which belonged to every Hellenic community. There was little chivalry or love of justice where strangers were concerned, and no love of peace. Among the Greeks, patriotism sometimes reached its highest, and sometimes fell to its lowest level. There were men who willingly died for their city. There were others, sometimes of the most brilliant gifts, who, like Themistocles and Alcibiades, did not hesitate, when exiled, to do their utmost to injure it. The power of money and the greed for money appears from the prevalence of bribery and the frequent embezzlement of the public funds. These Republics did not live by Virtue. Rather might one say that they lived by disbelief in it.

If the faults enumerated constitute a grave indictment of Greek democracy, let no judgment be passed till Greek oligarchy also has been examined. It had few of the merits and all the faults of democracy, except perhaps in the sphere of foreign relations, for in these policy is usually more consistent and foreseeing when directed by the Few rather than the Many. In the oligarchic cities there was less security for property and for personal liberty, and far less chance of justice, for the rulers took without scruple what they wanted, and everything went by favour. Oligarchs were as corrupt and more rapacious than any body could be in a democracy. The common man could not count on his own safety or on the honour of his family. Seditions and conspiracies were frequent, for not only did the mass of the people try to overthrow the oligarchs,— who, with the Greek aversion to compromise, did not, like the patricians of old Rome, know when to yield in time,— but the dominant families themselves quarrelled and fought against one another.

Aristotle condemns the rule of the Few as more pernicious than the rule of the Many. The only thing worse still was Tyranny, for which both he and Plato reserve their blackest colours. Liberty at least, Liberty as the unchecked development of the individual man, was secured by democracy, as Plato recognizes when he condemns its excess.[1]

Two facts stand out to the modern historian when he surveys these Republics from afar. One is this. They reached in an early stage of the political development of mankind the high-water mark, attained elsewhere only by the primitive communities of Switzerland, in the uncontrolled sovereignty of the whole people, and in the rule of the Average Man. If it was not a success, it was more successful than could well have been expected. The value of the lesson for moderns is no doubt reduced by the fact that the communities were small and that the lowest stratum of the population consisted chiefly of slaves. Yet high is the value that remains.

The other fact is that after all the changes of seventy-five generations the tendencies of human nature remain substantially what they were. Nowhere else do we find so vivid and various a record of these tendencies in their full and free play, embodied as they are in striking characters and dramatic situations. To those experiments in the government of the people by the people which the Greeks were the first to try, they brought an incomparable eagerness and resourceful ingenuity. Their fitful life, filled with wars and conspiracies and revolutions, was illumined by a blaze of poetry, philosophy, and art, which no subsequent age has equalled. Short indeed was the life of these republics, but it was intense, and it was wonderfully fruitful for all later generations. It has for us the unfading charm of showing human thought and passion in their primal simplicity. The stream, still near its source, runs with the clearness of a mountain spring welling up from the deep recesses of the rocks. We

---

[1] To see the best and the worst that could be said of the Athenian democracy, read and consider the two striking descriptions given by two famous Athenians, the statesman and the philosopher, the long funeral oration of Pericles in Thucydides, Book ii., and the description of democracy in Plato, *Republic*, Book viii.

To apprehend how the merits and faults of divers forms of government presented them to the imaginative but non-philosophical type of Greek mind, read the account in Herodotus, Book iii. chap. 80, of the alleged discussion of different forms of government among seven Persian nobles.

see men as Nature made them, obeying their first impulses, ardent and curious, full of invention, full of imagination. We see them unfettered by traditions and recollections, unguided by settled principles, without the habits and prejudices and hesitations which the memories of past failures implant, weaving theories, enriching the world with ideas and maxims as they move onward in the confident joyousness of youth.

CHAPTER XVII

THE REPUBLICS OF SPANISH AMERICA

THE Western hemisphere contains (besides the United States) twenty Republics, in all of which (except French-speaking Haiti and Portuguese-speaking Brazil) Spanish is the language of the dominant white race.[1] None of these States has had one hundred and thirty years of life, but into that short period they have crowded a series of vicissitudes and experiences which, for their number and the light they throw upon certain phases of human nature in politics, find a parallel only in the republics of ancient Greece and in those of mediaeval Italy. They have, however, received little attention from European historians, and still less from political philosophers. Most writers have been content to refer to them as awful examples of what befalls people who have cast themselves loose from monarchical institutions. Even Sir Henry Maine in his ingenious but elusive book on *Popular Government* (published in 1885) did not hesitate to make them the basis of his case against democracy. Now, whatever one might call them, they were certainly not democracies thirty-five years ago, and only two or three could be called by that name now. Plato and Aristotle would have described them as forms of Tyranny, *i.e.* illegal despotisms resting on military force. An account of them may, there-

---

[1] These may be classified under three heads:

Caribbean Republics, all tropical except the northern part of Mexico.

Mexico.	Salvador.	Panama.
Guatemala.	Nicaragua.	Colombia.
Honduras.	Costa Rica.	Venezuela.

Tropical South American Republics.

Ecuador.	Bolivia.	Brazil (the southern
Peru.	Paraguay.	part temperate).

Temperate South American Republics.

Chile.	Argentina.	Uruguay.

With three insular Republics also tropical — Cuba, San Domingo, and Haiti (French-speaking).

fore, seem to lie outside the province of the present treatise. Nevertheless they deserve attention here, for they indicate what happens when an attempt is made to establish popular self-government where the conditions necessary for its working are absent, and they also show, *per contra,* how a change in economic environment may bring about an improvement in political capacity, and lead communities towards a peaceful constitutionalism, even where intellectual and moral progress lag behind the advance in material prosperity.

When the colonial dominions of Spain began from A.D. 1810 onwards to throw off the yoke of the old Spanish monarchy, which had governed them with incomparable selfishness and stupidity, there were only two regions in which the bulk of the population was of European stock. These were the regions which are now Argentina and Uruguay, in each of which the native Indian tribes, though warlike, were few in number and so unfit to resist their conquerors that they had before the middle of the nineteenth century been either killed off or imperceptibly absorbed into the whites. In all the other States that arose on the ruins of the old Viceroyalties the pure European element was small, ranging from 5 to 10 per cent, the rest of the population being either pure Indian, speaking native languages, or of mixed blood, speaking Spanish. Political action existed only among the first and last of these classes, for the aborigines were either serfs working for Spanish masters on plantations or in mines, or else had remained in a tribal state, some of them practically independent, like the famous Mapoches (Araucanians) of Southern Chile and the warlike clans of Northern Mexico. Thus for the purposes of politics, those who may be called " the citizens " were only a small fraction, and in some regions an extremely small fraction, of the whole population.[1]

Since 1810 there has been much progress in parts of tropical America. But the population, such as it was and is, remains, in most States, scattered thinly over a vast area. Those of European stock, and those of mixed blood called *mestizos,* live mostly in small towns, lying far apart and separated by arid deserts or by densely-wooded tropical wilder-

[1] Slavery in the proper sense was practically confined to the negroes, a small element even in Peru and along the coasts of the Caribbean Sea. Brazil is the only country where the coloured people are a large element.

nesses in which man can scarcely make head against the forces of Nature. Railways (except in the temperate and well-peopled south [1]) are still few, and some large tropical areas remain almost unexplored. Not only the natives but a large part of the mestizos have continued in unlettered ignorance. They are citizens only in name, knowing nothing and caring nothing, except in a few cities, of what passes in the sphere of government.

There is no marked social distinction between the families of European race and the educated mestizos, and these two classes have little in common with the much larger mass of the aborigines. Every now and then an Indian of exceptional gifts, like Benito Juarez in Mexico, rises out of that mass to the top, and shows himself the intellectual equal of the white man. But otherwise the severance is complete, for the mestizo reckons himself a white, while the Indian remains an Indian, and in many districts practically a heathen in his beliefs, though he may worship saints and go to mass. [2]

The inhabitants of these Spanish colonies began their career as independent States without political training or experience. There had been no national and very few local institutions through which they could have learnt how to manage their own affairs. Spain had not given them, as England had given to her North American colonies, any town meetings, any municipal councils, any church organizations in which the laity bore a part. Associative bonds to link men together did not exist, except the control of the serf by his master. There were regions in which society, hardly advanced from what it had been in mediaeval Europe, did not possess even tribal communities much less any feudal organizations, such as those out of which European kingdoms developed. There was, in fact, no basis whatever for common political action, so the brand-new constitutions which a few of the best-educated colonial leaders had drafted on the model of the United States Constitution did not correspond to anything real in the circumstances of these new so-called republican States.

The long guerilla warfare, in the course of which the in-

[1] Including Southern Argentina, Chile, Uruguay, and Southern Brazil.
[2] The purely heathen population is small, existing chiefly in the tropical regions on both sides of the Equator; but even in Mexico Christianity is only skin-deep among the aborigines.

surgent colonists had worn out the resources of Spain till she gave up the contest in despair, had implanted in all these countries military habits, had made the soldier the leader, had accustomed the inhabitants to the rule of force. No one thought of obeying the law, for there was no law except on paper. Force and force only counted. The constitutions had provided elected presidents and elected legislatures, and courts of law, but what were such institutions without the sense of legal right, the means of enforcing it, and the habit of obedience to legally constituted authority?

These things being so, nearly all of these new States, except Chile, lapsed into a condition of chronic revolution. The executive head was of necessity a soldier, obliged to rule by the sword. If he ruled badly, or made himself otherwise unpopular, it was by the sword that he had to be overthrown. Military talent, or even fierce and ruthless energy without conspicuous talent, brought men to the front, and made them, under the title of President, irresponsible dictators. They were not necessarily wicked men, as were most of the Greek tyrants. They were what most fighting rulers almost inevitably become in such conditions, hard, selfish, and unscrupulous, because they live in the midst of violence, and can prevail only by a severity which in the more brutal natures passes into cruelty.

Although these Presidents were mere despots, the newly-formed States continued to be called Republics, and purported to be living under their formally enacted constitutions. The farce of electing a President was observed. The reigning potentate who bore that title usually secured his own re-election, or might occasionally put in a dependant to keep the place warm for him till he resumed official control. Sometimes, when he had accumulated and invested in Europe a sufficiently large fortune, he transferred himself, like Guzman Blanco of Venezuela, to Paris, to enjoy the evening of his days by spending there his ill-gotten gains. So, too, there was a legislature, usually of two Houses, elected for the prescribed legal term, but at the bidding of the President, who made sure of an ample majority, either by force or by fraud. The judges were his creatures placed on the bench to do his bidding, and allowed, when he had no orders to give, to levy toll upon or accept " gratifications " from the suitors. It was seldom necessary to lay heavy taxation on the citizens, because the dictator found it easier to raise, by loans in Europe at high rates of interest, the money wherewithal to pay his troops or, if he cared for the development of the country, to construct harbours and railways.   That a load of debt was thus imposed on his successors was of no concern to him, though it sometimes embroiled them with European governments unwise enough to take up the cause of the creditors. Meanwhile, what of the people?   The great bulk were indifferent, for the recurring revolutions scarcely affected them, and administration was no better and very little worse under one dictator than under another.   Politics were left to knots of intriguers and adventurers in the capital and a few other towns, while the rest of the better-educated class pursued the even tenor of their way on their plantations or in the petty commerce of the interior, since overseas trade was in the hands of foreign merchants, at first mostly British, afterwards German also, established at the seaports.   The great mass of the aborigines and the poorer mestizos scarcely knew of the political changes except when some army or marauding band swept past them, levying contributions on its way. The small armies who followed a revolutionary leader and maintained an intermittent civil war were chiefly composed of Indians, forced into the ranks or taking service at low pay, and officered by men of Spanish or mixed blood.   They fought fiercely, as was shown by a loss of life in the battles which was large in proportion to the numbers engaged.[1] Military habits were kept up not merely by internal but also by international strife, for some of the republics were often at war with their neighbours, the Northern States fighting on land, while Chile and Peru fought at sea also, each bringing its ironclad warships from Europe.   The civil war involved no political principles except to some extent the interests of the Church, which divided men in the Caribbean States, and to some extent also in Ecuador, Peru, Paraguay, and Uruguay.   I say " the Church " and not Religion, for as the whole population was, till a comparatively recent time, Roman Catholic in outward profession, the strife had noth-

[1] In the long war which Lopez, dictator of Paraguay, an almost purely Indian State, maintained against Uruguay, Argentina, and Brazil from 1865 to 1870, nearly the whole adult male population of Paraguay perished.

ing to do with doctrine but only with ecclesiastical privilege. In Mexico there was a strong clerical and latterly also a strong anti-clerical party. Not till the overthrow of the Austrian Archduke Maximilian, whom Louis Napoleon had in a luckless hour placed on the tottering throne of Mexico, did the anti-clericals under the native Indian Juarez win a decisive victory. Strangely enough, the racial issue between Indians and Europeans was hardly at all involved. The aboriginal populations, though they had retained a sullen aversion to the descendants of those Conquistadores who had followed Cortes or Pizarro, were too depressed and too unorganized to be able to act together or find capable leaders. Their last effort had been made in the great insurrection of the Peruvian Tupac Amaru (in 1781), which was suppressed with hideous cruelty by the Spanish viceroy of that now distant day.

Through this long welter of revolutions and dictatorships there appeared no men comparable for statesmanship or military genius, or for elevation of character, to the two heroes who won independence from Spain, the Venezuelan Bolivar and the Argentine San Martin. Conditions did not favour the growth of large minds animated by high purposes. But there were plenty of men of force and daring. Francia in Paraguay and Rosas in Argentina are conspicuous examples of strong dictators ruling by terror, who did nothing to help their countries forward. Barrios in Guatemala, who, like Louis XI. of France, is said to have carried his captives about in cages, has left the greatest reputation for cruelty; and Zelaya of Nicaragua, driven out by the United States a few years ago, is probably the last who maintained the tradition of torture. The lowest depth of savagery was reached in the Republic of Haiti, an almost purely negro country since it was lost to France in 1803.[1]

This state of things has lasted down to our own day in most of the twenty Republics, though of course in very varying degrees. The Caribbean States of Central and Northern South America (excepting Salvador and Costa Rica, but including Ecuador) have, together with Haiti, been on the

---

[1] Haiti has recently fallen under the influence of the United States, with a consequent improvement in its social as well as its economic conditions.

lowest level. Salvador, Bolivia, perhaps Colombia and Peru also, and now even Paraguay, slightly affected by its southern neighbours, are better. Cuba and San Domingo, under the protecting and steadying influence of the United States, are better still. Whether better or worse, however, and by whatever name the governments of these States may be called, none of them is a democracy. But it is one of the oddest instances of the power of a word that the less educated and even many of the more educated persons among the free nations have continued, especially in the United States, to believe them to be, because called " Republics," entitled to a confidence and sympathy which would not be given to a military tyranny under any other name. Chile, Argentina, Uruguay, and Brazil belong to a different category. They are true Republics, if not all of them democracies, and each requires a short separate treatment.

Chile has had a history unlike that of the other States. She has been from the first a constitutional Republic, some of whose features recall the oligarchy that governed England during the reigns of the two first Georges. Blessed by a temperate climate, a long stretch of sea-coast and (in her southern regions) a continuous cultivable area sufficient to support a large agricultural and pastoral community, every part of the country being in touch by sea with every other part, she has also enjoyed the advantage of possessing both a native and a Spanish stock of unusually sound quality — the Spanish settlers having mostly come from Northern Spain, many of them Basques, while the native Indians, though less advanced towards civilization than were the Peruvians, were of stronger fibre, as was proved by the valiant resistance of the never-conquered Araucanians. There is a good deal of pure European blood left in Chile, and the mixed race is both manly and industrious, with much independence of character. The leading families, holding considerable estates, have formed a sort of territorial oligarchy, keeping the government in their hands and getting on well with the peasantry, who, content to be guided by them in political matters, usually vote with their landlords. Though public peace was sometimes troubled in earlier days, the last sixty years have seen only one serious civil war, that of 1891 between President Balmaceda and the Assembly, in which the latter prevailed; and the Republic has seldom had to fear conspiracies or revolts. The army and navy have been kept highly efficient. The machinery of the constitution, under which the suffrage has been extended to include practically all adult males, an experiment which some Chileans have deemed premature, seems to work pretty smoothly. The President appoints and dismisses the ministers who are nevertheless held responsible to the legislature. Votes are honestly counted, but there is said to be a good deal of electoral corruption, though, as it is not confined to any one party, it does not prevent the general result from conforming to public opinion.[1] A system of proportional representation adopted some time ago appears to give satisfaction. The public credit has always been carefully guarded, so much so indeed that, during the civil war above referred to, both the contending parties tendered to the European bondholders the interest due upon the national debt. The men who lead in public affairs have been, as a rule, persons of standing and reputation in the country as well as of statesmanlike capacity. Neither Senators nor Deputies receive a salary.

Argentina, which had made a good beginning in the early days of the War of Independence when led by San Martin and Belgrano, relapsed after a time into a long period of disorder, and has now emerged therefrom mainly through the working of economic causes. She possesses in her Pampas a vast area of pastoral and arable land, equalled for its productive capacity only by that part of North-Western America which lies between the Rocky Mountains and the Great Lakes, and by the vast plain between the Irtish and the Middle Yenisei in Western Siberia. She has the further advantage of being peopled by men of an almost pure European stock, two-thirds Spanish, one-third, through recent immigration, Italian. The climate, hot in the tropical North and too cold for cultivation in the Patagonian South, is through most of the territory sufficiently temperate to enable these two South European races to work under the sun, and the industry of the Italians is now emulated by that of the immigrants who have recently flocked in from Spain. While the tyranny of President Rosas lasted, material progress was slow, because internal communications were wanting, and

[1] There is an educational qualification, but it is not strictly enforced.

foreigners feared to provide capital for creating them. But in the year that followed his expulsion in 1852 revolutions and civil wars became less frequent, the wild half-Indian Gauchos, from whom the bulk of revolutionary levies had been drawn, having begun to vanish, or be transmuted into peaceful cowboys. Immigration by degrees increased, English companies began to construct railways, the fertile lands were brought under cultivation, exports of hides, wool, and meat grew apace, and the growing trade brought the country within the range of European influences, intellectual as well as commercial. The value of agricultural land rose swiftly, especially after it had been found possible to obtain water from artesian wells in regions without surface streams. Its owners acquired with their accumulating wealth an interest in the tranquillity of the State. Everybody who felt the touch of prosperity — owners, traders, work-people — saw, as they watched a network of railways constructed by British capital spreading over the land, and Buenos Aires expanding into one of the great commercial cities of the world, that prosperity could remain only under stable conditions, which would draw more and more of foreign money and of foreign immigrants to supply the labour needed for the development of the country. The more industry there was, and the more prosperity, the smaller became the proportion of those who joined in revolutions, as men had been wont to do, from the love of fighting or to better their fortunes.

The long-continued antagonism of the provinces to the commercial centre of Buenos Aires gave rise to armed struggles which seem to have now died down. Since 1890 there have been some troubles, yet no serious or widespread disturbance of public peace, and the minds of men have accustomed themselves to constitutional methods of government. The change was marked by the fact that political chiefs who here, as in the other disorderly republics, had been mostly soldiers began to be mostly lawyers. Whoever looks through the annals of South American States will find that nearly every leader bears the title either of General or of Doctor of Laws. After Rosas, arms began to yield to the gown. The Presidents, if not always elected by unimpeachably legal methods, have not been installed by force. The constitutional machine works imperfectly, but it works. The old factions have gone: generals do not plan pronunciamentos: violence is going out of fashion.

The President is chosen by an electoral college modelled on that provided in the United States, and enjoys similar powers, including a veto on legislation which can be overridden by a two-thirds majority. He holds office for six years, is not immediately re-eligible, appoints the ministers who, being responsible to the legislature, countersign all his acts. They cannot sit, but can speak, in either Chamber. The Legislature consists of a Senate of twenty-eight, chosen by the provincial Legislatures and a Chamber of Deputies of one hundred and twenty members, elected, as are the Presidential electors, by universal suffrage, the term of Senator being nine, that of a Deputy four years. The elections used to be largely made by the Government in power, who respected forms by allowing a certain number of their opponents to be returned to the Chamber to discharge the functions of an Opposition, and recently a clause in the Constitution has been severely strained by the practice of what is called Intervention, i. e. the replacement of existing Provincial officials by Federal appointees, so as to enable a majority in the Legislature to be secured for the party to which the President belongs, there being a strong tendency in Spanish America to vote for the party which holds executive power. There seems to be now no taint of force and not much of fraud in the making up of lists and counting of votes; nor does bribery seem to prevail largely. Parties are still fluid and imperfectly organized. They are based less on principles than on attachment to leaders; and the bulk of the citizens showed no great interest in their civic duties until voting was made compulsory by a law of 1912.

The legislators (salary $1500 a month) are not very zealous in the discharge of their duties, and leave much to the President, who is at least as powerful as his prototype in the United States. Countries with only a short experience of constitutional government are apt, as has been recently seen in some of the new kingdoms of south-eastern Europe, to allow the Executive to overtop the Legislature. Municipal administration is described as fairly honest, i.e. there is not very much peculation but plenty of jobbery in the granting of contracts and the execution of local improvements.

The dispensation of justice is a weak point in South American as well as in South European countries. Legal proceedings are dilatory, and the Bench not always trusted, though it sins less by accepting pecuniary inducements than by yielding to the influences of family connection and personal friendship. Order is now tolerably well maintained throughout the country by a police as efficient as can be expected in vast and thinly peopled regions. Dynamite outrages were frequent in Buenos Aires some years ago, but the extremists who resorted to them have latterly been pursuing their aims by means of strikes on a very large scale. Labour unrest is, however, no greater than in Europe and North America, and needs mention only for the sake of indicating that so far from being due to economic distress it is now common in new countries where there is still unoccupied land, and wages have long been high.

The respect for legality and the general tone of public life have been sensibly rising in Argentina. Few of the recent Presidents and ministers have incurred suspicion of malpractices. Whether this can be said of the deputies seems more doubtful. Seditions arising out of angrily contested elections are now confined to cases in which the National Government intervenes because a provincial election is alleged to have been unfairly conducted, and such disturbances do not necessarily spread beyond the particular province. There has been little discontent except among the Socialists and Anarchists of Buenos Aires, for employment and prosperity abound. The increase in the number of small landholders, due partly to the equal division of estates passing by inheritance, partly to rise in the value of land which has led to the breaking up of purchasable estates into lots by industrious immigrants, is making for the stability of government, as it enlarges the class which has a motive for supporting public order.

Nevertheless, although the Government is democratic in form and not palpably undemocratic in practice, the rule of public opinion is not yet fully established. Men's minds are perhaps too much occupied by material considerations, the small cultivator thinking of produce and prices, the rich landowner enjoying the luxurious life of the capital, to give heed to politics. Under such conditions no high level of administration or legislation can be looked for. But this does not reduce the interest which the student of politics finds in watching the growth of institutions, and the development of what used to be a military tyranny into what is becoming a pacific self-governing community. The Argentine democracy, whatever may be the standard of public virtue they maintain, will possess the advantage of being free from external dangers, so that little of the revenue need go to military and naval armaments, and free also from pauperism, so that economic and social problems may be handled without the passion engendered by suffering. Here, as in the Australian States, the predominance of a single great city is too marked. One-fifth of the whole people dwell in Buenos Aires, whose excitable radicalism or socialism is apt to prevail against the more conservative provinces. It is to Argentina what Paris is to France, the centre of literature and the chief maker of public opinion by its ably written and powerful press.

Uruguay is another South American country in which a true republican Government, professing to be, and gradually becoming, a democracy, now exists. Its racial and physical conditions resemble those of Argentina [1] (of which it was at one time a part), and the broad outlines of its history, since it achieved independence, are not dissimilar. It is, however, very much smaller, and is a Unitary, not a Federal State. Its population is almost entirely of European stock, and its national sentiment extremely strong. In it also the progress of material development and the consequent growth of trade with Europe have worked for good. The creation of an excellent railway system, the influx of immigrants from Italy and Spain, the extension of education through a people now settling down to work, have begun to give the inhabitants, who were, till late in the nineteenth century, distracted by civil wars, an interest in order, and honest administration. Thus government has become more constitutional,[2] and elec-

[1] The climate, tempered by the ocean, has less marked extremes than Argentina, and the surface is more undulating.
[2] An interesting experiment in Government is now being tried under the new Constitution (1919) in the creation of a body called the National Council of Administration, consisting of nine persons elected

tions a better expression of popular sentiment. The Constitution is no longer a sham, though the initiative and power of the President still overshadow the Legislature. The factions that divided the nation since 1825, adherents of two rival Generals, are not yet extinct, one of them having become a more or less clerical, the other an anti-clerical party. In 1910 (when I visited the country) the Whites, enraged at the manipulation of the elections by the Reds, who then controlled the Government, started a short-lived insurrection. But clericalism is fast dying out, and the hereditary traditions of the Whites cannot keep it long alive. The statesman who has practically dominated the country, whether in office as President or out of it, is a person of advanced opinions, eager to try bold experiments which will take the wind out the sails of the (comparatively few) Socialists of Monte Video.

Brazil is (except Cuba, which was abandoned by Spain in 1898) the latest born of all the American Republics, for it retained its connection with Portugal till 1822 and did not dismiss its learned and amiable Emperor Dom Pedro II. till 1889. The change from a monarchical to a republican form did not mean much in substance, for the Crown had exercised very little power, and the masses have exercised quite as little under either name. The chief difference has been that revolts, unknown before, have occurred since, though none has risen to the dimensions of a civil war. The hereditary monarchy had the advantage of offering no occasion for attempts by military adventurers to seize the Presidency by violence, and the ties it maintained with Portugal had enabled European influences to play more freely on the country than was the case with the rest of South America after 1810. Material development has moved faster and political life has been more active under the new Republic, but the country is as far as ever from being a democracy.

Its area (3,300,000 square miles) exceeds that of the United States, but the population (estimated at 26,000,000)

for six years by direct popular vote, one-third retiring every two years. They appoint the ministers, and exercise all powers not expressly given to the President, who is popularly elected, and not re-eligible till after eight years. His veto on financial proposals may be overridden by a two-thirds majority of the Council. Manhood suffrage and proportional representation are established.

is extremely sparse, except in parts of the south and along the Atlantic coast. Most of the interior is a forest wilderness, in which a few towns, chiefly peopled by Indians, stand here and there along the great rivers. Of that population about one-sixth are aborigines, nearly one-third full blacks, another third blacks with more or less admixture of white blood, and a little more than one-sixth pure whites, about half of these of Portuguese stock, the rest Germans and Italians. The vast majority of the negroes and half-breeds are uneducated and below the level of a comprehension of politics or even of their own interests in politics. I mention these facts because they show why government cannot in such a country be really democratic, whatever the electoral suffrage. Power inevitably falls to the intelligent minority.

Brazil is a Federation, and properly so, considering not only its immense extent but the distance from one another of the few more thickly-peopled regions. The State Governments enjoy large powers and pursue their own policies, which are more or less wise according to the character of their respective legislatures, whose composition is better in the temperate Southern States, where the population is mostly white, than in the tropical regions, where a handful of whites control a multitude of coloured people. The Central Government consists of a President, elected for four years by direct popular vote; a Senate, elected for nine years; and a Chamber of Deputies, elected for three years. The suffrage excludes illiterates. The ministers are appointed by the President, are responsible to him, and do not sit in the Legislature. Elections are conducted with little respect for legality, and, when fraud fails to secure the desired result, a resort to force may be looked for. Not long ago the ballot-boxes in one of the greater States were, because it was feared that they would show a majority for a candidate opposed to the Government, seized by a body of police disguised as rioters, carried off to a distance and destroyed, whereupon the Governor of the State exercised his constitutional right of providing for the contingency of a loss of ballots, and appointed a Governmental candidate to the office which the election had been held to fill. There is plenty of ability, and an even greater profusion of oratorical talent, among the legislators, but intrigue rules, and, as M. Clemenceau observed after his visit

some ten years ago, " the Constitution enjoys a chiefly theoretic authority." An exceptionally skilful intriguer may,
like the strong leader who lately fell a victim to assassination, be effective master of the country.

The Republic is in fact an oligarchy, not of land-owning
families, like that of Chile, but of such among the richer
men, whether landlords or heads of industrial, financial, or
commercial enterprises, as occupy themselves with politics.
Like all oligarchies they use their power for their personal
benefit, yet with some regard to national interests also, for the
Brazilians are intensely proud of their magnificent country,
and claim for it the leadership of South America.   But between soaring patriotism and self-regarding schemes the
welfare of the masses receives less attention than it needs.
Something might be done for local self-government, unfavourable as the conditions are; and a large extension of
education is urgently required. The traveller is surprised
to find that in a country rich in poets and orators there does
not exist any duly equipped university. One is sometimes
reminded of the Slave States of the American Union as they
stood before the Civil War, where a government nominally
democratic was really the rule of a planter oligarchy.   It is
only thirty-two years since slavery was abolished in Brazil.
Were the States of the temperate South, where an industrious
population, mainly of European stock, has attained prosperity, to cast themselves loose from the tropical regions in
order to form a separate republic, they might create in time
a real democracy.

It remains to say a few words about Mexico, the greatest
of the northern republics and the one whose prospects of
peaceful progress have been most suddenly darkened by recent misfortunes. Much of the country, indeed nearly all
the northern territory, is a desert, being part of that arid
region which occupies a long strip of North America from
Canada to the Tropic of Cancer. Southern Mexico, however,
is a land of wonderful natural resources, with a delightful
climate on that high tableland where the barbarous tribes of
ancient Anahuac were passing into civilization when the
process was arrested by the invasion of Hernando Cortes.
Nearly two-thirds of the present inhabitants are Indians,
many of them still in a tribal state, some few heathens.   The

rest are mestizos, with about 250,000 of pure or nearly pure Spaniards. The country adopted its first constitution, a Federal one modelled on that of the United States, a century ago; and this instrument, amended in some points, has remained nominally in force ever since, though never put into effective operation. The extinction of the rule of Spain was followed by a long series of civil wars, in which one adventurer after another contended for power, the authority and possessions of the Catholic hierarchy being often involved. The capture and death in 1865 of the unfortunate Maximilian, when the French army that had supported him retired from the country under the menace of interference by the United States, sealed the defeat of the Church, which has never recovered from the blow. Juarez was presently replaced by Porfirio Diaz, who under the title of President ruled as a dictator (with one short interval) for thirty-five years, upholding the Constitution in form, and causing elections to be regularly held, on which occasions the soldiers were directed to drop a few voting papers into the ballot-boxes, lest they should be found empty.[1] Administrative work was conducted, better than ever before, by the Governors of the States under the President's general directions, while the political management of each district was entrusted to a person called the Political Chief (*Jefe politico*). In blood Porfirio was one-half or three-fourths an Indian, but no Spaniard of the Cortes type could have shown higher practical gifts. The country was pacified, brigandage, which had been rife for many years, sternly suppressed, and such of the brigands as survived turned into an efficient local gendarmerie (*Rurales*). Railways and harbours were constructed, mining developed, foreign capital attracted, the finances prudently handled, whatever could promote material development encouraged. The country became safe for travellers, for troops were always promptly despatched to any spot where the telegraph announced an outbreak, and when a robbery occurred the bad characters most likely to have had a hand in it were forthwith shot without trial. Every one extolled the wisdom as well as the energy of the now benevolent autocrat who had outlived the enemies of his earlier years and had ceased to need the methods by which he had

[1] So I was told when visiting Mexico in 1902.

reduced their number. He was one of the great men of his time, resolute, clear-sighted, swift in action. He even tried to induce his Legislature to pass measures on its own initiative, but found before long that it was unsafe to leave with them a power they were likely to use unwisely. Unfortunately he did not discern, or at any rate did not attempt, one task of supreme importance. In Mexico, as in most parts of Spanish America, the land (except where occupied by Indians in a quasi-tribal condition) has been since the Conquest in the hands of large proprietors, who work it by native labour. The Indian " peon " is a sort of serf, ill-paid and often ill-treated, discontented with his lot, but not knowing how to improve it. He and the poorer half-breeds, who are landless and little better off than the peon, are the material out of which robber bands and insurgent troops are easily made. It should have been the first aim of a wise policy to settle these people on the land as owners or as peasant cultivators with some security of tenure. The Mexican Indians are intelligent as well as good workers: the Spanish conquerors noted their superiority to the South American aborigines. But Diaz left this problem unsolved. The result was seen when the standard of revolt was raised in 1911, and he, being then over eighty years of age, allowed disorders to spread till he was himself obliged to quit the country, which then relapsed into an anarchy of general pillage and murder by revolutionary bands such as had prevailed before the days of Juarez. Could Diaz have found a successor who while following out his policy with equal energy would have given the land to the people and brought education within their reach, Mexico might within half a century have begun to be fit for constitutional liberty. Now, however, its first need is for a government strong enough to restore and maintain order, and when that has been done, and industry has revived, to remove the causes of economic unrest, give security for the employment of capital, and lay the foundations of local self-government.

The general moral of Spanish American history, for the sake of which these descriptions have been given, is almost too obvious to need stating. Why confer free self-governing institutions on a people unfit to comprehend or use them? The very notion of establishing a government by the votes of citizens and controlling the action of a legislature and an executive by holding the representatives responsible for the use they might make of their power, was not within the horizon of the vast bulk of the colonial subjects of Spain; much less could they work the elaborate machinery of two legislative Houses with an elected President and his Ministers. In such circumstances, power inevitably fell to the Executive head, the person whom the people could see and know, and to whom belonged the command of the army. The interest of the community required that this power, needed for the maintenance of order within and defence against aggression by violent neighbours, should be lodged in one strong hand. To subject it to a legislature of inexperienced and short-sighted men, probably selfish and practically irresponsible, because controlled by no public opinion, was to invite confusion and disaster. The people did not rule in these republics because they could not rule. Whatever the plans of theorists and the exhortations of the wise, every people comes sooner or later to that kind of government which the facts prescribe. Thus a nominally elective Presidency became a dictatorship. As each President was obliged to exceed his strictly legal authority because it would not have enabled him to cope with the situation, the distinction between his legal rights and the powers he was actually exercising was obliterated. He passed into a usurper, ruling and compelled to rule by force, so that those who attacked him by force, with or without a moral justification, could claim a title little worse than his own. The very conception of power *de iure* had no time to spring up and establish itself in the popular mind, for all power was *de facto* only. As the generation that had been accustomed to obey the Spanish Viceroys passed away, a new generation grew up accustomed to a régime of force. To create afresh that idea of obedience to duly constituted legal authority which is essential to a democracy was a slow process in a population a large part of which was in every State ignorant and semi-barbarous. In most of the tropical States this process has hardly yet begun; in none, except Chile, has it been quite completed. Regarding the more backward republics, such as Venezuela and Ecuador, and those in Central America, it is difficult to make any prediction. If the Western hemisphere were to-day in sixteenth-century conditions, these countries would probably be seized by some naval power and ruled as subject dependencies, as Holland rules Java and France Madagascar. Since that cannot happen now, we can but put our trust in that *vis medicatrix naturae* which slowly brings the public opinion of the world to bear upon the regions where its action is most needed.   If the political prospects for tropical America seem somewhat more hopeful to-day than they were seventy years ago, it is because economic conditions are improving.

What form of government would have been best suited to these communities after they had expelled the Spanish Viceroys ?

Those who look back with the experience of a century can see that the form which was adopted, suggested by the example of the United States Constitution, was unsuitable. No wonder it failed, for the conditions were entirely unlike those which the founders of English colonies in new lands had to their hand.   In the temperate parts of North America and in Australia there was no large aboriginal population living in a barbarous or semi-civilized state.   The colonizing communities destined to spread out and replenish the regions to be settled were English, carrying with them the habits and traditions of an old political system.

What would have happened if things had been left to take their natural course and no attempt made to imitate the United States Constitution ?   Among the various lines along which some sort of political organization might have developed itself I may mention three, any one of which might have better conformed to the social and economic conditions of the aboriginal peoples in the tropical regions.

One of these lines would have been the growth of small local, loosely connected or practically independent, communities, some with an urban centre, some semi-tribal, each ruled by a chief (native or mestizo) or by a group of the wealthier and more capable Spanish colonial landholding families. Such families represented the civilizing forces, and would have been obeyed by the Indians, some of whom were their tenants, some otherwise dependent upon them.   The rule of the chiefs or oligarchic groups would have been harsh and not very progressive, but there would have been some sort of order, with the chance of a peaceful aggregation of the communities into larger wholes as the country began to be developed and opened up to commerce.

Another possible line of development would have been the transmutation of each Viceroyalty into a sort of monarchy, the head of which would have had a legal power, thus continuing the tradition of obedience to duly constituted authority. Law and Fact would have been in a truer relation than under a government professing to depend on a popular election, which must obviously be a farce under the existing conditions. For the success of such a scheme there would have been needed in each country a man not only of force but of some statesmanlike quality and some military talent. It might have failed, as it failed when tried in Mexico. But it would have had at least as good a chance as the plan of representative bodies nominated by presidents who were usurping dictators.

A third form would have been that of an oligarchy composed of the leading families of the country. This came to pass, and has worked with comparatively little friction, in Chile, where no doubt the conditions were exceptionally favourable. It would have been difficult in Peru and Bolivia and Venezuela, owing (among other things) to the wide empty spaces between the small centres of population, and impossible in such a country as Haiti, where there were no families superior in knowledge and vigour to the ignorant and semi-savage masses. But in most of the countries it would have corresponded better to the elements of strength which the actual conditions presented, elements capable of governing and interested in good government, than did a sham Republic under the pretended control of an nominally elected Legislature. Such an oligarchy would have been likely to pass naturally, in the fulness of time and under the influence of the Time-Spirit, into a more popular form of government.

These are speculations. But about the moral of the whole story there is no question. Do not give to a people institutions for which it is unripe in the simple faith that the tool will give skill to the workman's hand. Respect Facts. Man is in each country not what we may wish him to be, but what Nature and History have made him.

One question remains. What is likely to be the future

of these new republics, and what the prospect that they will in time become true democracies? To answer this question let us see what have been the forces which have enabled some among the Republics to achieve real progress during the last half-century.

Chief among these has been the development in each country of its material resources. The growth of wealth through agriculture and mining has increased the number of persons interested in order and good government, and has led to the improvement of roads, railways, internal steam navigation. Education has followed, though slowly; universities have been founded; an indigenous literature has sprung up. Intercourse with foreign countries has grown, and has brought not only those loans which, though perhaps indispensable, were often a source of temptation, but also the ideas and mental habits of Europe and the United States into the Spanish American population. As the traditions of violence and disorder died down, free institutions and the way to work them began to be understood. Power passed peaceably from one president to another. The General is being replaced by the Doctor of Laws, and the man of law, even if he be tricky, is less dangerous than the man of the sword. Fraud is better than force, because fraud, however odious, does not disturb public order, and it is easier to prevent its recurrence than to break the habit of insurrection. It is in this way that Argentina and Uruguay have within the last forty years become politically civilized, and indeed more civilized than some States of Europe. In Mexico material progress had gone so far that if Porfirio Diaz, or a ruler of equal gifts, could have reigned for another forty years, and had grappled with the Indian question, the country might have been where Argentina and Chile are now. Bolivia has advanced, and in Brazil the southern states at least are capable of working a genuine popular government. Those who understand what South America had been under the Viceroys and what she was when she emerged from the long struggle for independence will not despond of her future.

FRANCE

CHAPTER XVIII

LAND AND HISTORY

AMONG the countries in which popular government prevails, France is in two respects unique. She adopted democracy by a swift and sudden stroke, without the long and gradual preparation through which the United States and Switzerland and England passed, springing almost at one bound out of absolute monarchy into the complete political equality of all citizens. And France did this not merely because the rule of the people was deemed the completest remedy for pressing evils, nor because other kinds of government had been tried and found wanting, but also in deference to general abstract principles which were taken for self-evident truths. Frenchmen have always shown, along with their gift for generalizing, an enjoyment of and a faith in general theories beyond that of the other free peoples. Thus the philosophical student of human institutions who desires to test political principles by their results finds a peculiar interest in examining the politics of France, for it is there, even more than in America, that the doctrines on which democracy is founded have told most upon the national mind, and been most frequently pushed to their logical conclusions. The history of the three Republics that have successively arisen since 1792 covers only sixty years in all. But within that space of time France has passed through many phases and tried many experiments. There has been much brilliant oratory, and endless political ingenuity. No period in history throws more light not only on the contrasts of theory with practice, but upon the tendencies which move and direct human society.

As the student of the contemporary politics of a country must everywhere try to understand the conditions, natural

and historical, amid which the form of government was established and is being now worked, so nowhere is such knowledge more essential than when one comes to speak of France.
We shall see that Nature has given her many things favourable to material prosperity and to immunity from external
attack, while the course of her history has produced economic
and social conditions which have profoundly influenced her
political development.

Let us begin by glancing briefly at the physical features
of the country, and then examine more at length the historical antecedents which still affect the State and its government.

France is naturally the richest of European countries, with
everything needed to secure the well-being of an industrious
people.[1]   Nearly all the soil is available for cultivation, or
for pasture, or for the growth of timber.   There is plenty of
coal and iron, chiefly in the north-east, fisheries on the coasts,
a climate eminently fitted for cereals in the north and centre,
and for vines in the centre and south, as well as for fruits and
other less important agricultural products.   The country is
washed by three seas, giving admirable facilities for commerce, and is guarded on the south and south-east by lofty
mountains difficult to traverse.   Only the north-eastern land
frontier is exposed to attack and has most frequently suffered from it.   The compactness of its territory, traversed by
no ranges high enough to interfere with free communication,
made Gaul appear to be one country even in the days of
Julius Caesar, and has enabled its people to attain, despite
differences of racial origin which survive in differences of
language, a more complete national unity than exists in Germany or Italy or Spain.[2]

The wealth derived from the soil and from the industrious habits of the people gave France in the Middle Ages a
place in commercial development hardly second to that of
Italy.   Prosperity brought in its train comforts and luxuries
beyond those of her Teutonic neighbours to the north and

[1] Russia has, of course, with her vast stretches of fertile land, a
greater productive capacity, but less variety of products and a less
genial climate.

[2] Breton is spoken in the north-west corner of Brittany and Basque
in a still smaller area in the Western Pyrenees, as well as German in
parts of Alsace.

east.   She rivalled Lombardy and Tuscany in the skill and taste of her artificers, qualities which have been so well maintained that she continues to be the purveyor for the whole world of articles of beauty.   The arable and vine or fruit-growing regions, well suited for *petite culture,* are very largely in the hands of small landowners, and both these and the tenant farmers have formed habits of thrift by which the pecuniary resources of the nation have been increased and pauperism kept within narrow limits.   Though a large manufacturing population has sprung up in the mining districts and great cities, the bulk of the nation is still agricultural, with the solid qualities and conservative instincts which everywhere belong to that class.   A larger proportion of the total wealth of the country is to be found in the hands of men with small incomes than in any other great European or American country.

Long as France has obeyed one government, there are marked differences between the races that compose the nation — Teutonic Flemings in the north-east with other Teutons on the eastern border, a strong infusion of Norse blood in Normandy, pure Celts still speaking a Celtic tongue in Brittany, Iberian and possibly Ligurian elements in the south.   These differences, however, which are as marked as those between the races that inhabit the British Isles, cause no political dissensions, serving rather to give variety, and the richness that comes from the presence of diverse elements, to the people as a whole.   This variety, noteworthy in the literature of France, is no less evident in French politics. Her statesmen show several types of character, two of which are especially conspicuous, the man of the north or east, and the man of the south — the former more measured and cautious, the latter more impulsive and brilliant.   These differences, however conspicuous in their extreme forms, are less significant than the intellectual character and habits of feeling and acting which have now come to belong to the nation as a whole: quickness of intelligence, a gift for oratory and a sense of style, together with a susceptibility to emotion not incompatible with shrewdness and a conservative prudence in affairs.   It was the French love of knowledge and aptness for speculation that made the schools of Paris foremost among the great universities of the Middle Ages, and led mediaeval writers to place in France the local home of Learning (*Studium*), as they assigned Priesthood (*Sacerdotium*) to the Italians and *Imperium* to the Germans.[1]

THE ANTECEDENTS AND DEVELOPMENT OF DEMOCRACY

In outlining the events and conditions that led up to the Revolution of 1789, when France made her first plunge into democracy, we need go no further back than the days of Louis the Fourteenth.   Before the end of his reign France, already long conscious of her national unity, was thoroughly consolidated, and had become the most powerful as well as the most intellectually polished country in Europe, with by far the most brilliant court.   Religious uniformity had been secured by the persecution or expulsion of the Calvinist Huguenots. Representative institutions had died out, for the ancient States-General had not met since 1614.   As Louis himself said, the King was the State.   No one talked of Liberty.

The seventy years that followed brought no changes in the constitution, but a complete change in opinion and sentiment. Protestantism did not revive, but scepticism spread widely among the educated classes, and affected even the clergy. The despotic system of government began to be freely criticized, especially after Montesquieu had pointed to English institutions as fit to be imitated.   It was ultimately discredited, first by the scandals of the court of Louis XV. and the careers of his successive ministers, then by the growing disorder of the finances.   Liberal opinions became fashionable.   After the influence of the American Revolution, to which France lent her aid in 1778, had begun to tell on Europe, they spread further and found fuller literary expression. The ancient monarchy, supported by the old noblesse, seemed to stand much as it had stood some centuries before, when feudalism was still a reality, but three changes of the utmost importance had in fact come to pass.   One was the loss by the nobles of their local administrative powers and functions. These had been absorbed by the Crown, which ruled the country by a King's Council in Versailles, the most important member whereof was the Comptroller in whose hands all

[1] In respect of the possession of the Papacy by Italy and of the Holy Roman Empire by the German kings.

financial affairs lay, and by Intendants, officials administering the provinces under the royal direction. The great landowners, having lost political power and administrative functions, retained over the peasantry feudal rights, which exposed them to the hatred of that class, a large part of which, though still liable to the old imposts and exactions, were even then owners of the soil they tilled. There was in the rural districts little of a middle class between nobles and peasants. The bourgeoisie were socially separated from the nobility, but less sharply from the classes below them, though the richer sort looked down upon the peasants whom they sometimes exploited, and who repaid them with suspicious dislike. It was the upper bourgeoisie, and especially the professional class among them, that supplied to the Crown its civil officials (other, of course, than the Court officials), so they managed to acquire plenty of real power and relieved their class from a good deal of taxation. Being by their attainments, their intellectual activity, and their education fully equal to the nobles, they felt their social disparagement all the more acutely. Thus in 1789 three political facts of the greatest moment had come into existence: (1) the centralization of all administrative as well as legislative authority in the King and his ministers, with a complete control of provincial as well as national affairs; (2) the arbitrary power of the Administration over the individual subject, who had no constitutional guarantees against its exercise; and (3) the antagonism of the richer and the poorer classes — contempt of the nobles for the bourgeois, contempt of the bourgeois for the peasantry, a dislike of the peasant and the workman for all who stood above them in the social scale. There was little local self-government either to draw the inhabitants of a district together into common work, or to accustom them to the exercise of a limited and subordinate executive power.

Then came the First Revolution, the great and terrible, yet beneficent, revolution. It swept away the feudal rights of the nobles, never to reappear. It overthrew, and for a time proscribed, the Church, abolished all titles and other distinctions of rank, and divided France into new administrative areas — the modern departments — cutting across and extinguishing the local life, enfeebled as it was, which had belonged to the old provinces.

In the seven turbulent years that succeeded the fall of the monarchy in 1792 there were, along with much destruction, some efforts, hasty and crude, to remodel the old or create new institutions. Systematic reconstruction came with Bonaparte, under whose strong hand a well-planned administration was erected on the foundations of the old régime, the centralization of power being retained and rendered more efficient, while the arbitrary power of the Crown, or its servants, was replaced by a law simplified and reduced to uniformity which, though it emanated from an autocracy, recognized rights substantially the same for all subjects. The old Conseil du Roi became the Conseil d'État, the old provincial Intendant was turned into the Prefect of the department, taking his orders from the central government and carrying them out with the same free hand as before.

When the Bourbon dynasty was re-established in 1814, the centralized administration and its arbitrary powers remained, and these have continued, though latterly somewhat reduced, down to the present day. This limited and quasi-constitutional monarchy of the Restoration was overthrown in July 1830 by the Second Revolution, the work of Paris rather than of France, which set up the monarchy of the House of Orleans, more constitutionally liberal than its predecessor, but on a narrow electoral basis. Its overthrow in 1848 by another Parisian insurrection — the Third Revolution — brought in the Second Republic, which proclaimed universal suffrage, but itself perished at the hands of its President, who had been elected in December 1848 by an enormous popular vote, before there had been time either to create local self-government or to provide guarantees for the freedom of the citizens. That President, Louis Napoleon Bonaparte, who by the " plebiscite " of 1851 got his Presidential power prolonged for ten years, succeeded by a second popular vote in turning it into the Second Bonapartean Empire, which was to be hereditary in his family. After he had been taken prisoner by the German army at Sedan in the war of 1870, a Republic, the Third, was hastily proclaimed by the legislative body then in existence. This fourth revolution expressed the feelings of Paris, but it was not made by the French people. In the following year a new Assembly, elected by universal suffrage in order to conclude peace, named Adolphe Thiers as "Chief of the Executive Power of the French Republic." [1]

Through these three monarchies, from 1814 to 1870, the centralized administration, as reconstructed by Napoleon, continued to exist, with the same autocratic powers. But the spirit of the First Revolution (1789–99) persisted in large sections of the urban population, and after 1830 its tendencies became more socialistic and aggressive. They burst into flame in the insurrection of the Commune of Paris in 1871, just after the Germans had evacuated the city. [2]

The nomination of Thiers was, and was understood to be, a purely provisional arrangement, and it hardly ceased to be so when the Assembly shortly afterwards elected him to be "President of the Republic." He did what he could, against the resistance of the monarchical majority in the Assembly, to secure the establishment of a republican form of government, and was aided by the successes of the Republicans at the elections that took place from time to time to fill vacancies in the Assembly. But the majority was still Monarchist, and its displeasure at his policy led them to overthrow him in 1873. He was replaced by Marshal MacMahon, a Bonapartist soldier who had joined the supporters of the ancient Bourbon dynasty. Every one felt that a permanent constitution ought to be enacted, but the divisions of opinion offered great obstacles. Among the Monarchists there were three parties. The Legitimists, adherents of the Count de Chambord (grandson of King Charles X.), who represented the elder branch of the House of Bourbon, were supported by the Church. The Orleanists pressed the claims of the Count of Paris, the grandson of King Louis Philippe, who, having in 1830 received the crown by a vote of the Assembly, had not asserted a title to rule by hereditary right. The Bonapartists sought to revive the Second Empire in the person of Louis Napoleon's son. These three sections, constituting the ma-

1 It would seem that the Assembly, in which there was a Monarchist majority, acquiesced in the use of the word "Republic," because they feared that if they proclaimed a monarchy forthwith, the monarch would have to bear the odium of signing the harsh treaty of peace which victorious Germany was imposing. See ch. i. of the *France contemporaire* of M. Gabriel Hanotaux.

2 The outline of events which occupies the next few pages seems needed to explain the parties that now exist in France and determine the character of its government.

jority of the Chamber, had combined to displace Thiers.
But, apart from the personal jealousies that divided both
them and the claimants they strove for, they represented
different schools of political doctrine and purpose. The
Orleanists were less reactionary and clerical than the Legitimists, the Bonapartists held to the Napoleonic tradition.
Each pursued its own aims. A reconciliation was at last
effected between the Count de Chambord, who was childless,
and the Count of Paris, the latter waiving his claim since he
became next in succession, but the former's subsequent refusal to accept the tricolor as the national flag, and his
accompanying declaration of his extreme Divine Right principles, destroyed the chance of a Restoration. As was said
at the time, " he lost the Crown of France for the sake of a
bit of calico." [1]

Accordingly the Republicans prevailed through the dissensions of their adversaries. A republican Constitution
was adopted in 1875, the decisive vote being carried by a
majority of one, on an amendment to give to the head of the
executive the title of "President of the Republic." The
Monarchist parties did not, however, abandon hope. President MacMahon, who had accepted in March 1876 a Moderate Republican (Left Centre) Ministry, was induced in
1877 to dismiss it and summon some of the leading reaction-
aries to form another. These bold men dissolved the Chamber, and ejected a large part of the administrative staff
throughout the country, substituting their own partisans, but
though prefects imposed restrictions on the press, putting
more than the usual official pressure upon the electors, a
large Republican majority was nevertheless returned. The
President, an honest man and loyal to the Constitution,
refused to attempt a *coup d'état,* and after an attempt to hold
on with a new Monarchist Ministry, called back the Moderate
Republicans to form an administration. Fourteen months
later the elections to the Senate having given a Republican
majority in that body, he resigned office, and an eminent
lawyer and politician, Jules Grévy, was chosen by the Chambers to fill his place.

[1] There was a story current that Pope Pius IX., when he learnt of the
failure of his hopes for monarchy in France (the Count of Chambord
having insisted on the white flag of his House), remarked, " Et tout
cela pour une serviette."

Since the Constitution of 1875 was established, there has been no attempt to upset it by force.   The Royalists, partly owing to their own divisions, partly through their blundering tactics, and partly also because the children of the Count of Paris were not attractive figures, lost ground in the country and in both Chambers.   The death of Louis Napoleon's son (in the Zulu War of 1879) destroyed the hopes of the Bonapartists.

Twice, however, has the republican form of government been threatened.   At the elections of 1885 several causes had been tending to weaken the advanced Republican party, whose leaders formed the Ministry then in power.   Gambetta, their strongest man, had died in 1882.   They were broken into two sections, and lost seats in consequence.   President Grévy, discredited by the corrupt practices of his son-in-law Wilson, resigned the presidency in 1887.   A party of discontent, not professedly Monarchist but aided by Monarchist funds, had grown up, and was advocating a revision of the Constitution for the purpose of strengthening the executive power.   It attached itself to a showy but essentially mediocre personality, General Boulanger, who had obtained some notoriety as Minister of War.   Originally put forward by the Radical Republicans, he gained the support of the Clericals and of all who for various reasons disliked the parliamentary system, and during a few months was a public danger, for his adherents had, by carrying him as a candidate for the Chamber at a succession of by-elections in the more conservative parts of the country, made him seem a popular favourite.   He even captured a seat in Paris.[1]   Ultimately, however, a vigorous Minister got rid of him by procuring his arraignment before the Senate sitting as a High Court of Justice.   Knowing that it would condemn him, he fled to Belgium, and shortly afterwards killed himself.   But it was a narrow escape for the Republic, since he seems, hoping for the support of the army, to have contemplated a *coup d'état.*

A few years later (1899–1902) the nation appeared to be drifting towards civil war.   There had been for some time

[1] The *scrutin de liste* system of election which had been introduced in 1885 enabled him to stand for a whole Department.   It was abolished in February 1889 in order to check this device, but has now been restored (see p. 241).

a notable revival of clerical activity, especially on the part of the religious Orders, for most of the parish clergy remained quiet. Pilgrimages were in fashion. A violent anti-Semitic agitation which had been originally directed against the great financial interests presently passed into politics. The Panama scandals, in which some Jewish financiers had played a part and some Republican deputies were involved, had shaken public confidence in the Chamber.

In 1894 a Jewish officer, Captain Dreyfus, was sentenced by court-martial to imprisonment for life on a charge of espionage and sent to Cayenne. In 1896 the question of his innocence was raised, and after a time became a political issue which convulsed France, the church and the army holding Dreyfus to be guilty, while the Republicans, though many at first hesitated, ultimately espoused his cause. He was pardoned by the President in 1899, and subsequently acquitted by the highest court after a civil trial. Excitement had by this time subsided. Though there had been no armed conflict, a bitterness of feeling had been disclosed afresh which seemed to imperil the stability of the Republic. In reviving the so-called " Nationalist " antagonism to the Parliamentary system, and in exasperating the anti-clerical Republicans, it led to the legislation disestablishing the Roman Catholic Church which, passed in 1902–5, was put into effect in 1906–7, encountering less resistance and creating less disorder than had been feared.

From the time when the restoration of the old monarchy ceased, because it had become hopeless, to be a real political issue, the relations of the Church to the State were the chief source of discord in France and made that discord passionate. The Church, which was exerting all its strength against the Republican party when Gambetta in 1877 uttered his famous phrase " Clericalism is the foe," continued monarchist at heart, and the more extreme Republicans regarded counter-attacks as the most effective form of defence. Education was the chief battle-ground, till the law of 1882, which made it compulsory, entrusted the elementary schools to lay teachers. Subsequently the Teaching Orders were dissolved by law. The course of the conflict was affected by the policy of the Vatican. Pope Leo XIII., fearing for the fortunes of the Church, counselled a conciliatory attitude as early as

1885, and in 1892 directed good Catholics to support the existing régime, observing that "on any theory the civil power is of God." Many Monarchists obeyed, but anti-Semitism and the Dreyfus troubles accentuated the antagonism, and it has continued to persist.[1]

In another way also religion and the Church told upon politics. When the risk of a monarchical restoration had disappeared, the Republican groups who had been united to oppose it began to fall apart. The more conservative section, described as the Left Centre, disapproving, some from religious feeling, some from policy, of the campaign against the Church, drew off from the larger and more advanced division of the party. Their numbers continued to dwindle as time went on, while opinions of a socialistic type more and more prevailed in the urban electorate. Divisions among the Republicans continued to increase as the chances of a monarchical restoration diminished, yet fear of the clergy sufficed to make the dominant sections hold together against the Church upon the main issues.

In the evolution of opinion towards more advanced views, and also as a result of the growth of manufacturing industry and consequent increase of a working-class population, a new school of thought and a new political party arose which became a significant factor, especially after the defeat of the Clericals left it more free to play for its own hand against the Republican parties which it had been supporting. Theories of the reconstruction of society on a communistic basis were scarcely heard of in the First Revolution, nearly all of whose leaders came from the bourgeoisie, and did not question the rights of property.[2] But at the Revolution of 1830 a Socialist party appeared among the working people, not definitely separating itself from other Republicans, but seeking to use a democratic republic as an engine for economic change.

[1] Anti-religious reaction has been strongest in those countries of Europe and America where ecclesiastical power had been most fully dominant. It was a political misfortune for France when the Huguenots were crushed by Louis XIV. Many of them were educated and thoughtful men, imbued with a liberalism which France could ill spare.

[2] Babœuf had proclaimed communistic doctrines during the First Revolution, but found little support for them. The National Assembly of 1789 in its declaration of the Rights of Man recognizes Property as a primordial right, along with Liberty, Security, and Self-Defence.

In 1848, when the Third Revolution overthrew the Orleans monarchy, doctrines of this type had spread widely, and the subsequent Parisian insurrection of June in that year was largely the work of Socialists. The same element appeared again in the revolt of the Parisian Commune against the Assembly of 1871, though the direct aim of the Communards was not so much economic as the setting up of a practically independent local authority for Paris. Thereafter Socialist opinions continued to grow, and although the party was frequently rent by disputes, its sections often drew together again, and came to constitute a body powerful not only by its numbers but by its disciplined cohesion. They have succeeded in obtaining from the Chambers much of the legislation they desire. Though their voting strength comes from the wage-earning masses, most of their leaders belong to the bourgeois class and are highly educated men. They would constitute an even stronger force in politics but for the fact that the agricultural peasantry compose the majority of the French electorate, own the land, and have every motive for maintaining the right of private property.

The general course of French political development from 1789 till 1900 cannot be more tersely stated than in the words following, which I quote from the valuable book of M. Seignobos [1] (vol. i. of English translation, p. 224):

The political development of the nineteenth century has been a series of ebbs and flows, but the tendency has been towards Republicanism. By repeated seizures of the government and an agitation more and more effective, the democratic Republicans have finally conquered France.

But the revolutions have been directed only to the structure of the central government and the possession of power. The social organization and the administrative mechanism have been preserved without serious change.

The democratic social organization, free from clerical control, established by the Revolution, was acceptable to the Republicans, and sufficiently popular to escape attack. The monarchical governments tried indirectly to revive the influence of the great landowners, the middle class, and the clergy, but they did not touch any of the social institutions — peasant proprietorship, equal division of inheritances, civil equality, eligibility for public office without distinctions of birth, exclusion of clerical control: France has steadily preserved the social system of the Revolution.

[1] *Histoire politique de l'Europe contemporaine, 1814–1896.*

The centralized and bureaucratic administrative system has also remained nearly intact. All the parties, when in opposition, have declared it to be oppressive, but, on attaining office, have preserved it as an instrument of power. Of the older Imperial régime France still retains:

(*a*) The central administration with its ministers, the departmental administration with its prefects and sub-prefects, and its control over the communes;

(*b*) The judicial organization with its body of court counsellors and its permanent judges, with its Ministry of Justice composed of advocates and prosecuting attorneys, with its antiquated and formal civil procedure and its secret inquisitorial criminal procedure, with the Napoleonic code almost unchanged (the granting of divorce is only a return to an institution taken away in 1815).

The survey I have given (necessarily brief and imperfect) of the conditions under which democracy was born in France, amid which it developed, and from which it has taken its colour, brings us to the point at which we may attempt to summarize the salient economic facts and the most potent intellectual and moral influences that were affecting the political life of the nation when the storm of war broke suddenly upon it in 1914. These conditions were:

(*a*) In the economic sphere:

In most parts of the country the land was in the hands of peasants who owned the soil they were tilling, who were intensely attached to its possession, and who shared with most (though not all) of the bourgeoisie an almost timorous conservatism.

Over against these conservative classes stood an industrial element, greatly increased during the last two generations, both in cities and in mining areas, which was largely permeated by socialistic ideas.

(*b*) In the governmental sphere:

Executive power remained highly centralized. The hand of the administration in Paris was felt everywhere. Local authorities had far narrower functions than in Britain or the United States, and the old provincial feeling which had given a certain local political and social life to the ancient divisions of the country, had, except in a few regions, almost disappeared, not having transferred itself to the Departments, artificial creations of the First Revolution.

(*c*) In the social sphere:

The influence of the old territorial aristocracy had vanished, except in the West, and over most of the country the poorer classes were permeated by jealousy and suspicion towards the landowners.

The old antagonism to the bourgeoisie of the poorer class, and especially of the town workers, continued, and had in many places become stronger with the growth of Socialism.

The tradition of the First Revolution remained strong in a section of the bourgeoisie as well as in a much larger section of the masses, and was ready to break out when passion ran high, but the habit of resorting to force had declined as the practice of constitutional government became familiar, for there was now a prospect of winning by peaceful means what in the older generation had been sought by street *émeutes* and barricades. Paris, always the mother of revolutions, lost its predominance, and could no longer force the pace for the nation. Few of those who had fought for the Commune in 1871 remained to revive the angry memories of that day. A new danger was, however, revealed in the more frequent resort to strikes on a large scale, accompanied by maltreatment of non-strikers and the destruction of property. The disposition to obey public authority was still strong in the population generally. The coexistence of this submissiveness with a proneness to violence, which, if noticeable chiefly in the less-educated class, is not confined to them, remains one of the curious phenomena of French character.[1]

Religious bitterness is intense. It is as strong in the enemies as in the friends of the Church, and is prone to express itself in petty persecutions which perpetuate themselves by creating fresh resentments.

Through all these changes of government and various forms of strife the French nation has remained intensely patriotic, united, when everything else tended to divide it, by its pride in France and its love of the sacred soil. It clung to the hope of recovering the provinces lost in 1871, and with scarcely a murmur accepted heavy taxation for military and naval purposes. It had become more pacific in sentiment towards the end of last century, and less was being heard of Alsace and Lorraine, when the aggressive attitude of its mighty eastern neighbour revived its martial spirit.

[1] Something similar has been observed in other peoples of Celtic stock.

Self-confidence had returned before the fateful day when that spirit came to be tested.

We may now proceed to examine the Constitution and government of the country, which have altered little in form, though considerably in methods, since 1875.

CHAPTER XIX

THE FRAME OF GOVERNMENT: PRESIDENT AND SENATE

THE Constitution of the French Republic is a Rigid one, distinguished from other laws by the fact that it is not changeable by ordinary legislation, but only by a special method to be hereafter described. In this it differs from the constitutions of the United Kingdom, New Zealand, Italy, Belgium, Holland, and the Scandinavian countries, for in all these countries the laws which regulate the structure and powers of government are not marked off from other statutes. It is not, however, set forth in a single instrument like the Rigid or Written Constitutions of the United States, Switzerland, Canada, Australia, and South Africa, but is contained in three Constitutional Laws.

One of these (Feb. 1875), assuming the President of the Republic as an official then existing under a law of 1873, enacts the method of electing him and his functions, and the mode of amending the Constitution. Two others of 1875 (one since partially repealed) deal with the legislature and the relations of the public powers, while two amending laws of 1884 introduce certain changes. The result of these enactments taken together is to create a legislature consisting of two Houses, a Senate and a Chamber of Deputies, who have the power (a) of electing, in joint session of both Houses, by an absolute majority, the President of the Republic, and (b) of changing the Constitutional Laws, not by the ordinary action of the legislature in each Chamber, but when sitting together in one body as a National Assembly. To enable them so to meet, each Chamber must have separately, either on its own motion or at the request of the President, declared, by an absolute majority, the need for a revision of those laws.[1] A later Constitutional Law (1884) provides

---

[1] The procedure for amending the Constitution has been used twice only.

that " the principle of the government cannot be the object of a proposal of revision." [1]

The provisions of the Constitution need not be set out in detail here, since they will appear in the description (to be hereafter given) of the Executive and Legislative organs. It is only matters relating to the structure and functions of the government that are dealt with in the Constitutional Laws. There are no broad declaration of political principles, such as appeared in the many earlier Constitutions of France,[2] no restrictions on the action of the legislature, nothing like what Americans call a Bill of Rights, guaranteeing those elementary and inherent rights of the individual which no power in the State is permitted to infringe. Taken together, these Constitutional Laws constitute the shortest and simplest, the most practical and the least rhetorical, instrument of government that has ever been enacted in France. Moreover — and this is a point of special interest to those who insist upon the sovereignty of the People — the National Assembly which passed these enactments in 1875 had received no mandate or commission from the French electorate to do so. It had been elected hastily, during the continuance of the war of 1870–71, in order to create an authority legally capable of making peace with Germany. As there did not then exist any authority competent to prescribe a suffrage for the election, recourse was had to the suffrage established during the Second Republic (1848–1852) which had been overthrown by Louis Napoleon. Neither this Assembly of 1871 nor any subsequent legislature has ever submitted for approval by a vote of the people the Constitutional Laws of 1875, and the question of so submitting them has been seldom raised, no one knowing what the result of a submission might be.

---

[1] *I.e.* that the presiding officer of an Assembly in which such a proposal is made cannot allow it to be discussed there. This law, though only negative, may be considered to be a provision of the Constitution meant to convey a solemn warning to any legislature invited to consider the abolition of the republican form of government. Were a legislature so disposed, it would of course begin by striking this provision out of the Constitution, and would then proceed to abolish the Republic just as if the provision had never existed. See as to a similar expedient in some ancient Greek republics, the Author's *Studies in History and Jurisprudence*, Essay III., pp. 205–207, of vol. i. of English Edition.

[2] See Chap. V. in Part I.

These features of the existing Constitution were due to those political conditions of 1875 which have been already described. In the one-chambered Legislature of that time the deputies who favoured a monarchical government and who had been hurriedly elected under the pressure of a terrible war, held a majority, but they were divided into three groups, Legitimists, Orleanists, and Bonapartists, corresponding to the three monarchies that had ruled in France; and each of these groups distrusted the others. Thus while the Republicans, though divided internally, were able to work together for some sort of republic, whatever character might subsequently be given to it, the Monarchist groups, each attached to one of several persons whose claims seemed irreconcilable, failed at the most critical moments to combine, and so drifted into a Republic which none of them desired. No party in the Chamber was strong enough to get all that it wanted: each had to consent to a compromise which it meant to be purely provisional. The more advanced Republicans acquiesced in a conservative Republic because they expected to change it in a radical direction. The Monarchists acquiesced in a seven-year Presidency, called a Republic, because they hoped thereafter to turn the President into a King or an Emperor.

The President

The President of the Republic is elected for a term of seven years by the two Chambers of the legislature meeting in joint session.[1] He is re-eligible for any number of terms. He is the head of the Executive Government, and has therewith:

The duty of executing the laws and power of proclaiming a state of siege.

The supreme control of the Army and Navy.

The conduct of foreign policy, through his right of negotiating treaties. Some of these, however, require legislative

---

[1] The description which follows of the structure and functions of the organs of Government in France has been made somewhat full because the French system may probably be imitated in the new republics which are now (1919) springing up in Europe, the new constitutional monarchies which were formerly in fashion having been discredited by the behaviour of the recently deposed kings who (or whose predecessors) had been given to rather than chosen by Greece and Bulgaria.

sanction, and he cannot declare war without the consent of the Legislature.

The power of appointing to all civil and military posts.

The power to pardon offences.

The function of representing the nation at all public ceremonies, and of presiding over them.

The right, concurrently with members of the Chambers, of proposing laws.

The power, with the consent of the Senate, of dissolving the Chamber of Deputies.

The power to summon the Chambers to meet in extraordinary session, and invite them to proceed, in joint session, to a revision of the Constitutional Laws.

The right of addressing messages to the Chambers. He cannot address them in person. Thiers had done so, but the Assembly, fearing the influence of his oratory, forbade this, and the prohibition has not been removed.

The power to adjourn the Chambers for a month, but not more than twice within the same session.

The power to require the Chambers to deliberate afresh upon a law they have passed. He has no veto.

All these powers, except of course those of a ceremonial nature, are exercised by or through his ministers, by one of whom every one of his acts must be countersigned. He is personally irresponsible and not legally removable by a vote of the Chambers, though they can practically make it difficult for him to retain office. But the Chamber of Deputies may accuse him of high treason, in which case he would be tried by the Senate, and would, if convicted, be deposed from office. Responsibility for executive acts done rests with his ministers, and it is to the Chambers, not to him, that they are responsible.

The position of the President in France is therefore entirely unlike that of the President of the United States. As the latter's title to power comes direct from the people who have elected him, he is independent of the legislature, and able to resist it. His ministers are his servants, responsible to and dismissible by him, and not responsible to Congress. Neither does the President of the Swiss Confederation come into comparison, for he is merely the Chairman of an Executive Council of seven ministers, with no more power than his colleagues. The real parallel is to be found in the Constitutional king of such countries as Italy, Britain, Holland, or Norway. In these countries the King reigns but does not govern, being the titular head of the State in whose name executive acts are done, while it is his ministers who are in fact responsible for them to the sovereign legislature. The French President is thus a monarch elected for seven years, but a monarch who has great dignity with slight responsibility and hardly any personal power. Of several rights vested in him little use has been made. Messages are rarely sent, not even at the opening and closing of a Parliamentary session. Only once has the Chamber been dissolved before the end of its natural term. The right of proroguing for a month has never been exercised, nor has that of calling on the Chambers to reconsider a Bill.

Two functions, however, there are, one of which he must fulfil without the intervention of his ministers, and the other of which has to be exercised upon the ministers themselves. The first is the selection of the person who is to be commissioned to form a ministry. When a Cabinet is defeated in the legislature and resigns, it is the President's duty to invite a leading deputy or senator to form a new administration. Custom prescribes that the President should first consult the President of the Senate and the President of the Chamber, because the aim in view is to secure a Prime Minister whom the legislature will be likely to support, and the chairmen of the two Houses are the persons best qualified to advise him on that subject. Heads of " groups," as well as other politicians of less mark, frequently call upon him to proffer their advice, but he need not regard it.

As regards the composition of the ministry his rights are less clear. There is nothing to prevent him from advising the person whom he selects to be President of the Council (Prime Minister) as to the men who are more or less fit, or unfit, to be invited to join the Cabinet; but, on the other hand, there is nothing to oblige the incoming Prime Minister to follow the advice given. As a rule, the President interferes very little, and he is certainly not held responsible for the structure of the ministry. The procedure is much the same as that followed in similar cases in England, where the Sovereign usually confines himself to sending for the statesman whom he asks to form the Government, though it some-times happens that he expresses a wish that some particular person should be included. The matter is simpler in England, where there have been, till recently, only two great parties, so that when a ministry containing the leaders of one of these has been overset, the choice of the Crown naturally falls on the leader (or one among the leaders) of the other; whereas in France there are in the Chamber many parties or groups, sometimes of nearly equal strength, and none commanding a majority of the whole body.

The other function of the President is that of advising his ministers in their conduct of public business. Being legally entitled to call for information as to all that passes in every public department, and especially in that of foreign affairs, he is able to advise, and has opportunities of expressing to his ministers his view on any subject. He thus holds a position between that of the British King, who reigns but does not govern, and that of the American President, who governs as well as reigns, but only for four years. There are two kinds of Ministerial meetings. One is the Cabinet Council (*Conseil de Cabinet*) held usually once a week, with the Prime Minister in the chair, to consider questions of current policy. It is like a British Cabinet. The other is the Council of Ministers (*Conseil des Ministres*), usually held twice or thrice a week with the President of the Republic in the chair. In it large political questions, including (besides matters purely formal) the measures needed to carry out the decisions of the Cabinet Council, are debated and determined. It is like an American Cabinet, save that in the latter the President can do what he likes, his Ministers being merely his confidential advisers.

What is the exact amount of power or influence which a French President exerts is an *arcanum imperii* which constitutional usage forbids either him or his ministers to disclose. The personal character of a President, his intellectual gifts, experience, and force of will make a difference in each particular case. Walter Bagehot, the most penetrating of British constitutional writers, indicated sixty years ago the value which the criticisms and counsels of a capable and experienced Sovereign, standing high above the strife of parties, might possess for his ministers. These counsels are in

England not often given, and not always followed when given,— they carry of course no legal weight — but an instance is still remembered when they proved valuable.[1] One can well believe that the advice of the President might be similarly useful in France, but there are two important differences. In France the President has always been a party leader, and may conceivably become one again; and the position he occupies, being less exalted in rank than that of a hereditary monarch, does not command so much formal deference. Advice from the President might therefore be less well received, and any influence exerted by him might be resented, not only by his ministers (who are said to be sometimes jealous even to the point of withholding information) but by the Chambers to which they are responsible. On the other hand, the President is sure to possess wide political experience, and is likely to be in general accord with his Cabinet, since he probably belongs to some section of the Left or Left Centre, as have all ministries since 1879. The Cabinet is usually what is called a *Cabinet de concentration, i.e.* one composed of the leading men drawn from various Left " groups," so that the co-operation between " groups " which Cabinets naturally aim at securing can be profitably assisted and prolonged by the influence of the President, judiciously exerted to avert breaches by which the Cabinet might fall. Taking all these things together, one may say that the Executive plays a useful and indeed indispensable part. Presidents prudently efface themselves in domestic matters, and, though believed to have occasionally proved helpful in questions of foreign relations, they have, so far as concerns the public, kept silence even from good words.

The election of a President, being in the hands of the Chambers and not of the people, and seldom having first-rate political importance, is usually carried through quickly and quietly, and excites no great interest in the nation at large. It is sometimes settled in a preliminary gathering of the " groups " belonging to the Left (a name used to denote the more " advanced " parties), which thus becomes what Americans call a " congressional caucus." Every Frenchman, except members of families that have reigned, is eligible for the

---

[1] On the occasion of a despatch addressed in 1861 to the United States Government regarding the *Trent* affair.

Presidency, but the persons chosen have, since Marshal Mac-Mahon, been all Parliamentary leaders and most of them former Prime Ministers, so their characters are well known to those who exercise the choice.[1] All have been men of high personal character, stained by no scandal. One only, Jules Grévy, was re-elected, but he resigned early in his second term in consequence of the malpractices of his son-in-law. Another (Casimir Périer) resigned in resentment at the vituperative attacks made by a section of the press on him and on the administration of the public services, against which (as he thought) the Chambers did not sufficiently protect him. Ten years later he expressed, in a letter to a newspaper upon a question which had arisen in the Senate regarding the powers of the Presidency, the view that the President of the Republic had no power which he could exert freely and personally except that of presiding at *solemnités nationales*. This notwithstanding, the dignity of the office is such that politicians of the first rank gladly accept it.

The constant recurrence in France of public ceremonial occasions of all kinds, and the value set upon the appearance of the Head of the State on such occasions, especially in the provinces, give him plenty to do, and enable him to feel that he is rendering real service to the country. That service is specially valuable when he happens to possess the dignity and affability which make his presence impressive or winning. He is an indispensable part of the constitutional machinery, for he represents the unity of the nation and the permanence of the executive power. In the words of Tocqueville, spoken long before the emergence of the Third Republic, "la grande ombre du peuple plane sur lui."

There are those in France who would like to turn the Presidency to fuller practical account as a motive force. It ought, they hold, to be real as well as ornamental, a power which could do something to guide the people and do much to restrain the legislature. This school of thinkers appeals to the principle, recognized in every French Constitution, of the separation of the legislative and executive powers, arguing that the predominance, which they call despotism, now ex-

[1] Here may be noted another contrast with the United States, where out of the Presidents chosen since Lincoln only four had sat in either House of Congress.

erted by the legislature violates that principle, producing weakness and instability in the conduct of affairs. The opposition this view encounters springs from the distrust and fear of an Executive Head which, long deep-rooted in the French mind, became intense during the rule of Louis Napoleon, who had abused his Presidential office to effect the *coup d'état* of December 1851. How, moreover, could the exercise of personal power by the President be reconciled with the provision of the Constitution which requires all his acts to be countersigned by a minister? An irremovable and irresponsible President cannot impose upon his ministers responsibility for acts which are his and not theirs, any more than they can lay on him the blame for acts which are theirs and not his. It is not merely because he is not chosen directly by the people that a French President has less authority than his American analogue, but rather because the Constitution-makers desired an executive figurehead which, standing in exalted dignity above the ebbs and flows of democratic sentiment, should not enjoy a power that might tempt him to overthrow democracy itself. Responsibility to the people cannot well be divided: it must rest either, as in England, with the Ministry, or, as in the United States, with the Executive Head.

Nevertheless, as will presently appear, discontent with the inconstancy and excitability of the Chamber of Deputies has created a wish, frequently asserting itself, to have a strong Executive and entrust him with a veto power. Those who call for a revision of the Constitution have this chiefly in their mind. That a President should be encouraged to advise his ministers more than he is known to do, and that they should give more heed to his advice, would not satisfy this party, which desires something much nearer to the American than to the British system, and holds that such a President, especially if elected by the people, would be well suited to a democratic country.

The Senate

The provisions which determine the structure and powers of the Senate were originally included in the Constitution of 1875; but a Constitutional amendment of 1884 took them out

of the category of " Constitutional Laws " and placed them
in that of those " Organic Laws " which can be altered in the
same manner as all other laws by the ordinary action of the
two Chambers.   This does not in effect make them more
easily changed, because when the two Houses agree to proceed together, as a National Assembly, to a revision of the
Constitutional Laws, the Senate, having only three hundred
members against the six hundred of the Chamber of Deputies,
is liable to be outvoted, whereas when other laws come up to
it in the regular course, it has a full power of rejection, and
is unlikely, being interested in its own prerogatives, to accept proposals which would reduce them.

By the Organic Law of December 9, 1884 (which is still
in force), the Senate consisted of 300 members elected in
the eighty-six departments of France, in Algeria, in the Territory of Belfort, and in the Colonies, by Electoral Colleges,
whose members have all been elected by universal suffrage.
To these there have been added 14 for Alsace-Lorraine, making 314 senators in all.   The Colleges consist of:

(a) The Deputies of the department.

(b) The members of the General Council of the department (*Conseil Général*).

(c) The members of the District Council (*Conseils d'Arrondissement*) within each department.

(d) Delegates chosen by the communes within each department, the larger communes being represented by a larger, the
smaller by a smaller number of delegates.[1]

The Commune of Paris has 30 delegates, some few other
large cities 24, while the large majority of the rural communes, often very small, have one each.   Even so, the dis-
proportion of delegates to population is startling.   A great
city like Lyons or Lille, for instance, may have no more delegates than a number of petty rural communes with a far
smaller population.   It therefore does not represent the people on a basis strictly proportioned to population, though it
approaches that basis much more nearly than do the American
and Australian Senates, where every State, large or small, is
equally represented.   The reason for this deviation from

---

[1] The Commune is in France the unit of local government in town
as in country.   It is a municipality presided over by a Mayor (Maire)
whatever its size, from great Paris down to a hamlet in an Alpine
valley.

democratic principle was the desire to give to the Electoral
Colleges that conservative character which was expected to
belong to the rural and especially the agricultural population;
and the laws of 1884 reduced this rural predominance chiefly
by assigning a larger number of delegates to the small towns,
in order to give a stronger representation to the bourgeois
element which now dominates them, while the rural commune
is in some regions under the influence of the local landowner.

In the voting of the Electoral College of each department
a majority of all the votes cast is required at the first two ballots for the election of a Senator, but on the third ballot a
plurality cast for a candidate is sufficient.   Voting is obligatory.   The expenses of the delegates who have to travel to
the capital of the department for the voting are paid out of
public funds (if asked for, as they always are), and are
estimated to cost, at each triennial election, about 900,000
francs (£36,000, $180,000).

The number of Senators returned from each department
varies from two to ten, according to population, the Algerian
departments and the Colonies having only one each.   A Senator's term of office is nine years.   The Senate is a permanent body, never dissolved as a whole, but renewed by one-
third every third year, the departments being arranged in
three sets, each set holding an election at one of the three
fixed dates.   Eligibility for the Senate begins at the age of
forty.   No other qualification, not even that of residence, is
required; but in practice a person is not likely to be chosen
unless he be connected with the department, either by origin
or by residence.

The legislative powers of the Senate are equal to those of
the Chamber of Deputies except as regards financial Bills.
These must originate in the Chamber, but when they reach
the Senate it can amend them by way of rejecting or reducing items in taxation or appropriation.   Whether it can also
increase the expenditure proposed except by reinstating items
which, proposed by the Ministry, the Chambers had struck
out, is matter of controversy.   It has sometimes done so,
but the Chamber usually protests, and the Senate, knowing
its case to be weak, usually yields.

It has also two special powers.   One is to give or withhold its consent to a dissolution of the Chamber of Deputies by the President before the legal time for the election of a new Chamber has arrived. This power has been exercised only once, in 1877. The other is to sit as a High Court of Justice when summoned to do so by the President of the Republic, for the trial of grave offences against the State. It has sat twice for this purpose. No special functions in connection with foreign affairs or with appointments (such as belong to the Senate of the United States) have been assigned to it.

The Senate in its actual Working.— When the Constitution was being formed, the more advanced Republicans preferred a single chamber system, such as had existed in the short-lived Second Republic of 1848–1852. But the Monarchist sections, and most of the moderate Republicans, insisted on having a body calculated to give stability, and would hardly have accepted universal suffrage without the check of another Chamber. Gambetta, eager to have a republic at once, acquiesced. Thus, after long discussions, in which nearly every possible way of creating an Upper House was considered, the example of the United States caused the election of three-fourths of the Senators to be vested in local authorities, while the selection of the remaining fourth was assigned to the National Assembly, which was to nominate them before it disappeared, subsequent vacancies among the nominees being left to be filled up by the Senate itself. This fourth were to sit for life. Indirect election, though suggested by the wish to have a comparatively conservative Assembly, was justified as giving a representation of the people not merely by numbers but by local social groups, each of which had a common interest and so a collective opinion. The idea was in so far a good one that it brought in many men of personal distinction, who gave lustre to the body in the eyes of the nation and helped to form in its members habits of decorum and gravity as well as to set a high intellectual standard in its debates. Of these nominated Senators and their co-opted successors the last died in 1918. The extinction of the class in 1884 was due, not to any complaints made against them, but to democratic theory, which disapproved of life tenure and demanded a popular, even if indirect, election. The present system works smoothly and is criticized by those only who object to Second Chambers altogether. Not much public interest is aroused either in the choice of delegates — the Maire is usually chosen in rural communes — or in the voting when it takes place in the Electoral Colleges. Although the delegates of the smaller communes still constitute almost everywhere a large majority in these Colleges, it is not they but usually the deputies and members of the *Conseil Général* who put forward and carry candidates. Nearly all the electing delegates belong to the so-called bourgeois class, *i.e.* they are neither nobles of ancient lineage nor working-men. Voting goes mostly on party lines, yet local connections and local influence count for much. The same local party committees which we shall find concerned with elections to the Chamber are at work here also. Bribery is rare, but it is alleged that the influence of the Prefect tells upon the delegates of the communes, which have (as will be seen presently) much to expect from his favour, the Prefect being usually the instrument through which the central administration works its will. The bulk of the Senators have of late years been professional men, chiefly physicians and lawyers, with a few agriculturists. The higher walks of commerce, landed property, and industry are not largely represented. Few men begin their political career in the Senate. Many have been deputies, who seek in their advancing years an easier life than falls to the lot of one who has to court a quadrennial re-election; many have been leading members of the *Conseil Général* or possibly of the *Conseil d'Arrondissement*. Thus nearly all come in with some measure of political training. The character of the Senators differs from that of the deputies chiefly in the fact that they are older, have had a longer experience, and are on the average rather better off. They keep in a touch with their constituencies which need not be quite so close as that of the Deputy, since he sits for four years only, the Senator for nine.

Most of the numerous parties into which French politicians are divided are represented in the Senate, but the extremes at both ends, Monarchists and Socialists, are relatively weaker than in the Chamber, for there are few departments in which either of those parties could carry an Electoral College. So also the smaller " groups " or subdivisions of the chief parties, which we shall find in the Chamber are less well marked — some indeed scarcely exist — in the Senate. Partisanship is less pronounced, the temperature lower, outbursts of passion unusual. The general character of opinion, which used to be Conservative Republican or what the French call " Left Centre," has become, since the end of last century, more anti-clerical and generally Radical, but Radical in a strongly Republican rather than in a Socialist sense. Averse to constitutional change, not directly amenable to popular pressure, disposed to support authority and to maintain a continuity in policy, it examines proposals by the light of experience and good sense rather than by their conformity to democratic theory. Its members, mostly bourgeois, and largely rural bourgeois, represent and value respectability. Being often men of local consequence, they know their departments well, but are less occupied than the deputies with local patronage, so that their labours are lighter. They are also somewhat more independent of party ties and party leadership. Few are re-elected more than once. Occupying apartments in the fine old palace of the Luxembourg, more than two miles distant from the Palais Bourbon where the Chamber is lodged, they see less of its members than the Lords see of the Commons in London or the Senators see of the Representatives in Washington.

The relations of the Senate to the Chamber are determined by its powers, which are weaker in fact than they seem on paper. Subordination in the realm of finance debars it from controlling the Executive, though it has twice caused the fall of ministries, in one instance, however, because the ministry wished to fall, as the Chamber did not rally to its support. Since it is only in the second degree the creation of universal suffrage, its claim to express the will of the people is less strong. Thus, while feeling the natural and inevitable jealousy of a Second Chamber towards a First Chamber, it recognizes its own inferiority and seldom challenges its rival to a duel. Not venturing to stem the current that runs strongly towards democracy, it has accepted a position inferior to that for which it was designed. But though it has less force, it has more finesse. Its expert parliamentarians, many of whom are familiar with the Chamber in its ways and its weaknesses, know when the latter can be successfully resisted, and choose their battle-ground with skill.

When the Chamber seems seriously interested in a Bill, or
when the ministry intimate that they are resolved to press
it, having public opinion behind them, the Senate gives way,
curbing its own repugnance.   When, on the other hand, it
thinks that the Chamber will be absorbed by other objects,
or has passed the Bill only in deference to momentary clam-
our, it quietly shelves the measure, or proceeds to amend it in
a leisurely way, returning it to the deputies after their zeal
has cooled down and popular interest has subsided.   Thus
many bad bills are slowly killed, sometimes after having gone
twice or thrice backwards and forwards between the Houses.
These tactics are least successful in the case of financial proposals, because the Chamber, perhaps of set purpose,
largely from its methods of business, which are alternately
dilatory and precipitate, often keeps back the Budget of the
year till the latest possible moment, so as to leave the Senate
no time for consideration and amendment unless it assumes
the responsibility of driving the Ministry to a provisional
levy of taxation needing to be subsequently confirmed.   This
habit of ousting the Senate from the financial control which
the Constitution meant to entrust to it is the more regrettable
because finance is a subject which the Senate understands.
The reports of its Commissions on the Budget are always
careful and usually sound, but they have little effect in
checking either the extravagance or the fiscal errors of the
deputies.

Ordinary Bills seldom originate in the Senate, whose best
work is done in the way of revising, both in substance and in
form, measures brought to it from the Chamber.   It is so
assiduous and competent in this function that the Chamber
is said to pass not a few demagogic Bills in the hope that
the Senate will eliminate their worst features.   Its dislike
of State-Socialism has sometimes induced it to discourage
legislation designed to improve the conditions of labour.   It
hated, but it feared to reject, the Bill for the purchase by the
State of the Western Railway, and long stood out against an
income-tax, the *bête noir* of capitalists and of the richer class
generally.

The only method provided for settling controversies between the Senate and the Chamber is that of a conference between two " Commissions," one appointed by each House,

these two bodies debating together but voting separately. If this method, seldom resorted to, fails to bring about agreement or to effect a compromise which each Chamber ratifies by its vote, nothing further can be done, for there exists no Referendum for ascertaining the opinion of the people. Should the Chamber persist in its own view, that view will be likely to prevail, especially if there be evidence that the popular House has the people behind it.

Though it is from among the deputies that most members of French Cabinets come, there are usually three or four taken from the Senate, and these distinguished men, perhaps Prime Ministers. Veterans of renown seek its less troubled and turbid waters. Instead of the atmosphere of strife in which the larger House lives, and which makes its debates exciting, there reigns in the Senate a sedate and sometimes almost languid tranquillity befitting the comparatively advanced age of its members.[1] Some critics say it has the obsolete air of a *théâtre de la rive gauche,* or describe it by terms corresponding to the American " side show," because it wants the vivacity of the Chamber, and draws far less of the attention of the nation. Nevertheless the position of a Senator is coveted, and his authority considerable. The level of the discussions is well maintained, not only as respects matter but also in the form and diction of the speeches. Brilliant oratory has been rare, but no other legislative body has in modern times shown a higher average standard of ability and knowledge among its members.

Devotees of the doctrine of absolute popular sovereignty through universal suffrage still demand the abolition of the Senate. It incurs some unpopularity by stifling, or cutting down, Bills which the Chamber lightly passes at the bidding of some section of opinion, and so comes to be denounced as reactionary. But it excites no very general hostility, and is indeed valued by most thoughtful men. It had once the honour of saving the Republic. When in 1888 General Boulanger and his partisans were trying to force a general election of the Chamber likely to result in giving him the support he needed for his grasp at power, the refusal which it became known would proceed from the Senate to any request

[1] The average age of Senators is sixty-three.

for a dissolution checkmated the scheme.[1]   This service gave
the Upper Chamber a claim, not yet forgotten, to the support
of good Republicans.   Appearances indicate that it will hold
its ground; and this appears to be the hope of the most reflective minds in nearly every party.   Gambetta, who had
rather reluctantly accepted it in 1875, said some years later
that a bicameral system was a " principe constitutif de tout
gouvernement parlementaire, et encore, malgré les errements
antérieurs, principe constitutif de tout gouvernement démocratique."   Stable in its composition and habits, it forms a
counterpoise to the haste and volatility of the more popular
Chamber.   Its half-century of life has not entirely fulfilled
the hopes of those who created it, for the faults of what the
French call Parliamentarism have been only mitigated and
not restrained.   Of the intellectual lights that adorned its
earlier years none are left now burning, and those who have
replaced them seem less brilliant.   There are some who
think it might have shown more courage in resisting the rash
action of the Chamber, and made itself more representative
of the sober and cautious elements in the nation.   But the
astute statesmen who lead the Senate may be credited with
knowing their own business.   They prefer the power of frequently securing delay and obtaining compromises to the risks
which a bolder attitude of opposition would involve.   A stage
is provided from which a man kept out of the popular Chamber by his temperament, or advancing years, or aversion to
the methods by which constituencies are captured and held,
may address his fellow-citizens, establish a reputation, and
serve the people not only by improving the quality of legislation but by discussing large issues with less risk of ruining
his prospects than might deter a deputy from trying to stem
the tide of temporary passion.   Thus most even of persons
opposed in theory to a bicameral scheme, as well as all of
those who would like the Senate to show more boldness, are
agreed in holding that it has justified its existence.   Things
would have been worse without it.

[1] It subsequently, as a High Court of Justice, found him guilty of
high treason, he having fled from France.

CHAPTER XX

OF the laws which regulate the election and powers of the Chamber, those only which provide for its election by manhood suffrage, and determine its relations to the President and the Senate, form a part of the Constitution. Ordinary laws have supplied the rest, directing that the Chamber is to be elected for four years, and fixing its number, which is at present 626, of whom 24 represent Alsace-Lorraine, while 6 come from Algiers and 10 from various colonies. The normal electoral area had been, since 1889, the Arrondissement, a division of the Department for local administrative purposes; but now the Department has been substituted, the voting for the numerous candidates being by a form of proportional representation tried for the first time in 1919. Under this new plan, however, the strength of each party in the Chamber does not exactly represent the strength of the parties in the nation. It was adopted as a compromise between the opponents of proportional representation and those of its advocates who desired to see their principle more boldly applied, and the latter think it has not gone far enough. Registration is performed by the local authorities. They have been known to falsify the register, but this is not common enough to be a serious evil. A man with more than one place of residence can choose at which he will vote, no one being permitted to vote in more than one area whether for the Chamber or for local purposes.

France has tried many electoral experiments in the arrangement of constituencies. Three times she established the system of making the larger area of the department the electoral division, assigning to each department a number of seats based on its population, for all of which the voting took place together on one list, with a second balloting where no candidate obtained an absolute majority. This plan is called the

Scrutin de liste. Three times this method was dropped and replaced by the *Scrutin d'arrondissement* (the scheme of one-membered constituencies). Now the *Scrutin de liste* has returned once more. Gambetta, among others, supposed that the larger electoral area would tend to raise the quality of candidates and diminish the power of local cliques and wire-pullers, but this did not prove to be the case. Whether it will do so now remains to be seen.[1]

The election arrangements are comparatively simple and inexpensive, and in rural areas the polling-places are numerous, there being one in every commune. It is usually the hall of the Mairie. Polling always takes place on a Sunday. The machinery of the polling and counting are a public charge, nor is there any legal maximum fixed for the candidates' expenses. Voting is by ballot, supposed to be secret, but in the rural communes the Maire can usually see how the peasant votes, and the peasant generally believes that his vote is known to the priest, the school teacher, and the landlord. Election frauds are not very frequent, though sometimes gross. They generally take the form of dropping into the ballot-box, probably with the collusion of the presiding officer, two or three extra voting papers concealed within the single paper which the voter hands to that functionary. Pleasant anecdotes are told of the way in which these things are sometimes done in southern France. On one occasion the clerk of the Maire, finding that the votes given were not sufficient to elect the candidate desired, remarked to his subordinate, " It is for you to complete the work of universal suffrage." Disturbances sometimes occur in which the ballot-boxes are seized by a group of rowdies, carried off and tampered with, but this is rare, and seems to be known only in the hot-headed south.

Bribery is sporadic, thought necessary in some places because otherwise the voters will not come up, and in other places useless because it would make no difference to the result. It seems less frequent than it was in England before the Corrupt Practices Act of 1882, or is now in some parts of the United States and Canada. Sometimes men defend or excuse it as a counterpoise to the exercise of undue

---

[1] In the election of 1919 out of 626 seats all but 50 were filled on the first balloting. For these a second balloting took place.

influence by officials or (formerly) by ministers of religion. "Treating," which is delicately described as "libations at the expense of the candidate," is infrequent, though the village *cabaret* is usually the meeting-place of political committees. An experienced friend told me that illicit expenditure could hardly be a growing evil, for the tendency had of late years been to an increase of the votes given for candidates of advanced opinions, who are nearly all poor men, unable to spend money on elections, and receiving little or no help from party funds.[1] Neither is there now in most parts of France any intimidation worth regarding by employers or landowners, though meetings are sometimes broken up and the polls disturbed by the violent opponents of a candidate. There are districts, however, especially in the west, where the landlord does exert influence on the tenant, and the master on the workman, and the priest on the parishioner.[2] Clerical persuasion no longer takes illegitimate forms. The force that may seriously pervert elections is the quiet pressure of local functionaries under the direction of their superiors or at the bidding of the sitting deputy.[3] Though there are not to-day any "official candidatures," such as those which were shamelessly practised under the Second Empire and revived under the Monarchist ministry of 1877, it is common for public functionaries or employees, from the Prefect of the department down to the local gendarme or road-mender, to do what each can to further the election of the person whom the ministry in power approves. There is much less pressure on individual voters than there was in Louis Napoleon's days, but the district or the commune is made to understand the wishes of the Government and led to expect favours from it in the way of expenditure upon local public works, from a parish pump up to a bridge or a town hall. As Parliamentary majorities are fluctuating, so that every vote in the Chamber becomes of consequence to ministers, the latter exert

[1] The great banks and financial companies are said to subscribe to the funds of some of the parties, but apparently not to such an extent as that which led to the legal prohibition in the United States of such contributions.

[2] André Siegfried, *Tableau Politique de la France de l'Ouest.*

[3] A darker (and, so far as I can judge, overdrawn) picture as respects bribery, intimidation, and election frauds is presented by Hasbach, *Moderne Demokratic*, pp. 560–563, who, however, describes southern France rather than northern.

themselves not only to secure the election of their professed supporters, but to propitiate as many deputies as possible. The Prefect and under-Prefect and all the persons in local public employment know this, and do their best, whether expressly instructed or not, to promote the candidature of those on whom the ministry counts, or whom it seeks to oblige. In recent years the candidate, if he feels himself strong, has been wont to require these services from the Prefect, whose fortunes he may make or mar by his influence with the Government, and he sometimes lords it over the local officials. In 1902 a deputy whose election was being disputed, on the ground of the governmental influence exerted on his behalf, was reproached with having had himself everywhere presented to the voters by the Prefect. " Quite the reverse," said he, " it was I who presented him."

The most active because the most omnipresent and often the most intelligent agent in pushing the interests of a candidate, especially one of advanced opinions, is the village schoolmaster. He is usually also the clerk of the Commune, and has his own reasons for being a strong Republican, because he is the natural rival of the parish priest.

However willing a Prefect may be to turn his administrative machinery to party purposes, he is often embarrassed by the fact that the ministry's hold on office is so weak that the party of the candidate whom he has been opposing may, by some turn of the Parliamentary wheel, come into office and punish him for his action. The worshipper of the Sun must make sure that it is not a setting sun whom he worships. Thus a Prefect may show deficient zeal for ministerial candidates,[1] and could, when the arrondissement was the electoral area, throw out anchors to windward by earning merit with candidates of different political stripes who were standing in different arrondissements of his department. Nevertheless the supporters of the Government actually in power have on the whole the advantage, and thus a threatened ministry usually strives to retain office till the Chamber expires by effluxion of time, so that it may be able " to make the elections." Yet it sometimes happens, in the constant shift-

---

[1] M. Felix Faure (afterwards President of the Republic) said in 1893 that functionaries are often more preoccupied in giving satisfaction to the Ministry of to-morrow than to that which they actually represent. (I quote from Mr. J. E. C. Bodley's *France*.)

ing of Parliamentary majorities, that the Minister of the Interior finds after a few weeks that he has secured a majority for his successor.

When a return is contested on the ground of irregularity or fraud or undue influence, the matter goes first to a Committee of the Chamber chosen by lot, and then to the full Chamber. The Committees are said sometimes to decide impartially, after weighing the (unsworn) evidence laid before them. The majority in the Chamber is less scrupulous and seats or unseats the members elected in obedience to party motives.[1] It is remarked that at the subsequent fresh election the unseated candidate is usually returned, for the French voter has a touch of the *frondeur* in him, and sets little store by the decisions of the Chamber, given in the spirit which is known to animate it.

Unsatisfactory as is the condition of things here described, there is little talk of mending it. The Chamber would not part with its control of disputed elections, nor would any one suggest that it should, as in England, be transferred to the judges, for it is held that only a body itself the child of universal suffrage can be entitled to deal with the results universal suffrage purports to have given. As regards official interference, the excuse made under the Second Empire that in a country so changeful as France it was the first duty of every Government to work for the stability of institutions, is one to which Republicans who acclaim the sovereignty of the people are hardly entitled to resort. If the people is all-wise as well as all-powerful, it ought to have its way. The practice is in fact constantly denounced by all parties, but it continues, because no ministry wishes to be the first to part with an advantage which it finds ready to hand in the far-reaching power of the central government. The command of the machinery makes the temptation; and the defence made for yielding to it dates from the earlier days of the Third Republic, when the gravity of the issues then before the Chamber seemed not only to Royalists, who had seen it unscrupulously used by Louis Napoleon, but even in some measure to Republicans also, sufficient to justify practices theoretically

---

[1] That this frequently happened in England sixty or seventy years ago was one of the grounds alleged for transferring the trial of election petitions to the judges in 1867.

indefensible. The system is really of old standing, having its roots in the excessive power over local officials vested in the Government of the day. As an eminent politician observed when inveighing against the evil, " It is not the Government I accuse, but Centralization; not the heir, but the heritage."

Let it be here mentioned, before proceeding to examine the rules of the Chamber and their working, (*a*) that a deputy must have attained the age of twenty-five and have all the qualifications of a voting citizen; (*b*) that members of families that have heretofore reigned in France cannot become candidates; (*c*) that no one can be a candidate at the same time in more than one constituency; and (*d*) that salaried officials, except a few of the highest, are ineligible. Ministers of religion are sometimes elected. Bishops have more than once been prominent figures.

The Chamber lasts for four years, meeting automatically in January, and has once only been dissolved before the expiration of its term. It is required by law to sit for at least five months in each year, but in fact has usually held a continuous session, interrupted by short vacations at different times in the year. It is convoked, not by the President of the Republic, though he may summon it for an extraordinary session, but by its own President.

This high functionary resembles the Speaker of the American House of Representatives rather than the Speaker of the British House of Commons, for he is not expected to display that absolute impartiality which is the distinguishing note of the latter, and he may rebuke, sometimes with pungent sarcasm, deputies whose language he disapproves. Custom has allowed him to favour, yet with due regard to fair play, the party to which he belonged before his elevation. He has not in recent years intervened in debates, but he keeps his eye on his own political future, often aspiring to the Presidency of the Republic, and sometimes called from the Chair to become the head of a Ministry. He is assisted in a general direction of the business of the Chamber by a Bureau or Standing Committee, consisting of the four Vice-Presidents (any of whom can preside in his absence), the eight Secretaries, and the three Questeurs, who have charge of financial matters. All these are deputies and chosen by the Chamber.

At its first meeting the Chamber divides itself into eleven

sections called Bureaux, the members whereof are chosen by lot and similarly renewed monthly in the same way. Their chief function used to be to create what are called " Commissions," bodies corresponding generally to the Committees of the British Parliament and the American Congress, but now it is the " Groups " (hereinafter mentioned) who nominate, each in proportion to its numerical strength, deputies to represent them on a Commission. Every Bill introduced is referred to some one of these bodies, which may alter it in any way, after hearing it explained and defended by the introducer. A member of the Commission, called the Reporter, prepares and submits to the Chamber a report upon it as amended, stating the reasons for the form the Commission has given to it.[1] When it comes before the full Chamber he takes charge of it, sometimes almost entirely superseding its introducer, even though a Minister. As the membership of an important Commission is much sought for, the post of Reporter on an important Bill is an avenue to distinction, or a proof of distinction already achieved. Under this system, the Chamber through its Commissions exercises a control over administration as well as legislation, for they can enquire into all the work of a department, summoning its functionaries before them, and recommending or refusing the measures the department desires. The authority of the ministry is reduced, for its bills may return from the Commission in a form different from that which they originally had or which ministers approve. The majority of the Commission need not be supporters of the Ministry, or anywise disposed to meet its wishes.

The inconveniences attending this system of the dual control of ministerial measures are most manifest in the case of the Budget. Financial proposals made by the Executive come before a Commission of thirty-three members, which can alter them at its own pleasure, refusing some appropriations, adding others, so that, unless it condescends to defer to the representations of the Finance Minister, it may produce, after long secret deliberations, a Budget very different from that which he submitted. So when the Ministerial

[1] I omit many details regarding these Bureaux and Commissions which are not necessary for a comprehension of the working of the Chamber.

scheme comes before the Chamber, the Reporter appears as a sort of second and rival Finance Minister, whose views may prevail against those of the Cabinet. The Government of the day has little influence, except what it may personally and indirectly exert, upon the composition of the Commissions, which may contain a majority of members opposed to its general financial policy, or to the view it takes of particular measures. The natural result is to render legislation incoherent, to make the conduct of financial policy unstable and confused, and to encourage extravagance, because ministers cannot prevent expenditure they think needless or mischievous. A further consequence is to reduce the authority of an Executive which can be easily overruled, the jealousy which animates the deputies leading them to disregard its wishes, perhaps to enjoy the rebuffs it suffers. The power of those persons who seem responsible because they were the original authors of a measure, or who can be made responsible to the public because they hold an office, being thus so reduced or destroyed that they cannot fairly be treated as responsible, actual control has passed to bodies whose members, debating in secret and holding no office, are not effectively answerable. The nation cannot, if displeased, punish the latter and ought not to punish the former. In these practices there is visible a deviation, due to the tendency of an Assembly to encroach wherever it can, from the doctrine to which lip-service is paid in France, of the separation of legislative from executive power, for an Executive is impotent when the funds needed for administration are withheld.

Here let a curious custom be noted. Only since 1885 have the names of deputies voting in a division been regularly recorded and published.[1] Voting is by ballot-papers of two colours, white denoting assent, blue disapproval. These are collected into an urn passed round by the attendants. A deputy may abstain from voting, though present in the Chamber, and can even vote by proxy, entrusting the function of dropping into the urn his paper to a friend who will vote

[1] The names were occasionally published between 1871 and 1885. The official record now states the names of deputies who did not vote, or were absent on leave, or were detained by attendance at the Budget Commission. The names of members voting in divisions in the British House of Commons were not recorded before the passing of the Reform Act of 1832.

white or blue according to what he conceives to be the wishes of his colleague. A case was mentioned to me in which an obliging deputy deposited the votes of more than thirty of his colleagues.

So much for what may be called the procedure of the Chamber. Let us pass to the men who run the machinery. As the Chamber is the centre of the whole political system, exerting a more complete control than does any legislature in any other government, we must examine in some little detail the persons who work the system and whom the system forms.

Though social as well as political equality reigns in France, there are still differences of rank, more significant in their disabling than in their recommending effect. Very few deputies come from the ancient nobility or from the large landowners, a section numerous in the West. That financial manufacturing and commercial plutocracy, which is called in America " Big Business," has few representatives, and among these extremely few persons of great wealth. The largest element consists of professional men, lawyers, physicians, journalists, retired functionaries, and professors or school teachers, this last class being the fewest.

There are not many to speak for agriculture, and even fewer had worked with their hands before they entered the Chamber. Most of the Socialists belong to the professional or commercial class. The Chamber is no more plutocratic than it is aristocratic. It consists chiefly of the same upper strata of the middle classes as does the United States Congress or the Parliament of Canada, the chief difference being that in those bodies there are even more lawyers, but hardly any physicians or teachers or journalists.[1] Few of the barristers have achieved distinction in their profession, for the building up of a large practice would be hardly compatible with attendance in the Chamber, but advocates who have succeeded there sometimes return to the bar and utilize at it their political fame while retaining their seats. Literature is represented almost entirely by journalists. If it be true, as French critics complain, that there are now few such intellectual displays as adorned the Chamber in the days of Louis Philippe, or in the first Assembly, elected in 1871, of

[1] The Chamber elected in 1919 contained 140 advocates, 44 journalists or men of letters, 4 Catholic priests, and 3 Protestant clergymen.

the Third Republic, there is plenty of keen intelligence and especially of oratorical talent. It is not so much universal suffrage that has brought in men from what Gambetta called the *nouvelles couches sociales* as the diffusion of secondary education, which has made easier the upward path for ability, especially of the literary and rhetorical kind. An English or American observer is impressed by the large number of deputies who possess not merely fluency but the gifts of lucid exposition and readiness in debate. Whether a man has much or little to say, he seems to know how to say it, not indeed in that choice or stately language which delighted auditors in the Assembly of 1871, but with readiness, force and point.

Such being the Deputy, whence comes he and how does he become a deputy? Though a man gains by being a resident or in the electoral area, or connected with it by birth, candidates are not, as in America, restricted to the place of their residence, and men of eminence have sat for districts with which they had no personal tie. The large majority, however, have spent their earlier life in the places they represent, and have begun their political career by acquiring influence among their neighbours. They enter local councils, and thus become known in the canton, the arrondissement, perhaps the department. They serve as Maires of their commune; they are active in local party work, and alert in looking after local interests generally. An ambitious doctor or lawyer may give gratuitous consultations or otherwise ingratiate himself with a local clientèle. To belong to a Masonic lodge, or even to an angling society or a gymnastic club,— all these things help. Broadly speaking, the personality of a candidate counts for much, and of course counts for more when political issues are least exciting and where convictions are least strong. One must not only cultivate an easy and genial manner, but observe, at least in the provinces, a decent regularity of life, avoiding, especially in the northern parts of France (for the South is indulgent), whatever could shock the *âme rigide de la province*. If one has money to spend on local purposes, so much the better, particularly in the mountainous districts where people are poor; but as local candidates are seldom affluent there is less than in England of what is there called " nursing a constituency."

When an aspirant has in these ways established his position, it is for the party committee of his district to put him forward as candidate, since the central party organizations count for little (except among the Socialists) and do not send down a candidate or supply him with the sinews of war. When the election comes, the candidate, except in great cities, will usually talk more about local affairs and the services he expects to render to the constituency than about national politics or the merits and programme of his own particular section of the Republican party. The authority of party leaders has been little invoked since the death of Gambetta, the last statesman who had a name to conjure with. Though contests evoke much heat, sometimes expressing itself in personal abuse, perhaps even leading to a duel, the bulk of the citizens may be languid, and many will not sacrifice their Sunday holiday to come to the polls. The vote cast has been light, according to the standards of Britain, Switzerland, or America, rarely however falling below 60 per cent of the qualified voters.[1] In 1919 it stood high, only 30 per cent having failed to vote.[2]

Once in, the deputy's first care is to stay in. This must be achieved — and here I refer less to large towns than to the ordinary rural or semi-rural constituencies — by a sedulous attention to the interests not merely of the district but of the individual residents in the district, especially of those to whom he owes his seat. Every kind of service is expected from him. He must obtain decorations for his leading supporters, and find a start in life for their sons and sons-in-law. Minor posts under Government and licenses to sell tobacco have to be secured for the rank and file. All sorts of commissions to be performed in Paris are expected from him, down to the choice of a wet nurse or the purchase of an umbrella. Several hours of his day are consumed in replying to the letters which pour in upon him, besides the time which must be given to the fulfilment of the behests he receives.

This is slavery. But there are compensations. Apart

[1] Between 1881 and 1910 the percentage of abstentions ranged in Western France from 24 to 32 per cent.

[2] The numbers were for Continental France, without Alsace-Lorraine — electors, 11,048,092; votes cast, 7,801,879; and for Alsace-Lorraine — electors, 397,610; votes cast, 328,924.

from his salary, which to the average member is a thing to be considered, he has power. He is one of the nine hundred odd who rule France. Though he is the servant of his electors, he is often also their master, respected and deferred to in his district as at least the equal of the Prefect, and perhaps stronger than his local party Committee. He is the fountain of honour, the dispenser of patronage, inspiring a lively sense of favours to come. So long as he helps the Department, and his friends in it, to the satisfaction of their desires, he is not likely to be disturbed, unless some sudden revulsion of political sentiment should sweep over the country. If he is well off, his subscriptions to local purposes help him; if poor, people feel it would be hard to turn him out and send him to seek a new means of livelihood. Accordingly, provided he keeps on good terms with the local wire-pullers, and is not involved in a scandal which would reach the constituency, he is likely, at least in rural areas, to hold his seat, and may in the fulness of time transfer himself to the calmer waters and longer term of the Senate. A sitting member is, like a British member, generally selected by his party to fight the seat, so the bulk of members in each Chamber have sat in a preceding one. In 1919, however, 340 new members were elected.

Next to that of staying in, the chief aim of our deputy is to get on. His best course is at first to eschew the *grande politique,* and be content with establishing his position by securing a place on one or more of the best Commissions, and establishing friendly relations with as many as possible of his colleagues, primarily of course with those who share his opinions, but if possible with other sections also. He usually begins by inscribing himself as member of one of the numerous " groups " into which the Chamber is divided. This brings us to consider the parliamentary parties.

I have already traced in outline the history of the movements of political opinion in France since 1871. It would be tedious, and for our present purpose needless, to describe the successive evolutions and modifications, the splits and recombinations, by which the broad division of politicians into Monarchists and Republicans passed into the more numerous now existing parties. It may suffice to enumerate these as respects the Chamber of Deputies, for it is only there (and to a less degree in the Senate), not in the country, that they are clearly marked. The French habit has long been to describe parties by names which had their origin in days when Conservatives sat on the right hand of the presiding officer, and Liberals on the left; and these names have the advantage of being colourless, while terms bearing a reference to particular tenets or a particular spirit frequently change their meaning, as the title " Progressive " has come to denote persons who are really Moderates, even perhaps Clericals, and " Radical," once a name of terror, has been so softened down that men talk of " Radicaux Modérés " or " Radicaux Conservateurs." So the name " Socialist " is so far from being equivalent to " Collectivist " or " Communist " that one has heard of " Socialistes anti-Collectivistes "; and when a party calls itself " Independent," its independence always inclines to the Right, or conservative, rather than to the more " advanced " side.[1]

The nine groups which existed in 1914 and the eight which existed at the beginning of 1920 might be broadly described as being fractions of four larger parties, or rather subdivisions of four types of political opinion — first, the Monar-

[1] In 1914 the party groups in the Chamber of Deputies were the following. I give them as from Right to Left:

Monarchists (all more or less Clerical in sentiment).
" Action Liberale populaire."
Progressive Republicans.
Republican Union (Fédération Républicaine).
Democratic Left.
Federation of the Left.
Radical Left.
Radical Socialists.
Independent Socialists.
United Socialists.

In 1920 there were stated to be besides twenty-one " non-inscrits " deputies more or less detached, but classifiable in a general way with the Left, the following eight groups:

1. Independents.
2. Progressists.
3. Republicans of the Left.
4. Republican Democratic Left.
5. " Action républicaine et sociale."
6. Radical Socialists.
7. Republican Socialists.
8. United Socialists.

Of these the largest were No. 4 with 93 and No. 6 with 86 members. At the election of 1919, which took place under the influence of a reaction against Socialism, there was a certain co-operation between the Right and the Centre parties.

chists; secondly, the Moderate Republicans (sometimes called Liberals); thirdly, the Advanced Republicans, cherishing the traditions of the First Revolution; and lastly, the Socialists, whose professed aim is an economic reconstruction of society.[1] The groups from time to time dissolve, or unite, or re-form themselves under other names. They may be — indeed they are sure to be — different in 1925 from what they are in 1920. It is therefore not worth while to describe their vaguely defined tenets or their always varying composition.

Let us now look at the Parliamentary group only as a wheel in the Parliamentary machinery. There is nothing like it in the American Congress, and only occasionally has something like it appeared in the British Parliament.[2] It is nominally a political organization, holding certain views which it desires to advocate. But it is also personal. Having a social side and directly practical aims, it concerns itself with the fortunes of its members. It claims for them places on the more important Commissions, and if a new ministry has to be formed, the incoming Prime Minister will be likely, if the professed opinions of a group do not differ widely from those he professes, to strengthen his position by inviting one or more of its members to accept a portfolio. A new deputy may therefore be guided in joining a group not only by his own political predilections, or by a wish to play up to the general sentiment of his constituents, but also by his estimate of what the group can do for his own career. Some few remain outside the regular groups in the class of " deputies not inscribed," and they also, it is said, act together on behalf of the personal interests and claims each desires to push. Though the members of a group have a Chairman and a Committee, and though they sometimes meet to consult on their collective action and usually vote together, they have not what the English call " whips " to bring them up to vote on a division. It is only among the Socialists that the obliga-

[1] Of the " Nationalists," who can hardly be described as a party or group but who represent a tendency affecting the members of several groups, I shall speak later.

[2] There was in the House of Commons a so-called Radical group from 1870 till 1880, and a sort of " Neo-Conservative " group from 1880 till 1885, the latter very small but very active, and containing men of importance. Of the present House and its varying groups the time has not come to speak. British Parliamentarism seems to be entering a new phase of development.

tion to act as one disciplined body is recognized and enforced by the threat of excommunication.

Besides these political groups there are, or have been, others formed on the basis of a specially keen interest in one subject, *e.g.* the French colonies, lay instruction, national defence; and also other groups devoted to the protection of some material interest. Such is the Agricultural Group, the Sugar Group, the Vine-growing Group, the Group of physicians. These aggregations form a sort of cross division of the Chamber. Most of them have nothing to do with party politics, and exert pressure on the ministry only for the advancement of their special industrial or commercial aims. The Colonial Group has large ambitions, and is frequently active in influencing governmental policy in the Chamber as well as in prompting the press.

As the groups are numerous, and no one of them commands one-third of the Chamber, no ministry expects to possess a majority which it can call its own. It must rely on a combination of two or more groups, constituting what is called, when it has reached solid stability, a Block. While the Block holds together, Ministers are reasonably safe. But the fluidity of each group imports an uncertainty into the action of every combination, so that when a new issue suddenly arises, due perhaps to displeasure at some act of the ministry, or to any other cause which creates temporary passion, the majority may crumble and the ministry fall, even without the open dissolution of the combination. It has also sometimes happened that the extreme groups, such as the Clericals on the one side and the Socialists on the other, hostile in principle, suddenly coalesce, and turn the balance of votes on a division. The union of extremists against the men in the middle is specially dangerous, because seldom predictable. These causes, taken together, explain the kaleidoscopic changes of government.

Another feature of the system, surprising to a British or American observer, is the absence of recognized leadership. Though every Group has its president, who to some extent directs it, who negotiates on its behalf with the existing ministry and with other groups, and is presumptively the person who will be chosen to represent it in a new ministry, he exerts less authority than Parliamentary leaders do in Britain or,

Canada or Australasia. This seems due not altogether to the absence of political issues sharply defined as between the various Republican groups, but partly to an exaggeration of the sentiment of equality combined with the French tendency to the assertion of individual will. So soon as any one statesman shoots ahead of others by his oratorical gifts or forceful personality, he excites first jealousy and then envy. His colleagues render to him no more allegiance than their own interests or those of the Group prescribe. His enemies talk of him as aiming at a sort of dictatorship, and the charge gives secret pleasure to some of his adherents. Thus Gambetta fell at the moment when he seemed strongest. Seldom has a Parliamentary chief so strong a hold on the country outside as to find in its support a means for securing the loyalty of his following in the Chamber. At general elections, the names of the chief statesmen are no talismans: they may, indeed, be scarcely mentioned. No one since Gambetta, except perhaps Waldeck Rousseau at the election of 1902, has been a popular figure, a name wherewith to conjure, in the same sense as were Peel, Palmerston, Gladstone, Disraeli, in Britain, or as Macdonald and Laurier were in Canada, or as Parkes in New South Wales, or Seddon in New Zealand.[1] This fact has something to do with the atmosphere of personal intrigue which has long suffused the French Chamber. If parties were tightly organized, they might find an advantage in having a recognized leader and making much of him. But only the Socialists are so organized, and they are the last who would seek to exalt one man above his fellows.

This passion for equality, this dislike of authority, this incessant striving for prominence and influence among the deputies, each descrying a ministerial portfolio at the end of the vista, finds another expression in the constant struggle on the part of the Chamber (and its Committees) to assert itself against the ministry and grasp more and more of executive power. The Commissions are already even stronger than the Committees of the Senate and the House in America, and their leading members are wont to express surprise that

[1] The constitutional arrangements of the United States and Switzerland scarcely permit a comparison between leadership in France and leadership in those countries.

there is not a similar effort in the British House of Commons to overbear the ministry.

The every-day work which the Chamber performs may be classified as (a) legislation, (b) criticism of executive departments, (c) displacement of ministries. In legislation the contrast between measures introduced and measures passed is startling. A deputy finds their introduction an easy means of attracting notice, and can thus please his constituents, whom he deluges with copies. A first and second reading are readily granted on the plea of urgency, but the great majority go no further, being stifled or shelved in the Commissions. Proposals on subjects of importance brought in by a minister have a better chance, but may emerge from a Commission so changed as to be scarcely recognizable. Comparatively few are passed into law. Questions of the first magnitude, debated session after session, remain long unsettled. This happens in all legislatures, but perhaps most frequently in France, not merely because the Commission system and the group system hamper the power of a ministry, but for a deeper reason also, viz. the existence of the Civil Code, which has permanently fixed so many principles of private civil law as to induce a dislike of innovations, for in the French mind, which superficial observers have called volatile, there is a strong vein of conservatism. New questions, economic and social, have emerged, especially during the last half-century, which the Code does not cover, but the Chamber does not find in legislation its chief interest, as is realized by those who notice how scanty is the attendance when important Bills are under discussion. Its delight is in personal matters and those "live issues" which affect the fortunes of a government. Any mistake made by a Minister, any conduct which can be represented as having either a pro-clerical or an anti-clerical tendency, any act which either offends the Labour Unions or betrays subserviency to them, leads to animated debates which may shake the ministry if it be weak, or accentuate hostility if it is defiant. Such acts furnish pretexts for resorting to that favourite method of attacking a Cabinet which is called the Interpellation. The deputy gives notice that he will interrogate a minister on some declaration made or administrative act done by him. The interpellation consists of a speech denouncing the conduct or the policy blamed, and asking the Prime Minister, or the Minister personally responsible, for an explanation. Neither the Cabinet nor the particular Minister is obliged to accept the debate on the spot, so usually a later day is fixed for the interpellation. When that day has arrived and the debate has run its course, a motion is made for passing to the Order of the day (*i.e.* proceeding to the next business on the paper). Then arises the opportunity for defeating the Cabinet. The *Ordre du jour* can be either *pur et simple* or *motivé*. The *Ordre pur et simple* is a motion stating, without any word of praise or blame for the Administration, that, the debate being at an end, the House resumes its previously appointed work. The *Ordre du jour motivé* adds to this resolution some words approving or condemning the conduct of the Ministry, the favourable resolutions coming from the friends, the unfavourable from the enemies of the Cabinet. The skill of the Opposition is shown in so phrasing their motions as to rope in the largest number possible of groups hostile to the ministry, while introducing something against which a group likely to befriend the ministry will find it hard to vote. Before the division the Ministry declare which of these *ordres du jour* they are disposed to accept. If they carry it, they are back into smooth water. If defeated, their bark goes down. These interpellations are the field-days of politics, rousing the greatest excitement, and drawing crowds of spectators. If the Cabinet has lost moral authority, or if it becomes known that it is riven by internal dissensions, almost any pretext will serve. Such a pretext is seldom found in matters of foreign policy, for an honourable tradition disposes men to avoid anything that could weaken France in the face of the outer world. Ministries fall more frequently by these interpellations than in divisions on legislative or financial measures, and they may fall quite suddenly, perhaps by an unexpected combination of groups, perhaps by want of promptitude in accepting, or themselves devising, the *ordre du jour motivé* which will carry them safely down the rapids.

The public business of the Chamber is not, however, the chief care of the deputy. He has private work to do which affects not only his own personal fortunes but the exercise of the functions discharged in public sittings. The relations (already described) which he maintains with his constituents oblige him to be in constant contact with the administrative departments. Only from the latter can he obtain the favours which he owes to the former. Ministers dispense the honours, the medals and ribands, the administrative posts, mostly of small consequence, the tobacco licences, and even the college bursaries. To them the deputy goes when the commune or the arrondissement desires a bridge or a road, when a farmer wants to be compensated for damage done to his vines by a hail-storm, when a taxpayer disputes the taxgatherer's claim, when a parent wishes to have an indulgent view taken of his son's performances in an examination, when a litigant thinks that a word of recommendation might help him in a court of justice.[1] The constituent writes to the deputy and the deputy approaches the minister, and when either a grant of money to the commune, or a riband, or a salaried post is in question, the minister is made to understand that the deputy's support at the next critical division will be affected by the more or less benevolent spirit the Administration displays. Thus besides the great game of politics played by the parties in the Chamber, besides the pressure of the Commissions upon the Administration, there is a continuous process of triangular trafficking between the constituents, the deputy, and the ministers, which is, to the two latter, always vexatious and often humiliating. A somewhat similar process went on once in England, and is not extinct, though now much attenuated, in the United States. Its prevalence in France, where the grosser forms of corruption are comparatively slight, is due to the concentration in the National Government of the whole administrative machinery of the country, every local functionary being appointed from Paris, and the cost of most kinds of local, public work being defrayed by the national treasury.[2] A French Administration might well desire to have less far extended power, for its power is its weakness.

[1] It is not to be supposed that in these latter cases justice suffers. It is easy to write a letter which can be read between the lines.

[2] M. Poincaré, speaking in the Chamber in 1912 (June 25) observed: " Nous sommes obligés d'employer la plus grande partie de notre activité à des besognes fastidieuses, à des démarches ingrates et nous en arrivons sous la passion des influences locales à considérer comme une nécessité vitale pour conserver notre mandat notre ingérence quotidienne dans toutes les questions administratives."

The Chamber is full of talent because, though many of the members have come from narrow surroundings and retain narrow views, the quickness and flexibility of the French mind enable them to adjust themselves to the conditions of a large assembly more readily than would most Englishmen or Americans. When an exciting moment arrives, the debates reach a high level of excellence. Repartees are swift and bright, and great tactical skill is displayed in escaping dangers or forming combinations on the spur of the moment. Turbulent scenes occur, but none worse than have once or twice occurred both in Congress and in the House of Commons, nor has violence approached the pitched battles of Buda Pest, where benches were broken, and inkstands hurtled through the air. There is little personal rancour, even among those who are most bitterly opposed in politics. Deputies will abuse one another in the Chamber and forthwith fraternize in the corridors, profuse in compliments on one another's eloquence. The atmosphere is one of a friendly *camaraderie,* which condemns acridity or vindictiveness. Parisians say that the level of manners has declined since 1877, and the style of speaking altered, with a loss of the old dignity. Wit may be as abundant, but one misses that philosophic thought by which the Assemblies of 1848 and 1871 impressed the nation and won the admiration of Europe.

Every deputy and senator receives a salary of 27,000 francs a year. The sum used to be 9000 francs, but in 1906 the deputies raised it to 15,000 francs, rather to the displeasure of the country, and after the great war it was increased to its present figure. Are they then fairly described as professional politicians? The mere fact of payment does not make them so, any more than it does the members of the British and Australian Parliaments. Comparatively few have entered the Chamber merely to make a living, though there are many whose effort to remain there is more active because they have abandoned their former means of livelihood. It would have been practically impossible not to pay those who quit their avocations to give their whole time to politics. Payment may not have done much to lower the moral standard of political life: it may indeed have enabled some to resist the temptations which surround them, yet it necessarily tends to make them eager to keep their seats, and in so far affects their independence.[1] They are not, as a rule, closely held to the terms of their electoral professions of faith, though proposals have been submitted to the Chamber that the popular mandate of any one who has disregarded these professions should be deemed, and if necessary judicially pronounced, to have been forfeited. It is customary for a deputy to appear before his constituents at least once a year, as in England, and to give a review of the political situation, which furnishes an opportunity for questioning him on his conduct. It is not, however, by his action in the *grande politique* of the Chamber that a deputy (other than a Socialist) usually stands or falls. Those few who are supposed to represent great financial or commercial interests need not greatly fear the attacks of extreme partisans in their districts, for they are likely to have the means provided them of securing by various influences the fidelity of the bulk of their constituents.

The chief differences between the professional politician of France and him of America is that the latter depends even more on his party organization than on what he secures for his constituents, that he can seldom count on a long tenure of his seat or of an administrative post, and that he can more easily find a business berth if he is sent back to private life. The number of those who belong to the class described in America as " professionals " is of course far larger there than in France, for it includes a host of persons who are not members of legislatures, most of the work they do being of a humbler kind.

---

[1] Rousseau wrote: " Sitôt que le service public cesse d'être la principale affaire des citoyens, et qu'ils aiment mieux servir de leur bourse que de leur personne, l'État est déjà près de sa ruine " (*Contrat Social*, iii. 15).

CHAPTER XXI

CABINET MINISTERS AND LOCAL PARTY ORGANIZATIONS

THREE powers rule France: the Deputies, the Ministers, and the local Party Committees. We may now pass to the second of these three forces that are incessantly contending or bargaining.

The Cabinet ministers are in practice, though not by law, either deputies or senators, and all expect, when their brief span of office has ended, to return to their functions as private members and resume the rôle of critics till the time comes for them to succeed their successors. Herein France resembles the British self-governing Dominions, in which every minister sits in Parliament,[1] and is unlike the United States, where a minister not only cannot sit in Congress but has, more frequently than not, never sat there. Thus the minister is by temperament, ideas, and habits first and always a member of the legislature. He knows his Chamber's ways, and has an intimacy, in which there may be little enough of friendship, with most of its members.

The person who has been summoned to form a Cabinet as President of the Council, selects his colleagues, choosing most of them from his own particular group, but generally adding one or two or more from other Republican groups by which he expects to be supported. The differences in their views and affiliations do not prevent the persons thus selected from getting on together and presenting a united front to the opposing faction. Self-interest prescribes this, and the political cleavages between the Republican groups are not very deep. Consistency is one of the lesser virtues in politics. A recent

---

[1] In England, the custom which requires a Minister to be a member of one or other House of Parliament has been sometimes departed from, though only for a time, since the prolonged absence of a person responsible for the management of a department would be highly inconvenient. I take no account of the cases which occurred during the war of 1914–19, for the conditions were then quite exceptional.

French Prime Minister observed, " Les necessités font éclater les dogmes."

The qualities which bring a deputy into the class of " *Ministrables* " [1] do not much differ from those which lead to Cabinet office in every democratic country and popular assembly. In France they may be summed up as — Ready eloquence, alertness of mind, Parliamentary tact, personal popularity, general adaptability. In the allotment of posts knowledge counts for something, and most so in the departments of finance and of the naval and military services. But adaptability counts for more. [2] Dignity of character and a spotless reputation are a valuable asset, especially in a Prime Minister, yet their absence does not prevent a man from rising high.

The Cabinet offices vary in number — in 1913 there were twelve — all of the same rank and carrying the same salary, but there may be (and in war time were) ministers without a portfolio, so the deliberative Cabinet might be of any size, though it had never, up to 1914, exceeded seventeen.

French ministers cannot well be compared with those of the United States, for the latter do not sit in the legislature, and are often selected less for their capacity than because they belong to States which the President wishes to gratify by giving them representation in his Cabinet. An American minister usually disappears from Washington after his four years' term of office, and may be no more heard of in the world of politics, while in France the ex-Minister holds on; and the wealth of the nation in former occupants of high office grows so fast by frequent Cabinet changes that there are plenty of tried men from whom a Prime Minister may make his selections. Talent is never lacking, though it is more frequently of the showy than of the solid order.

The dignity of a Minister is, next to the Presidency of the Republic and the Presidencies of one or other Chamber, the goal of a politician's ambitions. It carries the title of Excellency, and its possessor is received with every mark of honour when he visits a provincial city to perform some pub-

[1] A word probably suggested by the Italian adjective *Pa=papibile* (of a man fit to be chosen Pope) ; and an equivalent of the American phrase, " Cabinet timber."

[2] True of England also, where a Minister is (in normal times) very rarely selected with any regard to his special knowledge.

lic function. The power which belongs to it is more exten-
sive than a like office enjoys in any other free country, for
nowhere else are the functions of the Executive so far-reaching. But this power is greater in semblance than in reality.
The machinery of French administration is so complicated
that the permanent official hierarchy, deferential as they are
to their chief, can impede his action when they think that
he is breaking through their settled practice, for want of
expert knowledge may make him helpless in their hands, not
to add that he is generally deposed, or transferred to some
other post, before he has had time to learn to " know the
ropes." If he tries to understand everything he is asked to
sign, work accumulates, and the machine stops. While he
is struggling to master his duties, he has not only to face his
critics in the Chamber but to endure the daily plague of
requests from deputies to do this or that job for the benefit
of their constituents. High-minded and courageous as he
may be, he is obliged to think of the fortunes of the ministry,
and must yield to many an unwelcome demand in order to
secure the vote of the deputy who himself seeks to secure the
vote of his constituent. Nor are the deputies the only people to be feared. The financiers and heads of big business
enterprises, partly by the power of their wealth, partly
through the newspapers or the deputies, whom they can use as
tools, may bring to bear a formidable pressure.

Two other complaints are heard in France. One is that
the minister brings with him, or is soon surrounded by, a
swarm of personal dependents, private secretaries, and various hangers-on. These constitute what may be called his
private political and patronage staff, who help in his parliamentary work, deal with the press, keep an eye on places to
be disposed of, and are what physicians call a *nidus* for
intrigue as well as an annoyance to the permanent officials of
the department. The other charge is that the tendency of
local officials to refer everything to Paris continues to grow,
delaying business and increasing the risks of jobbery, because the Minister, who cannot know the facts as well as the
Prefect on the spot, is at the mercy of interested representations.

The " expectation of life," as insurance agents say, of a
French Ministry is short. Between 1875 and 1914 there

were 48 administrations with an average duration of nine months and twenty-two days.   Only one ministry since 1896, that of M. Waldeck Rousseau, had lasted for more than two years.   A change of Ministry makes little difference to the country, and cannot — as it often can in England — be deemed to indicate any change of popular opinion.   When a Ministry falls it does not lose a public confidence which it may never have possessed.   This is a phenomenon which Frenchmen deplore as harmful to the nation, because it prevents ministers from acquiring a grasp of their departmental duties, delays legislative progress, and creates a general sense of instability, defects which have done much to discredit Parliamentarism in the eyes of the people.   Yet they are less serious evils than they would be in other countries, and that for two reasons.   They do not disorganize, though they disturb, the general course of administration, because the great machine goes steadily on its way, being worked by a strong and competent bureaucracy which is as little affected by changes at the top as the equally strong and competent bureaucracy of the Roman Empire was disturbed in the provinces by the frequent accession to supreme power of one military adventurer after another.   They affect but slightly the foreign policy of France, for its general lines have been prescribed by the necessity of maintaining unity in the face of a threatening enemy.   They are an evil less serious than the inner malady of which they are the visible symptom.   What then are the causes which make ministries so unstable and changes so frequent?   Those which appear on the surface have been already stated, viz. the number of groups in the Chamber, the want of discipline in these groups and shifting of deputies from one to another, the suddenness with which political crises arise, the tendency of extreme groups to unite for the momentary aim of defeating a ministry which they dislike for opposite reasons, the impatience which makes deputies desire a change for the sake of a change.   But behind these there are other causes of wider scope, due to permanent conditions.   Some of these may be enumerated.

(1) Regional divisions of opinion in the country, making the political tendencies of the West, of the North and East, of the South, and (still more markedly) of the South-east dif-

fer so much from one another as to prevent a general consensus of view on fundamental questions.

(2) The antagonism between the strongly Roman Catholic proclivities of certain sections of the population and the anti-religious, or at least anti-clerical, vehemence of other sections.

(3) The hostility of the industrial masses, especially in the manufacturing and mining areas, to the employers and to the richer sort of people generally. But for the outside pressure, enforcing national cohesion, a class war might have broken out in many places, as indeed it has done at intervals in Paris, and to a less extent in other industrial centres.

(4) The indifference to politics of a large part of the agricultural population. This has its good side in so far as it has prevented party passion from seizing on the bulk of the nation and making the struggles of the Chamber provoke outbursts of violence over the country. But it has been also unfortunate in having failed to keep the deputies in order, to condemn intrigues, to discourage the creation of small groups, to make the parties feel their responsibility to the nation. If Parliamentary parties were formed on well-defined and permanent lines, the policy approved by a majority at a general election might be steadily pursued (as in England or Holland or Canada) until the country changes its mind, or some conspicuous error brings about the collapse of a ministry.

(5) To these causes one may perhaps add the fact that since the death of Gambetta no single leader of dominating personality has arisen. Democracies need men who by their genius, or by the strength and worth of their characters, can become not merely leaders but inspirers of a party.[1] The foremost men of the last forty years have been parliamentary rather than popular chiefs. Some of them (I speak of course only of those who have passed from the scene) have shown brilliant talent and great force. But none have had that sort of hold on the country which enabled Pitt or Peel or Gladstone in England, Calhoun, Clay, Webster, and Lincoln (not to mention later statesmen) in America, to become

[1] Jules Ferry seemed for a time to be coming near to this position, and Waldeck Rousseau, a finer character, came still nearer.

national figures, who were as necessary to their parties as their parties were to them. To the causes which prevent the development of leadership in France we must presently return.

After the deputies and the ministers comes the third and largest set of the actual though unconspicuous rulers of France, those who all over the country keep the machine of party government running, managing the elections by which deputies are chosen and ministers are installed in power. To understand the part played by the local committees we must recur to the political parties as already enumerated.

. These parties, though more or less organized in the Chamber of Deputies, do not extend over the country at large, or, to speak more exactly, they exist in the country as tendencies or *nuances* of opinion rather than as political organisms. For the purposes of France as a whole one must think of those four parties, or rather four schools of opinion already noted — the Right or Clerical Monarchist, the Centre or Moderate Republicans, the Radicals or Advanced Republicans, and the Socialists. Of these four only one, the Socialists, constitute a cohesive party in the English or American sense, for they alone have created and maintain a well-knit organization extending over a large part of the country and gripping its members tightly together outside as well as inside the Chamber. Of the other three, the Clericals or Monarchists hold well together, but the number of those among them who profess Legitimist principles has been much reduced, and their organization is confined to certain areas. The other two, Moderate and Advanced Republicans, are divided into the sections already described. Some of these sections have a central party committee as well as a certain number of local committees which carry on a propaganda, publish literature, and look after elections. No party group or section has, however, an organization ramified through all the constituencies like the three parties (Tory, Liberal, and Labour) which divide Great Britain or the still better drilled and more constantly active two great historic parties of the United States. There would be no use in trying to work a Socialist organization in the agricultural parts of Brittany, nor a Monarchist party in Marseilles. Accordingly no section dreams of running in every electoral district candidates of its own particular colour, but confines itself to those in which it has a reasonable chance of success.

If you ask an average French citizen about his political views, he is as likely as not to say that he does not meddle with politics; "Monsieur, je ne m'occupe pas de politique." If, however, he has views and is willing to express them, he will probably prove to be, in the rural parts or small towns of the west and north, either a Conservative of Clerical leanings or a Moderate anti-Clerical Republican; in the south-east, the central, and the eastern regions or small towns, either an Advanced or a Moderate Republican; in the mining districts and the great industrial centres, either an Advanced Republican or a Socialist. There are of course nearly everywhere some men of Socialist views, and everywhere some few Clericals or Monarchists, usually of a Legitimist colour. Candidates, therefore, whatever group in the Chamber they mean to join, belong to one or other of these four types of opinion, and do not — always excepting the Socialists — usually announce themselves to a constituency as adherents of any one Republican group in particular. It is between the four types that the electoral battle rages. The candidate may be sent down, or be financially aided, by the central committee of a group, but he does not necessarily appear as their man, nor (unless he be a Socialist) as selected by a local committee of a particular stripe. He stands on his own account, just as candidates did in Britain in the middle of last century, before parties had begun to be locally organized. When he issues his address, it is accompanied by a list of his chief local supporters, who constitute a sort of general committee, but it is only a few of the more active among them who form, along with the candidate and his agents, the working committee. Other candidates may come forward belonging to the same or a nearly allied section of the Republican party, each recommending himself less by the particular character of his views than by his personal merits and by the fervour of his promises to serve the material interests of the constituency. Candidatures are numerous because not generally costly. There used to be three, four, or five (or possibly more) aspirants to the single seat, perhaps a Monarchist and a Socialist, and three Republicans of slightly different shades, but now under the new system of election by departments with proportional representation, the number is larger. All went to the poll; and when, as frequently happened, none secured an absolute majority, it was usual for the one among the Republicans who had received the fewest votes to retire, so that the Republican party might have the best chance against a Monarchist or a Socialist. There is, however, no established practice in these matters, and an Advanced Radical may feel himself nearer to a Socialist than to a Republican of a less vivid hue, while some moderate Republicans differ but slightly from Conservatives.

Acute French observers distinguish two types of election. In one there is a more or less avowed coalition on the platform of anti-clericalism by the various groups of the Centre and the Left against the groups of the Right. The other type shows a sort of combination or co-operation of the Centre, or Moderate Republicans, with the Right on the platform of anti-Socialism and " social order " against the Socialists and more advanced Radicals. The election of 1906 belonged to the former type, the election of 1919 to the latter. In it the Socialist party suffered a set-back, owing to the uneasiness created by the language and policy of their most extreme men. In France, even more than elsewhere, extremists produce by their activity and vehemence the impression that they speak for the whole party, and thereby damage its cause.

In most constituencies, or at any rate in those dominated by the Advanced Republicans, political committees are kept alive during the interval between one election and another in order to look after the interests both of the party and of the candidate, and work if necessary in local elections, whenever these are fought on political lines, as well as in Senatorial elections for the Department. Such committees are not, as in America, Great Britain, and Australia, elected by the local members of the party, and though often in touch with the Central Committee in Paris of the group with which they are in sympathy, they do not take their orders from it. It may excite surprise that in a country where democratic principles are so ardently professed and where the disposition to work out every principle with consistent logic is so strong, the local committee which conducts the business of the party should not be officially created, and from time to time [1] renewed, as is done in the United States, by a vote of all the local members of the party. The reason is that the bulk of the citizens are less definitely committed to any one party than they are in the English-speaking countries, and that the groupings in the Chamber are not generally represented by like groupings over the country at large. The local committees are rather what used to be called in Scotland " cliques " — small camarillas of persons whose political activity is due either to the fervour of their attachment to a certain set of doctrines or to a desire to secure local influence and obtain the best of what is going in the way of honours and benefits for themselves and their kinsfolk or friends. Such good things are obtainable (as already observed) from the Administration through the deputy, who is the Fountain of Honour. The clique goes to him. He presses the ministry, or tries to overawe the Prefect. Sometimes there is in the clique a strong man who fills the place of the American Boss, but more frequently the deputy is himself a sort of Boss, being in constant and confidential relations with the chiefs of the committee and dependent upon their support, just as they are dependent on him, for without him they could not get those favours the dispensation whereof is the basis of their local power. The men who compose these local cliques — minor officials or ex-officials, shopkeepers, lawyers, doctors, teachers, journalists — constitute, along with the deputies and a few rich men, financiers, chiefs of industry and owners of great newspapers, what are called the *classes dirigeantes* of France, the practical rulers of the country, though of course more or less controlled by that public opinion which they bear a large part in making.

From this description, however, I must not omit two other political forces, the one clerical, the other aggressively anticlerical. In many places, especially in the Catholic West, the *cure* (the priest's house, or what is called in England the

---

[1] Local political party committees in France are a creation of the Third Republic. When universal suffrage had been established and the party system had " got into its stride," some kind of organization became necessary; but the conditions of the country have prevented it from developing to the extent attained in the United States, or even in England and Australia.

parsonage) is the natural centre for ecclesiastical and pro-ecclesiastical action, and there are also some Catholic unions and associations, with numerous branches, which exert power, though probably less power than their antagonists credit them with. Over against these clerical organizations stand the secret Republican societies, and especially the Freemasons. This ancient order, which in America is non-partisan, and in England rather Conservative than Liberal in its proclivi-ties (so far as it has any), is in France, as in Italy and Spain, Republican and anti-religious, and as such is condemned in those countries, as well as in Ireland, by the Roman Church. Its Lodges are in France rallying-grounds for the Advanced Republicans, and are believed to possess immense influence, which (as always happens with secret societies) is sometimes perverted to personal ends. These underground organiza-tions, ecclesiastical and anti-ecclesiastical, create an atmos-phere of mystery and suspicion in local politics not favour-able to the free expression of opinion, and tending to keep sensitive men out of local politics, just as the intrigues of the Chamber deter such men from entering Parliamentary life.

CHAPTER XXII

JUDICIAL AND CIVIL ADMINISTRATION

THE Judicial Bench is one of the oldest and most respected of French institutions, adorned in time past by many
illustrious names, and constituting under the *ancien régime*
what was called the *noblesse de robe*. It is not, as in English-speaking countries, virtually a branch of the profession
of advocacy, but, as in most parts of the European continent,
a distinct calling, which young men enter when their legal
education is finished, instead of being the crowning stage, as
in England, of a forensic career. Englishmen and Americans naturally prefer their own system, which restricts judicial appointments to those who have had experience at the
Bar. This plan would, if applied to republican France, have
one serious drawback. Advocates who were also deputies
might recommend themselves for judicial posts by political
services in the Chamber, and would be likely to retain on
the bench their political proclivities. The British system is
doubtless exposed to the same risk, but both in England and
in Scotland tradition and the fear of professional disapproval have been so strong for more than a century that
though judges are sometimes appointed as a reward for party
services, public opinion keeps them straight. They may
sometimes have a slight half-unconscious bias, but they would
not lower themselves to do the bidding of a government.

Both the higher French judges and the lowest rank, called
juges de paix, are appointed by the Minister of Justice.
Under the old Monarchy judicial posts were purchased; and
Montesquieu defended the system by the remark that if they
had been in the gift of the Crown they would have been bestowed upon Court favourites, probably less competent and
less trustworthy than the sons of judicial families whose
parental purchasers had imbued them with judicial traditions. The appointment is permanent, for, in principle and

as a rule, a judge cannot be removed except with the consent of the *Cour de Cassation,* the highest Court of Appeal. Removals for incompetence or delinquency are rare. But there have been times when the government of the day, fearing the anti-Republican tendencies of some of the judges, has required them to swear fidelity to the Republic, or has, after passing statutes suspending the rule of irremovability, gone so far as to displace a number of those whom they distrusted. This process, called a " purification " (*épuration*), was applied between 1879 and 1883 to remove a considerable number of judges and other legal officials whose loyalty to the Republic was suspected.[1] So bold a step, being the act of a dominant party, gave a shock to public sentiment; but it must be remembered that in a country where the form of government itself is an issue between parties, as was at that time the case, the need for defending existing institutions is deemed to excuse extreme measures. In A.D. 1745 an English judge known to belong to the party of the exiled Stuarts might conceivably have been deemed a potential rebel and extruded from the Bench by an address of both Houses of Parliament.

An easier method of making vacancies to which there can be appointed persons whom a ministry desires to have as judges in any particular court is found in promoting an existing judge and filling his place with the person desired. The hope of promotion from a lower to a higher court is an influence which a minister can, and sometimes does, bring to bear upon a judge. It is in one way or another his interest to stand well with the Government, and, to some extent, even with the deputies from the district in which he sits, which is usually, if he can so arrange, the district to which he belongs by birth or adoption, and where he dwells among relatives and friends. One hears other ways mentioned in which governments or persons of influence with governments have been known to interfere with the ordinary course of justice, such as transferring a case from one court to another, or in the assignment by the *Procureur-Général* (Attorney-General) of a case to a particular *Juge d'instruction* [2] or to the president

1 The number has been given at 982 of the former and 1763 of the latter class.

2 The title given to the official charged with the investigation and

of a particular tribunal; but there seems to be little basis for such charges, for the rules of judicial administration are uniform and pretty strictly observed. Deputies and others who possess influence, political or financial, are reported to approach judges, or give letters recommending litigants to their attention, a proceeding which, though disapproved, is not stamped out.

France has been so proud of her judiciary as to be extremely sensitive to its honour. This makes even small delinquencies noticed and lamented, and engenders suspicions that there may be more delinquencies than the public knows. So far as a stranger can judge, they appear to be rare. The judges are poorly paid, but the dignity of the office attracts capable men of high character, and a laudable standard of legal science is maintained in the decisions, those of the higher courts being reported as carefully, if not as fully, as the judgments of British or American tribunals. The judges in these courts are conspicuous social figures, taking rank among the first citizens of the communities within which they reside. If the government of the hour sometimes gets a little more than it ought from the judges, it gets so much less than it desires, that it has sometimes threatened another " purification." This seems improbable, unless an extreme party should obtain control of both Chambers. Great as is the power in France of abstract democratic theory, no one seems to suggest the direct election of judges by the people. Such a change would be unwelcome to deputies and ministers, who desire to retain all possible kinds of patronage.

THE CIVIL SERVICE

The Civil Service of the country consists, as in England, of a small branch which is political, including the offices which change with each ministry, such as the under secretaries in the central departments, and of that far larger

preparation of a criminal case. This could happen only in those few places where more than one *juge d'instruction* is attached to a tribunal, and the function of the official is only to report if there is a case for a prosecution. The French judicial system, with its separate administrative courts and special treatment of the military and naval services, presents more varieties than are found in English-speaking countries.

It need hardly be said that much less use is made of trial by jury in civil cases than is the practice in England and the United States.

branch which is permanent, carrying on the regular administrative work.

The civil administration is the oldest institution in France. Established under Richelieu and Louis XIV., it was interrupted and, for the moment, shattered, by the first Revolution. Reconstructed by Bonaparte during the Consulate, it has remained little changed in essentials since his time. No more need be said of it than will suffice to indicate the relation it bears to the democratic character of the government. It has suffered at the hands of democracy, yet has shown itself strong enough to mitigate some of the faults it cannot cure.

The Civil Service of France is larger in proportion to the population than that of any other free country, possibly, indeed, than that of any country in Europe or America, because the sphere reserved for local self-governing authorities is so narrow that nowhere else, not even in Germany, is so much work thrown upon the central administration. Men's eagerness to enter even the humbler walks of official life has led to the multiplication of posts by governments tempted to increase their patronage, and has made the competition for posts extremely keen.[1] Elective administrative offices, such as exist in the United States, are unknown, all appointments being made, as in England, by the Executive. Admission to most branches of the service, including those for which special knowledge or training is required, is by competitive examination, while the comparatively few places of a political character, whose occupants change with a change of ministry, lie outside the examination rules. To these the minister appoints at his discretion, probably influenced, at least where the post is of some consequence, not only by the politics of the aspirant, but also by private pressure exerted on his behalf. Promotion within the service is understood to go partly by seniority, partly by merit; but it is also largely governed by the political inducements which the deputy or some other important supporter brings to bear. In this way the less deserving may climb high, while efficiency suffers. No one can be displaced, except for some fault, though vested interests may be preserved by transfer or promotion

---

[1] It is sometimes said that the equal division of inheritances, believed to have the effect of discouraging emigration, tends to increase the eagernesss to obtain posts under government.

to some other post so as to create a vacancy for the man whom influence pushes upwards. The observance of this rule is secured by public sentiment, and especially by the strong corporate spirit of the service itself, which few ministers would venture to offend. The permanent heads of the chief departments are men of proved capacity and high social standing. Their knowledge and experience are indispensable to every government; and, like British officials, they render loyal service to the government of the day, whatever their personal predilections.

The salaries paid to the permanent civil servants are low in proportion to the cost of living, which had risen in France even before 1914; and it would be hard to secure adequate competence but for the widespread desire, extending even to the lower ranks in the official hierarchy, for that social importance which State employment confers. Complaints made relate chiefly to the routine and formally precise or bureaucratic methods which prevail in France almost as much as in Germany. The deeply ingrained habit of obedience to official orders makes these methods endured more patiently than they would be among English-speaking men. The delays that occur in the working of the administrative machine are not altogether the fault of the permanent service, for it is the pressure exercised on ministers for favours that makes the local official await orders and shirk responsibility, since he fears to take any action which might interfere with his chief's desire to oblige.

One branch of the Civil Service has an importance peculiar to France, viz.: that which consists of the teachers in elementary schools, all of whom are appointed and may be dismissed by the Executive. In the course of its conflict with the power of the clergy, the Republican party has by a series of statutes established lay teachers in every public school, and found in them powerful allies. They have organized themselves in a sort of union, and recently sought, against the wishes of the Government, to join the General Labour Federation in order to improve their pay and position. This insubordination — as it is called by the chiefs — is not confined to the teachers. Others among the rank and file of the public employees ask to be allowed to agitate for higher pay and better conditions, arguing that by becoming employees they do not cease to be citizens. The question that has arisen how far such action is compatible with the discipline (said to be already impaired in the Customs department) necessary for efficiency, is serious, and has raised trouble both in Great Britain and in Australia. In the villages the teacher is usually the best-educated and best-informed layman, who adds to his influence over the pupils that influence which belongs to him as being (in most communes) the clerk to and adviser of the Maire. In the State secondary schools and universities no religious instruction is given; but in these public opinion secures perfect freedom for the teachers, and no complaints are made regarding favouritism in appointments or the exercise of political control.

In France the railroads nearly all belong to private companies, but recently one great system, that of the West, was taken over by the Government. Its management became more costly, and the inefficiency charged against it is used as an argument to meet the Socialist demand for the " nationalization " of all railroads. Few other " public utilities " have been undertaken by the State. It draws revenue from a monopoly of tobacco and matches.

The chief local administrative official is the Prefect, a figure to whom there is no one to correspond in any English-speaking country nor in Switzerland. It is he who in each of the eighty-six departments represents the Government for civil purposes.[1] He is appointed, and may be removed, by the ministry at its discretion, no examination or other special qualification being required, since the post is a frankly political one. For his helpers and advisers he has a Prefectural Council, exercising a local jurisdiction over employees and minor administrative affairs; and under him there are Sub-Prefects also, appointed and removable by the ministry of the day, one for each arrondissement, of which there are in France 362. Through these functionaries a ministry carries out its wishes and fills most of the local posts, often consulting the Prefect, but (as already observed) chiefly influenced by the deputy, who has latterly become the stronger through his political hold on the ministry.

The rules of the permanent Civil Service forbid its mem-

[1] Excluding Alsace-Lorraine which stands for the present outside.

bers to take an active part in politics, but when they quietly
work for ministerial candidates they need not fear its disapproval. The Prefect and Sub-Prefect lie under no similar
disability, and frequently go round with a Governmental
candidate.

Two other significant features of the French system must
be here noted. One is the wide legislative power entrusted to
ministers. Statutes are as a rule drawn up in general terms,
leaving many details to be subsequently filled in. This happens to some extent in the United Kingdom, but there the
statute expressly delegates to the Sovereign in his Privy
Council, or to high officials — as for instance to the council
of judges of the Supreme Court, or to the Home Secretary —
power to issue Orders or Rules for carrying out the purpose
of the statute, which, if made within the limits prescribed,
have the force of law. In France, however, ministers are
competent without such special authorization (though this is
sometimes conferred) to issue ordinances binding not only
their subordinates in the administration but the citizens generally. The more important of these are promulgated in the
name of the President, as Decrees. Minor matters are dealt
with by various functionaries, not only individual ministers
but Prefects, and even Maires as heads of communes. These
are called *arrêtés*. The President's power extends to some
slight extent even to the authorizing, in urgent cases, the
borrowing of money (up to a certain limit) by the public
treasury.

The other feature, unknown to English-speaking men
though not to several continental countries, is the recognition of what is called Administrative Law. An official
charged with some dereliction of duty, whether against his
superiors or against a member of the public, is not liable, as
in Britain or the United States, to be either sued or prosecuted in the ordinary Courts for an act done in the course of
his official work. Complaints must be brought before the
Administrative Tribunals, which are constituted of officials,
the jurisdiction of these bodies covering many matters withdrawn from the competence of the ordinary Courts. This
system, an inheritance from the old monarchy, is defended as
required by the principle of the division of powers into Legis-

lative, Executive, and Judicial.[1]   To permit the ordinary
Courts of Law to try a functionary for an administrative act
would be, in French eyes, to allow the Judiciary to interfere
with the Executive, so the very same doctrine which in America secures the independence of the Judiciary from the Executive is used in France to secure the independence of the
Executive, nominally as against the Judiciary, but really as
against the public, for the agents of the Executive thereby
escape direct liability to the citizen, being themselves, through
their special Courts, not only judges of the facts of a
case but also interpreters of the law to be applied.

This rather undemocratic arrangement is an illustration
of the width of the power wielded in France by an executive
which is not only centralized but autocratic.   Yet the exercise of power, since liable to be checked by the legislature,
becomes uncertain in any particular case, for ministers, the
creatures of a large and fluctuating body, exercise their patronage at the wishes of the individual members of that body
and hold their own places at the caprice of its collective majority.   With restricted functions their position would be
more independent and more stable.   But a strong executive
is congenial to French ideas, and every government, be it
republican or monarchical, feeling bound to maintain at all
hazards its own form, has clung to a power which helps it to
repress attempts at revolutionary change, supported by the
feeling of the middle classes that public safety must be
secured.

A part of the administration which deserves mention, because there is nothing analogous to it in any English-speaking
country, is the Council of State.   Founded by Napoleon, this
useful and highly respected body consists of a number of
eminent persons appointed and dismissible nominally by the
President of the Republic, but practically by the ministry of
the day, though it is in practice not frequently changed in
composition.   Its functions are to advise upon certain classes
of ordinances and divers other matters of an administrative
nature, and to sit as a final Court of Appeal from the decisions of administrative tribunals.   This latter duty, which
belongs only to one class of the councillors, seems to be now

[1] The system was on this ground maintained in the Constitution of
1791.

the more important, for advice given on other matters need
not be followed by the ministry.   This Council has won the
commendation of some English writers, who think that some
similar institution might usefully be formed out of the
British Privy Council.   In France itself there are those who
hold that it could well be used more largely than it is for the
purpose of drafting or revising projects of legislation, and
regret that the Ministry and the Chambers are too jealous
of their own powers to share them with a nominated body.

CHAPTER XXIII

LOCAL GOVERNMENT

It has already been pointed out that pre-Revolutionary France had no system of local institutions similar to those of England and the United States. Certain ancient rights of jurisdiction belonged to the noblesse; and local judiciaries existed in the *Parlements* of some of the greater provinces, but administration, civil and financial, had passed into the hands of the officers of the Crown. When the welter of the Revolution ended in 1799, Napoleon, in reconstructing the administrative system of Louis XIV., so strengthened it as to make the hand of the Central Government felt in every part of the country. There was no thought of creating local institutions, still less of putting them upon a popular basis. France was cut up into Departments, on lines which in some cases ignored the old provinces.[1] The departments were artificial divisions, with no corporate tradition, such as still belong to English counties, and awakening no local patriotism. Only one relic of antiquity remained in the rural Commune, a civil as well as an ecclesiastical unit, which, now that the severance of the Catholic Church from the State has extinguished its religious character, remains as the basis of civil organization. To it we shall return presently, when the larger unit of the Department has been described.

Democratic principles require some sort of self-government, so in each Department there has been created an elected council, the *Conseil Général,* chosen by universal suffrage, each canton returning one member who sits for six years, one-half of the whole Council being changed every three years. There are two sessions in each year, one lasting for a month, the other a fortnight. If an extra session is called, the sit-

[1] Often, however, as in Normandy, Brittany, Gascony, Provence, a group of departments corresponds pretty closely with the ancient Province.

tings must not exceed a week.   Its taxing powers are strictly limited, and it can be dissolved by the Government, should it incur their displeasure.   Its chief functions are the care of the departmental roads, a class of highways intermediate between the national roads and the so-called " neighbourhood roads " (*chemins vicinaux*), as well as of the schools and asylums, and it can give subventions to railways.   The narrowness of its sphere is due to the wide powers exercised by the Prefect as the agent of the Central Government.   Not only does he appoint the departmental officials and manage the public institutions, dealing with many matters left in England or the United States to locally elected authorities, but his is the executive hand by which the decisions of the Council have to be carried out, and his power over the Council itself is considerable.   It cannot take action without having received his report on the matter proposed to be dealt with.   Its decisions on certain subjects can be annulled by the Central Government, whose approval is required for its tax levies, and for their appropriations to particular objects. Notwithstanding these limitations, there is considerable competition for seats on the Council, partly because they open a path to public life.   The elections are fought upon the lines of national party, and thereby embittered.[1]   Local would-be leaders find a field for making themselves known, and do so the more easily because the substantial citizens show little interest in the conduct of Departmental business.   A statute of 1884 withdrew from the Councils, as liable to partisanship, a part of the control they had possessed over the affairs of the communes.

The Arrondissement, which is the next largest local circumscription, and was till 1919 the electoral area for the election of a deputy to the Chambers, also possesses a Council (members elected for six years), but of slight importance, since it has neither revenues nor expenses of its own.   So, too, the canton, a still smaller division for judicial and military purposes, need not concern us.

Thus we arrive at the Commune, a local entity which is

---

[1] The fact that the Councils have a part in choosing the Senate has contributed to bring national politics into local elections.   A like result followed in the United States from vesting the choice of the senators in those State Legislatures from which it has been now withdrawn.

over nearly the whole of Central and Western Europe the basis of rural life, bearing in Germany and German-speaking Switzerland the name of *Gemeinde*. It corresponds to the Town or Township of the Northern and Western States of America. In England it was represented by the Parish, but after the middle of the seventeenth century that area had little significance for non-ecclesiastical purposes, until a statute of 1894 created Parish Councils with some civil functions. English and American readers must, however, beware of thinking of a French Commune as if it were what they understand either by a Parish or by a Township. The Commune is just as much urban as rural. It is a municipality capable of holding property as a corporation, and may be as large as Paris or as small as an Alpine hamlet. It has a Communal Council, varying in size from ten to thirty-six members, unpaid, elected for four years by universal suffrage, and themselves electing their Maire,[1] who, besides being the chairman, has administrative functions both as the agent of the Central Government, carrying out the directions of the Prefect, and as the executive in matters falling within the sphere of the Communal Council. In some of these matters the Prefect can interfere to annul the acts of Maire or Council; and he may suspend either, or both, from office for a month, while the Central Government can remove him and dissolve the Council altogether. Subject to this control the Council has a general management of local affairs, though official approval is required for the sale of communal property and nearly all other financial business.[2]

The Commune, or as we should say, Municipality, of Paris is specially regulated. It has a Council of eighty members, but the executive authority belongs partly to the Maires of its twenty arrondissements, who are appointed by the Central Government, partly to two high officials, the Prefect of the Seine and the Prefect of Police. Paris has been too formidable a factor in the political life of France to be left to wander at its own sweet will.

The Councils both of the Departments and of the large

[1] I use the French name, because the word Mayor is to English and American readers indissolubly associated with a city or borough.

[2] Some of the smaller and poorer communes occasionally receive subventions from the public treasury.

urban Communes differ greatly in composition and in competence. In villages the Maire is said to be often imperfectly educated and obliged to lean on the schoolmaster. It is alleged that in some large cities, especially where the Socialists have captured the council, local demagogues have found their way into the councils by profuse promises of benefits to the poorer citizens, that rash experiments have been tried, the legal limits of taxation exceeded, heavy debts contracted, patronage misused in the interests of personal friends and parties, improper advantages, such as free tickets for theatres, given to the councillors. If such abuses have been tolerated by the Prefect or the Minister of the Interior, this is ascribed to political motives, because the Administration may hesitate to quarrel with its friends. About the load of debts which presses many of the large municipalities — debts often contracted with little foresight, and sometimes from electioneering motives — there is no doubt, but the other evils just mentioned do not seem to have spread widely. Serious scandals are rare, and have nowhere reached the dimensions of those, now less frequent than formerly, which have disgraced many North American cities. Honest city government has not been one of the great political problems of France. There is probably some want of skill and of judgment, and a readiness to outstep the limits of the law in pursuing what are believed to be the interest of the masses, but peculation is seldom charged. Both French and German critics of democracy are so trenchant in their censure of the Parliamentary Republic that one cannot but suppose that where there is hardly any smoke there can be little fire.

The reader may ask why in a country democratic in spirit and logical in pushing its principles to their conclusions so little has been done for local self-government. The sovereignty of the people is the corner-stone of the Republic. Why trust a nation of forty millions to deal with questions vital to national existence, and refuse to trust the inhabitants of departments or communes with the management of their local affairs, affairs in which a little mismanagement will not greatly matter?

The first answer is that the permanent Civil Service, a bureaucracy holding power and liking power, doing their work well and believing that the people would not do it nearly so well, resist schemes of decentralization.

The second answer is that ministers and deputies cling to the patronage by which the latter keep their hold on their constituents and the former can win the support of deputies.

The third answer is that all who have ruled France since the Directory which Napoleon overthrew in 1799 have had to fear an insurrection which might change the form of government, whether that form was a Monarchy or a Republic. "Self-preservation is the first law of life. Whatever happens, the Monarchy, or the Empire, or the Republic (as the case may be) must be preserved. All the means needed for that supreme end must be used. The control of the whole administration of the country from the centre is such a means. We have it, we need it, we will keep it. It gives us the police as well as the army. It enables us to fill the local posts with our friends, safe men who will serve us at a pinch. It prevents local bodies which might be at a given moment disaffected, from becoming local centres of open resistance or secret conspiracy. If such bodies commanded large funds, or controlled the police, or were in any way strong and conspicuous enough to influence the masses of the people, they might be a danger. We must not give them the opportunity."

Furthermore, the people of France have not asked for a larger measure of local self-government. They have no such dislike to being governed as used to exist, and to some extent exists still, in England and America; and they care much more for being governed well than for governing themselves. Political philosophers and practical political reformers, from Tocqueville eighty years ago to Taine in our own time, have held up to them the example of the United States as fit to be imitated. Novelists have told them that centralization has injured local social life as well as political life all over France.[1] They have listened unmoved, making no such demand as stirs a ministry to action. No political party could by carrying a full-blown scheme of self-government gain enough credit to compensate for the difficulties of the enterprise, and for the troubles that might be expected before the

[1] See, for example, a striking passage in Octave Feuillet's story, *M. de Camors*, published as far back as the Second Empire.

people had learnt to use self-government wisely. There are
those who tell the observer privately, though few would proclaim it, that little could be gained by entrusting wide functions to communities most of which have not been fitted by
history, and are not fitted by existing social conditions, to use
those functions wisely, for the direction of affairs would be
likely to fall into the hands of plausible demagogues or wily
schemers, the motive forces would be self-interest tempered
by fanaticism, predatory in some places, religious or anti-
religious in others. Local self-government ought not to be
given till the people have learnt to use it. Yet how will they
learn to use it except by trying? This is the old problem
which has always divided thinkers as well as politicians.
Swimming can be learnt only by going into the water, but
if you go in before you can swim you may be drowned.
Those who know the history of Switzerland, America, and
England do not deny the risk, but think it well worth taking.

There has recently arisen a movement called Regionalism,
aiming at the division of France into a number of large administrative governmental areas to be formed by grouping departments on geographical lines in accordance with their respective economic interests and historical traditions, and proposing to confer upon each such area a measure of local au-
tonomy sufficient to relieve the Central Government of many
functions.[1] Considerations already referred to may seem to
recommend such a project, especially if accompanied by a
scheme enlarging the scope of self-government in the existing minor local divisions such as the Arrondissement. But
the idea had not in 1920 so far won popular support as to
make it probable that the legislature would give practical
effect to it at a time when other grave questions were occupying the public mind.

[1] Seventeen such local divisions, each containing from 3 to 10 departments, have been suggested.

CHAPTER XXIV

PUBLIC OPINION

WHAT has been said in preceding pages regarding the history of France and its political parties may serve to explain the characteristics of public opinion in France as compared with other democratic countries.

Public opinion, as we have already seen,[1] is a better ruler, when its will can be ascertained, than is the ballot. But its rule works best when it is National, *i.e.* national in two senses of the word, as being the product of nearly the whole nation, irrespective of local divisions, and as possessing a certain unity and generality of colour and tendency which includes or overrides or mitigates the inevitable divisions of view created by the existence of social classes and political parties. Where each type of class opinion or party opinion is sharply opposed to other types, one can hardly talk of the public opinion of the country at large, so the statesman who desires to obey the national will is driven to estimate the respective strength of each type, treating them as conflicting forces, and to strike a sort of balance between them, according to their power of supporting or resisting a given policy.

France is a large country, in which, strong as is the sense of national unity, marked differences of race and temperament are still discernible. The men of the North-west are unlike those of the East and South-west, while both are unlike the passionate South-east and the more phlegmatic North-east. The Normans are almost a distinct type, but less so than the Basques. In economic conditions also there are contrasts. Large estates remain in parts of the west and centre: in other regions the land belongs in small lots to the peasants. The population of the great manufacturing centres is as excitable as that of the quiet agricultural districts is sluggish and averse to change.

France, moreover, resembles a region where volcanic forces

[1] See Chapter XV. in Part I.

have been recently active. Here and there the ground is seared by explosions. Deep chasms have opened: rumblings are heard which may betoken fresh eruptions. The passions roused in three revolutions are not extinct. The bitterness of the workman against the bourgeois is exceeded by that which rages between the friends and the enemies of the Church. Thus in France public opinion is more profoundly divided than in any other great State. Even in the smaller countries, like Ireland or Australia, one finds no parallel. In Great Britain, though there have been hot conflicts between the two great parties, there have always been many questions outside the party sphere; and there have been plenty of citizens who thought and voted with independence, shifting the balance from one party to another, according to their judgment on the issues prominent at the moment. An acute and dispassionate observer could, not indeed always, yet generally, tell the direction in which the national mind was moving. This is even more true of the United States [1] and of Switzerland and of Canada.

France presents another peculiar feature. In Britain and the United States, as in most free countries, it is chiefly the men who think, speak, and write that form public opinion. Though only a small minority of the population, they are not a class, but shade off imperceptibly into the general body of the nation, the bulk of which, though in very varying degrees, takes some interest in politics. And of those who do the thinking and the speaking, in the capital and all over the country, a comparatively small proportion are members of the legislature or otherwise directly occupied with political work. Still more is this the case in Switzerland, where everybody is expected to possess some sort of knowledge and show some sort of interest in public questions. Not so in France, according to the reports of most foreign observers, who declare that a large section of the population, especially in rural districts and in the smaller towns, cares little about politics unless when some question arises directly affecting their occupation,[2] and that many of those who vote at a gen-

[1] In the United States one must of course except nearly all the coloured people and most of the recent immigrants, many of whom cannot speak English.

[2] Such as was the condition of vine-growing, which produced the angry demonstrations of the "viticoles" some years ago.

eral election, because they are brought up to the polls, give
so slight an attention to public matters that definite opinions
cannot be attributed to them. Their local newspaper contains scarcely any political news. To them business, family
affairs, and social pleasures cover the whole of life; so,
though they count as possible voters, they do not count for
the purpose of expressing (except almost mechanically at
elections) a real popular will.

Frenchmen, however, declare that the foreign observers referred to exaggerate this apparent indifference. The peasant
and the *petit bourgeois* does not wear his opinions upon his
sleeve. Even when he has no clear and decided view on a
particular question or the merits of a particular politician,
he is governed by tendencies, generally persistent, as is
shown by the constancy with which many electoral districts
adhere from one generation to another to candidates of a particular type, be it clerical, or moderate conservative, or that
of the advanced republican parties. The election of 1919 is
cited as indicating the existence of a large body of opinion
which, alarmed by the attitude of the Extreme (or Socialist)
Left, came to the polls in unusual strength, and swung back
from the Left towards the Centre or the Right. Evidently
these voters had been thinking.

There is also a class important by its talents and influence
rather than by its members, which eschews parliamentary
politics. It consists of the men of letters and science, and
includes most of the teachers in the universities and higher
schools, as well as many of those who follow the learned professions. These men seem to stand more apart from the practical political life of the country, both national and local,
than does the corresponding class in Britain or Switzerland
or the United States. They have, however, and they deserve to have, a very real influence in the formation of opinion. They have knowledge and capacity, an admirable power
of expression and a patriotic interest in the country's fortunes. But they are (except the journalists) in little direct
touch with the legislators, less than Englishmen of the same
type would be, so their opinion, though powerful and respected, tells comparatively little, or at any rate not directly,
on the conduct of affairs from session to session.

Premising these facts, let us see what are the chief cur-

rents of political opinion in France. I have already enumerated the parties in the two Chambers, and have indicated
the four main types of which the parties are subdivisions.
The first of these is the Catholic Legitimist, which cherishes
the traditions of the old Monarchy and the Church as they
stood in the days of Louis Quatorze. Though attached in
theory to the ancient dynasty, nearly the whole of this section has ceased to hope for a Restoration. It is now much
more Catholic than Legitimist, three-fourths at least of its
adherents having accepted the Republic. Its real principle
is attachment to Catholicism; and the hostility shown by the
more advanced Republicans to the clergy, even since the dis-
establishment effected in 1903–5, gives it grounds for holding together to defend religion. Most of its members do not
seek to re-establish the Church, but would be content with a
reasonable concordat, the recognition of a place for the teaching Orders in the instruction of the people, and the cessation
of the present anti-Catholic intolerance. Respectable by its
sincerity and by the social influence it can still put forth, it
is not a force of the first order, except in some parts of the
West and North,[1] and in the army, chiefly among the officers.

Such authority as men of a second type of opinion exert,
springs rather from the eminence than from the numbers of
those in whom it is embodied. These are the moderate Republicans, whose ideal, influential in 1848–49 and again in
1870–75, of a conservative Republic, upholding the rights of
property, repressing attempts at disorder, and carefully hus-
banding the national revenue, has lost favour in France. It
has still some distinguished literary exponents and the sympathy of a large part of the cultivated bourgeoisie; but its
force, scanty if we regard the votes it can command, is felt
chiefly in the unseen restraint which it imposes, largely

[1] An extremely interesting study of the political character of the
western and north-western parts of France may be found in the book
of M. André Siegfried, *Tableau politique de la France,* and some valuable articles on the same subject by the Count de Calan have appeared
in the *Revue politique de l'École Libre des Sciences politiques* during
recent months. The persistence of political attitude since 1789 shown
by constituencies in the south-west, north-west, and south-east of France
is remarkable. There is more changefulness in the Central regions. It
is to be wished that some British student would undertake a like local
enquiry into the political proclivities of British counties and cities, and
the causes thereof.

through the official class, upon projects of rash change. It has even a certain distant tenderness for the Church, less from religious sympathy than from a sense that religion exerts a steadying influence. It acquiesces in the existing Constitution, fearing that something worse might follow were that to be tampered with, but it disapproves the methods by which deputies and ministers work the system, and recoils from some of their proposals.

No sharp line can so far as respects specific articles of political faith be drawn between these Moderates and the third main type composed of the more numerous Advanced Republicans of the Left. But there is a difference of temper and tendency. The Radical school of opinion professes more faith in the masses, and is committed to semi-socialistic experiments planned in their interest. It looks back to 1791–93 as the Moderates look back to 1789–90, and cherishes the memories of the revolutions in which Paris overthrew four monarchies in succession. If any one type of opinion can be said to dominate the country it is this, for it is strong in the east and south and in most parts of the centre.

Finally, there is Socialist opinion. Of those who profess it, some are more, some less, attached to the doctrines of Proudhon or to those of Karl Marx, some more ready than others to resort to the general strike and even to violence. But all agree in desiring an economic reconstruction of society upon a collectivist or communistic basis. Many, probably most, of the leaders are not themselves hand-workers, but literary or professional men. Though the Socialists, being the best organized and best disciplined of all the parties, may be deemed a well-defined body, socialist opinions are not confined to that organized party, and the more advanced Radical views melt into those of the less advanced Socialists. While many Radicals are permeated by collectivist doctrine, not a few eminent Socialists have from time to time quitted the party to enrol themselves in the Radical ranks, either modifying their former views or recognizing that the time has not arrived for translating theory into practice.

Let it be noted that all the sections of the Republican Left, whatever their differences, have a bond of union in their hostility to Clericalism, and therefore to Monarchy which

they associate with Church power.   This is the dividing line
that goes deepest.

Besides these various schools of political thought, a tendency has now and then emerged which is not so much a
Doctrine or Programme as a manifestation of discontent with
the existing system of government.   A few sentences may
serve to explain its origin.

When Louis Napoleon's *coup d'état* overthrew the Second
Republic in 1851, he hastened to legalize his position by asking for, and obtaining, a plebiscite or popular vote of the
whole nation,— for universal suffrage then already existed,—
by which he was chosen President for ten years.   A similar
vote taken in 1852 made him Emperor, the majorities being
large on both occasions.   Many Frenchmen have been captivated by the notion of a popular dictatorship, a government
by one man, democratic in its source, because it springs
straight from universal suffrage, but uncontrolled in its exercise, because not dependent on the favour of a legislature.   Despite the calamities which the Second Empire
brought upon France, this idea kept alive a large party,
which called itself Bonapartist, and commanded many votes
in the Chamber down till the death of Louis Napoleon's son
in 1879.   Thereafter the party declined, there being no representative of the family whose personal merits recommended
him as its standard-bearer, and for many years past candidates for the Chamber have ceased to offer themselves as
Bonapartists.   But the type of doctrine, the tendency which
prefers not a constitutional monarchy but a popular dictatorship to the rule of a legislature, has persisted as a protest
against Parliamentarism, cherishing a desire to strengthen the
Executive, whether by conferring greater powers on the
President or by setting up some new kind of authority
through which the country, delivered from the intrigues of
the Chamber, may stand stronger and more united in the
face of foreign foes.   It was this tendency which, suddenly
developing with unsuspected force, made a hero of General
Boulanger, who was supposed to have in him the makings
of a dictator.   It reappeared in the days of the Dreyfus conflict, when the anti-Semites and the rich and the timid clamoured for strong government.   Never definitely embodied in

a party, it has gained support from every quarter in which
there was discontent. Monarchists favoured it: Clericals
welcomed it, and so did a large section of the army, of which
it frequently proclaimed itself the champion. It drew votes
from a section of the Radicals, even from a section of the Socialists. Blossoming into a party, it took the name of Nationalist, but as it found no leader who could be put forward
as a candidate for the Presidency, much less for an avowed
dictatorship, it presently withered and subsided as an organization. Yet the tendency remains, for it is on its practical side an inevitable reaction against the faults of " Parliamentarism," and on its theoretical side an expression of
democratic faith in universal suffrage and the direct action of
the people through the man of their choice. It finds vent
in the proposals frequently launched for enlarging the powers
of the President, so as to give him a leadership and authority
independent of his ministers. It has to be reckoned with as
a real, though a variable and unpredictable force. How far
the experiences of the Great War will affect it remains to be
seen. None of the military chiefs who won fame in that war
has sought to turn his influence to any political purpose.

Through what organs do these types of opinion express
themselves, and how is their respective strength to be gauged?
All are represented in the two Chambers. All appeal to the
public through the press, and by meetings, though these are
less frequent, excite less interest, and play (except in the
great cities) a smaller part in public affairs than popular
gatherings do in Britain or America. It is naturally the
more numerous and the more advanced parties, especially
Radicals and Socialists, who make most, and the Conservative
Republicans who make least use of popular demonstrations.
An army moving to the attack will shout or sing: that which
stands still stands silent.

All these types have their exponents in the newspaper press,
of which, as being both an index and a moulder of opinion,
some words must be said.

The French Press presents forms of excellence and forms
of turpitude more extreme than can be found in other great
countries. The worst journals live by blackmailing and
other base arts. The best reach a dignity of manner not surpassed and a perfection of literary expression hardly equalled

elsewhere. Their articles may not contain more knowledge and thought than did two or three of the ablest newspapers of Vienna, of Buda Pest, and of Germany, but they are better written, the French language being singularly adapted to this form of literature, for which the ablest French pens of the last hundred years created an admirable tradition. In these best newspapers one finds a wide outlook, a philosophic insight, a familiarity with the politics of other European countries, and a felicity of phrase which have rarely, if ever, been found combined in the press of any capital save Paris.

This is an old characteristic: two other features of the French Press are more recent. One is the business character which the newspapers of the largest circulation have assumed. They are great commercial enterprises, returning immense profits to their owners, and it is the profits that come first in the minds of their owners. Nowadays a newspaper lives by advertisements rather than by circulation, so it becomes necessary to secure advertisements. Circulation is desired because it draws the advertiser. These things being so, the owner is obliged both to propitiate that part of the business world whence advertisements come, and to avoid whatever is likely to reduce his circulation by offending any large body of readers. Hence — so it is alleged — a great journal cannot to-day show so much independence as formerly. Some one has said, " When the opinions of a journal begin to count, it ceases to have opinions." There are other ways in which newspapers are subject to influences. They like to stand well with the powers that be in the world of commerce and finance. They desire the latest, most exact, and most secret political news from abroad. Since this is in the gift of the Government, one must be on good terms with the Government in order to have it. A tacit understanding with ministers suits both parties, for ministers, when they obtain press goodwill, have a guarantee against attack, imperfect, no doubt, yet worth something, while the journal gets what helps its circulation. It is good policy to receive the proprietor or editor when he asks an interview, and to take reporters around in the special train when the President goes on a tour. The deputies follow suit, and confide to the newspaper such news as they can impart. Even the judicial bench seeks praise from the press.

While noting the above facts, generally true as regards the influence of newspapers in the country and at normal times — so far as any times can be called normal — another fact also is to be remembered. The small circle of persons who in Paris habitually occupy themselves with politics, *i.e.* with ministerial intrigues and changes, with gossip about foreign affairs, and with schemes for reaping pecuniary crops on that field where business and politics meet — this small crowd of ministers and deputies, with the buzzing swarm that surrounds ministers and deputies, is much influenced by the Parisian newspapers, especially at the arrival of a ministerial crisis. A scathing article may destroy the chances of an aspirant or wreck a possible combination. The incisive skill of French journalism which inflicted such wounds on Napoleon III. in his palmiest days, shows itself at these moments with unabated force. It permits itself much licence, but without that licence many truths which need to be told might remain unspoken.

These phenomena are not confined to France. Similar causes have been producing them everywhere. More peculiar to France is the ownership of a journal by some eminent politician, who writes in it or uses it as his organ, so that it gives currency to his views and becomes identified with his plans and aspirations. This is fairer to the public than a secret league between a newspaper and a minister, who is expected to reward it (as happens in some other countries) by an appointment or the bestowal of an honour. The open advocacy of the views of a particular statesman, or group, by his or its newspaper, supplies to some extent the decline in the freedom and earnestness with which politics are handled in the most widely circulated journals, which would appear to be to-day less purely political than they were thirty or forty years ago. As financial interests have grown more powerful and financiers have thrown their tentacles over politics, those newspapers which finance can use have in losing independence lost much of their value, both as critics and as leaders.[1]

It must not, however, be forgotten that the influence of

[1] Not a few journals, even among those of importance, are believed to have succumbed to the wiles of " interests," foreign or domestic, but the truth of these allegations is not easily ascertained.

the Parisian press, which alone most foreigners see, great as it is in and in a circle around the capital, declines rapidly when that point in the circle is reached where it is the local newspapers that the householder reads before the day's work begins.   Cities like Lyons and Nantes, Bordeaux and Marseilles, have powerful and well-written journals which escape some of the temptations that beset the capital.   They follow the proceedings of the legislature closely and, like the newspapers of Manchester, Liverpool, Birmingham, and Scotland, deal effectively with general as well as local issues.   It is often said that both these leading provincial papers and their readers take politics more seriously than do the Parisians.

Men ask in France whether it is the press that guides public opinion or public opinion that guides the press.   Both processes go on, but the ability of a journalist is shown, not so much in following and heightening the sentiment of the moment as in presaging the course which any sentiment is just beginning to take, and heading his ship that way before his rivals.

The type of opinion which most needs the help of the press is the Conservative Republican, because though strong in intellectual resources it is weak in numbers and organization. The stranger who admires it as literature is apt to overestimate its influence.   In reality neither its organs nor those of the extreme schools already enumerated (always excepting the Socialist papers read by Socialist workmen) reach the masses of the people.   But there are papers read by them, and especially those read by the rural voter, which do not make politics their main concern, since it is not for their politics that men buy them.   Local affairs, agricultural affairs, conspicuous crimes, and what are called *faits divers* form the staple of their news.   The proceedings of the Chambers, scantily reported in nearly all journals, are in these barely adverted to, so when an important speech is delivered by a Minister which the majority in the Chamber desires to bring before the people, it is printed on a broadsheet and sent down to all the communes, to be pasted up on the wall of the Mairie to be read by the good citizen.   Whether the good citizen spends much time in perusing it there may be doubted. I have never seen him so engaged.   These things seem to show that the press, or at any rate the Parisian press, is no sure index to the views or probable action of the agricultural electors.

How, then, is opinion formed? Among the industrial workers of the towns largely by the Radical or Socialist press which developes, as events occur, views of the type its readers already hold. To some extent, among the upper section of the professional and commercial class, by one or more of the leading journals of the capital, and among the middle or poorer sections of the bourgeoisie generally, by talk in the cafés of the town where they live, or perhaps at their clubs (*cercles*), for the French, being a sociable people, spend more of their evenings in one another's company than do the English or the Americans, and if they care at all about politics, discuss current events eagerly. Opinion seems to be formed more than in England by talk and less by the printed page, though of course each man's paper supplies the facts, or its version of the facts, upon which the discussions of the café proceed. The power of any single newspaper over its readers may be less than it has often been in England and in Australia. But the press can probably do more than it could in those countries to disparage or discredit a politician whom it seeks to ruin, for the French public is suspicious, apt to presume some foundation for charges positively brought, while the law of libel is notoriously ineffective where politics are concerned. Able and judicious as are some of the newspapers in each of the great provincial cities, the capital has been the chief factory in which political opinion is made. Though Goethe was fond of dwelling on the immense value of Paris as the meeting-place of philosophers, writers, and artists, it might be better for the country to have independent centres of political thought such as Germany has had, and as are guaranteed to America by her vast extent. They give to opinion a greater variety, and tend to soften the asperities of conflicts waged too exclusively on the same parliamentary battlefield.

Returning to the main issue, we have to ask how far public opinion, as compared with the legislative and executive machinery of government, is fit to direct the domestic and foreign policy of France. In the United States and Switzerland public opinion rules. To a less degree it rules in England also. Does it rule in France?

France differs from these three countries in two ways. In all of them a large majority of the voters are interested in public affairs, so a statesman of insight can usually discover the general trend of their views and wishes, even when he cannot predict precisely the result of an election, for many secondary questions affect different sets of voters. Opinion is so widely diffused among the more passive sections as well as among the more active, that it can be tolerably well tested in all classes. It is in the air which men breathe. But in France a somewhat larger section of the voters have few positive opinions, but are moved rather by tendencies, grounded on habit or a vague sense of their own interests, or on a feeling for or against the Church or the château, or on a dislike of the bourgeoisie. Such tendencies, even when they determine their permanent attitude to a party, do not necessarily prescribe their votes on every current issue, some of which may not affect personal interests or appeal to religious proclivities.

On the other hand, that part of the French people which, holding definite views, cares for and watches public affairs, is sharply divided into different schools of thought and (less sharply) into political parties. The extreme schools differ on fundamentals, even on the form of government and the economic structure of society. Thus when we take all these schools and groups in the aggregate, we find in them no general public opinion, but rather a congeries of dissident opinions, incapable of being brought into harmony. It is an orchestra of clashing instruments. So sharp is the clashing that, whereas in America and England one can reckon on a disposition to acquiesce in the decision of the majority once that decision has been given, one cannot so reckon in France. The will which an election reveals may remain the will of the strongest factions only, not of the nation as a whole. The statesman has to keep his eye on the conflicting parties as abiding factors and calculate their present or prospective strength. He cannot make a national harmony out of the discordant notes and try to sing in tune. To this, however, there is the one exception, which I have already mentioned. On the main lines of foreign policy there has been a truly national public opinion. Differences of course there must be as to the prudence of any particular diplomatic step.

Differences there were before the war as to the extent of the military precautions required; but these differences rarely weakened the Executive in its conduct of foreign relations. Pride and patriotism imposed silence on factions.

Secondary issues are, however, too much left to the Chambers and the group of political journalists who manufacture opinion in Paris. Here, as in England, the knowledge of foreign affairs and the interest felt in them have been too slender to enable the people to hold in check the schemes of adventurers pressing for the assumption of responsibilities abroad, and to exercise that control over foreign policy which is needed for the doing of justice and the maintenance of peace. The journals and coteries of Paris are in this sphere not sufficiently restrained by the opinion of the provinces.

It may help the reader to comprehend the peculiarly complicated phenomena of France if I try to present the forces and influences at work on politics in yet another form of classification, enumerating six classes or sets of citizens of most importance.

First come the peasantry, more than half of the total number of voters, knowing little, and often caring little about politics, but, shrewd in their way, thrifty almost to excess, and of a conservative temper.

Secondly, the working men in cities and other great industrial centres. Knowing more and caring more about public matters than do the peasants, but also regarding them chiefly from the side of their own interests, they are not generally revolutionists, but eager for changes that promise to better their condition.

Thirdly, the commercial sections of the middle classes, forming the great bulk of the bourgeoisie, thinking first of their business, valuing the stability of institutions, and, like their peasant neighbours, suspicious of novelties.

Fourthly, the professional classes, who while in one sense a part of the bourgeoisie, are more generally highly educated men, many of them occupied with letters or science, well qualified and disposed to take a lively interest in politics both foreign and domestic.

Fifthly. Across and through all these classes and the material interests by which each of them is moved, strikes the influence of religion and the Catholic Church, an influence whose appeal to tradition and emotion is capable, at moments, of thrusting aside or overriding all considerations of material interest — the peasant's passion for the land, the bourgeois' love of a quiet life, the intellectual detachment of the scholar or man of science.   Among the workers also there are those over whose capacity for idealism socialistic doctrines can exercise a power like that of religion.

Lastly there are the plutocrats of finance and industry, insignificant in number, but strong by the influence which wealth always confers, and which it here exerts, chiefly in secret, through the press.   There are, probably, among them some disinterested patriots, but, taken as a whole, they are more distinctly " out for themselves first, last, and all the time," than any other section of the community, and this concentration of effort on a single definite end is one of the sources of the power of wealth, apparently greater in France than anywhere else in the world.

CHAPTER XXV

THIS survey of the persons by whom France is ruled and of the methods which deputies, ministers, and officials are wont to employ, needs to be completed by a few words on public life as a whole, its purity and its general tone. All that foreign observers have said in censure of the two former classes has been surpassed in acrimony by critics who are themselves Frenchmen. The stranger who seeks to discover the truth from books and newspapers feels bound to discount much of what native writers say about their countrymen, as due to that warmth of partisan feeling which has for forty years been more intense here than elsewhere in Europe. Some faults, moreover, which belong to politics in all countries, and were at least as evident under the three preceding monarchies, are now held up to scorn as if peculiar to the present régime. But how much, then, are we to discount the sum total of the iniquities charged against the Third Republic? I have tried to correct the exaggerations of political polemics by the opinions of impartially minded French friends, but while the conclusions to be here stated seem to me generally true, it is with the greatest diffidence that I submit them.

Let us begin with the ordinary citizen. Is his vote at an election purchasable? The Commissions which investigate these matters take evidence laxly, and the Chamber is influenced in its decisions by party motives. But the upshot seems to be that the giving and receiving of bribes is rare. Few candidates can afford to spend money in this way; and though here, as in other countries, the voter may see little harm in making something out of his vote, the process is too costly to be often employed in the large constituencies universal suffrage has created.

As respects members of the Legislature and Ministers, for

these classes may be considered together, it is especially hard to speak positively.   The resounding explosion of the Panama affair, in which it was proved that immense sums had been diverted from the making of the Canal to private gains, and that some of these had gone to purchasing support in the Chamber, possibly from a few ministers and certainly from some deputies, created an atmosphere of suspicion which lasted for years, like the smoke that continues to hang over the spot where a high explosive shell has struck the ground. A scandal so tremendous seemed to confirm the vague suspicions that had existed before: and it tended to render probable charges subsequently made.   That very few persons were ultimately convicted scarcely diminished the effect, because it was known that some of the accused had escaped justice, either for want of evidence or through official connivance, and no one could be sure how many these might be.   Nothing similar has occurred since, yet the memory of Panama has remained to be used as a reproach against Parliamentary government, even by those who know that there were scandals in the days of Louis Philippe, when the intellectual character of the Chamber stood high, and more numerous scandals in the eighteen years' reign of Napoleon III. than the Republic has seen during the last fifty.

That there are some corruptible members of the Legisture is probable.   Such men are to be found in every large assembly, though in a few the standard of probity has been kept so high that they seldom venture to affront it.   Some sources of temptation are absent.   Those private Bills, promoted in the interests of some commercial or industrial enterprise, or granting a valuable concession of public rights to private undertakings, which are the chief source of corruption in American legislatures, scarcely exist in France. Few new railroads have been constructed of late years: few projects are brought forward which affect business men sufficiently to make it worth their while to approach legislators. Those who seek their own interests in the imposition or reduction of protective duties on imports generally pursue their aims openly.   Nevertheless it does happen that large financiers, or firms desiring to develop undertakings abroad, as for instance in Turkey, or in the colonies, do attempt to bring improper influences to bear: and sometimes they succeed. Persons who ought to know assure me that the percentage of purchasable deputies is trifling, but that a good many are not above using their position for gainful purposes, as an advocate may extend his practice by his position in the Chamber, or as a deputy can profit by indirectly helping a commercial company. Some evidence of the anxiety which the connection of senators and deputies with business undertakings has been causing may be found in the bills introduced to declare certain positions incompatible with that of a legislator. The provisions of the existing law declare the ineligibility for a seat of any one who exercises a public function paid by State funds (with a very few exceptions for Ministers and others), of any one who is a member of a "Commission Départmentale," or chosen by a *Conseil Général,* and of a director of three great steam-packet companies which hold postal service concessions from the Government. It was proposed by a bill of 1917 to extend this ineligibility to persons discharging either any function paid by the funds of the State, or of a Department, or of a Commune, or of a Colony, or any function to which a person may be nominated by the State in any financial, industrial, or commercial company or enterprise; and the bill would also forbid members of either Chamber, Ministers, and Under Secretaries of State to take part in any bargain or adjudication to which the State, or departments, or communes are parties in respect of work to be done or goods to be supplied. One can conjecture the evils at which such provisions as these are aimed.

The name of a deputy on the directorate of an incorporated company has lost what value it once possessed, because confidence has been shaken. A deputy may possibly, and a minister will usually, know facts enabling him to speculate in stocks with a prospect of success, and the opinion of his fellow-members deals leniently with this form of what is called *tripotage.* Though it is thought unbecoming for a politician to be mixed up with business matters, a slur on his reputation does not shut the door of office against him. The deputies and ministers who lack private fortune are not those round whom suspicion most frequently hovers, nor has the receipt of a salary lowered the moral standard, except in so far as it creates a further motive for giving an unconscientious vote in order to retain a seat. Public opinion is sensitive on the subject of pecuniary gains by politicians: it is only a talent which approaches indispensability that obtains impunity for transgressors. When stories are profusely circulated censoriousness tends to defeat itself, because if many accusations are made and remain unproved, people begin to treat the subject lightly, giving weight only to a few charges, and not troubling themselves to discriminate between the rest, for in despair of reaching the truth they cease to probe matters to the bottom.

A singularly fair-minded French observer, who tells me that during the last forty years the intellectual level of the deputies has slightly risen, while their moral level has slightly fallen, attributes this to two causes which have little to do with politics. The diffusion of higher education among the middle and lower middle and even the wage-earning classes has enabled a larger proportion than formerly of able men of humble origin to enter Parliament. Such men are less responsive to the standards set by a highly cultivated society because they have never belonged to it. They have brought with them less polished manners and less refined tastes, and they represent that new spirit which, pursuing merely material aims, is indifferent to religious or philosophical principles, a spirit which, though deemed characteristic of the generation that has grown up under the Republic, is not necessarily due to the Republic. There was plenty of irreligion and of licence, as well as plenty of corruption, under the Second Empire. The philosophic enthusiasts who championed liberty against Louis Napoleon believed that the Republic would bring purer morals and a loftier public spirit. But these things the Republic has not yet brought.

As respects the public departments, it has been already observed that their management has been on the whole honest and efficient. The branch in which lavish expenditures, with inadequate results, have most frequently occurred is the navy, but in all countries jobs or peculations may be looked for where large contracts are placed. Even the admirably organized and strictly disciplined public service of Germany has not been exempt. The eagerness to concentrate fire upon Parliamentarism may dispose French critics to spare their Civil Service, but certainly one hears few charges brought against its members. They have a pride in their work and a sense of professional solidarity which makes the upper ranks of the service at any rate feel that every man is the guardian of the honour of the profession as well as of his own.

The same may be said of the Judiciary. It is above pecuniary seductions. Yet the statements heard from many quarters, that judges are sometimes affected by political influences, proceeding either from the government, or from persons in touch with the government, cannot be disregarded. On the other hand, cases are quoted in which governments have demanded from the judges what the latter have refused to give. It would seem that though little harm may have so far resulted there is need for watchfulness. Public opinion is perhaps too tolerant of attempts to affect the impartiality and independence of the Bench. The habit of writing letters to judges about cases that come before them is a dangerous one, and the practice of promoting judges from lower to higher posts creates temptations, since it provides a motive for trying to stand well with the Government.[1] Some promotions of course there must be. They exist in England, where the most capable High Court judges of first instance are raised to the Court of Appeal, and in the United States, where District and Circuit judges are sometimes sent to the Supreme Court. But in both these cases the public opinion of the Bar, from which all judges are taken, provides a safeguard against favouritism. As French judges are not drawn from the Bar, it knows less of them and takes less interest in their careers.

When we come to what is called the Tone of public life it is still harder to form a correct estimate. What does the term mean? It can be felt rather than described, being something whose presence is, like a scent, impalpable but unmistakable. It is a quality in the atmosphere, delightful when it stimulates, depressing when it lowers intellectual or

---

[1] A veteran statesman, candidate for the Senate, describing himself as "ni libéral ni progressiste, ni radical ni socialiste," but "tout simplement républicain," wrote in November 1911 as follows: to the electors "Trouvez-vous que la justice soit assez indépendante, l'armée assez protégée contre les influences politiques, la masse grossissante de nos fonctionnaires est-elle assez pénétrée du sentiment de la discipline? Le scepticisme et l'apathie des citoyens paisibles ne font-ils pas de redoutables progrès, et l'audace impunie des autres? . . . Vous sentez-vous assez gouvernés?"

moral vitality. It is open-minded, free from prejudice and intolerance, governed by the love of truth. It is also imaginative and emotional, feeling the greatness of a nation's life, gladly recognizing the duty and the privilege of serving the State. It is patriotic in that sense of the word which implies that a nation ought to aim at righteousness as well as at power. Even in ambitious men it restrains the promptings of mere self-interest. It insists that those to whom the people have given their trust as representatives or as officials, should show themselves worthy of a nation's best traditions, sets a high standard for those who come forward as leaders, expects from them not only good taste and decorum, but also honour and a respect for one another's honour, requires them not only to apply the principle of *noblesse oblige* to themselves, but also to assume that opponents are to be treated with respect till they show themselves unworthy. Whoever has sat for many years in a representative assembly comes to know what its " tone " is by noting what acts or words it permits or condemns, what persons it admires or distrusts, and he learns how to discriminate between the tone of one parliament and another, as an ozonometer might be used to test the health-giving quality of air on a hilltop or in a swamp.

" Tone " in this sense is formed partly by tradition, which has by long observance set up a standard whereto public men are expected to conform, partly by the number and weight in the political life of a country of those who, admitted to be above all mendacity or treachery in the relations of private life, carry the same sense of honour into their public action. Such men are found in every class and every social stratum. They are also wanting in every class, in the socially highest as well as those who would be called the humblest. But as it is those of social standing who are most easily made amenable to the opinion of their own class and to the standards that class recognizes, it is an advantage to a country when such men, possessing also the intellectual gifts which make them eminent, are numerous in its public life, for they are obliged to respect the rules of conduct imposed by the society in which they move.

The political atmosphere in which French politicians live is not easily described. Everywhere in the world divergent views are expressed regarding the morals and manners of public men, and veterans are prone to note and lament a decline.   But in France the vehemence of partisanship makes the divergence specially marked, for those who dislike the present political system begin by decrying its products. What does seem tolerably clear is that the public men of to-day, and especially the deputies, receive less respect and deference than did their predecessors in the first ten years of the Third Republic.   The dignity of the Chamber has sunk. Vituperation abounds; injurious charges are bandied to and fro, and seem, because so frequent, to be little resented.   The odour of intrigue, never absent from any legislature in any country, seems rank in the Palais Bourbon,[1] and the talent for intrigue counts for as much as does oratory or administrative capacity.   A man universally distrusted may be among the busiest in contriving combinations to oust successive ministries in the hope that before long his own turn of office will arrive.   Whether it is better to have or to want that hypocrisy which has been described as the tribute Vice pays to Virtue, is a question often debated.   Here, at any rate, there is little of it.   Yet corruption, judicially proved, does exclude a man from office, and the possession of a stately and unblemished character commands authority as well as respect.   Even those who do not imitate can admire.

A minister who goes touring in the provinces is welcomed with external marks of deference far exceeding those that would be offered to a British or an American official of equal rank, for in France authority is honoured.   But the individual man who holds the authority may not receive at other times the confidence and respect of his fellow-citizens.   He is assailed — even Presidents have been assailed — in language rare in America and unknown in Switzerland, rare even in England, where personal attacks have been latterly more malignant than they were seventy years ago.   Though the conception of the State as a supreme and all-embracing power may inspire in France a sort of awe unknown in those countries, and posts under the State are more eagerly sought, the fact of serving it does not implant a higher sense of responsibility and duty.   There are a few religious idealists and a few Socialist idealists, but apart from these and from

[1] The building in which the Chamber sits.

that reverent devotion which the thought of France and her position in the world inspires, one is struck, no less than in the legislatures of America or Australia, by the pervasively materialistic spirit.   In a new country like Australia it is not surprising to find a certain commonness in political life. But France is the country which has at times seemed to live by its ideals, and which in bygone days set to Europe the standard of chivalric honour.

This state of things, often complained of by Frenchmen, is sometimes treated as a result and sometimes as a cause of the comparative paucity among present day politicians of such students, writers, and thinkers as adorned the legislatures of the Restoration, of the Orleans Monarchy, of the Second Republic, and, indeed, of the earlier years of the Third Republic.   True it is that neither Congress nor the British House of Commons is richer in such men than is the French Chamber.   It is chiefly by comparison with its former brilliance that the latter seems nowadays to shine with faint or few lights of genius.   Yet a country so fertile in spiritual independence and keen intellectual activity ought to see more of its most gifted sons seeking to enter its governing assembly.   Why do comparatively few enter?   Partly, men say, because the position of a deputy no longer carries social distinction outside the district which he represents, while the daily work of a deputy is laborious and humiliating.   A scholar, a university professor, a scientific investigator, even an advocate in large practice, would have to renounce his pursuits in order to hold his seat by such arts as are forced on the deputy.   Many who would like to enter are practically debarred by the want of local connection, for having their home in Paris they may be unable to recommend themselves elsewhere.   Partly also because men of this type have little chance with constituencies.   The good graces of local cliques are more easily won by the local doctor or lawyer or business man who will devote himself to local interests, or, where there is room for a stranger, by a wealthy manufacturer or financier from some great city.   It is also alleged that in parts of the country a man of old lineage or polished manners suffers from his social status.   The rural or small town electors want some one of their own class, while the wage-earners regard a wearer of a black coat as a natural enemy.   These tendencies, discouraging to men of refinement or of a philosophic cast of mind, would operate still more widely but for the diversity of social conditions in different parts of the country. The monarchical and Catholic West, for instance, though not more susceptible to ideas than other regions, offers a better chance to members of old landed families, often more independent of their constituents than a member can be where the masonic lodge or other local clique rules.

CHAPTER XXVI

WHAT DEMOCRACY HAS DONE FOR FRANCE

H<small>E</small> who should try to set forth and weigh against one another the defects and merits of popular government in France
under the Third Republic would himself err and mislead
others if he failed to remember the conditions under which
it has had to live since 1870. These conditions have been
made by the past, and by it only can they be explained.
Without repeating the historical sketch presented in Chapter XVIII., I will try to show, by briefly comparing the results of political development in England with those visible
in France, the advantages which the former has enjoyed for
working democratic institutions.

In England the compact framework of society changed
very slowly from A.D. 1500 to 1900. The ancient aristocracy
of land and birth passed by degrees into a new aristocracy of
wealth. The old ties that held each class to those that were
above it or below it, though slowly changed in character, were
never roughly broken.

In France the old feudal order lasted down till 1789,
though it had become a hollow shell. It continued sharply
cut off from the bourgeoisie, and the bourgeoisie were also, if
less sharply, cut off from the peasantry and the artisans.
Since the First Revolution there has been going on what the
French call a *morcellement* within each class, a dissolution
of each social stratum into social atoms.

In England there was, except at a few crises, such as Wat
Tyler's rising in 1381, very little class hatred and no permanent class antagonism. Neither is there to-day. It has
appeared in one of the British colonies, though in no acute
form, and its appearance there surprises the British visitor.[1]

In France the three classes disliked one another before the
Revolution. The old aristocracy of birth is now reduced to

[1] See chapter on Australia, *post*.

comparatively few families, and the new industrial and financial plutocracy which has arisen out of the bourgeoisie cannot look down on its immediate parents. But that plutocracy is hated by the industrial masses, and it fears them.

In England there were traditions of the independence of the legislature and of its power to assert popular rights going back to the fourteenth century; and since the middle of the seventeenth the privileges and usages of Parliament had become familiar to the nation. Every man who entered the House of Commons knew, or soon learnt, how to work the Parliamentary machine.

In France the ancient and cumbrous representative institution of the States-General had died out, and a new start was made at the First Revolution, without experience and in the midst of excitement.

In England the national mind was from early times pervaded by the idea of the supremacy of Law, a law based on the old customs of the people, a Law of the Land which operated not only as between the king's subjects but against the king himself if he sought to transgress it. When the day came for restricting the power of the king, that which was taken from him went to Parliament, and the last thing which Parliament desired was to entrust any discretionary power to the State — a word seldom used in England — or to any State-appointed local officials.

In France the Crown was not restrained. The ideas of Justice and Law were clearly grasped, and justice was skilfully administered as between subject and subject, but the conception of what law should be between subject and sovereign was clouded by a feeling that public interest must prevail against private interests, perhaps also by the texts which lawyers and judges drew from the law of imperial Rome. Thus no well-defined line was drawn limiting the powers of the State, and *Raison d'état* was allowed to justify the overriding of the subjects' rights. When that argument was used, law was affected as is the needle when a magnet is brought near to a compass. The men of 1789 found this doctrine and practice existing; they used it and let it pass on to their successors. The argument of *Raison d'état* has continued to hold its ground.

In England there was an old system of local self-government in counties and boroughs. This had, before the end of the eighteenth century, become very rusty and practically oligarchic. But it had sufficed to exclude the control of the central government and had fostered a sentiment of local patriotism.

In France such slight self-government as existed in the provinces and the towns before the First Revolution was subject to be controlled or overruled by the Crown. The only force that tried to resist Louis XVI.'s financial measures was the Parlement of Paris.

In England the central government had few posts to bestow outside the capital; and when many new offices began to be created in the nineteenth century as the functions of government went on expanding, a system of competitive examination was set up which took them out of the sphere of favouritism and made their occupants a practically permanent civil service. Members of Parliament, who had been worried by the demands of their constituents to be recommended for appointments, gladly acquiesced in the loss of what brought them more trouble than advantage. Political patronage finally disappeared in the later Victorian days.

In France the number of places under the central government is extremely large, and the political influence of officials at elections and otherwise is so great that it has been deemed necessary, by all governments and parties in their turn, to confine appointments as far as possible to persons who can be trusted to support the existing form of government, whatever it may be.

In England, down to 1876 and 1886 (when two successive schisms broke up the old Whig party), each of the great rival parties which had existed since the seventeenth century included large bodies of persons belonging to each of the social classes. There were plenty of the poor in the Tory party, plenty of wealthy nobles among the Whigs. (The Labour party dates only from 1906.)

In France political parties did not exist before the First Revolution; and since then nearly all the large landowners and most of the rich have belonged to one of them, and the large majority of the working-men to the more advanced sections of the other.

In England abstract ideas have counted for very little in

politics, because the struggles of the Whigs and the middle class against the power of the Crown took the form of an assertion of rights some of which were as old as Magna Charta, and the habit thus formed of relying on precedents and making reforms bit by bit, as each occasion called for them, became a tradition and a part of British character. Only at rare moments did reformers appeal to Natural Rights.

In France, on the other hand, theory came before practice, dazzling inexperienced minds. When the old monarchy fell, the traditions, such as they were, of feudal independence and local self-government had been forgotten, so there were no foundations, save those of abstract doctrine, on which to build. Practice has never been able to keep up with theory, and theory has always been apt to stand in the way of slow and small reforms. It discredited them as inadequate.[1]

In Great Britain the strife of jarring creeds and churches was fought out and all but settled in the sixteenth and seventeenth centuries. Such antagonisms as continued between the Established Church and the Nonconformists were of slight political moment. The nation has, since 1688, been practically of one faith, and persecution went out of fashion in England and Scotland because there was no occasion for it.

In France the reaction against the dominant Church, which had continued to persecute till within thirty years of the Revolution, was violent enough not only to overthrow the Church, but for a time to crush down religious observances. Ever since, the hostility of Catholics and Voltaireans, or atheists, has divided the nation, causing an exasperation more bitter than mere political quarrels provoke. There are not enough of Protestants and of Republican Catholics to form a middle term between the extremes of Clericalism and Secularism.

These differences may all be traced to the different course which events took in each country. They may have been also affected by racial qualities inherent in each people. But where history supplies a sufficient explanation, why hunt for causes in the far more obscure phenomena of racial heredity? More may perhaps be attributed to the insular position of

---

[1] People sometimes allege that there is a fondness for abstract theory in the Celtic mind and a preference for practical expedients in the Teutonic. But no Celtic gathering ever produced more theories and showed more viewiness than did the Frankfurt Parliament of 1848–9.

Britain, and something also to the fact that the law of imperial Rome, never adopted there, did not lend its sanction
to the doctrines of absolutism.   It is not merits in one stock
of mankind nor defects in the other, but a set of geographical facts and a series of historical facts, for which neither
country is to be praised or blamed, that gave Britain conditions more favourable to the working of that democratic system into which she passed in 1868 and 1885 than those amid
which France has had to live.   Some of the defects in French
government are due to those conditions and not to democracy.
It is still too soon to say whether Britain, which now finds
herself swept into an epoch of change, will make the most of
the advantages she has inherited.,   These differences in the
preparation of France and of England for a Parliamentary
democracy need to be remembered when we come to appraise
the merits of Republican government in France.

French critics, detached philosophers as well as reactionary politicians, complain of what they call " Parliamentarism."   That system is on the face of it a government by
ministers responsible to the Chambers (virtually to the Chamber of Deputies) who are assumed to represent the views of
their constituents, and thus to give effect to the wishes of the
majority of the nation.   Thus described, it resembles the
system of Britain and her self-governing Dominions.   In
practice, however, it is largely worked by the personal relations of deputies to the majority in their constituencies, or to
those who appear to lead that majority, and of ministers to
deputies.   Deputies hold their seats by obtaining favours for
constituencies or individual constituents, ministers hold their
places by granting these favours to deputies, a process which
depletes the Treasury, demoralizes the legislature, and weakens the Administration.   It is government by patronage.   It
is aggravated by the division of the Chamber into so many
parties and groups that for many years past no ministry has
been able to command a majority all its own, and every
arrangement has a provisional character.   Sometimes (as in
1901) a combination is formed, but its permanence cannot
be reckoned on.   This, in making Cabinets unstable, compels
a minister to think constantly of every vote, frequently even
of one to be caught from among his opponents.   The group
system engenders and almost justifies intrigue, for how else

can a working majority be secured? French politicians are probably not less scrupulous than politicians in other countries, but they are driven to tortuous methods.

The jealousy which the deputies show of the Administration may be explained partly as a tradition from the days of the Second Empire, partly from the critical temper inherent in the French nature, partly from the corporate ambition which leads every body of men to try to extend their power. It is unfortunate as a further source of instability, though sometimes as, for instance, in war crises, stringent criticism is needed to keep ministers up to the mark.

The plan of conducting legislation by Committees of the Chamber has been censured as weakening the power of a ministry to frame and push through its measures, and as injuring their symmetry. But this is due to the increasing demands made on the time of legislatures. The same procedure has been forced on the American Congress. In the British Parliament the opposite method of legislation by the whole House led to a deplorable congestion of business, to cure which a system of committees is being now tried. The governing assemblies of all the large countries are oppressed by more work than they can dispose of.

Of corruption in the legislature I have spoken already. Though neither flagrant nor widespread, there is enough to show that republics do not necessarily, according to Montesquieu's dictum, live by Virtue as Monarchies live by Honour. A graver defect has been the mismanagement of finance, the extravagance of every government, and the increase of the floating debt. So far from securing economy, as John Bright and the English Radicals of his time fondly expected, democracy has proved a more costly though less incompetent form of government than was the autocracy of Louis XIV. in France or that of the Czars in Russia.

The Executive, pitifully weak in its relations with the deputies, is over-strong as against the individual citizen. Of civil liberty, as understood in Britain and America, there is not too much but too little.[1] The citizen is not safe from

[1] In recent years something has been done to provide better guarantees. But something still remains to be done. A high authority wrote in 1910: "Notre histoire politique des cent vingt dernières années se resume dans ce paradoxe irreductible énervant et sterile, loger un individu parfaitement libre heureux et satisfait dans un État puissant omni-

domiciliary visits and arbitrary arrests.   On the other hand, the press enjoys practical impunity for whatever charges it may bring against individuals.

The responsibility of officials to special administrative tribunals, instead of to the ordinary courts of justice, secures for them, not indeed indulgence, for the special courts do their duty fairly enough, but a privileged position which reduces the citizen's sense of freedom.   This is the more serious because the range of action of the centralized administration is so wide, stretching over the whole country, drawing trivial matters to Paris for decision.   The Prefect, a product of the old régime reproduced under Napoleon, has not had his wings clipped by democracy.   The local civil servant, ruled by the deputy through the Prefect, is expected to render help in elections, and is at all times liable to be accused of political partisanship.   The Executive, moreover, sometimes at the prompting or with the consent of the Legislature, has been inclined to infringe upon the judicial department.   Judges were once displaced on a large scale because of an alleged want of loyalty to the Republic.

These faults have been excused on grounds of political necessity.   Where the very form of government is in dispute, and attempts to overthrow it by force may be feared, the same measure of freedom cannot — so it is argued — be allowed to local authorities or to individual citizens as in countries where a well-settled order has long existed, for a centralized bureaucracy holds a nation compactly together and restrains tendencies to disunion.   To this it is answered that the policy of restraint is one to which republics ought least of all to resort, because, themselves founded on freedom, they claim that freedom assures the contentment of the people and their loyalty to free institutions.   But though every Government, in its turn, applies repressive measures, defending itself by the plea that its predecessors have used them, the average citizen does not resent such action.   If conservatively disposed, as are most bourgeois and peasants, he sees in them a guarantee of order.

The intolerance shown in religious matters and the spying upon officials, upon the army, even apparently upon judges,

potent et autoritaire."—M. Maurice Caudel, in the preface to his instructive book *Nos Libertés politiques*.

in which this intolerance expresses itself, and which in 1913 was charged on Freemasons who were believed to have practised it, are equally unworthy of a free Government. They are palliated on the same ground, viz. that the Roman Church, its clergy, and its aims are unfriendly to the Republic, so that a *sous préfet* who goes frequently to mass or lets his daughter sing in a church choir is presumably wanting in loyalty to the government he serves.

"Liberty, Equality, Fraternity" is still the motto of the Republic. Equality, civil and political, exists. Social equality is a thing which governments cannot establish, except by extinguishing all classes save one. Economic equality has come no nearer than elsewhere. Only a social and economic revolution could create it, and it is doubtful whether it could thereafter be maintained. Liberty is less secured than in some monarchies. As for Fraternity, one who notes the personal bitterness to which political and ecclesiastical partisanship gives rise is reminded of Metternich's saying: "If I lived in France I should prefer to have cousins rather than brothers."

Class hatreds, anti-religious intolerance, and the deficient respect for personal liberty have not been brought into France by democracy. They are maladies of long standing, for which it is responsible only so far as it has not succeeded in eliminating them. It is the misfortune not the fault of the Republic that antagonisms are stronger than affinities, that they impede the working of government, distract it from some of its social tasks, and create a general sense of unrest.

This may also be said of the alleged indifference to politics of a large section of the population. Four revolutions and the almost incessant turmoil of political life since 1788 have not sufficed to make the bulk of the peasantry, and a considerable percentage of the bourgeoisie, take that steadily sustained interest in public affairs expected from them when the Republic was established. This impairs the influence of public opinion. In some classes it is sluggish, while if one regards the whole country, the divisions are too sharply cut to be blent into anything approaching a general national will. Though these conditions are no worse than they were under previous forms of government — perhaps indeed less evident

than in the days of the Orleanist and Bonapartist monarchies — they are naturally disappointing to those apostles of
popular government who hold that the gift of political power
confers the sense of a duty to use it and the capacity to use
it wisely.   Happy faith, which the experience of a century
and a quarter has not shaken.

It is time to turn to the other side of the balance-sheet and
see what the democratic Republic has accomplished for
France since 1871.

Its achievements must be judged, not only by the adverse
conditions (already described), which the Past had bequeathed, but also by comparison with the performances of
previous French monarchies, and in particular with those of
the Second Empire, a period of material growth and widespread prosperity.   Has France risen or sunk since her government became popular ?   By how much has the individual
citizen been made happier and more contented ?

Civil administration has been, both in town and country,
reasonably efficient and generally honest.   There has been
less corruption and favouritism among officials than under
the Second Empire.   Some municipalities have been wasteful as well as lavish in expenditure, and that of Paris far
from pure; yet such scandals as have arisen are less than
those which, common in America from 1865 to 1900, have
not yet been expunged from its cities.

Public order has been creditably maintained.   When one
considers the flame of anger that has blazed up in more than
one political crisis, and in great strikes, among an excitable
people, one must admit that only an Executive armed with
large powers and bold enough to use them, even in the face
of denunciations in the Chamber, could have checked disorders threatening civil war.   The range of action and the
arbitrary methods allowed to the police shock the Englishman
or American, but they are seldom used with an evil purpose.
Civil justice is less costly than in Britain or America.   Few
complaints are made of its administration or of that of the
criminal courts, and the superior judges are generally trusted.
The procedure in criminal cases which foreign observers have
censured as harsh towards the suspected prisoner, and the
laxity of the rules regarding the admission of evidence, are

things of old standing in France, and unconnected with the form of government. Respect for the law and the Executive have prevented the growth of the habit of lynching.

It is hard to estimate the value of the legislation which the Republic has produced without passing an opinion on measures which nothing but experience of their working can test. The subjects which have chiefly occupied the Chambers have been education, controversial only so far as it affects the action of ecclesiastics, the relations of Church and State, the right of working-men to combine in unions, old-age pensions, sanitation, factory laws, and taxation, the most hotly contested point in which has been not the tariff, for Protectionist doctrine reigns, but the imposition of an income-tax. Upon these subjects statutes of wide scope have been passed. There are complaints that more has not been effected for the benefit of the masses, but whoever considers the atmosphere of incessant party strife in which the Chambers have had to debate and decide will not disparage the amount and value of the work done to improve industrial conditions. The total annual output of measures is said to be about the same as under the two preceding monarchies. Most of these have been noncontroversial and of minor importance, partly no doubt because the Code framed under Napoleon definitely settled many questions in the law of family and the law of property which have remained less clearly determined in English-speaking countries, where there has been little codification on a large scale.

One of the chief tasks of each successive ministry has been to provide for military defence. Though the results accomplished fell short of what was frequently demanded, and though pessimists declared that democratic habits could not but destroy obedience, these results have been creditable to a people which had renounced and did not wish to revive its old militaristic spirit. A superb line of fortifications along the north-eastern frontier was constructed in the 'seventies and 'eighties. Constant attention was given to the supply of artillery. Mobilization was efficiently carried through in August 1914, and the French Army acquitted itself in the war which then began with a discipline and spirit worthy of its best traditions. The management of naval affairs, in which France had shone in days now remote, was less satisfactory, while the performances of the fleet in war seemed scarcely proportionate to the sums that had been spent upon producing it, or to the ancient fame of the French naval service.

The colonial possessions of France have been largely increased under the Republic in North, in West, and in Central Africa. Madagascar has been annexed, and so have large territories in South-Eastern Asia. All these acquisitions (except Tunis and Morocco) are tropical, and would be unsuited for the settlement of Frenchmen, even if France had any surplus of population to send abroad. Whether they have the commercial value attributed to them, considering the expenditure which the maintenance of a navy to protect them implies, is a further question.

Foreign policy has been conducted, through many difficult crises, sometimes unwisely, yet with fewer variations of aim than have been visible in the lines followed by the other great European States. The two Chambers, in this respect reflecting and obeying the mind and purpose of the nation, have almost always strengthened and supported the Executive. When one considers the defects incident to the rule of popular assemblies, the restraint which the Chambers imposed upon themselves must elicit the respect of impartial observers. Foreign policy has been deemed, ever since (and even before) the days of Demosthenes, to be the weak point of a democracy. This charge finds little support in a study of French history between 1871 and 1914. Greater errors were committed and more weakness shown under the Orleans Monarchy and certainly under the Second Empire.

The chief praise, however, which may be given to the Third Republic is that it has lasted fifty years, more than twice as long as any preceding form of government since 1792.[1] Several times it has been in peril. But though the currents drove the ship very near to the rocks, she managed, by skill or good luck, to escape them unscathed, and her course during the present century has been steadier than before. It would be too much to say that the mass of the

[1] The monarchy of Napoleon lasted fourteen years (dating from the beginning of the Consulate), that of the Bourbon Restoration sixteen years, that of Louis Philippe eighteen years, that of Louis Napoleon Bonaparte nineteen years. The first Republic had a life of seven, the second of three years.

people are better contented than in previous generations, for the peasantry and a large part of the bourgeoisie were content under Louis Napoleon, to whom many looked back as the man "qui faisait vivre tout le monde," and large sections of the working-men are impatient for a socialistic Republic. But a long series of elections has shown that though there is a dislike of Parliamentarism and a hankering after a stronger Executive — I do not mean a dictatorship — the old monarchical parties are virtually extinct. The Republic, in one form or another, is the choice of France. Even Paris, which has so often made revolutions without the will, or against the will, of the country, could not do so to-day. Tocqueville asked, more than half a century ago, " Are we on the way to intermittent anarchy, the incurable disease of old peoples ? " But France seems no nearer to-day than in 1870 to that calamity. Many forces are struggling for mastery within her. But those that make for stability, a stability in those essentials which give life and hope, seem likely to prevail.

What are the lessons which the history of popular government in France can furnish to other countries ? Caution is needed in basing conclusions of general applicability on the experience of a country whose conditions are so peculiar, for the successes and the failures there may be due less to the system than to those conditions. But subject to this reservation some few morals may be drawn illuminative for the student of popular governments in general.

Democracy needs local self-government as its foundation. That is the school in which the citizen acquires the habit of independent action, learns what is his duty to the State, and learns also how to discharge it. The control of local affairs by the Central Government has in France lessened the citizen's sense of responsibility. It has multiplied the posts of which the executive can dispose, and thereby enlarged the field in which political patronage can run riot. Patronage may no doubt be employed and abused by local authorities also, and is so employed in America and elsewhere for personal or party ends. But this does less harm to the higher interests of the State, for the field of action is narrower, and the malady may be only sporadic, curable by the action of the local citizens themselves when they have been roused to a sense of its evils, as it is being cured to-day in the United States.

That democracy is not necessarily a weak government is proved by the vigour and firmness with which the French Executive has more than once repressed breaches of public order. Much of course depends on the support which the ministry may count upon from public opinion. Much depends on the individual minister. He may be timid, he may be strong. But the general truth remains that a forceful man whose motives are above suspicion will be supported. The masses value courage in their leaders.

The control of a single omnipotent Assembly is dangerous. A check on haste or passion is needed, be it that of a Rigid Constitution limiting the Assembly's powers, or that of a presidential veto, or that of a Second Chamber. Some high authorities would like to see the French Senate stronger, not merely in respect of its legal powers, but by the weight of the men who compose it. But taking it as it is, it has been a valuable safeguard.

Democracies, especially Parliamentary democracies, need the kind of leadership which creates compact and steady parties, one of which may constitute a majority capable of maintaining, for some while at least, a government that will pursue a settled and consistent policy. It fixes upon one or a few that responsibility which can no more be fixed on an Assembly than you can grasp a handful of smoke. France has suffered, since the death of Gambetta, from the want of such leadership. Jules Ferry had some of the qualities required. Waldeck-Rousseau had these in larger measure, and he pulled things together when they were falling into confusion. The leader may no doubt be a demagogue who can lead the Assembly or beguile the people into dangerous paths, but France is not a soil specially favourable to demagogism, less favourable perhaps than England. France is intensely critical. It is not from plausible Parliamentary or platform rhetoricians that the menacing spectre of a dictatorship has arisen.

Universal suffrage offers no guarantee against such a spectre. It installed Louis Napoleon as President for ten years, it subsequently made him emperor, it confirmed his power a few months before his fall in 1870, and on each occasion by a vast majority. It gave a good deal of support to Boulanger. Caesarism can attract the masses now as it did in the last days of the Roman Republic.

Secret societies, indispensable to the friends of liberty who conspired against the tyrants of Italy two generations ago, are regrettable in a country which has secured full constitutional freedom. Their influence on politics is unhealthy because irresponsible, prone to intolerance, and easily made the tool of selfishness or social persecution.

Individual liberty is not necessarily secured either by the sovereignty of the people, or by equality in private civil rights, or by social equality. In France the citizen has less security against arbitrary arrest and detention, or the searching of his house, or any act of discretionary authority on the part of police or other officials, than Americans think to be an essential part of freedom or than Englishmen enjoyed as such long before democracy was established in England. He is subject in peace time to some of those stringent restrictions which in most free countries are imposed only in days of war.

Whoever surveys the history of France from 1789 to our own time must be struck by the habits of thought and action which repeated revolutions engender. Each violent disturbance of the established order disposes men to another. That "sacred right of insurrection" which ought to be the last resort when other remedies have failed, is invoked on occasions which do not warrant it, and is likely, if successful, to carry destruction farther than is necessary. Weakening the respect for authority, it encourages ambitious adventurers to use it against a lawful government whose defects can be removed in a legal and peaceful way. The fear of it, terrifying the quiet and "respectable" citizens who think first of their comfort and their property, makes them rally to the usurping adventurer and support the government he sets up. The acts of violence that accompany it may leave behind animosities dividing the nation for generations to come.[1]

---

[1] Of Labour troubles and the advocacy of what is called "Direct Action" nothing need be said here because these phenomena have appeared in other democratic countries also. So far from being characteristic of democracy, the General Strike (as a means for compelling submission by a government) and Direct Action are attacks on the fundamental principles of democratic government. What they show is

All these things happened in France. That the Revolution was needed in 1789 few will now deny, but two or three generations passed before the spirit which the Revolution called up could be exorcised. Half a century of constitutional government seems to have now broken the habit of insurrection, for the people know that they can obtain by their votes whatever they desire. But they still suffer, if not from the disease, yet from what physicians call the *sequelae*. The venerable doctrine of the English Whigs that where constitutional changes are needed they ought to be effected with the least possible breach of continuity, may seem obsolete and moss-grown. Nevertheless there are countries in which it still finds its application.

Those who say that democracy has not brought to the service of the State enough of the best ability of the nation cannot mean that there is a lack of talent, for as George Sand was wont to say, " Talent is everywhere in France." Englishmen and Americans who live in Paris are struck by the sustained vivacity of French politics and the amazing cleverness they elicit. The Chambers are a theatre in which the actors are also the audience, enjoying as connoisseurs one another's performances. Some of this cleverness might, however, be usefully exchanged for an infusion of calm and reflective minds, with a wider outlook around and ahead, who could by their characters and attainments exert a steadying influence on opinion. Each democracy needs leaders of the qualities fitted to compensate its peculiar defects. There is no lack in France of men rich in knowledge, acute and vigorous in thought. No modern country has done more, if indeed any has done so much, to originate and develop philosophic thinking on politics. But the greater part of these stores of knowledge and wisdom are not used in political life, and those few statesmen who possess them seem unable to breathe freely in the circumambient atmosphere of passion and partisanship.

A sketch of what the Republic has done or failed to do for France cannot well conclude without some reference to its alleged effects upon the intellectual and moral life of the country. Edmond Schérer, writing in 1883, remarked,

that those fundamental principles are either not understood or not regarded by a section of those who consider themselves democrats.

as many had said before him and have said since, that democracy was producing mediocrity. Some able French writers of our own day, not Royalists or Clericalists, attribute to it that moral decline also which they discover in their countrymen. With all deference to these eminent persons, one may doubt whether forms of government have more than a slight and transient influence upon literature or art or philosophy. Proposing in a later chapter to deal with this subject, I will here touch but briefly on the case of France. Political freedom has not there borne those intellectual fruits which enthusiasts who lived under despotism expected, for great thinkers and teachers and statesmen are no more frequent now than they were in those days. Democracy may, in the sphere of politics, have levelled down as well as levelled up, and failed to produce many figures conspicuous for elevation and independence. But though it may develop some kinds of talent more than others, there is nothing to show that it reduces the volume of talent that any country possesses, still less that it retards the growth of science, or of art, or of learning, or of polite letters. These things lie outside politics. They bloom or wither from causes hitherto unexplained, perhaps unexplainable: they are affected by social environment and the general tendencies of the age. If it be a materialistic age, men whose minds feed chiefly upon newspapers, men occupied with business projects and leading a restless, leisureless life, are not likely to be creative in the higher realms of thought. Whatever tendencies happen to rule their world will find expression in politics also, and colour their ideals; but it is in the tendencies themselves rather than in the form of government that the cause resides. Why suggest that it is democracy which has refused to the France of the twentieth century poets of outstanding fame like Victor Hugo, or prose writers like Renan and Taine, when we note the same absence of exceptionally brilliant figures in almost every country, whatever its form of government. Ranke and Mommsen have had no successors of equal rank in monarchical Germany; nor have Wordsworth, Tennyson, and Browning had such successors in democratic England. The charge that may be with more force brought against democracy is that it has failed, as in many other countries, to bring to the front, in sufficient numbers,

men of high constructive gifts, fit to grapple with the increasingly difficult problems the modern world has to face.
Herein universal suffrage and the representative system have
not fulfilled the hopes of 1789.

With morals the case is not quite the same, since they
are affected by the standards which the law sets up and
which the habits of political life make familiar.   If law
gives a free rein to licence in writing or in conduct, it may
help to lower the tone of social life.   The law, or the application of it, has in these matters been far from strict under
the Republic.   But the standard of morality, public or private, is in practice no lower than it has often been under
monarchies or oligarchies.   Not to go back to the Regency
and Louis XV., those who read the records of the Restoration after 1815 or remember the Second Empire, will not
single out the Third Republic for censure.   Pecuniary corruption was far more general and more flagrant under the
Russian autocracy than it has ever been in any free country.
Sixty years ago the France of Louis Napoleon used to be
unfavourably contrasted with what were then believed to be
the superior morals of Germany.   Such a contrast between
the two countries would not be drawn to-day.   The increase
of divorce, arraigned as a blemish due to the legislation of
the Republic, is a feature of modern society in every country,
nor is morality any higher in the countries that forbid divorce altogether than in those which permit it.   There may,
however, be force in the complaint that recent French legislation discourages school instruction in moral duty by forbidding the teacher to make any reference to the existence of
the Deity, and by excluding everything of a religious nature
from the school-books.

Political philosophers have been apt to attribute too much
to the influence of forms of government upon the life of a
nation as a whole.   Foreign observers in particular are apt
to fall into this error, knowing less of the inner spirit and
domestic virtues of a people than they do of its government
and politics, for where a government is popular its defects
are patent to all eyes, and these defects are taken to be an
index to its character.   Seven years ago such observers
thought they saw in France a people torn by internal dissensions, religious and political, a legislature changeful and

discredited, a large part of the population indifferent to politics, only a small fraction of the finest intellect of the country taking part in its public life. They concluded that France was a decadent country, in which the flame of national life was already flickering low. Then suddenly a war more terrible than any known before broke upon the nation, and an invading army occupied large parts of its territory. Political dissensions continued, political intrigues were as rife as ever; ministry followed ministry in quick succession. But the Nation rose to confront the peril that threatened its existence, and showed that the old spirit of France had lost nothing of its fervour, and her soldiers nothing of their valour.

SWITZERLAND

CHAPTER XXVII

THE PEOPLE AND THEIR HISTORY

AMONG the modern democracies which are true democracies, Switzerland has the highest claim to be studied.[1] It is the oldest, for it contains communities in which popular government dates farther back than it does anywhere else in the world; and it has pushed democratic doctrines farther, and worked them out more consistently, than any other European State. Moreover, being a Federal State, it contains within its comparatively narrow limits a greater variety of institutions based on democratic principles than any other country, greater even than the Federations of America and Australia can show.

To understand Swiss institutions and their working one must know something both of the physical character of the country and of the history of the small communities, diverse in race and speech, which have grown into the Swiss nation. The natural conditions might seem most unfavourable to the creation of a State or even of a nation. The Swiss people, as they are to-day, dwell on both sides of a gigantic mountain mass, those to the north on a high plateau traversed by a series of ridges, the rest in deep valleys separated from one another by craggy heights and widespreading snow-fields. No natural boundary marks them off from the Germans to the north and east, from the French to the west, and from the Italians to the south. Ethnologically they belong some to one, some to another, of those three racial stocks, and have

[1] There are in English several histories of Switzerland, and several useful descriptions of the constitutional system, but there does not seem to be any systematic account of the practical working of that system, presenting a picture of the current political life of the nation. The sketch which follows is based on personal enquiries made in Switzerland by myself in 1905 and 1919.

no common language. It is a remarkable series of events, reaching back over more than six hundred years, that has brought men of these three stocks together, and made them not only a united people, but one of the most united, and certainly the most patriotic, among the peoples of Europe.

OUTLINE OF SWISS HISTORY

Towards the end of the thirteenth century three small Teutonic communities dwelling in secluded valleys to the south and south-east of the Lake of Luzern, entered into a league of mutual defence to protect themselves against the encroachments of the land-owning nobles of the lower country to the north, to whose exactions, based on more or less doubtful feudal rights, they would not submit. Turning to account the strength of their mountain fastnesses, they repelled the repeated attacks of the Counts of Habsburg, though never disputing the ultimate sovereignty of the Emperor, having indeed received favours from the great monarchs of the house of Hohenstaufen. Like the Englishmen who in the same age were wresting from the Crown a recognition of English liberties, they proclaimed no abstract principles of freedom, but stood on the foundation of their ancient rights. They lived off the produce of their own fields and woods and pastures, governing themselves by gatherings of the people in which every householder was the equal of every other. This was the beginning of democracy. After a time other rural communities and a few cities, some which, like Zürich and Luzern, may have come down as trading centres from Roman times, some which, like Bern, had grown up as hill fortresses in the welter of the Dark Ages, entered into alliance with these stalwart mountaineers, and by degrees fresh communities were added, all being allied to the original three, but not necessarily to each of the others. In 1353, when Bern joined, the League came to number eight cantons. In 1513 the accession of Appenzell raised it to thirteen, at which figure it remained down till the changes induced by the French Revolution. Before the end of the fifteenth century it had become a power in Central Europe. The religious dissensions of the Reformation put a severe strain upon its cohesion, for half the cantons embraced

Protestantism and half clung to Rome, but it survived the
strain, for the supreme interest of common defence held its
members together.   In 1648 the Confederation was recognized by the Treaties of Westphalia as an independent State,
the theoretical suzerainty of the Empire having by that time
become obsolete.   The internal political institutions of the
allied communities varied greatly.   The rural cantons were
pure democracies, governing themselves by meetings of the
people.   Of the cities, some, like Bern, were close oligarchies
of nobles: in others oligarchy was more or less tempered by
a popular element.   As the Confederation bound them together only for offensive and defensive purposes, each canton
had control of its domestic affairs.   The Diet met to deal
with external policy and divers matters in which the cantons
were jointly interested, and the delegates who sat in it acted
on the instructions given by their respective cantons.   There
was, as in the United States between 1776 and 1789, no
Central Executive.   Some cantons had by conquests in war
acquired territories whose inhabitants they ruled as subjects,
and to whom they granted none of the freedom they claimed
for themselves.

   The French Revolution ushered in a period of storm and
confusion.   In 1798 French armies entered Switzerland.
Much fighting followed.   The old system was completely
overthrown.[1]   A centralized Helvetic Republic was created,
and vanished when a Federal system, far closer than that of
the old League, was established by Napoleon in 1803.
Change followed change.   A new and larger Confederation
was set up in 1815; and even thereafter unrest and dissensions continued till, after the short Sonderbund [2] war of
1847 between the Protestant and Catholic cantons had ended
by the victory of the former, a new Constitution was created
in 1848, which turned what had been a League of States
into a Federal State, modelled in many respects upon the
lines of the United States Constitution.   This frame of national government was, after long debates, further amended
in 1874, and it is by the Constitution of that year (altered

---

[1] A succinct and lucid account of these events is given in Mr. Cool-
idge's valuable article " Switzerland " in the *Encyclopaedia Britannica*,
11th edition, vol. xxvi.

[2] The Sonderbund was the separate league set up by seven seceding
Roman Catholic cantons.

subsequently in certain points) that Switzerland is now governed. The territories formerly subject to particular cantons, as Vaud was subject to Bern and as the Italian districts now forming Ticino were to the three oldest Forest Cantons (Uri, Schwytz, and Unterwalden), were in 1803 raised into autonomous cantons, and all Swiss citizens now enjoy equal political rights under cantonal constitutions, and under the Constitution of the Confederation.

Differences, however, remain between the component parts, differences so marked as to make the unity of the Swiss nation a singular, perhaps a unique, phenomenon in history. Nearly two-thirds of the population speak German, most of the others French, a few Italian, a still smaller number Romansch or Ladin.[1] A considerable majority both of German-speaking and of French-speaking people are Protestants, the rest Roman Catholics. Fortunately the local boundaries of the religious confessions do not coincide with those of language, for in some Protestant cantons the people speak German; in some Catholic cantons they speak French; in some Catholics and Protestants are mixed, and both languages are spoken. Racial intermixture proceeds steadily though slowly, and the diverse elements are assimilated more through literature and migration and commercial intercourse than by intermarriage. Villages may be found in which the German-speaking inhabitants do not know French, nor the French-speakers German. Some are more advanced than others in political knowledge and experience, but all alike are devoted to Switzerland, proud of its history, resolved to maintain the liberties both of the Cantons and of the Confederation. The circumstances which detached them from the three great neighbouring peoples secured to the older cantons a freedom which they prized all the more because they alone among continental nations enjoyed it; and when the subject lands were emancipated this love of freedom and fidelity to national traditions spread from the older cantons to the newer. Thus have members of three races become one people.

But though united they are not homogeneous. Not only in language are there differences, but also in the occupations

[1] A form of Romance speech differing a little from the Romansch which is spoken, along with German, in the Grisons (Graubünden).

of the inhabitants, in the external conditions of their life, in religion, in character, in ideas and habits of thought; and with this diversity there is also a local pride which clings to time-honoured ways and resists the tendencies, strong as these have become, that make for uniformity. Here, therefore, are the salient features of the nation which the student of their institutions must keep always before his mind — a strenuous patriotism bracing up the sense of national unity, an abounding variety in the details of social, of economic and of political life, coupled with an attachment to local self-government, which, having been the life-breath of the original cantons, passed into the minds and hearts of the others also, making them wish to share in the ancient traditions, and contributing to the overthrow of oligarchy in the cities even where, as in Bern, it had been strongest. Thus one may say that the three Forest Cantons, the highland kernel of what was called in the sixteenth century the "Old League of Upper Germany" have, while each retaining to-day no more territory than they held in 1291, so spread out by their traditions and by the spirit they kindled as to be the creators of the new democratic State. Success in war, and the pride in common triumphs, counted for much in the earlier stages of the process, while in the latest the existence of four great States to the north, east, south, and west, had, so to speak, squeezed the Swiss together, keeping them always on their guard against dangers from abroad.

The diversity of those who inhabit this small area (15,976 square miles) has increased of recent years by the growth of manufactures. One-third of the total population (which was estimated in 1915 at 3,900,000) is still engaged in pastoral and agricultural occupations, and the number of persons owning land is given as about 500,000. Among manufacturing industries, textiles (silk and cotton) are most important, watch-making and the production of machinery coming next. There are practically no mines, except of salt. Although the country has to import its coal, and is only beginning to develop the water power furnished by many mountain torrents, the recent extension of factories and workshops has created a large working-class population in the towns, especially of the north-eastern cantons, and drawn in a crowd of immigrants, chiefly from Germany, many of whom have not be-

come citizens.[1]　This has helped to diffuse socialistic principles, as the immigration of Italians into the industrial districts and of French into the West has largely increased the
number of Roman Catholics.[2]　In Geneva, the city of Calvin,
these now form a majority of the inhabitants, though not of
the citizens.　The growth of the urban element as compared
with that of the country dwellers naturally affects political
parties, and the incoming foreigners do not at once imbibe
Swiss patriotism and Swiss ways of thinking.　But the rural
folk, with their traditions of a historic patriotism, their individualism, and their habits of local self-government, still
remain the dominant element and give to the nation its peculiar character of steadiness and solidity.

[1] In the district round Zürich there were said to be, in 1914, 50,000
Italians, the great majority of whom were not being assimilated by
the Swiss.　Of the total population of the Confederation 15 per cent
were in that year foreigners.

[2] The Protestants were, in 1910, 2,108,000; the Roman Catholics
1,594,000.

CHAPTER XXVIII

LOCAL GOVERNMENT — THE COMMUNE

As Swiss political institutions have been built up on the foundation of small communities, rural and urban, accustomed to control their own affairs, it is from this kernel that a description may fitly start. I begin with the Communes, passing on next to the Cantons and thence to the Confederation. The Commune is in some places as old as the Canton, in some even older. The history of its earlier forms, its control of the common lands, the various features it showed in different districts of the country, and the transformations it has undergone down to quite recent times,— these are matters so intricate that I must be content with observing that the commune was from the earliest times a potent factor in accustoming the whole people to take interest in and know how to handle local affairs, every man on a level with his fellows. It is still the political unit of the nation ·and the focus of its local public life. To be naturalized as a Swiss citizen, one must be a member of some commune, and this gives (with the approval of the cantonal authority) both cantonal and national citizenship. There are now over 3164 communes in the country, varying greatly in size and population, and roughly corresponding with American townships. They deal with many branches of local business (though not everywhere to the same extent) such as education, police, poor relief, water-supply, sometimes in conjunction with a cantonal authority. Usually, too, a commune holds property, and has, in rural areas, the supervision of the communal woods and pastures. In the German-speaking cantons it is governed, in rural places and very small towns, by a mass meeting of the citizens in which questions are debated as well as voted upon. Where the population is larger, and generally in the French-speaking districts, the main business is the election of the Communal Council, a standing body for conducting current business and making minor appointments. Its chairman (like the Maire in France) has often special functions and a certain measure of independent action.[1]

In parts of Switzerland some communes were, till the end of the eighteenth century, virtually sovereign States, tiny, but independent. Such was the hamlet of Gersau, east of Brunnen, on the shore of the Lake of Luzern, and now included in the canton of Schwytz, and such were the communes of the upper valleys of the Rhine and the Inn, which formed themselves into the three Leagues that, still later, united to form the canton of Grisons (Graubünden).

In the larger towns the commune becomes a municipality, governed by a council, which is elected, as a rule, for three years, and has complete control of city affairs. There is usually, as chairman of this council, a president or mayor, who, having little power, resembles an English mayor or Scottish provost rather than the more important mayor of America. In some places, however, certain executive functions are entrusted to him. Cities, like rural communities, enjoy a wide range of authority subject to general cantonal laws. Some of them have undertaken to supply water and gas or electricity, some own the tramways, Zürich leading the way in these municipal enterprises. Neither against councillors nor against officials are charges of corruption brought even in the largest cities which raise a considerable revenue. The councils are sometimes accused of trying too many experiments or of employing too large a staff, and now and then a little jobbing may occur; but the salaries are small, the work done is carefully supervised, and taxation is not excessive, though the debt tends to rise. It need hardly be said that Swiss thrift is even more characteristic of the rural than of the municipal administrators.

School teachers are elected by the people and usually for short terms [2]— a plan which has not been found to work well

---

[1] The rural circumscription called a District (*Bezirk*), which includes a number of communes, is an artificial area, established for administrative purposes, and needs no description here.

[2] I was told that the Teachers' Union is apt to protect teachers from losing their posts by preventing a commune, whose dismissal of a

in Zürich.   So in some Protestant cantons the law provides
for the election of pastors for short terms.

In the cities elections are apt to be fought upon political
lines, which, however, are seldom sharply drawn.   Contests are sometimes avoided by conceding to each party a
fair representation.   In rural areas, which are seldom troubled with questions of general policy, such as those which
divide individualists and the advocates of municipal socialism, politics are little regarded in the choice of officials, for
there are not, as in the United States, office-seekers demanding rewards for their services.

Local self-government has been in Switzerland a factor of
prime importance, not only as the basis of the administrative fabric, but also because the training which the people
have received from practice in it has been a chief cause of
their success in working republican institutions.   Nowhere
in Europe has it been so fully left to the hands of the people.
The Swiss themselves lay stress upon it, as a means of edu-
cating the citizens in public work, as instilling the sense of
civic duty, and as enabling governmental action to be used
for the benefit of the community without either sacrificing
local initiative or making the action of the central authority
too strong and too pervasive.

The Cantons

The cantons, twenty-two in number — or rather twenty-
five, for three are divided into half-cantons, each with its own
government [1]—are, like the States of the American Union,
very unequal in size and population.   Grisons has an area
of 2773 square miles, Bern of 2657, Zug of 92.   The population of Bern was (estimate of 1915) 665,000, that of
Zürich 538,000, while that of Uri was 23,000, and that of
Glarus 34,000.   In fifteen German is the language almost
exclusively spoken, in three (Neuchâtel, Vaud, and Geneva)
French, in one (Ticino) Italian, in two (Valais and Solo-

teacher has displeased the profession, from finding another person to
fill the vacancy.

[1] These three are Unterwalden, divided into Unterwald above the
wood (Ob dem Wald) and Unterwald below the wood (Nid dem Wald),
Appenzell, divided into Ausser Rhoden and Inner Rhoden, and Basle,
divided into Country and City (Basel Land and Basel Stadt).

thurn) each tongue claims about a half of the inhabitants, while in Bern German predominates, as does French in Fribourg. Three cantons (Unterwalden, Appenzell, and Basle) are split up into independent half-cantons, and in each the two halves, taken together, hold in the Federal Legislature the representation of one canton.

The rights and powers of a Canton correspond generally to those of a State in the American Union and in the Australian Federal Commonwealth, and are greater than those of a Canadian Province. It is sovereign in so far as it has not yielded up its sovereignty to the Confederation, so that in case of doubt as to which possesses any given power, the presumption is in favour of the canton. "The cantons are sovereign," says the Constitution, "so far as their sovereignty is not limited by the Federal Constitution, and as such they exercise all the rights not delegated to the Federal Government." These powers include taxation (except customs duties), education (subject to a certain measure of oversight by the Federal Government), industrial legislation, and so much of legislation on contractual topics (including trade and commerce), and on criminal law, as has not been taken over by the Federal Legislature in the exercise of its concurrent legislative powers.[1] Thus their sphere, though, as we shall see, reduced in many respects by the increased legislative authority conferred on the National Government when the latter chooses to exert it, is still wide; and the hold they retain upon the interest and affection of their inhabitants is naturally strongest in the older and more conservative cantons.

In describing cantonal political institutions no more need be said about the forms democratic government has taken than is required to make its practical working intelligible, and to explain the nature of the political life which continues to flow in the old local channels.

The cantons, whose differences in detail are too numerous to be here dealt with, fall into two classes — those ruled by primary, and those ruled by representative assemblies. Four, viz. two whole cantons (Uri and Glarus) and four

[1] A Civil Code for the whole country, in which the old Teutonic customary law has been skilfully combined with the principles of modern French laws, was enacted in 1912, and a penal code was in 1919 being prepared by a committee of the Federal Legislature.

half-cantons, all of them small and all among the older cantons, have retained or returned to the primitive Teutonic system of government by a primary assembly, in which every adult male citizen can speak and vote.[1]   The assembly, called a Landesgemeinde, recalls the old English Folk Mot, the Thing of Norway and Iceland, the Homeric Agora, and the Roman Comitia; while its manner of doing business resembles that of the Town Meeting in New England.   It meets once a year in the open air under the presidency of the annually elected Landamman, enacts laws or ratifies those previously passed by the Council, passes resolutions, settles current questions such as those that relate to finance and public works, and elects both the principal officials, including the judges, and (as a sort of standing committee) an Administrative Council.   In cantons where the number who attend the Assembly is not too large to be reached by the voice, every one can speak, and can present a proposition.[2]   A smaller council, which manages the less important current business, is chosen by the citizens in local divisions.   This is the oldest, simplest, and purest form of democracy which the world knows.

Of these four cantons, three, viz. Uri, the two Unterwaldens and the two Appenzells (especially Appenzell Inner Rhoden), are highly conservative in temper.   (This is less true of Glarus in which manufacturing industries have sprung up.)   They are agricultural or pastoral communities where men lead simple lives, no one rich, no one abjectly poor, all socially equal.   They cherish the memories of their ancestors who won freedom for them centuries ago, and are content to abide in those traditions.   The reader will have noted that both in the communes and in the cantons there is, except to some slight extent in the four Landesgemeinde cantons, where the annually elected Landamman is head of the State, no such thing as a single official head of the political community, nor indeed any other flavour of monarchy such

[1] The view that the Landesgemeinde has, as Freeman and other writers have held, descended from the meetings of the early Germans described by Tacitus, now finds less favour, and it is rather deemed to be a product, during the earlier Middle Age, of the conditions of collective life in small and isolated communities.

[2] Subject, in some cantons, to rules respecting notice to be given or which require a proposal to have been previously submitted to a smaller body.

as the Governorship in an American State. Authority is always vested in a Council, the chairman of which is a presiding officer and nothing more, with no wider opportunities of exerting authority than have his colleagues.

All the other cantons, including the half-cantons Basel Land and Basel Stadt, have each its own constitution or frame of representative government which its people have enacted for themselves, as prescribed by the Federal Constitution, and which they can change as and when they please, subject, however, to the assent of the Federal Government. In each a prescribed number of citizens can demand a revision, in which case the work is undertaken either by the Great Council or by a body specially elected for the purpose, and the draft is (as in the American States) submitted to the people for their approval. Particular amendments also require the approval of a popular vote, cast by all citizens, for manhood suffrage has been everywhere adopted.[1] The elected legislature is in most cantons called the Great, sometimes the Cantonal, Council. Current executive business is entrusted to a smaller body, consisting of from five to thirteen members, and called in the German-speaking cantons the Administrative Council (Regierungs Rath) or the Small Council (Kleiner Rath). The higher judges are in most cantons appointed by the Great Council, but those of lower rank are elected by the people, and always for comparatively short terms. Police belongs to the cantons, which are bound to execute Federal as well as Cantonal laws.

This kind of government is, as already observed, everywhere rooted in a system of self-governing communes, where the inhabitants administer all their local affairs, and is as completely popular as can well be imagined. The Swiss having reduced to a minimum the powers of any single executive official, there is no official to whom a veto power could be entrusted. No one can disallow laws, except the people themselves by means of the Referendum, *i.e.* the right of the citizens to vote directly upon measures passed by the Cantonal Legislatures. To this right I shall presently return, as it is an institution applicable to the Confederation also. There are, moreover, seven cantons which permit the people, by a

[1] The question of extending the suffrage to women was in 1919 being raised in Neuchâtel and Zürich.

specified majority, to demand the dissolution and re-election of the Great Council as no longer truly representing popular sentiment. This resembles the American "Recall" to be described in a later chapter.[1]

The members of the Great or Cantonal Council are elected in districts and frequently re-elected on the expiry of their term, which usually lasts three or four years. The payment allotted to them is small. Everywhere in Switzerland, though most conspicuously in the smaller rural cantons, salaries are extremely low and offer no prize for ambition. This Council, which meets twice a year, is a body so much in the eyes of the people that it is not exposed to that distrust which has led to the restriction of the powers of American State Legislatures, nor has it favours to dispense such as lie in the gift of those assemblies.[2] It exercises a general control of cantonal affairs, votes the budget, makes the laws, supervises the administration. Nearly half of the cantons (omitting those with a Landesgemeinde) entrust to it the choice of the Executive Council, while in the rest the more thoroughly democratic plan of giving that function to the people has been adopted.

The Small (or Executive) Council is legally subordinate to the Great Council, which can direct it how to act, or reverse its decisions; but its members are admitted to speak in the Great Council, and its position and knowledge secure for it great influence with that body. It reports, it submits measures, it drafts bills when required to do so. It has the strength which experience acquired by permanence in office, confers, for the persons who compose it are usually re-elected, term after term. This is, however, not invariably the case, because in some cantons the balance of parties oscillates, and an effort may be made to instal adherents of whichever party may happen to be dominant. Still, broadly speaking, the Executive Council is a business Board with little political colour; and good working relations between the two bodies seem to subsist equally where the Great Council and where the people elect the Executive. The fact that in the latter case the Executive holds by an independent title has not, as

[1] See chapters on the United States.
[2] Of the Cantonal Judges I shall speak when we come to the judiciary of the Confederation.

some predicted, encouraged it to resist the legislature.
Though in nearly every canton one or more representatives
of the minority or minorities find their way on to the Executive Council, despite the fact that the vote is taken by a
"general ticket" over the whole canton, still, in order to assure the representation of minorities, several cantons have
adopted systems of proportional representation, for every
body feels that each important section should have its spokes-
man and its share of office.[1]   Switzerland is specially fitted
for such a system, because nowhere are so many voters independent, some not reckoning themselves party men, and most
of them disposed to please themselves rather than their party
leaders.   Opinion, however, has not yet finally declared itself
for or against the plan.   Some cantons have refused constitutional amendments framed to establish it, its opponents
observing that it encourages minorities to put forward as candidates not the men, and especially the moderate men, whom
general opinion will recognize as the best, but the keenest
partisans who have worked hardest for the party.   Without
proportional representation, men of the former class would
have been nominated in the hope of their drawing votes from
the other side, but the latter sort can, under the proportional
system, be made sure of election anyhow.   Hence even those
who admit the right of minorities to be represented have
argued that this was attained in a better way under the present disposition of the majority to make room for good candidates who do not belong to their own party.

In comparing Swiss with American bodies one must always remember how great is the difference in size between the
average Canton and the average State.   In most Swiss cantons all the leading men are known to one another and to
everybody else so it is easier for the voter to form a judgment
on the merits of candidates.   To serve the Canton has been
regarded rather as a duty than as a privilege, and as in earlier
days men were often compelled to accept public office, so now
some cantons impose a penalty on citizens who neglect to vote.
There has hitherto been in many cantons no sharp division
between parties and but little party organization; and in
the more backward rural cantons the representatives, coming

[1] This view is indeed expressly recognized in the Constitutions of
Bern and Aargau.

largely from the less-educated class, are frequently chosen in
respect not of the political doctrines they profess, but of their
local reputation and influence.   In so far, party counts for
little in cantonal affairs.   But there are also some cantons,
such as Geneva, where the smallness of the area sustains the
warmth of political life, and where the element of personal
leadership comes more fully into play than it does in the
Assembly of the Confederation.   In these, and especially
wherever the growth of Socialism has alarmed the conservative sentiment of the peasantry and the richer townsfolk,
cantonal elections are fought with spirit upon party lines.

GOVERNMENT OF THE CONFEDERATION

The Federal Constitution

The Constitution of the Confederation was enacted and
can be changed by the people only, acting both as a Swiss
Nation and as the peoples of the several cantons.   The Legislature may, if both Houses concur, decide on a revision, and
then proceed to make it, thereafter submitting it to a popular
vote.   If, however, only one House desires it, or if it is
demanded by 50,000 qualified citizens, a popular vote is
taken as to whether there shall be a revision, and if this is
carried in the affirmative by a majority of citizens voting,
then, after a new election of the Legislature, the two Houses
proceed to amendment, and the amended Constitution is submitted to the people.   If it is approved by a majority of votes
of the citizens and also by a majority of the cantons, it goes
into effect.   Where no general revision but only a specific
amendment is proposed, either by both Houses or by 50,000
citizens, the preliminary vote of the people is not required,
but the amendment goes straight to the people for acceptance
or rejection.   The 50,000 may either propose their amendment in the form of a clause or merely state its principle
and ask the Legislature to put their idea into proper shape.
The Constitution of 1874 has been amended twelve times between 1874 and 1918, five amendments submitted between
those years having been rejected.

The Constitution is a longer document than is the Federal Constitution of the United States, on which it is largely
modelled, and enters more fully into details, some of which

belong to the sphere of ordinary rather than to that of constitutional legislation. Three of its features deserve special mention.

First.— The distribution of powers between the National and the Cantonal Governments is generally similar to that of the American and Australian Federations. The National Government has the control of foreign relations, save that the cantons are permitted, subject to Federal approval, to make with one another and with neighbouring foreign States agreements regarding border and police relations, not being of a political nature.[1] It declares war, makes peace, concludes treaties, manages the national army. (No canton may, without Federal permission, maintain a force exceeding 300 men.) It owns and works all the railways, except the Simplon-Loetschberg line from Bern to Domo d' Ossola, and some tourist lines running up the mountains. It administers all Federal property, takes charge of posts and telegraphs, of copyrights, of currency and national finance, of banking and of customs duties, controls water-power, and has a monopoly of gunpowder and of the production of alcohol. It legislates upon commerce (including bankruptcy) and upon contracts generally, except those relating to land, which are left to the cantons; and has now (as already observed) enacted a complete civil code. It determines questions as to the meaning and construction of the Constitution, including cases in which a canton is alleged to have transgressed that instrument. These are exclusive powers. It has also some concurrent powers exerciseable conjointly with the cantons, and can supervise the action of the cantons in certain fields, such as industrial conditions, insurance, highways, the regulation of the press and education, requiring the cantons to provide instruction which shall be compulsory, unsectarian, and gratuitous. When it exerts these concurrent powers its statutes prevail against those of a canton.

Secondly.— There is little in the nature of what Americans call a Bill of Rights, far less than in the Constitution of the United States. Trial by jury is not mentioned, but capital punishment for political offences is forbidden.

Thirdly.— The conflicts between the Roman Church and

[1] This provision was designed to prevent any attempt to create another *Sonderbund*.

the Protestant parties which so long distracted Switzerland
have suggested various provisions relating to religion. Freedom of belief and the free exercise of worship " within the
limits of morality and public order " are guaranteed throughout every canton. No one can be compelled to take part in
any religious society or religious act, nor shall his civil or
political rights be abridged by any ecclesiastical provisions,
nor shall religious views absolve from the performance of
civic duties, nor taxes be required from any one the proceeds
of which are appropriated to a religious body to which he
does not belong. No bishopric may be created without the
consent of the Federal Government. Ecclesiastical jurisdiction is abolished; burial-places are to belong to the civil authorities; the right of marriage is not to be limited on religious or economic grounds. Neither the Jesuits nor any Order affiliated with them shall exist; the participation of their
members in church or school work is forbidden, and the Federal Government may extend this prohibition to other religious Orders whose action endangers the State or disturbs
inter-denominational peace. These provisions, however, do
not inhibit a canton from maintaining what may be called a
State establishment of religion, and some in fact so do, the
civil authorities supporting by funds and to some extent
guiding or controlling the ecclesiastical organization. This
happens to a greater extent in several Protestant cantons than
it does in Catholic, because the Roman Church has an organization and authority of its own.

The Frame of National Government

The Federal Government consists of four authorities: (*a*)
the Legislature, viz. the National Assembly (Bundesver-
sammlung, Assemblée Fédérale), which is the supreme representative body; (*b*) the Executive, viz. the Federal Council (Bundesrath, Conseil Fédéral), an administrative body of
seven members; (*c*) the Judiciary, viz. one Federal Tribunal
(Bundesgericht)[1]; (*d*) the People of the Confederation,
which, being the final authority and empowered to act by its
direct vote, has the ultimate control of legislation, and through
legislation, of the government as a whole.

[1] The Judicial Department is not, however, as will presently appear,
a " branch of the Government " in the American sense.

The Federal Legislature

The National Assembly consists of two Houses: the National Council (National Rath, Conseil National) and the Council of States, *i.e.* Cantons (Stände Rath, Conseil d'États).

The National Council (corresponding to the American House of Representatives) is elected by the citizens of the cantons in cantonal districts and now (1919) by proportional representation. The smallest cantons and the smallest of the six half-cantons have each one member, while Bern has 32 and Zürich 25. The total number is now 189. All are elected by manhood suffrage,[1] on the last Sunday in October, once in three years, a church being frequently the polling-place. Each Chamber sits for three years, there being no power of dissolution. It meets regularly four times a year,[2] March, June, September, and December, choosing its President and Vice-President for each session, neither being eligible for the same office in the next consecutive regular session. Each member is paid twenty-five francs (about $5) a day for each day when he attends, besides his travelling expenses. The Chambers meet at 8 A.M. in summer, at 9 in winter, and the sessions seldom last more than three weeks.

The Council of States, corresponding to the Senate in the United States and in Australia, consists of two members from each canton, chosen by each canton according to its own laws, in most cantons by the people, in others by the Cantonal or "Great" Council. The term of service also varies, some cantons choosing councillors for one, some for three years, while Valais elects for two. Their salaries (nearly everywhere the same as those of members of the National Council) are paid by the cantons.

For some few purposes, such as the election of the administrative Federal Council and of its President, of the Chancellor, and of the Commander-in-Chief of the Army, and also of the Federal Tribunal, and also for the determination of legal questions, and the granting of pardons, the two Houses

[1] Excluding persons who have been deprived of their civic rights for crime, and (in some cantons) bankrupts and paupers.

[2] The Federal Council may convoke an extraordinary session should any emergency arise.

sit together as a National Assembly, the President of the National Council presiding.

The powers of the two Houses, legislative, administrative, and judicial, are equal, and (as in Australia, but not in the United States) the smaller House, which represents the cantons, is in practice rather the weaker of the two, men of energy and ambition preferring to sit in the National Council. There is no provision for deciding an issue on which the Houses may differ, but differences are neither frequent nor serious, because the Council of States is from its mode of choice practically no more conservative than the larger House. The ultimate control of legislation reserved to the whole people makes this omission unimportant. A member of one House cannot sit in the other also, but may hold any post in the government of a canton, even that of a judge.

Each House has what is called a Bureau, composed of the President and " scrutateurs " (four in the National Council, two in the Council of States). They take the divisions, and, with the President, nominate the Committees (called Commissions), unless the House itself does so. These last are appointed *pro hac vice,* there being no standing Committees.

Members may speak in any one of the three languages, German, French, and Italian, and every public document is published in all three, though nearly all educated Swiss know both German and French, and the Italian members can usually speak the latter tongue.

The normal Swiss member shows just the qualities we associate with the Swiss character. He is solid, shrewd, unemotional, or at any rate indisposed to reveal his emotions. He takes a practical common-sense and what may be called middle-class business view of questions, being less prone than is the German to recur to theoretical first principles or than is the Frenchman to be dazzled by glittering phrases. Yet his way of thinking is, if not more philosophical, rather more systematic and more guided by general principles than is that of the American or English legislator.

Within this general type a difference may be noted between the German-speaking and the French-speaking Swiss. These latter, who are by race partly Celtic, partly Burgundian, though differentiated from the more purely Celtic stock of East Central France through the larger admixture of Teutonic blood and the influence of Teutonic fellow-citizens,[1] still remain swifter-minded, more excitable, more disposed to acclaim and follow a leader than is the Germanic Switzer, yet are therewithal also of a conservative temper, not theorists in their politics. The German-speaking or " Allemannic " Swiss of Eastern and North Central Switzerland consider themselves to differ materially from the South German Swabians north of the Rhine, though this difference need not be ascribed to the fact that there is a good deal of the old Helvetic (Celtic) blood all over Switzerland.

These qualities of the individual have given its peculiar quality to the Swiss national legislature. It has been the most business-like legislative body in the world, doing its work quietly and thinking of little else. Each session lasts from three to five weeks. There are few set debates and still fewer set speeches. Rhetoric is almost unknown; and it is at once a cause and a consequence of this fact that manifestations of dissent or of approval are rarely heard. Speakers are not interrupted and rarely applauded. If after a spirited peroration some cries of " Bravo " are heard, the phenomenon is noted as unusual. Every member has his desk, and though neither of the two halls is so large as to make hearing difficult, many members seem in both to pay little attention to most of the speeches, usually delivered in a quiet conversational tone and with little regard for finish of form. In the National Council members speak standing, in the Council of States from their seats.

There are no official stenographers, and the debates are but scantily reported, even in the leading newspapers, though now and then an important discussion is, by order of the Houses, reported verbatim and published.[2] The alternation of speeches from German to French and back again reduces the vivacity of debate. The German speakers are said to be more long-winded than the French. Excellent order is kept; obstruction is unknown; and divisions are much less frequent than in the British Parliament or in Congress. In fact the

[1] Western Switzerland constituted in the earlier Middle Ages the kingdom of Transjurane Burgundy, formed by the Teutonic Burgundian tribes who came from the Middle Rhineland. It stretched from the Rhine above Basle to the Pennine Alps.

[2] This happened occasionally when important deliverances of opinion were made during and after the late European war.

proceedings, just because they are so business-like, because rhetoric is not in fashion, and men think rather of what they have to say than of how to say it, would be pronounced dull by a French Parliamentarian.   There is in them little of that cut and thrust, that brisk repartee, that personal element of invective and countercharge which adds keenness and pungency to all debates, and in which members of other legislatures find their most constant source of interest.

The very aspect of each House suggests reasons for this. Each hall is semicircular, and members of the same party do not necessarily sit together: indeed they usually sit by cantons.   There is no bench for a Ministry nor for an Opposition, since neither exists.   The executive officials, those Federal Councillors who will be presently mentioned, have seats on a dais right and left of the President, but, not being members, they are not party leaders.   Thus that strife for office and the sweets of office felt as always present in the background of debates in the assemblies of England, France, and other parliamentary countries, finds little place in the Swiss legislature.

Attendance is regular and punctual.   A member absenting himself without strong reasons would be deemed neglectful, and unless he furnishes such a reason for non-appearance at roll-call, does not receive payment for the day.   The city of Bern, where the legislature meets, presents few counter-attractions of business or pleasure to distract members from their duties; and rarely does it happen that any one is summoned by telegraph to a division.

Elections to the Federal Houses raise, for reasons to be presently stated, little popular excitement, and a member who seeks re-election is usually returned, for there is no great oscillation in the strength of parties, and the Swiss are the least changeful of all democracies, not lightly withdrawing a confidence once given.   Neither do they worry their representatives, who might well be envied by French deputies or American Congressmen.

There are few constitutional limitations on the power of the legislature, except of course those that are involved in the very nature of a federation the component parts of which retain legislative power.   Such limitations, not thought necessary when the Constitutions of 1848 and 1874 were framed,

are deemed even less needed now, because the power of the
people can, through the Referendum, be invoked to overrule
the legislature.   Moreover, just as the small size of the country, the small numbers in the legislative bodies, and the tra-
ditionally strict standard of honesty by which politicians are
judged, combine to render needless provisions against the
abuse of legislative functions for private ends, so public
opinion would at once check any attempt by the Councils
to extend their powers beyond the limits the Constitution
prescribes.

The parties play a rôle far inferior to that of a party in
France or England, because in the executive sphere the
Houses cannot displace the Ministers, and in the legislative
sphere the Houses have not the last word, since that belongs
to the people.   In both Chambers accordingly the parties
have but a loose organization, for though each has a leader his
functions and authority are slender.   There are no whips
nor any summonses like those which in England are daily
issued to members of the party.   A general concurrence of
opinion upon leading principles suffices to keep each party
pretty well together upon the graver issues raised in the
Assembly; while upon points which do not involve party
principles, a member votes as he pleases.   The Constitution declares that the member is not a delegate to be fettered
by instructions from his canton or his constituency, and
neither colleagues nor constituents complain unless he can
be supposed either to have sinister motives or to be practically
renouncing the doctrines for which the party stands.   When,
however, offices have to be conferred by vote of the Houses, it
becomes necessary that a party should meet in caucus to agree
on the candidate it will support.   These are important gatherings, since the seven Federal Councillors chosen every three
years, and the twenty-four Federal judges, chosen every six
years, are appointed by the two Houses sitting together.

To explain how legislation is cared for, though the duty
and function of preparing and proposing it belongs neither
to a party leader nor, as in the United States, to the Chairman of a Committee, let it be said that measures coming before the Chambers are of two kinds.   Some are administrative, being such as the Executive in the course of its functions finds necessary.   These are drafted and submitted by

the Federal Council, one or more of whose members attend to explain and recommend them. Others, of wider scope, may be demanded by public opinion, or by the wishes of the dominant party. At the instance of any member a resolution may be passed requesting the Federal Council to address itself to the subject and prepare a Bill. When so drafted, a Bill goes on its way through the Houses, sometimes, if it is complex or if enquiry is needed, being referred to a Committee. Financial Bills are of course in a special sense the business of the Federal Council, which has charge of revenue and expenditure. No difficulty seems to be found in making legislation keep abreast of the wishes and needs of the people. Indeed, it more frequently goes ahead of than falls behind those wishes.

There are in the National Legislature few Bills of the category called " private " or " local " in England and America, partly because these matters largely belong to the cantonal legislatures or to the Communes, partly because nearly all the great railways have been taken over by the Federal Government, and any considerable new railway enterprise would be undertaken by it. Such concessions as remain to be granted, e.g. for those tourist railways up mountains which have wrought such mischief to the scenery of Switzerland, seldom offer a prospect of profits so large as to involve the dangers which the granting of concessions brings in some countries, and against which the British Parliament found it needful to provide by stringent rules. Thus a formidable source of corruption is absent. What has been said above regarding individual politicians may be said of the legislature generally. It is free from even the suspicion of being used for the purposes of private gain. " Lobbying " (if any) is on a small scale. It may be thought that the customs tariff would here, as in the United States, and to a less extent in some European countries, give an opening for the pressure of selfish interests applying sordid inducements. The Swiss tariff was till recently a low one, as compared with those of its great neighbours, and originally a tariff for revenue, since the Federal Government did not then levy direct taxes. Though agriculturists and manufacturers are said to have begun to press demands for higher protective import duties, neither section has as yet done so in an illegitimate way, nor have rich manufacturers made those large contributions to party funds which became a scandal in the United States. Nor could they, seeing that there are no party funds except the trifling sums raised for election expenses.

Had there been between 1874 and 1919 a strong and compact Opposition, instead of three weak Oppositions, only one of which was really keen, proceedings in the Assembly would have been more lively, and the ruling party itself would have been knit more closely together. But the comparatively loose order in which that party was wont to march, and its disposition not to monopolize offices or to try bold experiments, mitigated the criticisms of the three Oppositions. They did not set themselves to hamper the Administration, so the wheels of progress were not clogged as in most parliamentary countries. The habit of considering measures in a non-partisan spirit has been wholesome for the nation, and did much to allay the hotter party strife which went on in a few cantons.

Why did not the dominant party, being so large, break up into sections? Partly because there were few motives of personal ambition leading to the creation of groups following a leader; partly because the existence of a compact, though comparatively small, minority, held together by religious sentiment, made them feel the need for cohesion. In the background there was always standing the recollection of the Sonderbund War. Hence constant vigilance to hold in check any designs the Catholic hierarchy might form.

To-day — I have been speaking so far of Switzerland up to 1920 — one hears it remarked that the intellectual level of the legislature has been declining during the last twenty years, and that public life shows fewer eminent figures. Welti, Ruchonnet, and Numa Droz are cited as instances of leaders who have not left successors of equal mark. If this be so, it may be partly due to the fact that the Swiss, having settled the great constitutional and political questions which occupied them from 1830 till 1874, were living in quieter times not so fit to call out men's powers. Those who succeed a great generation which fought and suffered for high principles usually fall below its moral and intellectual level, as happened in England after 1660, and in Italy when the heroes of the *Risorgimento* had passed away.   Nor is it to be forgotten that in Switzerland, as elsewhere, the development of manufacturing industries and of commerce and finance opened up careers which many men of talent and ambition find more attractive.   This is one of the reasons which may be assigned for the decline in legislatures observed in most countries.   Apart from this want of brilliance, neither of the two Houses is open to serious criticism.   They do their work efficiently; they maintain a good standard of decorum and manners; they retain the respect of the people; they work harmoniously with the Executive.

The Federal Executive

The Federal Council (Bundesrath) is one of the institutions of Switzerland that best deserves study.   In no other modern republic is executive power entrusted to a Council instead of to a man, and in no other free country has the working Executive so little to do with party politics.   The Council is not a Cabinet, like that of Britain and the countries which have imitated her cabinet system, for it does not lead the Legislature, and is not displaceable thereby. Neither is it independent of the Legislature, like the Executive of the United States and of other republics which have borrowed therefrom the so-called " Presidential system," and though it has some of the features of both those schemes, it differs from both in having no distinctly partisan character. It stands outside party, is not chosen to do party work, does not determine party policy, yet is not wholly without some party colour.

This interesting and indeed unique institution consists of seven persons, elected by the Federal Assembly for three years.   One of the seven is annually chosen by the Federal Assembly to be President of this Council, and another to be Vice-President, and neither may be re-elected to the same post for the following year.   Not more than one Councillor can be chosen from any one canton.   Custom prescribes that one Councillor shall always come from Bern and another from Zürich; and one is usually chosen from the important French-speaking canton Vaud.   One is also, again by custom, taken from a Roman Catholic canton, and (very often) one from the Italian-speaking Ticino. They cannot, during their term of office, sit in either House nor hold any other Federal nor any Cantonal post. To each member an administrative department is allotted, for which he is primarily responsible, but the Council meets constantly as a sort of Cabinet for the discussion of important business; all decisions emanate from it as a whole, as does the elaborate report which it annually presents to the legislature; and it speaks as a whole to foreign Powers. Its members appear, but do not vote, in both branches of the legislature. When business relating to a particular department is being there considered, the Councillor who manages that department attends, answers questions, gives explanations, and joins in debate.

The Councillor chosen President for the year has no more power than his colleagues, and is really only their Chairman. But he bears the title of President of the Confederation (Bundespraesident), is the first citizen of the nation, and represents it on all ceremonial occasions. His salary is 26,500 francs a year, that of each of his colleagues being 25,000 (about £1000, $5000).

Besides its general administrative (including financial) work, the charge of foreign relations and of the army, the Council supervises the conduct of the permanent civil service of the Confederation.

Another most useful function is that, already referred to, of drafting Bills to be brought before the Legislature. When a proposal suggesting legislation for a specified purpose is accepted, the Council prepares a Bill, and it frequently advises either House, at any stage, regarding the form or substance of measures submitted. It has also judicial duties, for since there are not administrative Courts, like those of France or Italy, such cases as arise regarding the behaviour of officials are not within the sphere of the Federal Tribunal, but are dealt with by the Council, subject, as a rule, to an appeal to the Legislature.[1]

The Federal Councillors are usually re-elected so long as they desire to serve. Between 1848 and 1919 there was only one exception to this rule, which had a good effect in sus-

[1] In 1919 a plan for the creation of a tribunal to deal with administrative cases involving complaints against officials was being considered in pursuance of a constitutional amendment passed in 1914.

taining friendly personal relations. Though they have been active politicians, they are chosen in respect of their capacity as administrators, not as speakers or tacticians. Since the National Assembly is the school of public business always before the eyes of the country, and in which men can show their ability to their associates, it is usually from among their own members that the Houses select. As there has been always (since 1891) one Catholic, so a Liberal has been frequently chosen, although the majority was Radical from 1848 till 1919. Eloquence is neither needed nor sought for in a Federal Councillor. It is administrative skill, mental grasp, good sense, tact and temper that recommend a candidate. That selections are well made appears from the practice of re-election.[1]

Were it their function to initiate and advocate policy, this continuity would be scarcely possible. Policy, however, belongs to the Assembly; though in practice the Council by its knowledge and experience exerts much influence even on questions of general principle, while details are usually left to it. In foreign affairs it has a pretty free hand, but the scrupulously neutral attitude of the country on these questions has been so plainly prescribed by the geographical position of Switzerland between four great military neighbours that differences of opinion on that subject seldom arose.[2] The bulk of its work is administrative, including not only the management of affairs distinctly Federal, such as the collection and expenditure of national revenue and the management of national undertakings, of which the railways are an important branch, but also a general supervision of the Cantonal Governments in order to secure that Federal law is adequately enforced everywhere. This task, always delicate and sometimes difficult, has been successfully performed because the Assembly supports the Council, and the Council has not only military force at its command, but can also reduce a canton to submission by withholding any subvention due to it from the Federal Treasury.

So important and multifarious is the work performed by the Council that visitors were, before the European War,

---

[1] One is sometimes told that this practice makes it hard to get rid of a Councillor who is no longer equal to his work.

[2] During the war of 1914–1918 difficulties did arise, but into these I need not enter, for the circumstances were most exceptional.

1914, surprised to find how small was the official staff attached to the several departments, and how limited the accommodation provided for the Councillors and their secretaries. Even the plainness of the arrangements that existed at Washington fifty years ago did not reach this austere republican simplicity.

A peculiar feature distinguishing this Swiss Executive from any other is that though the Council acts as one body, differences in opinion are permitted and allowed to become known. Its members occasionally speak on opposite sides in the legislature. Such differences rarely cause trouble, because if they turn on points of administration, these are compromised or perhaps settled in accordance either with the opinion of the Councillor in whose sphere the matter lies, or with what seems the wish of the Assembly, while if they touch legislation they are determined by that body. I have nevertheless heard it remarked that the need for compromise where views differ sometimes prevents a question from being dealt with on broad principles.

Not less surprising, to a foreign observer, than these internal relations of the Councillors, occasional dissidence with practically unbroken co-operation, are the relations of the Federal Council to the Assembly. Legally the servant of the Legislature, it exerts in practice almost as much authority as do English, and more than do some French Cabinets, so that it may be said to lead as well as to follow. It is a guide as well as an instrument, and often suggests as well as drafts measures. Nevertheless the Assembly occasionally overrules the Council, reversing its decisions or materially altering its Bills; and this makes no difference to the continuance in office of the Council nor to the confidence it receives, such is the power of usage and tradition in a practical people where public opinion expects every one to subordinate his own feelings to the public good, and where personal ambition has played a smaller part than in any other free country since 1848.

It is sometimes alleged that the influence of party has been visible in the tendency of the majority in the Assembly to support the Federal Council even when it may have gone astray. The Council has no power over that majority, for it cannot, like a British Cabinet, threaten a dissolution; nor has it the indirect control over members which the American Executive may exert by obliging or disobliging members in the matter of appointments, because appointments are few and not lucrative.   The suggestion rather is that as the majority has chosen, and is therefore in a sense responsible for, the Federal Council, it feels bound to stand by it, right or wrong.   The reluctance, however, to lower the authority of the Executive department by scolding it for a past error of judgment when it has turned into a new and safer path, is a pardonable and (within limits) even a useful tendency.   Although a dominant party is usually the better for having a strong Opposition to confront it, there has been seldom any disposition in the Federal Council or the majority of the Assembly, to abuse their respective powers in pressing business through.   The existence of the Referendum would anyhow prevent them from using those powers to pass measures against the popular will.   But apart from that peculiar institution, one can hardly imagine a majority in Switzerland making itself a tyrant, since nowhere would public opinion more promptly interfere to protect a minority.   The disposition to settle differences by arrangement is a noteworthy feature of the country.

In its constitutional position and working the Federal Council has been deemed one of the conspicuous successes of the Swiss system, for it secures three great advantages, specially valuable in a country, governed by the whole people.

It provides a body which is able not only to influence and advise the ruling Assembly without lessening its responsibility to the citizens, but which, because it is non-partisan, can mediate, should need arise, between contending parties, adjusting difficulties and arranging compromises in a spirit of conciliation.

It enables proved administrative talent to be kept in the service of the nation, irrespective of the personal opinions of the Councillors upon the particular issues which may for the moment divide parties.   Men opposed to the main principles on which the Assembly desires the government to be conducted could not indeed profitably administer in accordance with those principles, for a total want of sympathy with the laws passed would affect them in applying those laws.

But where differences are not fundamental, or do not touch the department a particular Minister deals with, why lose your best servant because he does not agree with you on matters outside the scope of his work? As well change your physician because you differ from him in religion.

It secures continuity in policy and permits traditions to be formed. The weak side of continuity and traditions is the tendency for administration to become " groovy " and so to fall behind new needs and neglect new methods. This is hardly a danger in Switzerland, where ministers are always accessible, and are in constant touch with the Assembly, while it is a real gain to avoid the dislocations which the arrival of new ministers causes, and to save the time lost while they are learning their duties.

To secure these two latter advantages is comparatively easy in countries like the (late) German Empire or Japan, where ministers hold office at the pleasure of the monarch rather than of the Parliament. They are to some extent secured in England and France through the existence of a permanent non-political head of each great branch of the Civil Service, whose experience illumines the darkness of the political minister who brings no previous knowledge, and perhaps nothing but fluent speech or (in former days) family connections, to his new functions. Switzerland is, however, the only democracy which has found a means of keeping its administrators practically out of party politics.

The Federal Judiciary

The Judiciary is in Switzerland a less important part of the machinery of Federal government than it is in the United States or in the Australian Commonwealth, and may therefore be briefly dealt with.

There is only one Federal Tribunal, consisting of fourteen judges appointed by the two Houses of the Legislature sitting together as a National Assembly. The term of office is six years, for in Switzerland democratic doctrine forbids extended grants of power, but the custom of re-electing a judge who has discharged his functions efficiently has established what is practically a life tenure. Though no qualifications are prescribed by law, pains are taken to select men of legal learning and ability, and while political predilections may sometimes be present, it is not alleged that they have injured the quality of the bench, any more than the occasional action of like influences tells on the general confidence felt in England and (as respects the Federal Courts) in the United States in the highest courts of those countries. The salaries, like all others in Switzerland, are low, £600 ($3000) a year, with an additional £40 for the President.

The Tribunal sits at Lausanne, a concession to the sentiment of the French-speaking cantons, since the Legislature has its home at German-speaking Bern. The jurisdiction of the Federal Court is less strictly defined by the Constitution than is the case in America or Australia, for the Legislature has received and used a power to extend it.[1] Originally created to deal with cases to which the Confederation or a canton is a party, its competence has been extended to other classes of suits, and it may be resorted to, by the agreement of litigants, in cases where the sum involved exceeds a prescribed amount. It has criminal jurisdiction, with a jury, in cases of treason or of other offences against Federal law. Its power further extends to certain classes of civil appeals (where the sum involved is of a certain amount) from Cantonal Courts, and also to matters of public law and the rights of citizens under either the Federal or a Cantonal Constitution. There are no inferior Federal Courts, because the bulk of judicial work continues to be discharged by the Cantonal judges, nor has the Tribunal (as in the United States) a staff of its own all over the country to execute judgments, this duty being left to the Federal Council,[2] acting (in practice) through the Cantonal authorities.

In two respects this Swiss Court differs materially from the Federal Judiciary of the United States. Those cases which are in continental Europe called Administrative, i.e. cases in which the application of administrative provisions is involved or in which Government officials are either charged with some fault or are sued by a private person for some alleged wrong, have been reserved for the Federal Council or Federal Assembly, whereas in the United States, as in

[1] The powers of the Tribunal are stated in Arts. CX. to CXIV. of the Constitution, in terms which it is not easy to abridge, except in a general and somewhat vague way.

[2] Constitution, Art. CII. 5.

England, they are dealt with by the ordinary courts.[1]   Secondly, the Swiss Tribunal cannot declare any Federal law
or part of a law to be invalid as infringing some provision of
the Federal Constitution.   It may annul a Cantonal law as
transgressing either the Federal or a Cantonal Constitution,
but the Constitution expressly assigns to the Federal Legislature the right of interpreting both the Federal Constitution itself and all laws passed thereunder, so that it can put
its own construction on every law which it has itself passed,
without the intervention of any judicial authority to correct
it.   This principle does not commend itself to American
lawyers, who hold that the powers of a legislature cannot
go beyond those which the people have by the Constitution
conferred upon it, and that there can be no security for the
observance of that fundamental instrument if the interpretation of the people's intentions, as therein expressed, is left
to be determined by the legislature which has passed a statute
alleged to contravene the Constitution, because that would
make the violating body the judge in its own case.   This
view, however, does not prevail in continental Europe, where
republican Swiss and French, as well as monarchist German, lawyers have clung to the tradition which subordinates
the judiciary to the executive and legislative powers.   Two
very high Swiss authorities, while admitting the American
system to be more logical, observed to me that in Switzerland
no harm had resulted, and that the rights of the people could
not be seriously infringed, because they can be at any time
invoked to protect themselves.   If a law of the National
Assembly is arraigned as a breach of the Constitution, a demand may be made forthwith under the Referendum for its
submission to a popular vote, which will either reject or confirm the law.   This remedy is, however, not available as
regards those laws which the Assembly has declared to be
either " urgent " or " not of general application."   In these
the Assembly remains uncontrolled, save by public opinion.
Constitutions are in Continental Europe not so strictly in-
terpreted, nor constitutional provisions so carefully distinguished from ordinary laws, as has been the case in America,

[1] A private citizen who is party in a civil suit may also contest before a court the validity of a Cantonal law alleged to transgress the
Federal Constitution.

whose example has in this respect influenced Canada and Australia, but not Switzerland.

It may be added that as the judges of the Federal Tribunal are appointed for six years only, there is an objection to entrusting them with the power of disallowing legislation, which does not exist where, as in the United States National Government, the judges are appointed for life. The American judge is independent; the Swiss judge might conceivably be influenced by the wish to secure his own re-election.

Here let me return to the Cantons to add a few words on their judges.

The Cantonal Judiciary

In the cantons we find (except in the smallest) a Court of Appeals, Courts of First Instance, and Justices of the Peace. All are chosen either by the people voting directly (this of course includes the Landesgemeinde cantons) or by the Cantonal (" Great ") Council, never by the smaller or Executive Council. The salaries are low, and though the term is short, usually three or four years, the custom of re-election prevails. There has been a controversy over the respective merits of these two modes of choice, some arguing that the Council can form a better judgment on the technical capacity of a candidate, others replying that the people are more likely to be free from personal favouritism or political bias. This assumes what is perhaps generally true in Switzerland, but would not be true in America, that the people will not be guided in their action by party organizations.[1] The persons selected are described as being usually of high character and competent, some cantons requiring evidence of considerable legal attainments. If they are not always erudite, it must be remembered that less value is attached to professional learning and " scientific " law in Switzerland than in such countries as England, France, and America, not only because the bar holds a less important place, but also because the Swiss dislike technicalities and refinements, preferring a rough, simple, " practical," or, as they say, " popular " (*volksthümlich*) sort of justice. The inferior courts are

[1] In Zürich, and probably elsewhere also, the Bar try to secure good selections.

expected to decide on the broad merits of the questions that come before them. Arbitration is largely used to avoid litigation. Unsatisfactory as the election of judges by the people for short terms has proved to be in the States of the American Union, it is not considered to work badly in the cantons, where it is argued that the Council might choose no better, that the people, not being influenced by political motives, have no interest except that of finding a trustworthy fellow-citizen to settle their disputes, that the vigilance which a small community exercises provides a safeguard for good conduct, and that there is no single high cantonal official, resembling the Governor in an American State, in whom the power of appointment could be vested with a certainty of making him responsible for its exercise. As an unfortunate choice can be remedied at the next election, displacement by such a method as impeachment has not seemed needful.

The institution of the jury, long prized in English-speaking countries, where it is a natural growth of the soil, is in Switzerland little used in civil cases except for those relating to the press, and in criminal trials for grave offences, but justice is made popular by sometimes appointing non-professional judges and by the practice of associating lay assessors with the regular judge and there are cantons in which it is administered gratis, or where legal advice and assistance are provided for the poor. Zürich tried to reduce the cost of trials by throwing the profession of advocacy open to all the world with no security for legal knowledge, but the experiment failed.[1]

The Swiss find no fault with their Cantonal judiciary. It may be, except in cities like Geneva or Basle, less learned than that of Germany, but it serves the everyday needs of the people. Its members are never charged with corruption, if sometimes with favouritism, nor are they below the level of the advocates who appear before them. Where a plaintiff (or a defendant) is a native of the canton where the suit is being tried, and the other party an outsider, the judge is said to be disposed to lean towards the native, because he fears to displease his fellow-citizens of the same canton. (In the United States, where the litigant parties belong to different States, a Federal Court can be resorted to.) The impres-

[1] Dr. E. Zürcher in *Moderne Demokratie*, p. 16.

sion left on the observer's mind is that choice by the Great
Council is safer than choice by the vote of the citizens, for
the popularly elected judge may be influenced, consciously or
unconsciously, by the wish to avoid offending a prominent
neighbour.   Taking purity and promptitude, cheapness and
certainty (*i.e.* the strict observance of settled principles and
rules) to be (apart from judicial honesty) the four chief
merits of any judicial system, the results of the Swiss system
may be deemed as good as or better than those of England
or of the United States as respects the three former of these
requisites, although in point of legal science both of the latter
may surpass the judges in the Courts of the smaller cantons.

The Civil Service and the Army

The Federal officials, both in the capital and throughout
the country, are (except a very few of the most important
which lie in the gift of the National Assembly) appointed
by the Federal Council, and are dismissible by it for any
dereliction of duty.   Appointments to the higher posts are
for a term of three years; but reappointment is so much the
rule that the Civil Service may be described as practically
permanent.   Very rarely is any one dismissed for political
reasons; nor do such reasons play any great part in selection,
though there may be a tendency to prefer those who belong
to the dominant party.   Thus nothing resembling the Spoils
System of the United States exists, a fact, however, attributable also to the meagreness of salaries and to the lack of the
social importance which office bestows in France and Germany.   Places are not worth struggling for, and public opinion would reprehend any attempt to appoint incompetent
men for party reasons.   Till the railways were acquired by
the Confederation, the Civil Service, consisting practically of
postal and customs officials, was small, and did not give, by
demands for higher pay, the sort of trouble which has arisen
in Australia among railway workers and in England among
postal and telegraph clerks.

Before quitting the Civil Service, a word must be said of
its relation to political life.   Federal officials cannot enter
the Federal Legislature, nor, as a general rule, can Cantonal officials sit in a Cantonal Legislature; but either set of

officials can sit in the other, *i.e.* Cantonal officials can and do frequently sit in the Federal Legislature, Federal officials much more rarely (and, I think, only with the leave of their superior) in a Cantonal. There are, however, exceptions. In Zürich, Cantonal officials may sit in the " Great " or Cantonal Council, and there review the proceedings of their official superiors, the Executive Council, although the members of that Executive Council are not themselves eligible for election to the Cantonal (Great) Council, but can only speak in it as Ministers. Even the judges of the highest Cantonal Court are eligible for the Council of their canton, being excluded from voting only when their own report is under discussion. This is a singular departure from the principle of separating the legislative from the executive department, the function of administering from the function of supervising. But the Swiss are not meticulous, allowing many deviations from principle to happen when no harm results. Custom and public opinion keep things fairly straight.

Both Federal and Cantonal employees are permitted to take part in political agitation and to work at elections. They are not indeed expected, as has happened in the United States, to be foremost in canvassing and organizing on behalf of the party which has appointed them, nor have they the motive of personal interest which exists there, for they are mostly re-elected or reappointed after the expiry of a term of service, not for party reasons, but because it is not the habit to disturb an actual occupant. Participation in party work by officials would be pernicious in England and is pernicious in America. In this singular Republic, however, no great practical evil seems to have followed. Though the Federal Government employs a host of voters on the railways it has acquired, these did not for some years apply pressure to members in order to obtain a rise in wages, and gave no trouble otherwise. It must, however, be added that when the State purchased the railways it forthwith raised the wages, theretofore too low, and it has been suggested that the prospect of a rise influenced some of the votes by which the people approved that purchase. More recently representatives have, at the instance of railway employees, been pressing the Federal Council for higher pay.

Only in a few of the large cantons is there any consider-

able body of civil employees, besides, of course, the police
and those engaged in collecting taxes or executing public
works.   What has been said of the Federal Civil Service
applies generally to these also.   Salaries are so low that there
is no such competition for governmental posts as in France,
and the Swiss aversion to whatever can be called " bureaucracy " prevents their multiplication.   Neither is there such
abuse of patronage for political purposes as exists in France
or Canada or the United States.   Appointments are made by
the Executive Council of the canton, and in cities by the
Municipal Council.   Though some cantons prescribe qualifications for posts requiring scientific or legal knowledge, no
great stress is laid on such knowledge.   Popular sentiment
does not favour pensions, partly perhaps because the Civil
Service is not legally a permanent one, but some cantons
offer their employees a subvention designed to encourage them
to insure their lives.   Taking the service as a whole, it is
both competent and honest, though less highly trained than
that of Germany.

The Army is an important branch of the national administration, and its organization has at times given rise to controversies.   Every citizen is liable to serve from his twentieth to his thirty-second year in the regular effective force
called *élite* (*auszug*), in which he is called out yearly for
manœuvres after having received a thorough initial training.
At thirty-two he passes into what may be called the Reserve
— Landwehr and Landsturm — until the age of forty-four.
This universal obligation to serve which had come down from
early days was never disputed, because the people felt that,
standing between great military nations, they must be prepared to defend their neutrality, not to add that the tradition of service in foreign armies, which had lasted from the
fifteenth century till forbidden by the Constitution of 1848,
had made the career of arms familiar.[1]   The law of 1907,
which now regulates military service, was accepted by the
people on a Referendum.   The cantons appoint the officers
up to the rank of major, these being in some cantons elected.
Officers of higher rank are appointed by the Federal Coun-

---

[1] Every soldier keeps his arms and accoutrements in his own house,
the pride of a Swiss in his arms being an old tradition.   This accel-
erates mobilization.

cil. Complaints have been from time to time made regarding favouritism, personal rather than political, in appointments, but on the whole the army may be deemed efficient and popular. The peasants in particular enjoy their term of training, and Socialists willingly become officers. The total strength of the *élite* was (in 1919) about 140,000, and that of the Landwehr about 60,000. The total cost of the army was £1,772,000, about one-third of the whole expenditure of the Confederation.

Closely connected with the supreme need of a country's defence is the duty of so directing foreign policy as to maintain good economic relations with its neighbours. Switzerland is almost the only European State that has no temptations to increase its territory, for that would be possible only if the people of Vorarlberg, or of Tirol, asked to be admitted to the Confederation,[1] or if France were to yield the part of Savoy which lies south of Lake Leman. Having no seacoast, it depends for food and for coal upon the goodwill of Germany, France, and Italy, and needs access through them to the markets of the outer world. Thus, though the scope of Swiss foreign relations is limited to few subjects, and though its lines are prescribed by obvious needs, skill is required to enable a small State to hold its own between neighbours often grasping and always mutually jealous. Such skill has generally been found available, nor has courage been lacking to defend the right of asylum extended to revolutionist refugees driven from their own countries. Questions of foreign policy have seldom led to serious political controversies over principles; and even in criticizing the methods used and the particular steps taken, public opinion has been temperate. In respect both of defence and of foreign relations, two branches of government in which democracies are commonly supposed to be inefficient or unstable, the Swiss have shown themselves as consistent and firm as their difficult position permits. Their permanent attitude to the

[1] In 1919 the people of Vorarlberg expressed their wish to be admitted as a Canton, but though the proposal had much to recommend it, it found no general favour among the Swiss, some of whom did not desire to strengthen the Roman Catholic party, while in the French-speaking districts a certain dislike was shown to the addition of a German-speaking Canton. It was believed at the time that the French Government would have opposed the plan had it ever been formally presented to the Paris Conference.

powerful neighbours is that of watchfulness tinged by suspicion. The Assembly has thought itself forced, by the protective tariffs of neighbour States and by the fear of being swamped by German competition in manufactures, to impose a tariff for the defence of what are taken to be the economic interests of Switzerland, which holds in this respect a position towards Germany resembling that which Canada holds towards the United States.

The actual merits and defects, or what may be called the everyday quality of the administration of a country, cannot be judged by a stranger, who is obliged to gather as best he may the sentiments of the inhabitants, and to gauge from their complaints the amount of dissatisfaction that exists. The Swiss, like the Germans, are not querulous, and their administration is so completely popular, so absolutely their own creation, reflecting their own qualities, that to blame it would be to blame themselves.   Anyhow, as they do complain less than either Englishmen or Americans or Frenchmen, though equally free to speak their mind, one must conclude that they are well satisfied, not only with the purity of their Civil Service, which is unquestionable, but with its competence and its diligence.[1]   This is the more noteworthy because they are, especially in the German cantons, not deferential to officials.   The right of the individual to personal freedom and immunity from interference by the State is not so fully safeguarded by law as in England or America, though this blemish is less conspicuous in Switzerland than in other parts of continental Europe where the Roman law had more power.   The Switzer is less " governed " or " regulated " than his neighbours in France and Germany.   He holds himself more erect in the presence of authority.   Indeed the word " bureaucracy " (*Beamtenthum*) and " centralization " rouse such antagonism that whoever proposes to extend the functions of government must at the same time protest that he hates the bureaucrat and desires that whatever has to be done should be done locally and not from the capital, and as far as possible by the people themselves.   The Swiss set no great store upon the technical training of offi-

[1] Here again I speak of things as they were before 1914, for censures were passed on the handling of some of the matters dealt with during the war.

cials, and their public service stands on a lower level of skill
than does the Prussian, and draws into its ranks less of the
talent of the country. Regarded as a career, it is unattrac-
tive; regarded as a hierarchy, it is not perfectly organized
and disciplined. But it is in touch with the common man,
and in no wise a caste, while at the same time it suffers less
from the influences of political party than does the civil
service in the United States or in France.

Government and Administration in General

Two merits strike all foreign observers. One is the cheapness of the administration. Finances have been carefully
managed both in the cantons and (except during the recent
war) in the Confederation, current administrative expenses
being kept down. The Confederation grew richer with the
growth of the country, and the rise in indirect taxation was
filling its treasury when the expenditure needed for the force
that was to defend the country's neutrality piled up a heavy
debt. Economy must now again be its first care, and may be
expected, for the people are not only thrifty, but inquisitive,
applying to public expenditure a rigorous standard such as
that which regulates a peasant household.

Purity, the other conspicuous feature, if partly due to the
absence of those temptations which richer countries sometimes present, is none the less creditable.[1] The Cantonal
governments, like the Federal, are practically free from corruption, for scandals, though they occur as in all countries,
are rare; and when they occur, the guilty person, however
strong his position had been, must quit public life forthwith.
In the United States, or in Canada, such a culprit might have
held his place, or recovered it after a few years. It may be
thought that in the small communities of Switzerland virtue
is easier because detection is more certain. But there have
been small communities elsewhere, in Spanish and here and
there in British and French colonies also, in which venality
almost ceased to be disgraceful.

Lest the shadows that fall upon parts of the landscape

---

[1] Aristotle, agreeing with the Hebrew sage who prayed he might
have neither poverty nor riches, would have applauded in Switzerland
an approximation to his model democracy in which power rested with
citizens of moderate means.

should seem to have been forgotten, it is proper to enumerate, before closing this sketch of the legislative and executive machinery, some of the faults which the Swiss themselves find in it.   I give those which I have heard from men entitled to speak, without venturing to estimate the extent to which the alleged blemishes exist, and the harm they do. Some are not serious.   But the duty of an enquirer, especially when he prosecutes his enquiries among a rather taciturn people, is to ask for the worst that can be said against the existing system.

1. The plan of granting subventions from the national treasury to the cantons is alleged to be wasteful, injurious to the cantons in impairing self-helpfulness, and liable to be perverted for political purposes.   The dominant party can, it is said, strengthen itself by these gifts, and bring a small canton too much under Federal influence.   Against this it is argued that the power of withholding a subvention is an engine for securing the enforcement of Federal law by a canton disposed to be insubordinate.   No great mischief has resulted so far, but the practice has its risks.   Local subsidies have been lavishly bestowed, and misused for political ends, in the United States and in Canada.

2. Through recent extensions of the sphere of government, as well as through the growth of the country, the Federal Council has been loaded with more work than it can overtake and has little time for studying large questions of policy. There are but seven Ministers, each with a small staff.   A well-paid and highly competent official, resembling the permanent Under Secretary of the great English departments, is badly needed.   But the people are slow to move.   They rejected in 1898 a law providing pensions for Federal employees.   The peasants, when they come to Bern, shake their heads over the handsome flight of steps which leads up to the legislative chambers.   So the Assembly has hesitated to spend more money on the hard-worked administration. Economy, rare in democracies, is characteristic of a country where the vast majority of the citizens not only pay taxes, but know and feel that they pay.

3. The Federal Council is alleged to have been influenced in the exercise of its patronage by party considerations, appointing, or promoting, persons who are recommended by

members of the Assembly as having served the dominant
party, and the steady increase in the number of administrative boards steadily increases its patronage. Such cases
doubtless occur in the case of small offices, but seldom with
regard to important posts, such as those in diplomacy, in the
higher ranks of the home service, or in the professors of the
famous Polytechnikum at Zürich. Occasional abuses of
patronage must be expected in every country, unless it selects
officials by competitive examination, and that method is not
easily applied to promotions in the higher ranks. The evil
is not frequent enough in Switzerland to lower the tone and
efficiency of the public service generally. More serious was
the complaint that the army suffered from having too many
officers who owed their position to their local influence or
political affiliations rather than to military aptitude. This
defect, for which the Cantonal authorities, who appoint the
lower officers, were largely responsible is believed to have
been cured by the legislation of 1907. The management of
the army is however still criticized, some holding that it is
too costly, others that it does not secure thoroughly skilled
officers.

4. When, as often happens, the Federal Government appoints a Commission, perhaps consisting of members of the
Assembly, to investigate and report upon some pending matter, such as a question of undertaking, or estimating the cost
of, some public work, those who conduct the enquiry are sometimes accused of needlessly protracting the sittings in order
to increase the compensation they receive for their trouble,
which is fixed at thirty francs per diem, *plus* travelling
expenses.

5. Another charge, which affects not the Federal but the
Cantonal and Communal Governments, is of wider scope.
There is said to be much petty jobbery and demagogism in
the towns, especially the smaller towns, and in some rural
areas. Sometimes by their talent for intrigue, sometimes by
plausible speech, men with more ambition than merit push
themselves to the front, become wire-pullers in local elections,
get small contracts for their friends, and perhaps end by
securing a local post for themselves,[1] for even a pittance

[1] A not too friendly picture of political party arts, as practised in
a city of French-speaking Switzerland, may be found in the novel

means something to the class of men, usually tradesfolk or the humbler kind of lawyers, who practise these arts. One finds a concurrence of testimony upon this point; nor is this surprising, for such things must be expected in any community (not composed of angels) where offices, too poorly remunerated to attract able men, are bestowed either by popular election or by Boards each of whose members is practically irresponsible.

Such place-hunting would exist even if there were no parties. It tends, however, to become involved with party action. Every party needs men, especially young men, who will undertake troublesome unpaid work, such as that of organizing meetings, looking after elections, propagating party doctrines. Though there is less of such work in Switzerland than in most democracies, some there must be, and it is natural for those who render such service to expect a reward in the shape of an office, natural that men of ambition, but no strong convictions, should join a party which has something to give, natural also for those who have been closely associated in political agitation to think first of their acquaintances when they have a post to bestow. This tendency to work politics for the sake of offices goes, in some places, hand in hand with the efforts of the Freemasons to advance their friends. Here, as in other parts of the European continent, this order is associated with radicalism. It is supposed to be strong in Switzerland, but all secret societies are, like the Jesuits, apt to be credited with more power than they possess. The proneness to push one's friends and reward adherents by office, though most often charged on the Swiss Radicals because they have had more opportunities, is nowhere stronger than in the Ultramontane canton of Fribourg.

The extent of this evil is differently estimated in Switzerland itself by different observers, who here as elsewhere can go on disagreeing, since the materials for a fair and exact judgment are unattainable. A stranger is led to believe that the malady, perhaps most evident in days when there

called *L'Echelle*, by M. J. P. Porret. There may be, but I have not found, a similar picture of cantonal politics in Zürich or Basle. M. Porret's description may be compared with the graphic and humorous treatment of New Hampshire (U. S. A.) politics in the *Coniston*, and *Mr. Crewe's Career* of Mr. Winston Churchill.

are no great issues bringing the best citizens to the front, is more widespread here than in England (a few boroughs excepted), or in Holland, or in Norway, or in the Australasian British colonies, but less common than in France, and far less common than it has been in the United States. Happily for themselves, the Swiss never contracted the American habit of turning out employees to make room for others who have " claims on the party."

CHAPTER XXIX

DIRECT LEGISLATION BY THE PEOPLE: REFERENDUM AND INITIATIVE

So far we have been studying those parts of the Swiss system which it has in common with other constitutional countries, viz. representative assemblies and an executive responsible thereto or to the people. Now, however, we come to an institution almost peculiar to Switzerland, one which deserves full examination, because it has profoundly modified Swiss government and has begun to influence opinion throughout the world. This is the method of Direct Popular Legislation, *i.e.* law-making by the citizens themselves and not through their representatives. Nothing in Swiss arrangements is more instructive to the student of democracy, for it opens a window into the soul of the multitude. Their thoughts and feelings are seen directly, not refracted through the medium of elected bodies.

Wherever in the early world we find a people governing itself, its power seems to have found its expression in the direct action of a primary assembly of the whole community, whether as tribe or as city.[1] Of the primitive Germans Tacitus says, " De minoribus principes consultant, de maioribus omnes." Such an assembly has, as already observed (see p. 337), maintained itself in some Cantons of Switzerland, and has parallels in other parts of the world, even among the Kafirs of South Africa.[2] In the Middle Ages these primitive gatherings died out, as large nations were formed out of small communities, so constitutional freedom, when evolved out of the feudal polity, passed into the form of representative assemblies. Only the Swiss Landesgemeinde kept up the ancient tradition and practice, and made

---

[1] In some Slavonic countries something similar seems to have existed, but apparently not among the Celtic peoples.

[2] A description of the Pitso (a primary assembly) among the Basutos may be found in the author's *Impressions of South Africa*, chap. xx.

the idea of direct action by the people familiar. Even the oligarchical governments of cities like Bern and Zürich occasionally referred questions of exceptional gravity to the communities over which they ruled, inviting their opinion,[1] and in Geneva (not till last century a member of the Confederation) the whole people exercised their right of enacting laws in the Conseil Général.[2] Rousseau, who argued that no government was truly popular unless the people acted directly and not through delegates, was doubtless influenced by the recollections of his own city as well as by what he had heard of the Landesgemeinde in the old Forest Cantons. He must, as a child, have accompanied his father to a meeting of the General Assembly of the Genevese in which the citizens voted on the laws submitted by their legislative authorities. The Swiss practice was seldom referred to by the constitution-makers of France from 1789 onwards. But it had impressed Napoleon.[3] In his treatment of the country he came as near to allowing himself to be influenced by sentiment as in any other part of his career, and he established in 1803 a Constitution for the whole country, then for the first time officially described as Switzerland, which lasted till his fall.

When the flood of change induced by the French Revolution had passed, and the Landesgemeinde were re-established in the mountain valleys which had known them from old time, their example, coupled with the new theories of popular rights which France had diffused, and perhaps also with the example of the American States, began to tell upon the minds of the larger cantons. In the period of change which lasted from 1830 to 1848, the new constitutions which the cantons adopted were submitted to the people and enacted by their votes, as a Federal Constitution had been submitted but rejected in 1802. Again, in 1848 it was the peoples of the

[1] As to these *Volksanfragen*, see an instructive discourse (published as a pamphlet) by M. Horace Micheli (of Geneva) entitled *La Souveraineté populaire*.

[2] See an interesting pamphlet of M. G. Wagnière, *La Democratie en Suisse*, p. 15. Throughout the eighteenth century a struggle went on in Geneva between the oligarchic government and the popular party which was endeavouring to assert, or recover, the rights of the mass of citizens. An interesting view of its latest phase may be found in Mr. D. W. Freshfield's *Life of Saussure*.

[3] I quote (in note at the end of this chapter) from M. Wagnière a passage from the First Consul's address to the Swiss delegates who came to Paris in 1801.

cantons that accepted the new Federal Constitution. The direct action of the people having thus become familiar, the practice extended itself from constitutions to other enactments. As early as 1831 St. Gallen adopted a scheme by which communes could vote to reject a law passed by the Assembly of the canton; and this so-called " veto " in one form or another was adopted by other cantons, till at last a system developed itself under which the people obtained in every canton but one (Fribourg) the right of accepting or refusing a law submitted to it by the Legislature. This is the so-called Referendum, a name drawn from the usage in the old Confederation by which the delegates to the Diet from a canton were entitled to withhold its assent to a resolution of that body till they had referred it to their own canton for assent or rejection.[1]

Concurrently with the process by which the people asserted their final voice in legislation, there appeared another by which they secured the power of themselves proposing legislation over the head and without the consent of the representative Assembly. In 1845 Vaud inserted in its Constitution a provision giving 8000 electors the right to require that the Cantonal Council should submit to popular vote any question of enacting or repealing a law, and other cantons followed by degrees. When the Federal Constitution was, after long and vehement controversy, revised in 1874, power was given to 30,000 voters to require that a Bill passed by the Legislature should be submitted to the people. This created the Federal Referendum. The possession by the people, since 1848, of the right to demand, by a petition signed by 50,000 voters, that the Constitution should be amended, suggested a new clause, enacted in 1891 and now in force, enabling that number of citizens to put forward a specific amendment to be submitted to the vote of the people. This is the so-called Popular Constitutional Initiative. These two institutions, Referendum and Initiative, represent an effort to return from the modern method of legislation by representative assemblies to the ancient method of legislation by the citizens themselves. In the Hellenic world the area of

[1] See as to the history of Swiss popular legislation, the valuable book of Th. Curti, *Le Referendum*, Paris, 1905, a translation, with additions, from the German original.

each republic was so small that the citizens could meet for debate, as they now do in the small Landesgemeinde cantons. Such oral debate being impossible in the Confederation and the larger cantons, the citizen can in these exercise his rights only by delivering his vote on paper.

Premising that there are also cantons in which communes, too large to determine issues by a popular vote in the communal meeting, send these issues to be voted on at a poll of the commune, and also some large cities in which municipal matters are similarly submitted to a popular vote of all the citizens, we may proceed to the more important and more instructive procedure employed for popular voting in the Confederation and in the Cantons, examining, first, the arrangements governing the employment of the popular vote by Referendum and Initiative in the Confederation and the Cantons; secondly, the figures recording the use made of it; thirdly, the actual working of the system; and lastly, the arguments used to recommend or disparage it, winding up with the conclusions regarding it at which Swiss opinion has arrived. It will then be possible to judge how far the example Switzerland sets is fit to be followed in other countries.

The arrangements now in force, complicated at first sight, become easier to follow when we consider separately *A* the Referendum and *B* the Initiative, and when in considering each of these we distinguish the application of each (*a*) to the Confederation and (*b*) to the cantons respectively, and also in both Confederation and Cantons (1) to Constitutions and (2) to laws respectively.

A. *The Referendum*

(*a*) In the Confederation the Referendum (*i.e.* the submission to popular vote, for approval or rejection, of a measure passed by the legislature) exists:

1. For all changes whatever in the Federal Constitution. This approval must be given not only by a numerical majority of the citizens voting, but also by a majority of the cantons.

2. For all Federal Laws (*i.e.* statutes), and for all Resolutions (*Beschlüsse, arrêtés*) (being of general application and not having been declared by the Legislature to be

" urgent "), whenever a demand for such submission to popular vote is made by either at least 30,000 citizens or by at
least eight cantons.

(*b*) In the Cantons the Referendum exists:

1. For all changes in the Cantonal Constitution.[1]

2. As respects laws and resolutions passed by the Cantonal
Legislature,

> In eight cantons for all laws and resolutions.   (This is
> called the Obligatory Referendum.)

> In seven cantons where a prescribed number of citizens
> of the canton (the number varying from canton to
> canton) demand its application.   (This is called the
> Optional or Facultative Referendum.)

> In three cantons there is a distinction drawn between
> different classes of laws, the Referendum being Obli-
> gatory for some and Optional for others.

> In one canton (Fribourg) there is no Referendum for
> laws.

In cantons, governed by a Primary Assembly of all citizens (Landesgemeinde), there is no need for a Referendum,
since that Assembly legislates.

It thus appears that the Confederation does not go so far
as do the cantons, for it submits laws to popular vote only
where 30,000 citizens (or eight cantons) ask for the submission, whereas all cantons but seven require either all laws or
all laws of a prescribed character to be so submitted.   It is of
course easier and cheaper to take a popular vote in a small
community than over the whole Confederation.   Only five
cantons have more than 200,000 inhabitants, a number less
than the population of some American congressional districts.

What Resolutions are to be deemed " urgent " ?   This is
a question which has raised much discussion, and as it has
been found impossible to frame a satisfactory definition, the
matter has been left to be decided by the Federal Assembly
in each case as it arises.   Broadly speaking it is only enactments of a temporary character or framed for some particular emergency that are deemed " urgent," [2] and so withheld

---

[1] The Federal Constitution prescribes (Art. VI.) that every Cantonal Constitution must be accepted by the people.

[2] It is sometimes alleged that this power of the Assembly has, especially in recent years, been unduly extended.   By giving the title of

from submission to the popular vote. Treaties have not so
far been submitted (save in the very exceptional case of that
by which Switzerland entered into the League of Nations constituted by the Treaty of Versailles of 1919), but the question whether they ought to be is to be presently determined
by a popular vote. Neither is the annual budget submitted,
nor decisions of a merely administrative character.

B. *The Initiative*

The Initiative (*i.e.* the right of a prescribed number of
the citizens to propose the passing of an enactment by popular vote) exists:

(*a*) In the Confederation —

For changes in the Constitution when a demand is made
by at least 50,000 citizens. They may make it either by
sending up to the Assembly a specific amendment, which the
latter then forthwith submits to the people, or by demanding
that the Assembly shall prepare an amendment embodying a
certain principle which they lay before it. In this latter
case the Assembly first submits to the people the question:
Shall the Assembly prepare such an amendment as is desired?
If this is carried the Assembly prepares it, and a further

Resolutions to enactments which are really Laws, and by declaring
such Resolutions to be either "urgent" or "not of general application," it can withdraw from the operation of the Referendum matters
not really urgent. Whereas between 1874 and 1913 the citizens used
the right of demanding a Referendum 31 times on a total of 284 Laws
and Resolutions passed by the Assembly, they used it only 3 times
on 62 Laws and Resolutions passed between 1905 and 1919. This
decline from a percentage of 11 per cent to 5 per cent may suggest that
the citizens found less occasion for the exercise of their right, but it
may also be due to the large use of the power of "declaring urgency,"
a power liable to be employed when the Assembly feared rejection by
the people. Of 1150 enactments passed by the Assembly between 1874
and 1919, upon only about 350 could the Referendum have been demanded. In a debate (in 1919) in the Assembly a member observed
"On raconte qu'un homme d'église qui voulait manger un poulet un
jour de carême dit à son poulet 'Je te baptise carpe,' et sa conscience
éttait tranquille. Le Conseil Fédéral et la Commission du Conseil
National font un peu la même chose pour leur poulet, pour ce projet.
Ils la baptisent 'arrêté,' et leur conscience démocratique est tranquille,
parce que si c'est un arrêté il n'y a pas besoin de le soumettre au
Referendum." On this occasion the remonstrance prevailed, and the
National Council changed the description of the enactment from
"arrêté" to "loi."

popular vote is then taken on the amendment so prepared and submitted.

(*b*) In the Cantons —

1. In all the cantons (except Geneva)[1] a prescribed number of citizens (varying in the different cantons) may either demand a general revision of the Constitution, or propose some particular amendments to it.[2]

2. In all the cantons except three (Luzern, Fribourg, and Valais) a prescribed number of citizens may either propose a new law or resolution, or submit to the Cantonal Council the principle on which they desire a new law to be based, asking the Council to frame the law desired. In the latter case the Council puts to the people the question: Shall a new law such as is desired be prepared? and if the people answer affirmatively, the Council prepares the law and it goes before the people to be decided on a second vote. If, on the other hand, the proposal as already drafted by its promoters goes straight to the people, the Council may oppose it, or may themselves draft an alternative new law on the same subject, to be voted on by the people along with the measure proposed by the demanding citizens.

The broad result of these arrangements is that in the Confederation, the wide area of which makes a frequent reference to the people troublesome, popular voting in the two forms of Referendum and Initiative is used for three purposes, viz.:

(*a*) For changes in the Constitution proposed by the Assembly.

(*β*) For changes in the Constitution proposed by 50,000 citizens under the Initiative.

(*γ*) For ordinary laws where 30,000 citizens, or eight cantons, make the demand under the Referendum.

In the Cantons, since they are smaller, it is natural to find it used more freely, viz.:

(*a*) For Constitutional amendments proposed by the Cantonal Legislature to the people.

---

[1] Geneva has an automatic revision of her Constitution every fifteen years.

[2] The Federal Constitution also prescribes (Art. VI.) that in every canton the absolute majority of the citizens (*i.e.* a majority of the whole number of citizens) shall have the right of demanding a revision of the Constitution.

(β) For Constitutional changes proposed by a prescribed number of citizens by way of Initiative.

(γ) In most cantons as respects Laws — (1) For all laws proposed by the Legislature (Referendum); (2) for laws proposed by a prescribed number of citizens (Initiative).

Where a revision of the Constitution is proposed by the citizens, the Cantonal Council is entitled to submit its own amendments also, and if the popular vote decides that there is to be a general revision, the work of making it is performed either by the Council or by a body (resembling the American Constitutional Convention) created for the purpose.

It will be observed that while the Confederation restricts the Initiative of citizens to changes in the Constitution, the cantons are less conservative and permit it to be used for changing the ordinary laws. There is, however, no recognized test for determining what is a constitutional change, *i.e.* for distinguishing constitutional amendments from ordinary laws. In this absence of a clear line between the two kinds of enactment the Initiative has been often used, both in the Confederation and in cantons, to pass under the guise of a constitutional amendment what is really an ordinary and not what lawyers or historians would deem a constitutional law.[1]

The procedure applied in the Confederation, as respects a Referendum on laws or resolutions, is the following. Every law when passed is published in the official journal and sent to the cantons to be circulated through the communes. Ninety days are allowed to pass before it can take effect. Within this period either eight cantons or 30,000 citizens may demand its submission to the people. The method of demand by cantons being rarely used, the opponents of the Bill proceed to collect signatures. If it excites little popular interest they must work hard to secure the requisite number, and organizations are sometimes formed for the purpose. Where the population is Roman Catholic, the clergy can give effective help; where it is Protestant, action by the pastors if they care to act (which

[1] The same difficulty has arisen in those States of the American Union which have adopted the Popular Initiative. To-day, the only distinction that can, both in Switzerland and these States, be drawn between a Law and a provision of the Constitution is that the latter can be repeated or amended only by a vote of the people.

they seldom do) is less efficient, attendance at their churches being less regular.   Sometimes, but by no means as a matter of course, party organizations take the matter up.   Agents may even be sent out to collect signatures, and paid ten or twenty centimes per signature.[1]   Where this happens, the signatures are not always above suspicion, and thousands of names have in some instances been struck off, either because written in the same hand or for want of the proper official attestation by the president of the commune to which the citizen belongs.   The Federal Council has decided that illiterates can sign by a mark, but the right of signing, since it is a part of citizenship, depends on Cantonal law.   When the number sent in has been recognized as sufficient by the Federal Council, it informs the Cantonal Councils, publishes the law all over the country, and fixes a day for the voting, not less than four weeks after the publication and distribution of the law.   Then an agitation begins, greater or less according to the importance attached to the law and to the interest which the political parties, as parties, take in it.   A copy of the law is sent to each voter, but no official explanatory memorandum accompanies it, the Federal Assembly having considered that it would be hard to secure an impartial one.[2]   Meetings are held at which members of the legislature and others advocate or oppose it, and the press is full of articles on the subject.   Nevertheless not every citizen is perfectly informed, for the debates in the Federal Assembly are so scantily reported that the arguments *pro* and *con* cannot be easily gathered from them.   However anxious a man may be to discharge his civic duties, he may possess, especially if he lives in an isolated spot among the mountains, no adequate data for judgment on matters perhaps technical or otherwise difficult.   This may be one of the reasons why the vote, when it comes, has been often disappointingly small.

[1] Professor Hilty mentions that, having asked one of the inhabitants of a remote valley why all his village had signed the demand for a Referendum, he was informed that a native of the valley who came to collect signatures told the people that he was to get ten centimes — one penny, two cents — for every signature. Having no opinion of their own on the matter, their courteous generosity enriched him by a gift which cost them nothing.

[2] A Memorandum is, however, issued in Oregon, U.S.A., for the information of the voters.

The arrangements for voting are in the hands of the cantonal authorities, though the ballot-papers and the copies of the law are supplied by the Federal Government. The voting, which always takes place on the same day over the whole country, and on a Sunday, is quiet and orderly, nor are complaints heard of bribery or of fraudulent counts. As the law has to be printed in German, French, Italian, and Romansch, and more than 600,000 copies are needed, the cost of taking the opinion of the people is considerable.

The cantons employ a procedure generally similar to that described for the Confederation. In most of them also a discretion is left to the Council to exempt from the Referendum resolutions which are temporary in their operation, and some nominations to office and resolutions of an administrative nature are also exempted. Appropriations of money beyond a certain sum (even if not of permanent operation) are in some cantons required to be submitted. In nine and a half cantons where the Referendum applies to all laws, there is of course no preliminary stage of collecting signatures. So soon as the law or decree (not being of an urgent nature) has been passed, or (in some cantons) at the end of the legislative session, notice is given of the day on which the popular vote is to be taken, and a copy of the law is (usually) sent to each citizen. In these cantons a sort of message or document explaining each law is prepared by the Cantonal Executive Council and delivered to each citizen with his copy of the law. Such messages are usually recommendations of the measure, but it seems that in one canton (Thurgau), where the Executive Council, being directly chosen by the people, is independent of the Great or Legislative Council, the former body has been known to criticize the law adversely.[1] Before a Cantonal, as before a Federal, voting there is plenty of public discussion, followed by the people with great interest, at least in the towns and in the more educated of the rural districts. The press, too, is alert. It is often accused of misrepresenting the issue; but newspaper misrepresentations, dangerous in the sphere of foreign relations, are less harmful in domestic affairs, where the

[1] Deploige, *Referendum in Switzerland*, p. 181 of English translation.

topic is more familiar and corrections can be promptly made. No European country has so many journals in proportion to its size as Switzerland, and no shade of opinion lacks its organ. Some cantons direct that public meetings for debating the law shall be held before the voting. In some, abstention from voting is punished by a small fine.

Where, as in seven and a half cantons, the Referendum is Optional, *i.e.* is taken at the demand of a prescribed number of citizens, the Cantonal Council may itself, without waiting for a demand, decide to take the opinion of the people on some particular measure which it has passed, and in some cantons a prescribed minority of the Council may require the measure to be so submitted. In Schaffhausen an official memorandum explaining the law is circulated to the people. In Fribourg the authorities of the Roman Catholic Church, powerful there, show no desire to introduce the Referendum.

In cantons where every law must be submitted to the people, an active legislature may lay a heavy burden upon the citizen. Most cantons fix one or two occasions in the year for taking a popular vote on the batch of laws passed at the last preceding sittings of the Council. Zürich has a regular spring and a regular autumn voting, but frequently adds a third, so its citizens are kept pretty busy. In Zürich, moreover, and also in Aargau, a law may (when the Cantonal Council so directs) be voted on in sections, so that the people can reject one part and adopt the rest, a useful provision in an intelligent and painstaking people. One canton (Basel Land) used to require for the acceptance of a law an absolute majority of the qualified citizens, but this requirement has been abandoned, since it often caused the loss of a measure, because a sufficient number of citizens had not come to the polls.

The procedure followed in the cantons where a law comes before the people by way of Initiative resembles (*mutatis mutandis*) that applicable to the Referendum where demanded by a prescribed number of voters. Copies of the proposed law are distributed to every citizen before the day of voting arrives, and in some cantons the arguments advanced by the proposers are also circulated at the public expense. The Cantonal Council can express its opinion on the project or put forward an alternative plan. The law, if and when passed, may like any other cantonal law be declared invalid by the Federal Legislature if they conceive it to transgress the Federal Constitution.

Some other features of the cantonal Initiative systems deserve to be mentioned.

Proposals for changes in the Constitution and those which submit ordinary laws may be differently treated. In the former case the work of revision is sometimes entrusted to a special body chosen for the purpose (resembling the American Constitutional Convention),[1] but more frequently the Cantonal Council undertakes it after its next re-election, and where the people have to vote, first whether there is to be a revision, and thereafter upon changes proposed, a prescribed interval must elapse between the two votings.

In Bern, when the suggestion for a revision comes from the Cantonal Council, a two-thirds majority in that body is required.

Some cantons permit the Council to advise the people against a general revision demanded by Initiative as well as to express its opinion upon particular changes proposed.

Since no sharp distinction is drawn in the cantons any more than (as already observed) in the Confederation between matters fit to be placed in a Constitution and those which belong to ordinary legislation, a Constitution may be loaded with provisions which do not affect the general frame of government and cannot be deemed Fundamental. This is inconvenient as well as illogical, but it has been found practically impossible (as in the States of the American Union) to define what properly belongs to a Constitution. In cantons where the people can initiate changes in the laws as well as in the Constitution there is less temptation than in the Confederation to propose what is really an ordinary Law in the form of a Constitutional amendment. It may be useful to give a few figures showing how these arrangements have worked.

In the Confederation the popular votings between 1874, when the Referendum was introduced, and 1898 have been as follows : —

[1] Swiss opinion does not generally approve the plan of a Special Convention, and it is not employed in the Confederation.

A. Votings on Constitutional Amendments, 10. Of these amendments, 7 were accepted and 4 rejected.

B. Votings on Laws and Resolutions passed by the Legislature, 25. Of these enactments, 7 were accepted and 18 rejected.

A. Between 1905 and 1919 the figures were: —

Votings on Laws and Resolutions passed by the Legislature, 3. Of these, all were accepted.

In all these cases the vote taken by cantons agreed with the decision of the popular vote.

The signatures demanding a Referendum ranged from 35,000 to 88,000 (in 1907).

It is convenient to give here the figures relating to constitutional amendments also, in order to compare the results when the Legislature proposes and when the citizens propose.

Proposals made since 1874 by the Legislature, 25. Of these 19 were accepted and 6 rejected.

Proposals made by 50,000 citizens, 12. Of these 5 were accepted and 7 rejected.[1]

The number of votes cast in both forms of popular voting naturally varies with the amount of interest evoked by the particular measure submitted. It has fallen so low as 30 per cent of the total number of qualified citizens, and has risen as high as 74. The average seems to be about 55 per cent. The number of signatures obtained for a demand for the submission of a law seems to be no index to the vote which will be ultimately cast against it. The largest number of signatures for a constitutional amendment was 167,000 (in 1908) in support of an Initiative for prohibiting the sale of absinthe. The proposal was carried by 241,000 against 138,000.

From these figures two things may be gathered.

One is that the power of demanding the submission to the people of a law passed by the Legislature is not abused. Within the forty-four years from 1874 to 1919 less than one law in the year was so submitted; and in the last fifteen the popular vote, only thrice demanded, affirmed each

---

[1] Two were withdrawn, and at the beginning of 1920 three Initiative proposals were pending on which the people had not yet voted (one of these has since been carried), and the question proposed by the Assembly of accepting the decision of the Assembly that Switzerland should enter the League of Nations had not yet been voted upon.

law. The cases in which attempts were made to obtain submission but the requisite number of signatures could not be collected, were not numerous.

The other is that the proportion of rejections to approvals between 1874 and 1898 shows that cases occur, even in this highly democratic government, in which the legislature does not duly represent popular sentiment.[1] This is of course no news to practical politicians. Even in Great Britain Bills are sometimes " jammed through " the House of Commons by a Minister, though everybody knows that the bulk of the nation dislikes them. I recall at least one case where even the majority that was supporting the Ministry was reluctant to pass its Bill, though it obeyed.[2]

Some examples may show how the people use their power. As the Swiss put into their Federal Constitution matters better fitted to be dealt with by ordinary legislation, we may consider together the cases in which constitutional amendments have been voted on, as they must be in every instance, and those in which a Referendum has been demanded on a particular law.

The people rejected twice a law making uniform the qualifications for the suffrage in Federal elections, with the result that this subject remains in the sphere of Cantonal regulation. This was due to a Cantonal sentiment averse to extension of Federal power.

They rejected several laws relating to banks and to patents which, not quite understanding the details, they thought faulty, and also a Federal resolution anent patents. This latter had been submitted along with a law on epidemic diseases, making vaccination, already compulsory in some cantons, compulsory over all Switzerland. The proposal evoked strong protests and was rejected by a large majority, and the harmless Patents Resolution, discredited by its neighbour measure, shared that neighbour's fate. They rejected a proposal for enlarging the powers of the Federal Government in educational matters, partly because it was denounced as " bureaucratic " and anti-religious, but even

[1] In one case a Bill passed by the Assembly with only a single dissentient vote was rejected by a large majority on a Referendum.

[2] The majority was wiser than the Ministry, for the measure damaged the party at the next general election.

more because it might have led to a secularization of the schools. Both Roman Catholics and many of the more conservative Protestants were intensely hostile, while the zeal of the (possibly more numerous) party that favours purely secular instruction was not active enough to overcome this resistance.

They rejected, by a large majority, a law providing pensions for Federal employees, the peasantry seeing no reason why these veterans of public service should have any better treatment than they had themselves. A reluctance to try experiments or enlarge Federal powers led them in 1891 to reject the proposed purchase of the Central Railway of Switzerland, yet seven years later they accepted a scheme for buying up all the lines of the country.

Other laws rejected had the following purposes: an increase in the expenditure upon the representation of Switzerland abroad; the creation of a Federal monopoly of the sale of lucifer matches, especially with a view to the sake of prevention of disease among the workers; the establishment of a State bank; alterations in the administration of the army so as to bring it more under Federal control; amendments in the military criminal law; a guarantee upon the sale of cattle (requiring such guarantee to be in writing); the creation of a system of compulsory insurance against sickness and accidents. In this last case it was apparently not so much the principle as the details that excited criticism, while the various private insurance societies organized opposition, and there were suspicions lest the Federal Government should use the scheme for party purposes. So 1903 saw the defeat of an amendment altering the constitutional provisions regarding the Federal alcohol monopoly, and of a law directed against newspaper incitements to escape the obligation of military service.

On the other hand, they accepted the following measures: A law making civil marriage compulsory and at the same time facilitating divorce. The former provision was so largely approved (though it provoked opposition among Roman Catholics) that it is believed to have secured the acceptance of the latter provision, notwithstanding some Protestant as well as Catholic dislike to a relaxation of the divorce law. The number of divorces rapidly in creased.

A measure amending the factory laws and fixing eleven hours as the maximum day's labour.

A general bankruptcy law for the Confederation.

A Constitutional amendment empowering Federal legislation regarding insurance against sickness and accidents.

A law granting a large subsidy to the Gothard railway, coupled with power to subsidize Alpine lines in Eastern and Western Switzerland.

Two tariff laws, successively raising import duties.

An amendment to the Constitution removing the prohibition to the cantons to impose the penalty of death which it had contained.

An amendment (1885) to the Constitution giving the Federal Government a monopoly of the production of distilled spirits, and a subsequent law (1887) framed in pursuance of the power so conferred.

A law for the regulation of railway accounts.

Constitutional amendments extending the supervision of the Federal Government over forests, and empowering it to legislate regarding foodstuffs and other articles of prime necessity in the interests of public health (both by large majorities).

Constitutional amendments (1898) enabling the Federal Assembly to prepare a uniform code of civil and another of criminal law for the Confederation. These long steps towards centralization were accepted by majorities exceeding two-thirds of the citizens voting (264,933 against 101,820, 266,713 against 101,712).

A Constitutional amendment empowering the Federal Government to grant subventions to schools in the cantons.

An amendment submitted by popular Initiative, and voted on in 1920, for the suppression of public gaming resorts.

A measure for the purchase and working by the Federal Government of all the great railway lines. This bold new departure, though notably enlarging the sphere of Federal administration, was carried by 386,000 votes against 182,000, the heaviest vote ever cast.

This list has been made full in order to convey to the reader the kind of questions which come before the Swiss people. Since in many instances the English or American reader has no means of judging whether or no the people erred, some remarks on the motives which seem to have influenced their action in Confederation votings may be useful.

The first question that rises to the mind will be as to the part played by political organizations in influencing the action of the people. In most democratic countries, and certainly in Britain,[1] it is hard to imagine a popular voting which would not be worked by the political parties. In Switzerland party sentiment seldom dominates the minds of the citizens. It is chiefly where a religious issue or a socialistic issue is involved that such sentiment tells, and then chiefly in Catholic districts. The Swiss voter, always independent, is most independent when he has to review the action of his Legislature. Still there are instances in which displeasure at the conduct of a party seemed to create a prejudice against measures it had put through the Assembly. In 1884 the Referendum was demanded on four laws passed shortly before,[2] none of which would probably have been required to run the gauntlet but for the irritation created in the minority parties by what was then deemed the rather high-handed behaviour of the ruling majority in the Assembly. All four bills were rejected, although two at least of them [3] were unquestionably, and one at least of the other two probably, beneficial. But the sequel was the oddest part of the affair. Immediately after these votings there occurred a general election, and the citizens returned to the Assembly a scarcely diminished majority of the same party which they had just censured by rejecting their bills. One would have expected the exact opposite, viz. that the innocent measures should be passed and the offending men dismissed. But the Swiss, who dislike changing their members, took their own way of expressing displeasure, and the majority profited by the warning. Cases occur in which the

---

[1] Nevertheless in those States of the N. American Union which use the Referendum, democratic as they are, voting does not closely follow party lines.

[2] As to these four instances, called at the time " the four-humped camel," see Th. Curti, *ut supra*, p. 334, and Deploige, English translation, p. 225.

[3] One of these two was a proposal to strengthen the staff of the Federal Department of Justice, the other to increase by £400 the expenditure on the Legation at Washington.

party dominant in the Assembly having by some law or by some executive act offended a large section of the citizens, this section engineers the rejection of some law submitted to it rather as a rebuke or manifestation of its anger than because it dislikes the law itself. This furnishes a convenient relief for the angry feeling, after the satisfaction of which things resume their normal course, and the people, having delivered their souls, can proceed on the next election to choose the same legislators whom they have just before rebuked.

So sometimes a law is defeated, not because the bulk of the people condemn it, but because the favour of the larger number is so much fainter than the hostility of a smaller that the latter bring up not only all their own voters but a percentage of the indifferent, while the less zealous majority poll less than their proper strength. As often happens, intensity wins against mere numbers. This is one of the ways in which minorities can make themselves into majorities.

Though now and then a harmless measure suffers from being put to the vote simultaneously with one which rouses opposition still, broadly speaking, each proposal is dealt with on its merits. Distrust of the men who have proposed it does not necessarily disparage it; and as a party cannot count on getting its followers to support its measures at the polls, so neither does it suffer damage from their rejection.

Independence, then, is the first quality of the citizen which the working of the system reveals. A second is Parsimony. Like the Scotch, the Swiss are not more avaricious than their neighbours, but they are more thrifty, and in public matters positively penurious. The Swiss peasant lives plainly and is extremely frugal. Averse to anything which can increase taxation — and all pay some direct tax — he does not understand why officials should be paid on a scale exceeding what he earns by his own toil. So laws involving an expenditure which would in England or France be thought insignificant in proportion to the results expected have been frequently thrown out by the votes of those who measure public needs by the depth of their own purses, and lack the knowledge that would fit them to judge financial questions.

A third tendency or motive is the dislike of officials and officialism. It has repeatedly led to the failure of bills for strengthening the administrative departments, and although such bills were sometimes needed, their failure checked for the moment the progress of what is called *étatisme, i.e.* State Socialism.

A fourth is jealousy of the interference of the Central Government with the cantons. Several instances have been given above. Yet the instances of the railways and the adoption of codes of law for the Confederation show that it is not always operative.

The quality we call good sense, the quality most important in a legislating nation as in a legislating assembly, is compounded of two things: judgment and coolheadedness, the absence of passion and the presence of intelligence. Now in the Swiss, a fighting people, but not (except the Italian Ticinese) a passionate people, long experience has formed the habit of voting in a calm spirit. They are an educated nation; nearly everybody not only can read but does read. They have solid rather than quick minds, and their best minds are more sagacious than imaginative. If few possess the knowledge needed to form an opinion on much of the legislation that comes before them, many have that consciousness of ignorance which is the beginning of wisdom. Hence their attitude towards a difficult or complicated measure is guarded or suspicious. *Omne ignotum pro periculoso.* Unless they have such confidence in the Assembly that passed the law, or in the advisers who recommend it, as to supply what is wanting to their own judgment, they are disposed to reject rather than to approve.

This is the explanation of what has been called the " conservatism " of the Swiss. They are cautious, not easily caught by new schemes, little swayed by demagogues, preferring, when something rouses their prejudice or eludes their comprehension, or points to dubious future developments, to vote " No." As the average voter has a slower and less instructed mind than the average legislator, who is always more or less a picked man and trained to his work, new ideas take longer to penetrate the voter's head. Study or debate convinces the legislator that some reform is needed, and he passes a law to effect it. But when the law comes before the voter, his attachment to old custom, unenlightened by study though partially enlightened by discussion, prompts a negative. This happens chiefly in the rural and especially the mountain cantons, much less in a manufacturing population such as that of Zürich or Basle, in which legislation is more active. Thus an intricate law, or one covering more than one subject or introducing new principles, is apt to be rejected on the first voting, yet subsequently accepted.

Under these conditions some laws are delayed, and some lost. But it is far from true to say that the citizen " in the long-run votes 'No' to every proposal." [1] He votes " No " sometimes because he dislikes the proposal on the merits, sometimes because he does not understand it, sometimes because he does not see where it will lead him. But of mere blind aversion to change there is little evidence, as appears from the instances cited in which sweeping measures have been adopted.

But though dogged conservatism is not the note of the Swiss voter, he is frequently more short-sighted than his representative in the Assembly. Wider views of policy would have sanctioned compulsory vaccination, reforms in the military administration, proposals for the better support of foreign legations and for pensions to Federal officials. Here it was parsimony and the want of an imagination that could realize conditions outside the voter's range that caused the mistakes. The former fault is so rare in democracies as to be almost a merit; the latter is inevitable when questions are addressed to a multitude of peasants and artisans who obey neither a party nor a leader. In Switzerland, however, no serious mischief has followed, for most of the laws rejected have been either afterwards adopted in a better form, or recognized to have been premature, because not sure to have behind them the popular sentiment which makes enforcement easy.

The working of Popular Voting in the cantons can be but briefly treated, because the data have never been fully col-

[1] Sir H. S. Maine, *Popular Government*, p. 97.

lected, even in Switzerland itself, and could be collected only by a long enquiry in the several cantons themselves. So far as can be gathered from the records of voting in a few of those larger cantons whose experience has been described by Swiss writers, the general conclusions to be drawn do not substantially differ from those which the Confederation furnishes.   Zürich, which I take as one of the most important, has had an Obligatory Referendum since 1869; *i.e.* all laws passed by the Cantonal Council have to be submitted to the people, who, in the words of their Constitution, " exercise the legislative power with the assistance of the Cantonal Council."   Between 1869 and 1893 the people voted on 128 proposals submitted by the Council, whereof 99 were accepted and 29 rejected.   Between 1893 and 1919 (inclusive) there were votings on 126 laws and decrees and 12 constitutional amendments submitted by the Council, and there were also votings on 15 proposals made by popular Initiative, 14 for laws, 1 for an amendment to the Constitution.   The average percentage of voters is estimated at 74,[1] but the use of proxies and the fact that in some communes abstention is punishable by fine makes Zürich exceptional.   When a Referendum vote coincides with an election to the Legislature, the average rises to 79.   The highest percentage of votes cast to qualified voters I have found is 87 per cent in 1891, and the percentage seldom sinks below 60.   Some measures aiming at useful objects have been rejected, as, for instance, laws for extending and improving education and the position of teachers, for limiting factory work to twelve hours a day and checking the employment of children, for establishing a system of compulsory insurance against sickness.   The Council in these cases seems to have gone ahead of the general opinion.   But when some of these proposals were subsequently submitted they were accepted, because better understood.   Thus a law fixing ten hours as the maximum time for the labour of women in shops and certain domestic industries was carried by 45,000 votes against 12,000.   Many other valuable measures have been similarly accepted, and according to

---

[1] When the Federal Constitution was submitted in 1874 the percentage who voted in Canton Zürich was 93.7, which seems to make a " record " in popular votings.

the Swiss writers who have treated the subject, possibly biassed in favour of their peculiar institutions, no permanent harm has followed rejections; the reforms really needed are ultimately carried, and usually in a better shape than they at first wore.

Anxious to disprove the charge of undue conservatism, the writers just referred to point to the fact that Zürich enacted a progressive income-tax which bears heavily on the rich. Such a measure, which would in some countries be cited to support a very different charge, was enacted in Vaud as a Constitutional amendment proceeding from the Legislature. It deserves to be remarked that although the people of Zürich are sometimes penny-wise in their dislike of expenditure, they have renounced the function of fixing the salaries of officials, vesting it in the Cantonal Council, and that they approved a proposal to spend three million francs on University and other new educational buildings in the city and canton. As an eminent and fair-minded citizen observed to me: " Reform would no doubt have moved faster without the Referendum. Yet the people are less stupid than we thought, when it was introduced, that they would show themselves. They reject some good laws, but fewer than we expected. Even prejudice and parsimony do not prevail against proposals whose utility can be made clear."

The general results of the use of the popular vote in the cantons, taken all together, show that the Referendum is used temperately in those cantons where it is compulsory.

Where it is optional, the demands for it are not numerous, and are particularly few in the French-speaking cantons, Vaud, Neuchâtel, and Geneva.[1] This fact seems to show either that there is no disposition to use the right of demand in a factious and vexatious spirit, or else that the legislatures of these cantons are in such full accord with the general sentiment that there is no occasion for an appeal to the people. It may also imply that the cantons which submit all laws do so rather in conformity to democratic theory than because there is any greater disposition in them than in others to distrust the legislature.

[1] In the thirty years ending with 1912, even Geneva used the Referendum only ten times and the Initiative only seven.

The proportion of voters who go to the poll is rather smaller than in the Confederation, especially in cantons where all laws are submitted. In Bern it has been as low as 30 per cent, and in Basel Land and Solothurn the average does not exceed 50 per cent. Religious issues call out the largest vote; laws involving increased expenditure, especially in the form of increased salaries, are those most frequently rejected.

The system of Direct Legislation excites so much interest in other countries, and has been so often recommended as an improvement on the parliamentary frame of government, that it is worth while, even at the risk of some little repetition, to enumerate and examine the arguments for and against it which Swiss experience has suggested. Its adoption and wide extension may be traced to two sources.

One is the theoretic doctrine of the Sovereignty of the whole People, which, as a theory, is of French rather than Swiss origin,[1] and found its first concrete application in Europe in the submission to the whole French nation in 1793 of the Constitution of that year, a Constitution never in fact brought into force. This suggested the similar consultation of the Swiss people in 1802.

The other source is the practice of the small Alpine communities. As the whole people had voted their laws in primary assemblies, it seemed conformable to ancient usage that when the number of citizens grew too large to be reached by one voice, they should be allowed to express their individual wills by voting at the spot wherein they dwelt. Men felt the independent personality of the citizen to be thus recognized in the wider, as well as in the narrower, compass. The law is his law, because he has taken a direct part in enacting it. As the direct control of the people has worked well in the sphere of local government it ought to prove equally sound in the canton and in the Confederation.

A third ground for introducing the system, strongly pressed in the United States, was little dwelt upon in

[1] Rousseau held that every law ought to be enacted by the citizens, but seems to have had in mind small communities, rather than a large nation. The doctrine that the People are the ultimate fountain of power descends from the ancient world, and was taken from the Roman law by St. Thomas Aquinas and other mediaeval writers.

Switzerland, viz. dissatisfaction with representative bodies as failing to embody and express the popular will. Few complaints were made that the Swiss Legislatures were perverting that will, and no one charged them with corruption or other sinister motives; but it was urged that the citizen knows better than his representatives what is for his own benefit, and that a law cannot but carry fuller moral authority and command more unquestioning obedience if it comes straight from the ultimate fountain of power. Here, it was said, is a proper counterpoise to that extension of the sphere of the Central Government which gives rise to disquiet, here is a safeguard against the influence which railway companies and other great commercial or financial interests may exert over the Federal Legislature.

To these arguments, which prevailed in 1874, others, drawn from the experience of the years that have passed since, have been added.

The frequent rejection by the people of measures passed by the Assembly shows that the latter does not always know or give effect to what has proved to be the real will of the people.

While the Assembly has not suffered in public respect, it has been led to take more pains to consult public sentiment, to anticipate objections, to put bills into the shape most brief, simple, and comprehensible by the average citizen. The citizen is supposed to know the law. Give him the best chance of knowing it.

A further benefit is secured for the people. Their patriotism and their sense of responsibility are stimulated, for they feel themselves more fully associated with the work of legislation, formerly left to a class which professed to stand above them, and they are the more disposed to support the law they have shared in making.

As the political education of the masses is thus promoted, so also that class in whose hands the conduct of government has mostly rested is brought into closer contact with the masses and can do more to familiarize the latter with political questions.

The influence of party is reduced, for a measure is considered by the people on its merits, apart from the leaders who have proposed it or the party in the Assembly that has carried it. Its approval by the people does not imply a strengthening, nor its rejection a weakening, of general legislative policy. Neither the Federal Council nor the Assembly is shaken because a Bill fails to become law.

Though some measures bear a party stamp and rouse party resistance, though displeasure at the action of a party may discredit the laws it has passed and lead to their rejection, though those who are accustomed to vote for candidates belonging to one party in the Assembly are predisposed to vote for the laws that party has passed, still, as the comparative weakness of party organization in Switzerland has permitted the habit of giving a popular vote " on the merits " to grow up, measures are more likely to be judged irrespective of those who advocate them than could well happen in any representative assembly where party leadership exists. In an assembly party solidarity and the hope of gaining party advantage disturb the minds of legislators. But the People have no gain or loss to look for save what the law itself may bring.

In a representative democracy there ought to be some check upon the legislature. The Swiss Constitution does not, like the American, give a veto to the Executive, and the two Chambers do not sufficiently differ from one another in composition and type of opinion to constitute their possible disagreement an adequate restraint on hasty action. Thus the only check available is that of a popular vote.

Finally, there must somewhere in every government be a power which can say the last word, can deliver a decision from which there is no appeal. In a democracy it is only the People who can thus put an end to controversy.

These considerations have not entirely removed the objections which a very few Swiss as well as some foreign critics continue to bring against the Referendum. Among such objections, which I state in order to present both sides of the case, the following, applicable to its use in the cantons as well as in the Confederation, may be noted.

The status and authority of a legislature must suffer whenever a Bill it has passed is rejected, for the people become less deferential. Its sense of responsibility is reduced, for it may be disposed to pass measures its judgment disapproves, counting on the people to reject them, or may fear to pass laws it thinks needed lest it should receive a buffet from the popular vote.

The people at large are not qualified, no not even the people of Switzerland, to form and deliver an opinion upon many subjects of legislation. "Imagine," said Welti, a famous leader, once President of the Confederation, "a cowherd or a stable-boy with the Commercial Code in his hand going to vote for or against it." [1] They may be ever so shrewd and ever so willing to do their duty, but they have not, and cannot have, the knowledge needed to enable them to judge, nor can the pamphlets distributed and the speeches made by the supporters or opponents of the measure convey to them the requisite knowledge. How can a peasant of Solothurn in a lonely valley of the Jura form an opinion on the appropriations in a financial Bill. Is the object a laudable one? Is it worth the money proposed to be allotted? Can the public treasury afford the expenditure? The voter cannot, as he might in the Landesgemeinde of Uri, ask for explanations: he must vote "Yes" or "No" there and then. The arguments advanced in the Legislature have taught him little, for its debates are most scantily reported. If it is said, "Let ignorant voters take the advice of their more instructed neighbours," that is an admission that the notion of referring these matters to the decision of the average individual who cannot judge for himself is wrong in principle, for it is the voter's own opinion, not some one else's, which it is desired to elicit.

The number of abstentions at Referendum votings is large enough to show that many a voter either cares little for his civic duties, or knows his unfitness to perform them. As the proportion of these abstentions to the number of qualified voters does not seem to diminish, has not the gain to the political education of the people been less than was expected?

The results of a popular vote cannot be always deemed a true expression of the popular mind, which is often captured by phrases, led astray by irrelevant issues, perplexed by the number of distinct points which a Bill may contain, and thus moved by its dislike to some one point to reject a measure which, taken as a whole, it would approve. No

[1] This the people did when that Code was, after Welti's time, enacted.

amendments are possible. The vote must be given for the Bill and for the whole Bill. Or again, a laudable measure may be rejected because it has been submitted at the same time with another which displeases a large section of the voters. Having first voted against the one he dislikes, the less intelligent citizen goes on to negative that which comes next, unregardful of its contents.

Frequent Referenda, not to speak of their cost, lay too heavy a burden upon the voter, who relapses into a wearied indifference or gives an unconsidered vote. This happens in those cantons which, claiming to be progressive, pass many laws. The citizen has other things besides politics to attend to, and the unrest and agitation produced by constant appeals to the people by Referenda as well as at elections disgust the quiet solid man.

When a law has been carried by a small majority, its moral authority may suffer more than would be the case had opinion been nearly equally divided in the Assembly. In countries where the legislature rules, a law passed is accepted because it comes in the regular way from the usual organ of the people's will, and few enquire what was the majority that passed it. But when it has gone to a popular vote, a section of the citizens are arrayed against it. They become its opponents, and feel aggrieved if they are overridden by only a few votes.[1]

The most comprehensive but also the vaguest argument adduced against the Referendum is that it retards political, social, and economic progress. This objection made some noise in the world when currency was given to it by Sir Henry Maine in 1885.[2] It particularly impressed Englishmen, of the class which had been wont to associate democratic rights with an aggressive radicalism. To find conservatism among the masses was to them a joyful surprise. The Referendum appeared as a harbour of refuge. On the other hand, some advocates of social reform, in Switzerland as elsewhere, complain that State Socialism and Labour legislation do not advance fast enough. To estimate the truth there may be in these opposite views

[1] No case was brought to my knowledge in which this had occurred. In Switzerland, as in America, minorities usually acquiesce quietly, perceiving that only thus can free government go on.

[2] In his book entitled *Popular Government*.

would require a careful examination, not only of the intrinsic merits of each rejected law, but also whether in each case the law was seasonable, suited to the sentiments of the people, and therefore fit to be forthwith applied with general acquiescence. Space failing me for such an examination, it is enough to observe that although prejudice or undue caution has in some cases delayed the march of economic or social reforms which the Assembly proposed, the best Swiss authorities hold, and hold more strongly now than thirty years ago, that no general harm has followed. Every system has its defects. Those who, knowing England or France, compare the legislation of those countries with that of Switzerland since 1874 will find in the two former instances in which progress has suffered from the pressure exerted upon members of the legislature by classes or by trades whose interests were allowed to prevail against those of the nation.

Some of the arguments here summarized are, like that last mentioned, not supported by Swiss experience. Some apply to the action of the people when they elect representatives hardly less than when they vote on laws, because an election is often (though less in Switzerland than in Britain or America) an expression of opinion on political issues as well as on the merits of the candidate. To others weight may be allowed. It is true that there are laws on which the bulk of the voters are not qualified to pass judgment, true also that demagogues might use the Referendum as a means of attacking a legislature or its leaders, true that the less intelligent voter is sometimes led away from the merits of a law by extraneous considerations, such as party spirit or religious prejudice, or even the prospects of the crops, which may have put him in a bad humour. Abstentions are so numerous that some cantons have imposed penalties, and of those thus driven to vote, many drop in a blank paper, having no opinion to express.

Here let me revert to the part which the system of Popular Voting plays in the constitutional scheme of Government. It disjoins the Legislative from the Executive Department more completely than any form of the representative system can do, because it permits not only the Executive Council (Federal or Cantonal as the case may be) but also the

Legislative body, which in the Confederation both chooses and directs the Federal Council, and which in some cantons chooses, and in all directs or influences the Executive Council of the cantons, to continue its normal action whether or not its legislation is approved. Where the function of ultimately enacting the law has been transferred from the representative body to the people, the people become the true Legislature, and their representatives merely a body which prepares and drafts measures, and which, in conjunction with the Executive Council, carries on the current business of the nation. Thus it follows that neither the Executive Council nor the Legislative Assembly need be changed because a law submitted by them is not passed. The people reject the law, as a merchant may reject the plan for a business operation which his manager suggests, but they do not dismiss the Assembly any more than the merchant dismisses his manager. The function of administering the laws continues to be smoothly carried on by the same set of officials, so long as their personal character and capacity makes them trusted.

Under the French and English system this does not happen, because the defeat of an important Bill which the Ministry has proposed means the displacement of the Ministry, while under the American system, although the President and his officials who administer public affairs cannot be ejected by the majority in Congress, yet since they have (through the President's veto) a share in legislation and are closely associated with one or other of the great parties in Congress, they practically share the fortunes of the parties, and cannot expect re-election when the party has incurred popular displeasure by its legislative errors or omissions, whereas the Swiss system tends to reduce party feeling because it makes legislation a matter by which a party need not stand or fall.

Neither in the Confederation nor in the cantons is it now proposed to abolish the Referendum on laws, nor has any canton discarded it, though some have specifically excepted financial laws. Statesmen who would like to restrict it to some classes of laws admit both the practical difficulty of defining those classes, and the objections to leaving discretion in the hands of a legislature. The people as a whole value the privilege. The party which long held a majority in the Assembly, though sometimes annoyed at its results, were and are debarred by their principles from trying to withdraw it; while the Conservative and Roman Catholic Oppositions, less fettered by theory, sometimes found the Referendum useful as a means of defeating Radical measures. The institution has become permanent, not only because the people as a whole are not disposed to resign any function they have assumed, but also because it is entirely conformable to their ideas and has worked in practice at least as well as a purely representative system worked before or would be likely to work now. There are differences as to the extent to which the principle should be carried, but although the Obligatory form has been adopted in most cantons, the opinion of some experienced statesmen prefers the Optional form because the constant pollings which the former involves weary the citizen, and make him less careful to give a well-considered vote. In the Confederation the objections to obligatory submission of every bill seem graver, for this would throw a heavy burden on the voters, producing more trouble and unrest than does the agitation needed to obtain signatures to the few demands for submission.

On a review of the whole matter the foreign observer will probably reach the following conclusions.

Any harm done by the Referendum in delaying useful legislation has been more than compensated by the good done in securing the general assent of the people where their opinion was doubtful, in relieving tension, providing a safety-valve for discontent, warning the legislatures not to run ahead of popular sentiment.

It has worked particularly well in small areas, such as Communes (including cities) where the citizens have full knowledge of the facts to be dealt with.[1]

There is nothing to show that it has reduced the quality of the members of the Assembly or Cantonal Councils

---

[1] Geneva was mentioned to me as a canton in which an independent committee of citizens had succeeded in defeating, on a popular vote, a scheme propounded by the Council, which they deemed likely to reduce the standard and variety of university teaching. Similarly, an ancient tower, associated with the history of the city, which the Council had meant to remove was saved by an appeal to popular vote.

or tended to discourage capable men from seeking a seat thereon.

It has served to give stability to the government by disjoining questions of Measures from questions of Men, and has facilitated the continuance in office of experienced members of the executive and the legislature. Taking its working over a series· of years, it would seem to have reduced rather than intensified party feeling.

It has helped not only to give to the governments of the Confederation and the cantons a thoroughly popular character, obliging each citizen to realize his personal share in making the. law he is to obey, but, so far from " atomizing " the nation into so many individuals, has rather drawn together all classes in the discharge of a common duty, and become a unifying force giving democracy a fuller self-consciousness.

It has shown the people to be, if not wiser, yet slightly more conservative than was expected. But their aversion to change has been due to caution, not to unreason, and seldom to prejudice.

In recognizing the success of the Referendum we must never forget how much the conditions of Switzerland favour its application. It is specially suited to small areas, and to small populations not dominated by party spirit.[1]

Working of the Initiative

The working of the Initiative, *i.e.* the right of a group of citizens to propose measures to be enacted by a vote

[1] A Swiss friend whose great abilities and experience entitle his opinion to high respect sums up to me his view as follows:

" The Referendum compels all citizens to occupy themselves with and pass a judgment upon the practical questions of the State, and thus draws the individual directly into the interest of the State, while anchoring the State in the People.

" This means for the individual citizen an enrichment of his personality, and, reciprocally, the State is obliged to keep the instruction of the People on the highest possible level.

" The Referendum makes all classes and districts in Switzerland partners in State tasks and duties and creates therewith a very strong feeling of membership in one community. Every Swiss submits himself to a decision by the people."

This sense of a common duty to the State seems to be stronger in Switzerland than anywhere else in the world. I remember that when long ago in a secluded Alpine valley I asked a peasant whether all of the people, needs to be considered apart from the Referendum, for though its theoretic basis is the same, the conditions of its application are different.

It claims to be the necessary development of the idea of Popular Sovereignty. The people, it is held, cannot truly rule if they act through representatives or delegates. The individual will of the citizen cannot be duly expressed save by his own voice or vote. His representative may, consciously or unconsciously, misrepresent him. The Referendum doubtless secures him against being bound by any law on which he has had no chance of expressing his own will. But the opportunity of exercising his volition against a law submitted confers a right of Negation only. He needs also the Positive Right of framing and placing before his fellows the law which expresses his own will and mind. Only thus is the freedom of each citizen secured.[1]

Abstract theory has been reinforced by the argument that since representative assemblies are apt to consist of one class, or to be dominated by class interests, they cannot be trusted to bring forward and lay before the people the measures which the people desire. As the Referendum protects the people against the legislature's sins of commission, so the Initiative is a remedy for their omissions. Individuals may propound excellent schemes and recommend them at meetings and through the press without affecting an indifferent or hostile legislature. If the People is really to rule they ought to have their chance of going straight to the People. This argument has force in those American States where great corporations know how to " take care of a legislature." But the Swiss advocates of the Initiative have been moved chiefly by abstract principles. Their strength lies in the universal acceptance of Popular Sovereignty as a dogma, whereof the Initiative seems the logical result.

We have already seen that in the Confederation, where it exists only for proposals to amend the Constitution, the

the dwellers had not the right to attend and vote in the Landesgemeinde, he answered, "Not the right merely, the Duty" (*Es ist ihre Pflicht*).

[1] An interesting abstract of the doctrines of Rittinghausen and Considérant, writers of the last generation who influenced opinion on this subject in their time, may be found in the (already mentioned) excellent book of Th. Curti, *Le Referendum*, pp. 200–207.

Initiative has been demanded only eight times and amendments proposed by it only twice carried. These cases are worth noting. They included a law to forbid the killing of animals without first stunning them by a blow. This, though proposed in the guise of a desire to prevent cruelty to animals, was really a manifestation of the anti-Semitism then rife in Continental Europe. It was carried against the advice of the Federal Assembly, and although a similar measure had, when passed by the Cantonal Councils of Bern and Aargau, been quashed by the Federal Council and the Assembly as inconsistent with the guarantees of religious liberty provided by the Federal Constitution.[1] Some cantons enforce it, but the Federal Assembly has never passed an Act imposing penalties for its breach. This was an inauspicious beginning. The next two constitutional amendments proposed by the popular Initiative were one declaring the " right to labour," another proposing to distribute the surplus of the Federal customs revenue among the cantons in proportion to population, two francs for each person. Both were rejected in 1894, the former by a vote of three to one, the latter by a majority of nearly three to two; and a like fate befell two other proposals made by Initiative in 1900, one to introduce proportional representation in the election of the National Council, and the other to choose the (Executive) Federal Council by popular vote, as well as one similarly made in 1903 to exclude resident foreigners in computing population for the purpose of determining the number of representatives to which a canton is entitled. But in 1918 an amendment introducing proportional representation was carried. This is the most noteworthy instance of a large constitutional change effected by the Initiative method against the will of the majority of the legislature.

In the cantons, where the Initiative has been much more freely used, it has held its ground, but does not seem to make further way. It has not been the parent of any reforms which might not have been obtained, though not so quickly, through the legislature, while it has sometimes placed unwise laws on the statute book. Zürich, where it

---

[1] This objection was of course overridden by the insertion of the amendment as a part of the Constitution.

can be demanded by 5000 citizens — a small number for so
large a canton — has resorted most frequently to it.   Sometimes the prudence of the Cantonal Council, dissuading the
people from the particular plan proposed and substituting
a better one, averted unfortunate results,[1] while in the case
of an ill-considered banking law the Federal authorities
annulled the law as inconsistent with the Federal Constitution.   Several times the people have shown their good sense
in rejecting mischievous schemes proposed by this method.
Not very different have been the results in St. Gallen, Bern,
and Aargau.   The French-speaking cantons use it less.

When the conditions under which the Initiative works
are compared with those of the Referendum we are not
surprised to find that the opinion of statesmen was for a
long time less favourable to the former.   Its opponents argue
that whereas a law submitted to the people by Referendum
must have already been carefully considered by the Federal
Council which drafted it, and by both Houses of the National Assembly, a Bill proposed by Initiative emanates
from a group of more or less intelligent and instructed
citizens, having never run the gauntlet of independent critics, possibly hostile, certainly competent by their knowledge
and experience.   It may be crude in conception, unskilful
in form, marred by obscurities or omissions.   It will often
suffer in practice from the fact that it has not proceeded
from those who will, as the Executive, have the function of
administering it, and are thus aware of the practical difficulties it may have to overcome.   It might be dangerous
if applied to agreements made between cantons or with
foreign States; and it would render the course of normal
legislation more or less provisional, because it may suddenly
cut across existing laws, its relation to which has not been
duly considered.   These objections, which the early history
of the Initiative tended to support, would not be conclusive
if it could be shown to be the only remedy against the prejudices, or the class selfishness, or the subjection to private
interests, that may prevent a legislative body from passing
measures which the people deliberately, and not merely by
a sudden impulse, desire to see enacted.   There have been
times in England, as in other countries, when a legislature

---

[1] This happened in the case of a proposal to forbid vivisection.

refused to pass laws which a majority of the adult male population, perhaps even of the registered electors, seemed to desire. Does such a state of things exist in Switzerland or in any of its cantons? If so, why do not the electors when choosing their representatives make known their wishes, and insist that the legislature shall carry them out forthwith? It is doubtless possible that parliamentary obstruction, or corrupt influences applied to members, or the pertinacity of a leading statesman who dominates his party and holds it back from some particular measure, may delay the gratification of the popular will. But (excluding large-scale corruption, unknown in Switzerland) such cases must be rare; such causes can have only a temporary operation. The Initiative has in recent years begun to be more frequently demanded in the Confederation,[1] so that men, noting that virtual effacement of the distinction between Constitutional Amendments and Laws which now permits all sorts of proposals to be submitted under the guise of Amendments to the Constitution, have begun to ask why the right of Initiative should not be extended to Laws. The requirement of 50,000 signatures might be retained for Laws because the number of Swiss citizens has risen greatly since 1891, and a larger number, say 80,000, might be required for the proposal of an Amendment. As things stand, the people, though they cannot propose a law when it is called a "law" can propose what is really a law by calling it an Amendment, and can repeal an existing Law by enacting an Amendment which overrides it. The change in form would not increase the volume of direct popular legislation, while it might help to preserve for the Constitution that character of a Fundamental Instrument which it is fast losing.[2] The critical period of a threatened strife of classes which has arrived for Switzerland as for other countries may suggest that the time is scarcely ripe for a final judgment on the system of Direct Legislation. But I must add that, revisiting the country in 1919, I found the opin-

[1] It is sometimes alleged that the habit of withdrawing enactments as "urgent" from the category of those which can be made the subject of a Referendum may have contributed to this larger use of the Initiative, but other causes also may be suggested.

[2] In the Canton of Zürich where the Initiative exists for Laws, enactments desired are usually proposed as Laws, and the popular Initiative in constitutional amendments is rare.

ion of thoughtful men much more favourable to the Initiative than I had found it in 1905. Many held it to be
valuable as checking the undue power of any party which
should long command a majority in the legislature: few
dwelt upon the danger present to the mind of statesmen in
other countries, that it may offer a temptation to irresponsible demagogues seeking by some bold proposal to capture
the favour of the masses.

The foregoing account will have shown that such success
as has been attained in Switzerland by the method of direct
popular legislation is due to the historical antecedents of
the Swiss people, to their long practice of self-government
in small communities, to social equality and to the pervading
spirit of patriotism and sense of public duty. No like success can be assumed for countries where similar conditions
are absent. A popular vote taken over wide areas and in
vast populations, such as those of Great Britain or France,
might work quite differently. The habits and aptitudes
of the peoples may not have fitted them for it. In Switzerland it is a natural growth, racy of the soil. There are
institutions which, like plants, flourish only on their own
hillside and under their own sunshine. The Landesgemeinde thrives in Uri; the Referendum thrives in Zürich.
But could saxifrages or soldanellas gemming a pasture in
the High Alps thrive if planted in Egypt? As, however,
the plan of Direct Popular legislation has been tried on a
large scale in the States of North-Western America also,
a general appraisement of its merits may be reserved till its
working there has been examined.

EXTRACT FROM AN ADDRESS DELIVERED BY THE FIRST CONSUL (BONAPARTE) IN 1801 TO THE SWISS DELEGATES

" Songez bien, Messieurs," disait Bonaparte, " à l'importance
des traits caractéristiques, c'est ceux qui, éloignant l'idée de ressem-
blanc avec les autres Etats écartent aussi la pensée de vous con-
fondre avec eux. Je sais bien que le régime des démocraties est
accompagné de nombreux inconvénients, et qu'il ne soutient pas
un examen rationnel: mais enfin il est établi depuis des siècles, il
a son origine dan le climat, la nature, les besoins et les habitudes
primitives des habitants; il ist conforme au génie des lieux, et il
ne faut pas avoir raison, en dépit de la nécessité, quand l'usage et

la raison se trouvent en contradiction, c'est le premier qui l'emporte. Vous voudriez anéantir ou restreindre les landsgemeinde, mais alors il ne faut plus parler de démocratie ni de républicains. Les peuples libres n'ont jamais souffert qu'on les privât de l'exercice immédiat de la souveraineté. Ils ne connaissent ni ne goûtent les inventions modernes d'un système représentatif qui détruit les attributs essentiels d'une république. Je vous parle comme si j'étais moi-même un Suisse. Pour les petits Etats, le système fédératif est éminemment avantageux. Je suis moi-même né montagnard; je connais l'esprit qui les anime.

" D'heureuses circonstances m'ont placé à la tête du gouvernement français, mais je me regarderais comme incapable de gouverner les Suisses. Il vous est déjà difficile de trouver un landamman; s'il est de Zurich, les Bernois seront mécontents et vice-versa; elisezvous un protestant, les catholiques feront opposition.

" Plus j'ai réfléchi sur la nature de votre pays et sur la diversité de ses éléments constitutifs, plus j'ai été convaincu de l'impossibilité de la soumettre à un régime uniforme; tout vous conduit au fédéralisme. Quelle différence n v a-t-il pas, par exemple, entre vos montagnards et vos citadins ! Voudriez-vous forcer les cantons démocratiques à vivre sous le même gouvernement que les villes, ou bien songeriez-vous à introduire dans celles-ci, à Berne, par exemple, la démocratie pure?

" La Suisse ne ressemble à aucun autre Etat, soit par les événements qui s'y sont succédés depuis plusieurs siècles, soit par les différentes langues, les différentes religions, et cette extrême différence de mœurs qui existe entre ses différentes parties. La nature a fait votre Etat fédératif, vouloir la vaincre n'est pas d'un homme sage."

In 1803 Napoleon wrote to the Swiss as follows:

" Une forme de gouvernement qui n'est pas le résultat d'une longue série d'événements, de malheurs, d'efforts, d'enterprises de la part d'un peuple, ne prendra jamais racine."

CHAPTER XXX

POLITICAL PARTIES

The stability and consistency which have marked general policy as well as legislation in Switzerland are often ascribed to the predominance since 1848 of one political party. The causes of this fact, as well as the other circumstances that affect the party politics of the country, need some explanation. Nowhere in Europe might there appear to be more abundant materials for the emergence of many parties and for their frequent regroupings or transformations, for where else can be found so many diversities of racial character, of religion, of speech, of forms of industry and of the conflicting economic interests to which such forms give rise? Yet nowhere has the ship of state been so little tossed by party oscillations.

Switzerland had her War of Secession in 1847. Seven Roman Catholic cantons who had withdrawn from the Confederation to form a federation of their own, were brought to submission in a short and almost bloodless struggle which was followed by no revenge. The Constitution of 1848 sealed the reunion of all the cantons and created closer ties between them. The Liberals of that day who framed the Constitution held a large majority in the country, and long held it. After a time, however, differences of temperament and opinion divided the party. The larger section is now known as the Left or Radical party, and the much smaller and less advanced section has retained the name of Liberal, though it is often called the Centre. Meantime the Catholic minority of 1846–48, the men of the Sonderbund, kept together and were ultimately consolidated by the political disputes which arose over the dogma of Papal Infallibility adopted by the Vatican Council of 1870. They form a third party variously described as Catholic or Clerical or Ultramontane. There were thus three parties. After 1880

Marxian doctrines began to spread in the industrial centres, and a Socialist party arose which, though strong only in a few populous areas, increases in numbers and is extremely active. Its growth has been favoured by the large immigration of German working-men. More recently some advanced members of the Radical Left detached themselves from it and became known as the Democratic Group, but they did not remain a distinct section. There were thus four or five parties; but that which was once the advanced wing of the Liberal party and is now the Radical party commanded in 1918 more votes in both branches of the National Assembly than did all the other parties taken together.[1] The League of Peasants party which has since appeared does not act as a political group except for the protection of agricultural interests, and it is not yet clear what its relations to the other parties will be.

It is a singular fact, and a fortunate one for the country, that the lines of party do not coincide with those of race and language. Though the strength of the Radicals lies in the German-speaking and Protestant cantons, it draws support from French-speaking areas also, such as Vaud and Geneva, while the Clericals find adherents equally in German-speaking Luzern and in French-speaking Fribourg. The Socialists are strongest in Zürich, and, to a less extent, in Aargau, Thurgau, and St. Gallen. The Old Liberals, also called Democratic Liberals, a small rank and file with able officers, come almost entirely from Protestant districts, and some have been returned to the Assembly in respect of their personal eminence, not because they had a popular majority in the districts for which they sit. This willingness to find room for men of distinction is an idyllic feature of Swiss politics without parallel elsewhere. In France and in English-speaking countries there is a cry of triumph when a party leader is defeated at the polls: in Switzerland

---

[1] In the National Council it had 102 members out of 189. In 1919 when the election was held on the plan of Proportional Representation this party, though remaining the largest, did not obtain in the National Council a majority of the whole, but only 63 members, the Catholic Conservative party securing 41 seats, the Socialists 41, while the new group of Peasants, Artisans, and Bourgeois party won 26, and the Liberal Democratic Group 9. Seven seats went to a so-called " Groupe de politique socialé," and two to Independents. The composition of these groups may, however, soon begin to vary.

his opponents take pains to provide against such a contingency.

It was in ecclesiastical, rather than in language or in class distinctions, that the foundations of these parties were laid. Ever since the days of Zwingli, religion has been a cause of division. It nearly broke in pieces the old Confederacy of Thirteen Cantons. But to this must be added the difference that everywhere exists between men of a cautious mind and conservative temper, and those who are more prone to change or more disposed to trust the masses of the people. The latter are the Radicals, the former either Catholics or conservative Liberals. Rich men are in most countries apt to belong to the former category, but in Switzerland the line of party division does not coincide with that of class. There are plenty of Conservatives among the peasants, plenty of Radicals among the educated and well-to-do. The Socialists are, broadly speaking, a class party, but they include not only many of the minor and poorly paid Government employees, but also some few philosophic democrats not belonging to the ranks of Labour; and though standing outside the churches, they find some sympathizers among Roman Catholic and also among Protestant pastors. Swiss Socialists are rather non-Christian than anti-Christian, most of them less anti-Christian than are those of France, and Swiss Radicalism is hostile only to Clericalism, not to Christianity.

The Radicals correspond broadly to the Liberal party in England, to the Left Centre and Democratic Left in France, and to the Liberals (now the National party) in Australia. Many shades of opinion may be found among them, but they are sharply distinguished from the Ultramontanes by their hostility to sacerdotal claims and less sharply from the Liberals by their greater readiness to extend Federal authority and to use it for promoting schemes of social reform. Despite their name, they have, like all parties which have long enjoyed power, a good deal of administrative conservatism. A Radical who has arrived is not the same thing as a Radical on the road.

The Liberals, who would in England be described as Moderate or Conservative Liberals, have lost ground in recent years, but are still influential by their intellectual distinction and social weight. Clinging to the orthodox economics and *laissez faire* principles of last century, they are effective critics, strong for resistance, furnishing a counterpoise to the Socialists and others who would accelerate the process of change and extend the functions of the State. In the past, when more largely represented in the Assembly, they furnished the Federal Council with many admirable members, highly qualified for administrative functions.

Political life, generally tranquil in the Confederation, is more active, and occasionally more troubled, in the cantons. In the mountainous and agricultural regions, which are largely Catholic, it is chiefly local questions that occupy the people. Things move slowly and quietly, except in the excitable Italian population of Ticino, where the struggle between priestly influence and revolutionary ideas has sometimes led to outbreaks of violence. In manufacturing cantons like Zürich, Thurgau, Aargau, and Basle parties are more active because the issues that arise are more various and stirring, but these issues are so numerous, one canton differing from another, that it is impossible to give a general description of cantonal politics. The parties are not necessarily the same as in the Confederation. They do not always even bear the same names. In Geneva, for instance, those who in Federal politics are called Liberals describe themselves as Democrats. National organizations have had no such all-pervasive power as in the United States or in Australia, so Cantonal elections are usually fought on Cantonal, not on National issues, yet similar influences and tendencies are visible, and the same types of opinion appear. The Catholic is ready to rally to his Church. The Socialist complains that labour gets less than its due, and urges that the canton or the commune should undertake new work and extend its grasp further and further over the means of production and the methods of distribution. Meanwhile the somewhat stolid peasant landowner and the respectable middle-class shopkeeper or banker's clerk look askance at these novelties, much as the same kind of man does in rural France and rural Germany.

Except in urban manufacturing communities, where new ideas and schemes are afloat among the workers and municipal elections are fought by the Socialists, party politics have roused little heat. In some cantons, Radicals are scarcely distinguishable from Liberals; in others, as in Geneva, Radicals may for election purposes work along with Socialists. Some of the older rural cantons are so purely Roman Catholic that one can hardly talk of any other party, while in others Radicalism has had practically no opposition to confront. In both sets of cantons there were slight oscillations affecting the complexion of the Cantonal Legislature, while the representation in the Houses of the Federal Assembly was varying little from one election to another.

Returning to the Confederation, let us note the questions on which controversy is most active. It is seldom perceptible as regards foreign policy, for this is prescribed by the general sense that a neutrality friendly to all its neighbours alike must be preserved. Even during the war of 1914–18 the strong sympathy felt all over French-speaking Switzerland for the Western Allies, and that extended by a part of the German-speaking population to the Central Powers, disturbed the country only for a few moments when the action of some military authorities, and, more rarely, that of the Federal Executive, was impugned. There is, as in nearly all Federal Governments, a division of opinion between those who favour the extension of Federal power and those who cling to cantonal rights, and this has grown more evident here since the Radical majority have leant towards *Étatisme, i.e.* an extension of the functions of government.[1] On the whole, the Radicals are Centralizers, the Ultramontanes and Liberals Cantonalists. A combination of these two latter parties, coupled with the conservative instinct of a large section of the rural Radicals, procured the rejection, at several votings by Referendum, of proposals for the assumption of new powers by the National Government, yet in the case of the acquisition of the railways this instinct yielded to the prospect of economic advantage.[2] In matters

[1] *Étatisme* has suffered in public favour through the failure in economy and efficiency, which here, as well as in England and the United States, were noted in the administration (during the recent war) of several departments which had to bear a severe strain.

[2] A further reason was that the holding by Germans of a large proportion of the shares in the Gothard railway, an undertaking of vast international importance, had made it politically desirable for the Swiss Government to obtain full control of that line; and to do this it seemed necessary to acquire the other lines also.

of social reform, each scheme is considered on its merits, and the cautiously progressive policy of the Radicals has been generally approved, though the Socialists and the small group of Radical Democrats desired to quicken the pace.[1] Economic issues have fallen into the background since a protective tariff was adopted: it is only some of the older Liberals who cast longing, lingering looks behind at the days of free trade. Religion, especially where it affects denominational teaching in the schools, excites more feeling. The leaders of the Radicals favour purely secular instruction, as do the Socialists, while the Clericals and most of the Liberals stand on the other side. As, however, the control of elementary schools is primarily a matter for the cantons, this battle is fought chiefly in those cantons where Roman Catholics and Protestants are fairly balanced. Almost the only question contested on purely party grounds, *i.e.* with a view to the effect which its determination may have upon party strength, was that of the representation of minorities. The dominant Radicals believed that Proportional Representation would weaken the hands of government both in the legislative and the executive departments by multiplying sections in the legislature and reducing the majorities needed to give stability. The Socialists, as well as the Ultramontanes and the Liberals, sections whose representatives in the National Council are smaller than their strength in the constituencies entitle them to, expected to secure by it an increase in their respective numbers. As already observed, it was carried in 1918 and put in force at the elections of 1919. Among other proposals for constitutional change the most prominent is that of transferring the choice of the Federal Council from the National Assembly to a vote of the whole people. Advocated as a logical development of the principle of popular sovereignty by the Socialists and more democratic Radicals, and by the Ultramontanes as a means of securing for them a better representation in the Federal Council, it is resisted by the bulk of the Radical party as tending to disturb that confidence and cordial co-operation which has enabled that Executive Council to work well with the Legislature. This is not the only mat-

[1] One does not hear of proposals to fix wages by law or to entrust the fixing thereof, as in Australia, to a Court of law.

ter in which the two extremes of Clericals and Socialists, sometimes reinforced by the Liberals, have stood together against the Radicals. Both these extreme parties favour female suffrage, both expecting to gain by it, for the Clericals count on the influence exerted by the priesthood upon women. Where there are several Opposition minority parties, there is always a likelihood of their joining forces against the majority. The same phenomenon has sometimes been seen in France, and it was seen in the British Parliament when in 1885 the Irish Nationalists united with the English Tories to turn out the Liberal ministry of that day.

The spirit of party being weaker here than in most democracies, and the questions that divide the nation rarely rousing passion, one is not surprised to find political organizations less tightly knit and less actively worked than in England or the United States or Australia. Only the Socialists have in their well-defined positive programme, in their Labour Unions, and in their propagandist zeal, both the motive and the means for building up a compact and militant system. These Unions constitute a network of associations and committees always available for political action. The sentiment of class solidarity and the hope of winning material benefits, coupled with the power of setting the whole voting machine in motion by pulling a few strings, give to this party, as they have given to the Labour party in Australia, a closer cohesion and stricter discipline than the other parties possess. It has moved like one man. Few internal dissensions have hitherto impaired its combatant efficiency but a divergence has recently (1919) appeared between the more and the less extreme wings. It puts forward its programme at every kind of election, National, Cantonal, Municipal, Communal, and requires its members in the legislatures to give an account to the party of their action there.

Next to it in this respect stand the Clericals. Supported by the church organization, with priests in every commune and bishops giving directions from behind the lines, Ultramontane Fribourg has been the chief headquarters, while Luzern, though less clerically minded, is a not less reliable centre for the action of Catholic laymen. The Radical party, with its stable majority in the Confederation, was not

equally impelled to strengthen itself by a system of local
Committees for enrolling adherents, selecting candidates,
and stimulating popular zeal. However, its general congress of delegates, chosen in each canton by the cantonal
party authority, declares the policy of the party; and appoints a central organ of thirty-two persons to give effect to
the resolutions they pass. There is also a Central Committee and (in nearly all cantons) a Cantonal Committee,
with its small Executive Committee, for handling current
business and keeping touch with the cantonal organizations,
as well as local Committees in the large towns and the more
populous rural areas. The Liberals have Committees in
some cantons, but in others are feebly represented, and
sometimes divided among themselves.

To an Englishman, and still more to an American, the
most conclusive evidence of the comparative insignificance
of party organization is the absence of party funds. Politics is run in Switzerland more cheaply than anywhere else
in the world. Were there any serious amount of regular
work to be done in organizing, in canvassing, in getting up
meetings, in diffusing literature among the voters, money
would be needed. Even the active propaganda of the Social
Democrats involves little special expenditure, for their Labour organizations, created for other purposes, do what is
needed in the way of instruction, drill, and electioneering
campaigns. This remarkable contrast with the phenomena
of the United States is easily explained by the absence of the
motive of personal profit. It is not worth anybody's while
to spend money on party work except for some definite public purpose. Nobody in Switzerland has anything to gain
for his own pocket by the victory of a party, for places are
poorly paid, Federal places do not change hands after an
election, Cantonal places are not important enough to deserve a costly fight, nor could the expenditure of money at
an election escape notice in these small communities. Only
where there is a public aim, rousing for the moment keen
public interest, must funds be raised.

To complete this brief view of the influence of party in
Switzerland, let us see how that influence works in the several modes and organs through which the people conduct
the government of their country. These are (a) popular

elections, (b) action by the Legislatures, (c) the action of the people voting directly on proposals submitted by Referendum and Initiative, and (d) the action of the Executive, which in the Confederation is the Federal Council, in the Cantons the Small Council.

(a) Elections are the matter with which British, French, and American parties chiefly occupy themselves. It is at and through these that they make their appeals to the citizens, arraign their adversaries, proclaim the benefits they propose to confer on the community.

In Switzerland elections are more numerous than in England or Canada, and quite as numerous as in France, though not so numerous as in sorely-burdened America. Terms of office are short, and many posts which in other countries are filled by the nomination of the executive or the legislature, are here in the direct gift of the people. In the Confederation the members of the National Council are chosen for three years; those of the Cantonal Great Councils usually for the same term. In many cantons the smaller or Executive Council and the judges, as well as some other officials, are elected by the people, and for short terms. There are also communal elections. This frequent invocation of the citizen has a good side in keeping his interest alive, and a less good side in exhausting that interest by making the exercise of civic rights occur so often that he may cease to scrutinize the merits of the candidates. One hears it said, " Our frequent voting tires the peasant and the workman: he cannot even have his Sunday for recreation." Judicious observers wish to see the number of elections reduced, but they admit that the evil is reduced by the habit of re-electing the occupant of a post.

The extent to which the interest of the voter is maintained can be gauged better in Switzerland than elsewhere by the percentage of the citizens who cast a vote, seeing that the parties (except the Social Democrats) seldom work hard to bring them up to the polls. Allowing for the absence of this factor, and remembering that with manhood suffrage the percentage of persons actually voting must be expected to be a trifle lower than where the suffrage is restricted to the slightly richer and less migratory part of the population, Switzerland stands well. The proportion of actual to possible votes is rather larger than the average of Great Britain or Australia, and as good as that of the United States; and it is said to be better now in cantons where all offices are filled by direct popular voting than it was or is under the old system of voting only for representatives. In Zürich the percentage now ranges from 70 to 80, whereas in former days it sometimes sank to 20. This, however, is a canton where proxies are permitted, where political life is comparatively strenuous, and in some of whose communes there are penalties for neglect.[1] In Appenzell failure to attend the Landesgemeinde (without reasonable excuse) is punished by a fine of ten francs, and some other cantons endeavour to compel voting by the imposition of fines for omission. Such provisions may seem to indicate indifference; yet they also indicate the high standard democratic theory sets up. Everywhere there will be " slackers," but no people shows so widely diffused and so constant an interest in the exercise of its political functions.

The rational will which the citizens are expected to possess and to express by their votes may be perverted in three ways: by Fear, when the voter is intimidated; by Corrupt inducements, when he is bribed; by Fraud, when the votes are not honestly taken or honestly counted. In Switzerland none of these perversions exists to an appreciable extent. Intimidation is unheard of. There are practically no landlords, and nowadays it would be impossible for employers to put pressure upon their workmen, and rarely possible for priests to drive in their flocks.[2] Neither do mobs terrorize the quiet citizen, for the polls are quiet and orderly. Only in one or two cantons have officials been occasionally charged with such interference as is common in France. Bribery is, if not unknown, yet uncommon, confined to some very few cantons, and that for three reasons. Few candidates could afford it. It is not worth a candidate's while, because there is no money and little glory to be had out of politics. It could hardly be kept secret in

[1] In these communes, if the citizen neither appeared to drop his ballot paper nor transmitted it in the official envelope within three days, it was sent for, and he was charged one franc for the trouble.

[2] Protestant pastors seldom seek to exert political influence, and in French-speaking cantons carefully abstain from even the appearance of doing so.

communities so small as nearly all the Swiss constituencies are; and when it became known, the briber would be punished by public anger and the bribed by public contempt.

The elections are by universal testimony fairly conducted. I have heard of a case in which persons were brought in and hired to give votes, and of another in which ballot-boxes had been tampered with and the election annulled on that ground. But such instances are extremely rare.

The cost is small. All those expenses which in England are called "official," viz. the provision of polling-places, boxes, clerks, etc., are borne by the State, and the candidate pays hardly anything for the hire of rooms, for agents, or for advertisements. Before 1918 a candidate for one of the large county divisions in England was legally entitled to pay almost as much to get returned to Parliament as all the candidates for the National Council taken together would pay at a General Election over all Switzerland.

Note that the practice of "nursing" a constituency, by spending money in it some while before an election, or by giving large subscriptions to local purposes, generally charitable or otherwise directly political — a practice which has during the last thirty years become common in England — is unheard of in Switzerland. To be in politics costs nothing beyond the loss of time involved in absence from a man's home work. Neither is a member expected to render those services which are demanded from a deputy in France. There are no decorations to be procured for constituents by voting in support of Ministers. And just as no candidate or member gains favour with his constituents by getting favours for them, so there are no titles or other marks of distinction by which the party dominant in the Federal or in a Cantonal Legislature could reward either the fidelity of its supporters or any pecuniary service rendered to its organization.

(a) The functions of a party in an election begin with the choice of a candidate. This gives less trouble than it does in Britain and has long done in the United States, and though any citizen may present himself to the electors uninvited and unrecommended by an organization, this is unusual and might be deemed unbecoming, so the local party Committee selects a person whom they think suitable, and submits his name to a meeting, which, albeit open, will be attended only by members of the party. Precautions to exclude other persons are not found needful. At such a meeting other names may be proposed, but in general the nominations made by the Committee are adopted. Among the Social Democrats, who are thoroughly, and the Clericals, who are (in most places) tolerably well organized, the recommendation of the Committee is followed as a matter of course. As regards the two other parties, things are in much the same condition as they were in Britain before the new system of representative party Committees began to be created between 1870 and 1890. The process is all the smoother in Switzerland, because the habit has been formed of re-electing for a fresh term the member of the legislature, or official, or judge whose post becomes vacant. He can thus easily observe the etiquette which prescribes that a member wishing to speak on politics should do so in some other constituency than his own. Rarely is a member desiring re-election rejected by the Committee, unless either his personal character or his general fidelity to the party has been seriously impugned. Rarely is he rejected by the electors unless some marked change has occurred in the political sentiments of the constituency. *" Semel electus, semper electus"* is, broadly speaking, the principle observed.

In selecting a candidate, a local resident, or at least a man connected by family with the locality, is preferred. Very seldom does a citizen of one canton become a member of the National Council for a constituency situate in some other, and of course no one but a citizen of the canton would be chosen for the Council of States. But localism, though stronger than in England or Australia, seems less strong than in the United States. Every party tries to select good candidates, for the voter is more independent than in America or France, and values the man more than the label he bears.[1] One whom his neighbours respects for his character

[1] I have, however, heard it remarked that the slight decline noticeable in the intellectual quality of representatives is due to the recent tendency to prefer docile candidates to men of more independent character. It is also said that sensitive men sometimes refrain from candidacy, because the personal criticism to which politicians are subjected is more disagreeable in small constituencies, where everybody is personally known, than it can well be in large communities.

and attainments will often have the support of those who
do not agree with his politics. Sometimes, when an election
is at hand, the leaders of the chief parties, holding it right
to give every section of opinion a fair representation, will
agree upon a list of candidates, and though this is mostly
settled on the basis of the voting strength each party commands, it may happen that eminent citizens are put on the
list and carried who could not have been elected on a regular party vote. The difference between Switzerland and
the countries where issues are fundamental and party spirit
runs high is best shown by the large number of uncontested
constituencies. There have been years in which more than
half the seats in the National Council were not fought.
Sometimes, because one party has a large and permanent
preponderance, sometimes because no issue is acute, the
voters care more to be represented by their best citizens
than by those most exactly in accord with their views. Being in Zürich in 1905, I found that there were in the
Executive Council of the canton three Radicals, three Liberals, and one Social Democrat, though the Radical vote
was decidedly larger than the Liberal, and the Socialist vote
was not then strong enough to have carried its man. All
had been elected without a contest. So at the same time
there was in the city of Zürich a Council consisting of four
Liberals, two Radicals, and three Socialists, all chosen practically without opposition:[1] and the two other parties had
joined in electing a Social Democrat to the Supreme Court of
the State from the feeling that it was only fair to let that section of the inhabitants have one of themselves on the bench.

Sometimes — I have known it happen in Zürich — Radicals and Liberals agree to support one another's lists in
Cantonal elections, and in Federal elections combine, under
the name of the *Freisinnige Partei,* to issue a joint list.
The proportion of the voters who remain outside any party
organization is larger than in England, and far larger than
in America, yet this does not necessarily make the result of
contests unpredictable, for these unattached voters change
their attitude very little, and usually support the sitting
member.

---

[1] Such little opposition as there was turned upon personal not political reasons.

(*b*) We now come to party action in the Legislature. Up to 1918 the Radicals held a majority in both the National Council and the Council of States, smaller in the latter body (in 1918 it was 25 against 19), because some of the less populous cantons always return Roman Catholic members. But, as already noted (p. 409), the elections of 1919 changed the situation, giving no party an absolute majority, though the Radical party with its sixty members was the largest. The preponderance of one party, as well as the fact that when several parties unite in desiring to defeat a Bill this is best done by attacking it on a Referendum vote, had tended to keep party feeling at a low temperature. Things may now be different. When a question arises on which it is thought proper that the party should act together, the nominal leader does not issue a command but calls a meeting of the " fraction " (as it is called), to settle how its members should vote. Measures are, as a rule, discussed on their merits, with little regard (except on questions of constitutional change) to their effect on party interests, seldom deeply involved, since the last word rests with the people if the stage of submission by Referendum is reached. The general absence of passion has tended to make things move gently and facilitated compromise. It was chiefly when offices were in question that party motives came into play, as for instance when a vacancy in the Federal Council had to be filled, and then (as already observed) the Radicals, while keeping a majority, recognized the claims of the minority parties. Other posts filled by the vote of the two Houses sitting together are the chancellorship, the headship of the army (when a general commanding-in-chief is needed),[1] and the seats in the Federal Tribunal. In these cases party feeling may affect, without necessarily determining, the selection.

(*c*) The Executive Federal Council is said to be sometimes influenced by party proclivities in making civil or military appointments, but the daily conduct of its business seems little disturbed thereby. Though discharging most of the functions of a Cabinet, it lacks that solidarity of opinion (professed if not always existent) which is the note of French or British Cabinet Government. Its members

---

[1] In ordinary times there are only colonels.

are expected to work together, and do work together, whatever their differences of view. The opinion of the majority is the opinion of the Council, even if councillors should speak discrepantly in the Legislature.[1]

(d) The action of the People exercising their legislative power in voting on questions submitted by Referendum or Initiative has been already dealt with. Where the nature of the subject permits, the parties use their influence, and if the question raises issues either religious or socialistic, it may prove effective. Yet even on these questions a popular vote does not necessarily test the respective strength of the parties, for the Swiss voter not only thinks for himself on the merits of the issue, but has also, and especially in rural areas, an aversion to novelties. When in doubt, he prefers to " stand upon the old paths."

These remarks, however, apply much less to the Socialists, who, being well organized, cast a solid vote both at elections and in Referenda, and rather less to the Catholic Conservatives than to the other parties in which party allegiance is less strong.

What has been said finds an application to cantonal party politics, subject, however, to the qualification that party feeling is warmer in most of the cantons than in the Confederation. Leaders are apt to exert more influence, being better known personally, and in closer touch with the people. As a small kettleful of water boils more quickly than a large one, so the temperature of public sentiment rises faster in small communities, and the issues, being more frequently affected by local or personal considerations, make a more direct appeal to the people. Since national issues do not prevail everywhere, as in the United States or Canada, cantonal parties are more changeful, cantonal elections more uncertain. Elections call out a heavier poll than does a Referendum, because the issue has usually more interest for the average citizen.

As respects the Communes and municipalities, national or cantonal issues count for little, local issues and the merits

---

[1] Even in Great Britain it may happen that members of a Ministry are permitted to oppose one another in debate. I recall a case in which this happened when Woman Suffrage, a subject on which the Cabinet had not delivered a collective opinion, was being debated in the House of Commons.

of individual candidates for a great deal. The Socialists can, however, deliver a solid party vote, because their platforms are largely applicable to communal policies. In Swiss, as in nearly all Canadian, in Scottish, and in many English cities, there is a practical good sense which prevents national political partisanship from warping the mind of the citizen who desires capable administration.

Why Party is not a Strong Force

The comparative weakness in Switzerland of that party system by which government is worked in all other modern democracies makes it worth while to sum up the causes which have made it here and here only a secondary force.

First.— For half a century or more there have not been before the nation any vital issues, such as was that of Monarchy *v.* Democracy in France, or that of Slavery in the United States. The form of government has, in its outlines, been long well settled, the bed-rock of democracy reached. There are no questions of colonial, hardly any of foreign policy.

Secondly.— There has been little discontent with existing economic conditions. Such resentment as the spread of socialistic doctrines reveals, does not (as in some countries) spring from poverty, much less from misery, among the workers, but mainly from theoretic considerations, and the wish to distribute more equitably the products of labour. Being fairly satisfied with their lot, the bulk of the people have been disposed to let well alone.

Thirdly.— The old ecclesiastical antagonisms, if not effaced, for the Catholics complain of the treatment accorded to the religious orders, are not very acute. In the Confederation religious equality reigns, subject to the provisions of the Constitution regarding bishoprics and religious orders. As the cantons may (subject as aforesaid) regulate ecclesiastical matters, Catholic cantons can do what they please, so long as they do not transgress any guaranteed right, and no Protestant canton thinks of interfering with its Catholics.[1]

[1] I know of a commune near Geneva in which Protestants subscribed to the erection of a Catholic Church, and Catholics to that of a Protestant.

Fourthly.— Class hatreds have been absent. Differences of wealth exist, but there are no millionaires, nor any such displays of wealth as excite envy in countries like France or America. The desire to equalize conditions and instal the "proletariate" in power has created an aggressive party, but less bitterness has been aroused than is seen in other parts of Europe.

Fifthly.— Personal ambition and personal leadership in public life are less conspicuous than in any other free country. The Swiss seldom acclaim or follow individuals. They respect ability and they trust one whom they have long known as honest and courageous, but enthusiasm and hero-worship seem foreign to their natures. The national heroes are far back in the past. No statesman has ever created a party called by his name. No Pitt, no Gladstone, no Gambetta, no Deák, no Jefferson or Clay or O'Connell or Parnell.

Sixthly.— That "sporting instinct," as one may call it, which in the English-speaking peoples stirs the members of a party to fight for it because it is theirs and they want it to win, the same instinct which goes to wild lengths in baseball matches or athletic competitions, is faint among the Swiss. Politics are a serious matter, a business matter, not a game.

Seventhly.— The prizes which public life offers to the individual member of a party are few and hardly worth striving for. Public service has not the attraction of social importance which counts for much in France, nor the pecuniary rewards that dangle before American politicians of the lower type.

Eighthly.— The graver questions of policy are settled in the last resort by popular vote, so that the dominance of any one party in the Legislature or in the Executive Council (be it in the Confederation or in a canton) is a secondary matter, and can but rarely involve any great benefit or harm to the country.

Ninthly.— For two generations one party commanded so decided a majority in the Confederation that the other parties, instead of trying to dethrone it, confined themselves to resisting such of its particular measures as they disliked. As it seldom provoked them by abusing its strength — for this would have endangered its own position — their re-sistance was conducted with moderation.

Lastly.— Patriotism, a patriotism which puts the inter-est of the nation above all domestic differences, holds all the Swiss together. In Britain and America, as well as in Australia and New Zealand, there were during last cen-tury no foreign neighbours to fear, so party spirit could disport itself freely. Here the pressure of four great mili-tary Powers keeps compact a people composed of the most diverse elements.

Taken together, these considerations explain why party feeling, which in some democracies can swell to a raging torrent, has in Switzerland been since 1848 no more than a rippling brook.

Absence of " Professional Politicians "

That the absence of acute partisanship in the legislative and executive authorities should make the daily movement of legislation and administration steadier and smoother than in countries where it is the function of a parliamentary Opposition to criticize and arraign, sometimes even to ob-struct, the action of the ministry,— this is a natural and obvious result over which a people may rejoice. But in Switzerland it shows another result, which distinguishes it from France and from some English-speaking countries. In no other democracy (except perhaps Norway) is there so small a class of professional politicians. Hardly any per-sons are occupied in working the non-official political ma-chinery. The class who in Britain are called " political agents," employed either by party organizations, central or local, or by sitting members, or by prospective candidates — a class which, though still small, has increased in recent years — is scarcely noticeable. In the United States there exists a vastly larger class which busies itself not only with the manufacture of public opinion, but with the forming and working of local committees and the selection of party candidates for all elective offices, and the conduct of elec-tions, National, State, and Municipal. Neither is that class to be found in Switzerland, although the number of cantonal and communal offices which lie in the direct gift of the people is large in proportion to the population. Two facts already mentioned account for the difference. In Switzerland the offices are not greatly sought for vacancies are few, owing to the practice of re-election, and the average voter is but slightly influenced in his choice by the coincidence of a candidate's politics with his own. Even in elections to the legislature he regards personal merit as well as party profession, for in small areas such merit can be known and judged. Thus one may say that in Switzerland there are few " politicians " in the American, French, and English sense of the word, except the members of the legislative bodies, Federal and Cantonal.

Character of the Members of Legislature

How stands it, then, with these members? Is politics for them a career? From what classes and occupations do they come? How do they commend themselves to the electors? What standard of intelligence, knowledge, and uprightness do they reach?

As political life is not in the pecuniary sense a profession, so too it is hardly a career. There is practically nothing to be gained from a seat in the Legislature, for a man of the average member's talents would earn more in a profession. The Federal offices which it gives a prospect of obtaining are few in the Confederation, being virtually confined to places in the Executive Council and in the Federal Tribunal. Though these posts are legally held only for three years and six years respectively, the habit of re-election makes vacancies so few that the chance for any given member is scarcely worth regarding. Nobody, therefore, embarks in politics as a lucrative calling. What able man would enter a legislature for the sake of twenty shillings a day during sixteen weeks in the year? In the cantons the phenomena are fairly similar, though in some there are more opportunities than the National Government offers for using a seat in the Legislature for personal advancement. A lawyer may increase his practice either by showing his talents for speaking or by becoming a person of some local importance; a business man may improve his standing in the business world; and there are posts which, though scantily remunerated, may be worth having when other plans break down or other careers are closed. It remains true, however, that politics, by itself, is not an avocation. Practically every legislator has his own business or profession, and lives by it. The motives which lead him into public life are much the same as those one finds in England. There is an interest in public questions, and a desire to serve the causes he cares for: there is an ambition, which the sternest moralist will hardly condemn, to make effective such abilities as he possesses and win distinction by them: there is the longing for some sort of power, and among some few there is the hope of turning a public position to account in the world of business or, more frequently, in winning social estimation, for in Switzerland the position of a deputy, though carrying no sort of rank, witnesses to the respect which fellow-citizens have accorded, seeing that the Assembly has always stood high in the esteem of the people.

All classes are represented in it, but the large majority are well-educated men, about half of them lawyers or cantonal officials who have received some legal training. The old nobility, such as the Junkers of Bern, do not offer themselves, and might not be returned if they did, either in the cities which they ruled as a patrician oligarchy, almost till within living memory, or in most of the rural areas. But in some few cantons, such as Uri and Schwytz and Grisons, the ancient noble families who have been associated with the history of the canton for four or five centuries continue to enjoy great respect, sometimes even political influence, and their descendants are still chosen to fill the highest cantonal posts or returned as members to one or other Federal House. Broadly speaking, though wealth may sometimes aid a candidate and rank may sometimes expose him to suspicion, neither makes much difference. A man is elected on the strength of his local standing, his character, and his capacity. Nowhere in Europe, except perhaps in Norway, where there was never any ennobled class, and in Bulgaria and Serbia, where, while the Turk still ruled, everybody was a peasant without civil rights, is social equality so complete as in Switzerland, complete enough to need no asserting. In cities the families of

ancient lineage cherish their traditions in silence, and the
newer well-born families of mercantile origin have also a
certain pride of ancestry, but both (speaking broadly)
stand apart from public life. These excepted, the members
come from all classes, though in the National Assembly
there were, till the Socialists arose, no working-men, and
hardly ·any peasants. Rich men do not eschew politics, as
in Australia, or find that difficulty in getting a seat which
is experienced in America, but they are usually too much
occupied by their business as manufacturers or hotel proprietors to give attendance in Bern while the Assembly is in
session. The large majority are men of moderate means
and simple life, fair specimens of the upper middle class
of the nation, with its characteristic shrewd sense and plain
way of living. The Assembly is equal in knowledge and
capacity to the French and English legislatures, though
without the oratorical brilliance of the former.

Both in the Confederation and in the cantons members
are respected and trusted. Imputations of corruption or
of the grosser forms of jobbery have been rare, and convictions still more rare, except perhaps in two or three cantons, which it would be invidious to name. The term " politician," though a Bernese Junker might use it with the
sort of scorn for a parvenu which the patrician Catilina
showed for Cicero,[1] carries no faint tinge of such suspicion
as it awakens in France and in some States of the American
Union. This holds true of the official class also, including
the judges of the upper courts. If a man has been proved
to be dishonest, his public career comes to a perpetual end.

The so-called " tone of public life " is best conveyed by
comparing it with that of other countries. When the visitor enters the· halls in which the Federal Assembly meets,
and watches the proceedings and talks with the statesmen,
he notes the absence of that air of pomp and ceremony
which custom and tradition have preserved in France and
England and Hungary. Few forms are observed: little
appears of the dignity with which the historic greatness of
a country invests the men who guide its destinies, whatever
their personal worth. All is plain almost to bareness. As
in earlier centuries the courtiers and diplomatists of France

[1] " Civis inquilinus urbis Romae " (according to Sallust).

and Austria disparaged the republican manners of Holland
and Switzerland, so one notes a blunt homeliness and want
of external polish which censorious tongues would call
roughness.   But there is less acridity, less unfairness in
controversy, less of wounding insinuation than in the
Chambers of France, less commonness and rudeness, sometimes descending to vulgarity, than in those of America and
Australia.   One feels in Switzerland the presence, along
with a sort of rustic simplicity, of a natural rough-hewn
dignity, the product of a long tradition of national independence and individual freedom, and rooted in a sense of
equality which respects itself without disparaging others.
The observer finds nothing in the proceedings or externals
of the Swiss Chambers to touch his imagination, as the imagination of American students is touched by features of
the British Parliament so familiar to the Englishman that
he fails to mark them.   But the visitor's judgment is impressed.   He sees solid thoughtful men, with strong and
cool heads, trying to do their best for the country which is
the first love of their hearts.   There is an atmosphere of
reciprocal respect.   Representatives do not inveigh against
their colleagues.   They trust the Federal Councillors.   The
people trust both.   Taking the country as a whole, the tone
of public life in the Confederation, in most of the cantons, and in the communes, is healthier than what one finds
in France, Italy, or Brazil, or many States of the American
Union, and provinces of Canada, and not inferior to that
of Britain, of Australia and New Zealand, of Holland, Norway, and Chile.

If this be so — for a stranger fears to dogmatize on a
subject to which even the inhabitants find it hard to apply
positive tests — the soundness of Swiss public life is, as
must always be the case, mainly due to the vigilance of public opinion.

CHAPTER XXXI

PUBLIC OPINION

THE public opinion of a people is the expression (as applied to politics) of the intelligence and taste, the temper and the moral feelings of the individual citizens. In trying to understand Swiss opinion we must therefore begin from the Swiss citizen.

How are we to form any general estimate of character of a nation composed of very different elements? Race differences go deep: we see that in Spain. Religious differences go even deeper: we see that in France, where they divide the stream of opinion at its source. Nevertheless in countries where racial distinctions are so marked as in Great Britain, and even in a vast country like the United States, in the northern, southern, and western parts of which men live under widely diverse economic conditions, there may be a general and pervasive opinion which expresses the national thought and purpose, creating out of the various elements that temper one another a real and fruitful unity. This is the case in Switzerland. The majority of the people are of Teutonic stock, the minority of Celtic or Italic. There is a Protestant majority and a Roman Catholic minority, with the recollection of an acute conflict only seventy years behind. Yet religious antagonisms have softened, and racial differences cause no enmity, but may even seem to give a greater variety and breadth to the character of the people. The Allemanic or German-speaking part of the population has a steady and persistent German thoroughness, with rather less sentimentality and certainly more independence than characterize the typical Middle German, as, for instance, the Rhinelander or Thuringian or Saxon. The French-speaking population has a Burgundian strain, which gives it less mobility and vivacity than one finds in natives of Southern and West Central France. Still, though the contrast between the French-speakers of Vaud and Geneva and the German-speakers of Zürich and Luzern is less marked than is the unlikeness of the German of Cologne to the Frenchman of Lyons, a certain contrast remains. In turning from a journal of a German city like Basle to a journal of Lausanne one perceives a difference deeper than that of language, a difference in mental habits and attitude.[1] Each element does of course modify the other, but apparently less by personal contact than through and by literature. This was to be expected. What is more remarkable is that the new cantons, French and Italian, have appropriated the historical traditions of the original cantons, which were all Germanic. The children of those who two centuries ago were held as subjects have inherited the glories of those who ruled their forefathers. This is a fruit of Liberty and Equality.

Let us see now what all Swiss have in common, whether through the influence of history, institutions, and literature, or from any other source.[2]

They are all alike imbued with the spirit of liberty, not only in the sense of civil, religious, and political liberty, but in the sense also of individual independence. The peasant or workman stands on his own feet and goes his own way. He may be led, but he will not be driven. He has also learnt the two first lessons freedom ought to teach, respect for the rights of others and the correlation of Duties with Rights. Thus he is generally tolerant of opposition, not hurried into violence, open to argument, ready to consider a compromise. Nowhere so fully as here (except perhaps in the United States) has what may be called the fusing power of free institutions shown itself so powerful. Diverse as are the human beings in other respects, they have been, for the purposes of politics, melted together in one crucible and run into one mould.

[1] The German-speakers are said to be more prone to accept governmental direction, and to favour the extension of state functions than are the inhabitants of "*Suisse romande*," who dislike "*reglementation*."

[2] I speak only of the native Swiss, not including the recent immigrants, mostly still unassimilated.

Another spirit common to both sections of the nation is the spirit of rural conservatism. A large majority of the French-speakers, a considerable though diminishing majority of the German-speakers, live by agriculture or by pastoral pursuits. The habits of such a life, secluded and touched by few new ideas, make men averse to change, and resentful of any attempt to hustle them. This quality, combined with the tolerance already referred to, produces a cautious moderation of temper which would be stolid if it were stupid. The Swiss peasant, however, though less intellectually alert than the Italian, is slow rather than stupid. His views may be narrow, like the valley whose steep sides pen him in. But he can think, though it may take some time to set his thoughts going in the direction desired. Alpine climbers, British and American, have often noted the intelligence of their guides, sometimes well-read men, from whom one can learn much in conversation.

That taste and capacity for local self-government which began with the old rural cantons has passed into the whole nation, strengthening independence, intelligence, and the sense of civic duty. They have formed the habit of judging everything upon its merits, and this has contributed to reduce the influence exerted by individual leaders. Though it has produced some remarkable statesmen, the history of the country is the history of the people, not of its foremost figures, and could not be written in a series of biographies, as one might write the history of England or Scotland or France. No single man since Zwingli has exerted any decisive influence on the fortunes of the nation or become a great European figure. Geneva was not in Calvin's time, nor in Rousseau's, a member of the Confederation, though in close relations with it. No one has been even so much of a hero as Ferdinand Lassalle was to the German Socialists forty years ago. This feature of Swiss character, taken along with its coolness and comparative insensibility to rhetoric, makes the country no good field for the demagogue. A few such have occasionally figured in Cantonal, but none in Federal politics. They would be discounted. If sweeping economic changes come, it will be by appeals made to self-interested cupidity or to the doctrine of human equality in its extreme form, not through any personal fascination or oratorical arts that may be used to recommend them.

Social Equality has been long established, and the attachment to it has become a part of national character. It is, as already observed, compatible with a respect for ancient lineage, and does not make the peasant or workman aggressively hostile to the richer class, as the latter is in France to the so-called " bourgeois." There is neither subserviency nor self-assertion : each man is taken for what he is worth, not in money, but as a citizen. Life is plain and frugal in all classes. The ostentatious luxury of the rich foreigners who flaunt themselves at Luzern or Zürich would be censured in a native Swiss.

How, then, does Social Equality affect the relations of the people to the politician ? Does he play down to them by an affection of rustic simplicity, as often happens in the United States ? Do they distrust him if he is better off or better educated ? Do the compliments paid to the " practical common-sense " and " great heart " of the people, usual in all democratic countries, give them a conceit of their universal competence and extinguish any deference to special knowledge or long experience ?

There is something of all this, but less than might be expected in a country so pervaded by the spirit of equality, for the practice of self-government seems to have worked to temper the theory of popular sovereignty. The citizen has so long been accustomed to the former that the strong wine of the latter does not go to his head. He has perhaps too little sense of the value of technical knowledge, especially when he is asked to pay for it, does not realize the intricacy of modern economic problems, cares little for shining qualities and might resent any assumption of superior capacity. But he knows the worth of good men, desires his community to retain their services, respects the opinion of those who impress him as honest and thoughtful. A Swiss professor [1] once told me that having delivered an address in a village on some current question that was to come before

---

[1] Dr. Karl Hilty, one of the sagest as well as one of the most lovable Swiss I have ever known. He died in 1908.

the people for their decision, an old farmer came up to him after it was over and said, " Don't suppose that we agriculturists think poorly of you learned men. We like to see you and to hear you: you have things to tell us we don't know."

All classes are less prone to be moved by abstract ideas than either the French or the Germans. Though Rousseau was a Genevese, his doctrines were making more impression in France, and even in North America, than his own city, till its government, with genuinely oligarchic folly, ordered the *Contrat Social* to be publicly burnt. In the first years of the French Revolution Geneva saw a popular outburst, which overwhelmed the aristocracy and spread into West Switzerland. But this was due rather to the contagion of France than to Rousseau's teaching; nor has any subsequent dissemination of ideas ever lit such a blaze. The Socialism of German-speaking Switzerland is comparatively recent and due to the Marxian propaganda from Germany, strengthened by the immigration of German working-men, most of whom, however, have not become citizens. A like immigration from France and Italy has had a similar, though less marked, effect in the western cantons. More prudent than the Americans, the Swiss are chary in admitting aliens to full civic rights.[1] They are, moreover, not of a speculative turn of mind. They have produced great mathematicians like Euler, great moralists and critics like Vinet, but no first-rate metaphysicians or political philosophers. Nevertheless the dogma of popular sovereignty, coinciding with the love of equality and the practice of local self-government, has counted for more in recommending the Referendum and Initiative than have any actual grievances those institutions might have served to abate.

As the habit of following public affairs with personal interest is more widely diffused in Switzerland than in other European countries, so it seems probable that they fill a larger space than they do elsewhere in the mind of the average citizen. This is partly due to the small size of governmental areas, the Commune, the Canton, the Con-

---

[1] To be a citizen, one must be admitted to a commune, and though poor communes welcome rich applicants, all communes are careful not to burden themselves with those whom they might have to support.

federation itself, but something may be attributed to the
comparative absence of sources of interest present in other
countries.   Commerce, manufactures, finance have been on
a small scale, except in a very few urban centres.   Athletic
sports do not occupy the thoughts of the youth as in England and America.   Competitions in rifle-shooting rouse
some interest, but this, from its connection with the army,
is a form of patriotism.   Among the richer people there
are hardly any devoted, like so many Englishmen, to some
form of " sport," hunting, shooting, horse-racing; nor has
amusement become a passion among the less affluent.   Life,
though it grows more strenuous, is more sedate, and the
eagerness for new sensations less acute, than in the cities
of France, Germany, or America.   Even gaiety takes quiet
forms.   There is some leisure for thinking, and some perception of the relative importance of public duty and private self-indulgence.

Let us see how far these features of national life and
character tinge, or are reflected in, the opinions of the people
on political subjects.

They are averse both to centralization and to State socialism, yet willing to take a step in either direction when
a tangible and tolerably certain benefit is set before them.
Cantonalist feeling seems almost as strong as State feeling
was in the United States before the Civil War, and rather
stronger than it is there now.

They are parsimonious, unlike in this respect to all other
democracies, except those of the two South African Republics in their days of independence.   Life has been hard for
the peasant, his income small, his taxes, light as they are,
an appreciable part of his expenditure.   Proposals which
could raise taxation are *prima facie* repellent, except to
those Socialists who regard progressive taxation as a step
towards communism.   Religious partisanship exists, but in
a mild form, milder than in any other country (except
Hungary) where there is a strong minority of one faith opposed to a majority of another.   Protestant hatred of the
Jesuits and fear of other religious orders is a dislike of
what may become a political power working in secret, rather
than an expression of intolerance.   Nevertheless the instance of the Initiative vote against the Jews in 1893 (see

above, p. 403) shows that it is possible to arouse and play upon religious or racial prejudices.

The humanitarian sentiment characteristic of modern democracies led to the abolition of capital punishment by the Constitution of 1874, but was not strong enough to prevent the Constitution from being so amended as to permit a canton to restore that penalty, some shocking cases of murder having induced a reconsideration of the subject. Few cantons, however, have availed themselves of the permission. The tolerant spirit of " Live and let live " is exemplified in the scantiness of compulsory legislation, even as regards intoxicating spirits, though there exists a strong temperance party. One discovers no signs of that Tyranny of the Majority which Tocqueville discovered in America and which J. S. Mill feared as a probable feature of democracy everywhere. On the other hand, there is a willingness, surprising to English observers, to allow to the Executive, for the maintenance of public order and for dealing with suspected offenders, larger powers than English practice has shown to be sufficient.

In judging public men — and this is, after all, the most important of all the functions public opinion has to exercise — the Swiss are shrewd and on the whole fair and just. Confidence is not lightly given nor lightly withdrawn. The qualities most valued are those which characterize the nation — balance, caution, and firmness, coupled of course with integrity. The judgments which the people render are moral rather than sentimental. Newspaper criticism of leading politicians can be stringent, but it is more temperate than in any other democratic country, except perhaps Holland and Norway.

Here let the meed of praise be noted which foreign observers agree in bestowing on the Swiss press. It is well conducted, intelligent, tarnished neither by blackmailing nor by personal virulence. Four of the chief dailies, two published in French, two in German, are among the best in Europe. They do much to guide opinion and to sustain the level of political thinking. All classes read. In no European country are there so many journals in proportion to the population. No single paper, however, seems to exercise a political power such as some have done in Australia and as several now do in Argentina and Brazil. Some are keenly partisan, but none seems to be owned by, or devoted to the interests of, any particular statesman.

How far, then, for this is the point of moment, are we to say that public opinion governs Switzerland, and what relation does it bear to that method of direct legislation at the polls in which the popular will finds its most direct expression?

It might be unsafe to treat a vote on a Referendum or Initiative as exactly reflecting the popular mind, for, although it gives a better means of judging opinion than is found elsewhere in Europe, one must always allow for the influence of party, which can compress into a definite channel the wandering waters of half-formed notions and impressions. Many people can be made to vote, even in Switzerland, who do not contribute to the real opinion of the nation. When a conservatively minded peasant votes "No," he may mean only that he is not yet prepared to say "Yes." Views embodied in votes tell us less than we desire to know as to the trend of thought, but views publicly expressed have the effect which belongs either to the authority of the person they proceed from or to the intensity of conviction which will fight to make them prevail. Thus there are times when a skilled observer can discover that an opinion is already or may soon be dominant, though it does not secure a majority at the polls. It is nevertheless true that the Referendum comes nearer than any other plan yet invented to a method of measuring the public opinion of the moment, for it helps the statesman to discern what is passing in the popular mind. It supplies sailing directions by which he may shape his course, warns him off submerged shoals, indicates better than an election how far the education of the public mind upon a given subject has progressed.

The popular vote by which the people in May 1920 accepted the proposal of the Legislature that Switzerland should enter the League of Nations excited an unprecedentedly and thoroughgoing keen discussion all over the country, and the voting upon it was the largest ever known, exceeding in six cantons 80 per cent of the qualified

citizens.[1]   Both the earnestness with which the people approached their duty and the result of their thought on the
subject were of good omen.

[1] A Swiss friend wrote to me during the progress of this contest:
"Le pacte de la Société des Nations est distribué à tous les citoyens
avec diverses annexes. Les articles de journaux, les conférences se
multiplient. Dans la moindre auberge on entend des discussions
acharnées sur tel ou tel article que des citoyens tout à fait simples
savent par cœur tout comme ils connaissent et invoquent les commen-
taires qu'en ont donné les plus grand juristes. J'ai été interpellé dans
la rue par des citoyens modestes qui tiraient de leur poche leur exem-
plaire du pacte tout crayonné des remarques et qui exigaient des ex-
plications détaillées sur tel ou tel article." The debates and the voting were an aid to political education such as no other European country has seen, and when the proposal, which was opposed by the
Socialists and by the great bulk of the Conservatives in the German-
speaking cantons, was carried by a majority of 414,000 to 322,000, the
decision was at once accepted with a good grace by the minority.

CHAPTER XXXII

CONCLUDING REFLECTIONS ON SWISS POLITICAL INSTITUTIONS

The interest of a general survey of Swiss institutions in their constitutional framework and in actual operation consists not only in the unlikeness of these institutions to those of other modern States, but also in the fact that their daily working has produced results that could not have been predicted from their form. This has been due to two causes. One is the growth of usages which have essentially affected and come to govern that daily working. The other is the comparatively small influence exerted by the power of political party.

Both of these are visible in the Swiss habit of handling their Constitution. That instrument is less precise in its distribution of powers between the National Government and the Cantonal Governments than are the Constitutions of other Federal States. It grants concurrent powers over many branches of legislation, and it permits the National Government to disallow cantonal laws. Controversies may be raised regarding doubtful points of interpretation which in most Federal countries would give rise to friction. In America they would be brought before the Judiciary, there an independent power, which can by judgment raise issues susceptible of final determination only by an amendment of the Constitution. In Switzerland, however, comparatively little trouble has arisen. The Legislature endeavours to adjust matters, keeping as much as possible in general accord with the provisions of the Constitution, where these are clear, yet in such wise as to mollify the canton concerned or the interest affected, and find a solution which will work smoothly all round. Thus a laxity which Americans or Australians would not put up with gives little trouble in Switzerland, and a deviation from the sound principle that no legislature should be allowed to be the judge of the constitutionality of its own action becomes harmless, because every one knows that the Assembly would not abuse a power whose misuse could be promptly corrected by the people.

The frame of National Government creates a Legislature with a term of only three years, and an Executive of seven persons chosen by that Legislature with the same term. These executive officials have not, like the British Cabinet, the advantage of being members of the Legislature, though they can address it. Such a scheme would seem calculated to produce constant changes in men and in policy, as well as to weaken the authority of a Ministry short-lived and dependent on a short-lived Legislature. But neither of these things has happened. Owing to the habit of re-election, the Federal Council stands practically unchanged from one three-year period to another. So, too, the composition of the Legislature itself has hitherto changed little. It is in close and friendly touch with the Executive, profiting by the latter's counsel and administrative experience, leaving minor affairs to it, but in large matters directing its course and taking responsibility for the conduct of business, while within the Federal Council custom has established the rule that each of its members accepts the decision of the majority, or, if the matter has gone to the Assembly, the decision of that body. Because it is not a party body, this Federal Executive of seven is a virtually permanent Cabinet, and the nation gains by retaining the services of its most experienced administrators; though it is perhaps too apt to shift them from one department to another. These benefits are due to a practice or convention not embodied in any provision of the Constitution, but formed by usage, and commended by the results. It is an interesting illustration of the extent to which the legal provisions of a Constitution are modified in their working by what Professor Dicey [1] has called the " Conventions of a Constitution," usages which are worked by a sort of understanding arrived at between politicians and so well settled by practice as to become virtually, though not legally, imperative. Such " understandings " generally grow up in oligarchical rather than in democratic Governments. It was largely by them that the ex-

[1] *The Law of the Constitution.*

tremely complicated constitution of the Roman Republic,
in its legal aspect a mass of apparent contradictions, was
worked.   It was by them, as they were formed under the
oligarchic régime of the eighteenth century, that the British
Constitution was, and is to some extent still worked.   Such
conventions fare well so long as their moral authority lasts,
but in the long-run break down when unduly strained.
They broke down at Rome because ambitious leaders, in a
period which was becoming revolutionary, disregarded them,
and having military force at their command pushed to an
extreme the powers which the letter of the law gave to a
magistrate.   They have largely lost their force in England,
because parties in the Legislature, under the influence of
passion, have disregarded them and have exerted to the full
the powers which majorities in a ruling legislature possess.
Switzerland is a remarkable instance of a government in
which they grew up after it had become democratic, for
though there were doubtless plenty of such non-legal usages
among the oligarchies in cities like Bern and Zürich before
1848, the new Constitution did not take them over, as the
purchaser of a business takes it over as " a going concern."
It was the Liberal statesmen of 1848 who created them for
their own use.[1]   The absence in Switzerland of the friction
between the Houses of the Legislature, so common in two-
Chambered Governments, is, however, due not to conventions or understandings but chiefly to the fact that for many
years the same party held a majority in both Houses, the
members of both being, moreover, drawn from the same
class, elected, either directly or indirectly, by manhood suffrage, and neither House having any special interests, economic or ecclesiastical, to defend.   Their differences are
only such as naturally arise between any two bodies of men
debating apart, though holding opinions and guided by motives substantially the same.

What has been said of the Confederation seems generally
true of the cantonal governments also.   There is less
smoothness in the working of the latter, because in few has

[1] Something similar happened in the United States during the first
half-century of the Constitution.   Convenience established, among the
then small number of leading men in Congress, usages many of which
have held their ground (see the author's *American Commonwealth*,
vol. i. chap. xxxiv.).

any one party a permanent majority in the legislative Great
Council, and because in some cantons the Executive Council
is chosen not by the Legislature but directly by the people.
Nevertheless, as party oscillations are seldom sudden or
violent, and as those executives which are chosen by the
people are usually chosen at the same time as the legislatures, these two authorities get on well together. In the
cantons, as in the Confederation, the suspicion that power
may be abused has prescribed the assignment of all business to Boards.[1] Nowhere is there what Americans call a
" One Man Power," not because the Swiss, like the Greek
republics, dreaded a possible Tyrant, but because they love
equality, and have not been compelled to secure responsibility to the people by fixing it upon a single man who can
be held to strict account more easily than can a Board.[2]
In these small communities representatives and officials all
stand near the people and work under the people's eye.
Public opinion controls everybody. The Legislature, moreover, though legally the centre of all power, is thought not
to need those constitutional checks which the American constitutions impose, because its action can be reversed by the
Referendum or superseded by the Initiative. Thus the system of government by Executive Councils in touch with
Legislative Councils has worked well. The people are, at
any rate, contented. Some changes have indeed been proposed. There are those who would assimilate the Federal
system to that of the more democratic cantons by transferring the election of the (Executive) Federal Council from
the Assembly to the people, a change which while it would
on the one hand give more of independent power to the
Council, might on the other make it, under the plan of proportional representation, unable to work as effectively as
heretofore. Others again would make the Referendum applicable to all cantonal laws in every canton, and would ex-

[1] A similar feeling operated at Athens (see above, Chapter XVI.).
There are similarities between the Greek republics, at their best, and
Switzerland, just as there are also similarities between them, at their
worst, and the more backward of the Spanish-American republics.

[2] Perhaps also because in mediaeval Switzerland there was never
any monarch nearer than the Emperor, so that no monarchical tradition was formed which in other countries made a single Head of the
State, however limited his powers, seem a natural apex of the governmental edifice.

tend the application of the Initiative in the Confederation to laws as well as to Constitutional amendments. Some foreign observers, weary of the perpetual strife which troubles their own politics, will be disposed to ask: " Why try further experiments merely for the sake of giving fuller extension to direct popular sovereignty, considering how wide are the powers the people already exercise? Why disturb a system which has worked usefully, with an absence of friction which other countries admire? Might not a warning from the oracle which bade the people of Camarina leave well alone be sometimes serviceable?"

The merits which such observers discover in the government of Switzerland as compared with other full-fledged democracies, ancient and modern, may be stated as follows:

Its stability, remarkable in the Confederation, not so complete, yet pretty general, in the cantons also.

The consistency with which its policy has been directed to the same broad aims.

The quality of the legislation it produces, steadily progressive in the Confederation, more irregular, but on the whole sound and useful, in the cantons also, and in both, be it more or less progressive, a genuine expression of the popular will.

An administration, economical beyond all comparison, and generally efficient.[1] The economy is a part of the efficiency, for the close scrutiny of expenditure induces care to see that money's worth is got for money spent.

Ample provision is made, except in a very few cantons, for all branches of Education.

Public works are not neglected. The roads are excellent, considering the difficulties of a mountainous country, liable to landslips and to floods from melting snows. Order is well preserved. Justice is honestly, and above all cheaply, administered, though with less technical perfection than in some other countries.

Municipal government is pure and usually efficient.

Adequate provision is made for national defence, and the citizens recognize their duty to render personal service in arms.

---

[1] Except in so far as small salaries fail to secure high special competence in officials.

The liberty of the individual is respected. The tone of public life is maintained at a high standard, and politics is not tainted by corruption. The strong sense of civic duty is seen in the large amount of unpaid public service rendered in cantons and communes.

To these let us add certain other points in which Switzerland is to be commended, and which, though not directly attributable to the form of its government, have at any rate grown up and thriven under that government.

Social as well as civil equality exists, and is accompanied by good feeling between the richer and the poorer. Nowhere is the sense of national unity stronger.

There are no marked inequalities in wealth, and wealth, *per se,* is not an object of hatred. Its power is less felt in legislation than in any other modern country except Norway.

There has been for seventy years little party passion and little religious bitterness.

There are no professional politicians, and comparatively few local demagogues.

Rings, Bosses, Caucuses are rarely discernible, and where visible, just sufficiently so to make their rarity noteworthy.

Except in one political group, growing, but not yet large, contentment reigns. Contentment is not always a good sign, for it may be a mark of apathy, indicating that men have not awakened to the possibility of bettering their conditions and developing their faculties. But no one can call the Swiss apathetic.

The last preceding pages have embodied the impressions formed during a visit to Switzerland in 1905. When I revisited the country in 1919 shadows from passing clouds were beginning to fall upon parts of the landscape. Apart from the shock which there, as elsewhere, had been given by the Great War to hopes of the peaceful progress of the world, the Swiss were realizing their especial dangers from powerful military neighbour states, from the influx of immigrants who were strangers to their own traditions, from the rise of prices, from labour troubles — a formidable general strike having been only just averted by the energetic promptitude of the Government — from the contagion of poisonous foreign influences, from a load of debt incurred

during the war, from defects in the governmental handling
of economic and administrative problems the war had raised.
Cautious persons were alarmed by the spread of communistic doctrines, as well as by the tendency to centralization,
and by an extension of bureaucracy which seemed to threaten
cantonal rights and local self-government. Some, while admitting the force of the arguments for proportional representation, feared that it might enfeeble government by
breaking up the legislature into groups, and might make it
difficult for the Federal Council to maintain the harmony
and general continuity of policy which had proved valuable
in the past. Nevertheless there was among thoughtful men
more cheerfulness than one could find in 1919 in any other
European country. Faith in the good sense and good temper of the people, and in the patriotism which gave unity
to them, made them believe that whatever troubles might be
in store, patriotism and good sense would deliver Switzerland out of all the troubles that might await her, as they had
often saved her before. The visitor was reminded of the
persistent optimism of the Americans. Optimism has sometimes lulled democracies into a false security; yet a people's
faith in itself may be a well-spring of vital energy.

Against these advantages which the country enjoy, what
defects are we to set on the other side of the balance-sheet?
Perfection is not to be expected in any government, however popular, nor does one find the Swiss claiming it for
their own. They admit that the doctrine of equality is
pushed too far in disregarding the value of special knowledge and skill in officials. Some think that in certain cantons the rich are overtaxed, and indeed so overtaxed as to
drive wealth, or the industries which capital is needed to
maintain, out of the canton.[1] Others regret the existence
of petty political cliques with selfish aims, of the habit of
place-hunting, of local jobbery in the giving out of contracts,
and abusing, for some personal end, the position a man
holds in a Cantonal Council or as a Cantonal official. Favouritism has been alleged to exist in the granting of commissions in the army to persons who have what is called in

[1] I do not venture into the controversial question as to what proportion of their income the rich ought to contribute to the services
of the State, but state the complaint as I heard it in Switzerland, and
as it is heard now in many other countries.

America " a pull." As such evils must be expected in every country, doubtless they exist here; but exactly how far they exist in the cantons chiefly impugned it would be hard even for a Swiss investigator to determine.

Being in Bern in 1905, after expressing my surprise at the excellence of the government of the Confederation, I asked a well-informed and judicious Swiss friend to tell me frankly what he thought were its faults. " You must have some faults," I said, " and you can afford to let me know of them." After a little reflection he replied: " We have a practice of referring a difficult question on which legislation is desired to a Committee — like one of your Royal Commissions or Parliamentary Committees in England — which is charged to enquire into and report on the subject. Such a Committee frequently chooses to conduct its investigations at some agreeable mountain hotel during the summer months, and lives there at the public expense longer than is at all necessary. This may not often happen, but we consider it a scandal." " If you are not jesting," I replied, " and this is the blackest sin you can confess, then think of Paris and Montreal, Pittsburg and Cincinnati, and, in the words of our children's hymn, bless the goodness and the grace that have made you a happy Swiss boy."

To what causes may be ascribed the exemption of this Republic from the evils that have afflicted many others? Some causes have been already indicated. The course of Swiss history has formed in the people an unusually strong patriotism and sense of national unity, creating traditions of civic duty which have retained exceptional strength. Those traditions, fostered and made real by the long practice of local self-government, have become part of the national mind. The practice of self-government has also given the best kind of political education, teaching men to associate duties with rights, to respect one another's convictions, to subordinate personal feelings to the common good, to prefer constitutional methods to revolutionary violence. The country has been poor; and though here as well as elsewhere money can tempt virtue — and money coming from abroad used to count for much in old Switzerland — the domestic tempters have been few and have had little to offer. The largest element in the nation consists of peasant proprietors, interested in guarding their own rights of property, and averse to large or sudden changes. Wealth is more equally distributed than in any of the great European countries, and those who have wealth owe it more often to their frugal habits than to large industrial or financial operations.

Much is also to be ascribed to some features of national character. The people are not impressionable, not of an impulsive temper, not open to the charms of thrilling eloquence or of a fascinating personality. Though the grandeur of the scenery that surrounds them has inspired poets like Schiller and Coleridge and Byron, they are themselves not an imaginative people, and it is patriotism, not the splendour of nature, that stirs their hearts. They have, moreover, some qualities specially valuable in politics,— shrewdness, coolness, that hard clear perception of the actualities of life which it is the fashion to call "realism." Even the French-speaking part of the people show these qualities when one compares them with the Celts of Ireland, for instance, or with the Slavs of Poland or Serbia. The Romans, far inferior to the Greeks in artistic gift, had a greater aptitude for politics and law.

Another question follows. How far do the successes of democracy in Switzerland entitle us to hope that other peoples may by following like methods attain a like measure of stability and prosperity? Will Swiss institutions bear transplanting; or will the peaceable fruits of righteousness they have borne ripen only under the conditions of their native home?

Where an institution has succeeded with one particular people and in one set of economic conditions, the presumption that it will suit another people living under different conditions is a weak presumption, and affords slight basis for prediction. Similarly, if an institution works well because it has been worked on certain lines fixed by custom, one must not assume that it will work equally well in a country where a like custom could hardly be created. There are cases in which the custom has become a part of the institution. Strip it away and the institution is not the same.

It is sometimes asked, Is it to men or to institutions or to surrounding conditions that the success attained by a nation is due? These three things cannot be separated. The con-

ditions do much to make the men, and the men learn how to
use the conditions; the institutions are the work of the men,
and become in turn influences moulding the characters of
those who work them.

Among the governmental institutions of Switzerland
there are at least two which might furnish a model fit to be
studied by other free governments, and ought to be considered by some of the new States that are now springing up
in Europe.   One of them is the vesting of executive power
in a small Council, chosen for a short term and not part of
the legislature, instead of in a single President (as in the
United States and the Spanish-American Republics), or in
a Cabinet composed of members of the legislature (as in
France, Britain, and the British self-governing Dominions).

The Federal Council has worked efficiently in this small
country with a small legislature, where the leading men are
familiarly known to a large proportion of the citizens, and
in this poor country where there are no millionaires or
gigantic joint-stock companies greedy for benefits which governments can bestow.   Would such a Council succeed in the
United States or in a German republic?   The advantages
which the Swiss scheme has displayed largely depend upon
the habit of re-electing its members every three years, the
legislature which elects being itself little changed from one
election to another.   This habit of re-election has in its
turn depended upon the predominance of one party in both
Houses of the National Assembly, on the small size of constituencies, and on the comparatively low temperature at
which partisanship stands in the country.   Could the advantages which the Swiss scheme yields be looked for in
France, where for many years past no party has commanded
a majority and party divisions cut deep?   As a former
President of the Confederation observed to me, " The plan
fits a small State where party feeling does not run high.
Would it work well elsewhere?"   And he added: " Where
grave decisions on foreign policy have to be suddenly taken,
would a Council composed of men of different tendencies
be able to take them effectively?"

Even in Switzerland is it certain that the conditions
which have favoured the Council will endure?   Were the
smaller parties in the Assembly to become bitterly antag-

onistic to the Radicals, still the largest, or should the Radicals themselves be divided by the emergence of new issues into various sections, it would be hard, perhaps impossible, to prevent the (Executive) Federal Council from becoming either a purely party body, to which men were elected for party reasons and in which they acted on party lines, just as Cabinets do in England and Australia, or else an ineffective body, living by a series of compromises, unable to pursue a decided and consistent policy, as heretofore? I was told that when the Municipal Council of Zürich contained one member of a party fundamentally opposed to his colleagues the situation became very difficult.[1] Nevertheless the Swiss example ought not to be forgotten by those who in England complain that a man who has shown eminent capacity for finance or for the conduct of, let us say, foreign or colonial affairs is displaced when his party loses its majority in the House of Commons. Still more does it deserve regard in America, where the disconnection of the President's Cabinet from Congress makes it possible for him to obtain the ministerial services of those who do not belong to his party and need not possess the gifts of speech.

The other Swiss institution which can be, and has already begun to be, imitated in other countries is the direct action of the people in voting by Referendum and Initiative. Here again let us note the circumstances which in this particular country have given to the Referendum such success as it has attained. Chief among these is the small size of the community called upon to vote. The largest canton has a population smaller than that of Lancashire or Rhode Island. The Confederation has little more than half the population of Australia, one-fourth of the population of New York State, one-tenth of the population of Great Britain; and even in Switzerland the popular vote does not often exceed 60 per cent of the citizens, though the level of political knowledge and interest stands higher than anywhere else in the world. Add to this that the influence exercised by the parties has been slighter than is to be expected in any of the three countries above named, so that the Swiss

[1] In 1920 the Federal Council contained five Radicals and two Catholics. The Socialists having refused to work along with the other members, there was no Socialist. There were four members from " Suisse allemande," two from " Suisse romande," and one Italian.

people deliver a judgment less likely to be perverted by party affiliations or partisan representations. Would the Referendum work equally well if Party were to become a stronger force in the Confederation than it has been since 1874? This season of fair weather may not last. There have been periods in other countries when the light breezes of party sentiment that were scarcely ruffling the surface of politics suddenly rose into a succession of gales, which tossed the ship of State for many a year. Should the Socialist party, already eager and active, develop its organization further, the other parties might be obliged, as lately happened in Australia, to create organizations fit to cope with the young antagonist. Or, again, schisms might arise to divide the party now dominant, and one of its sections might form an alliance with another party which would change the whole situation.

Are there any other matters in which other nations may profit by Swiss experience?

To look elsewhere for geographical and physical conditions which would produce economic and social phenomena resembling those of Switzerland would be idle. To create the moral and intellectual conditions that have formed the political character of the people would be, if possible at all, a difficult and extremely slow work. It is related that an American visitor, admiring the close, smooth greensward of the Fellows' Garden at Trinity College, Cambridge, enquired how the college came to have such a lawn. The answer was: "We have been watering and mowing and rolling it for three hundred years." Six hundred years have gone to the moulding of the political thought and habits of the Swiss. Nevertheless there are points in which other States may learn from Switzerland. The habit of re-electing to the Legislature or to official posts, irrespective of their party ties, men who have given good service, might usefully be imitated in the States of the American Union, so that the influence of national parties should be removed from local elections with which national issues have nothing to do. Party has its value, and is in some branches of government inevitable; but in Britain and France, as well as in America, it has been worked to death.

Both Englishmen and Frenchmen would do well to note

the absence in Switzerland of any grants by political authorities of titles and decorations, ribbons, medals, and other such marks of distinction. To reserve these honours for persons who have really deserved them has, both in France and in England, been found impossible. When they lie in the gift of a party chief, they are sure to be used for party purposes, and therewith they not only lose their value as rewards of good service, but become instruments of a sort of corruption. Canada has done well to deprecate their introduction into its public life. In a free community the truest — and a sufficient — honour any one can win is the respect of his fellow-citizens.

The constant teaching in the schools of civic duty and the inculcation of the best traditions of national history is a wholesome feature of Swiss life. In no country does one find that the people know so much about and care so much for their historic past. Englishmen have overlooked this side of education so far as regards the masses of the people; and among the educated class it has been frequently turned, as sometimes in America also, to the service of a vainglorious Jingoism from which Switzerland is exempt.

The sense of citizenship finds expression in the willing acceptance of universal military training as a national obligation. If the peace-loving peoples of the world are condemned to endure in the future the same apprehension of attack by aggressive military States as has afflicted the hearts and drained the resources of Europeans during the last two generations, they may have to impose a similar obligation.

Two other things which have greatly contributed to the excellence of government in Switzerland may be commended to the attention of British and French, and indeed also of Spanish-American statesmen.

Great Britain has long admitted, but has also long neglected to fulfil, the duty of trying to divide large estates so as to create a race of small landowners cultivating the soil they dwell upon. It is this class which furnishes the most stable element in the population, now swollen by a mass of new immigrants, of the United States and Canada. It is a class hardly to be found in Argentina and Mexico, and not sufficiently numerous in Germany, Spain, and Italy.

France, and Britain also, have done too little to extend

and develop a system of local self-government, especially in rural areas. Jefferson saw that in the presence of such a system lay the political strength of New England, in its absence the weakness of Virginia.[1] It is the foundation of all that is best in the political life of the Swiss democracy.

It may be asked: " If the success Switzerland has attained in creating a government which has escaped the evils from which other democracies have suffered be due to a singular concatenation of favouring conditions not existing elsewhere and unlikely to be reproduced elsewhere, of what value is her experience for other countries ? "

Its value is to have shown that merits may be attained by a government genuinely popular which those who have followed the history of other governments meant to be popular might have dismissed as unattainable. Citizens may be more animated by a widely-diffused sense of public duty, legislators and officials may more generally resist temptations offered by self-interest, party feeling may be kept within safer limits than has been heretofore found possible elsewhere. A government by the whole people which shall honestly aim at the welfare of the whole people, win their confidence and create in them a sense of contentment with their institutions, is not a mere dream of optimists, not an unrealizable ideal. To have established and worked such a government, even if not perfectly, is to have rendered a real service to mankind, for it cheers them with hopes, putting substance into what those who have followed the hard facts of political history have been wont to dismiss as illusions.

The scanty attention which Swiss institutions have received, and the inadequate recognition of their value to students of political philosophy, seem largely due to the unexciting and what may be called the prosaic humdrum character of Swiss political life. There are no sensational events to draw the eyes of the outer world; no Cabinet crises, as in England; no brilliant displays of oratory, as in the French Chamber; no dramatic surprises, as in the

[1] Jefferson, however, must have seen, though he thought it safer not to add, that it was not merely the Town meetings but also the quality of the men who composed those meetings, educated land-owning farmers, members of Congregational churches, that vivified the local politics of Massachusetts and Connecticut.

huge national nominating conventions of the United States. Most readers of history find their chief enjoyment in startling events and striking personal careers, however quiet their own lives and however pacific their tempers. They are thrilled by feats of strategic genius like those of Hannibal or Belisarius or Marlborough, and by political conflicts where defeat is suddenly turned into victory by brilliant oratory or resourceful statesmanship. In reading of these things few stop to think of the sufferings war brings, the bitterness and waste of effort that accompany internal strife; and many dismiss as dull the pages that record the steady progress of a nation in civil administration along well-drawn lines of economic progress. So the achievements of modern Switzerland, just because they do not appeal to imagination or emotion, have been little regarded, though directed with unusual success to what ought to be the main aims of government, the comfort and well-being of the individual, the satisfaction of his desire for intellectual pleasures, the maintenance of peace and kindly relations between social classes. The virtues of Swiss government, clad in plain grey homespun, have not caught the world's eye. But the homespun keeps out cold and has worn well.

The future of Switzerland opens up a dim and distant vista of possibilities. Her fate lies not entirely in her own hands, for she cannot but be affected by the great nations that dwell around her. The next decade may be for her people, as for the rest of Europe, a stormy time, testing institutions and character as they have not been tested during the last two generations.

There were moments in the later Middle Ages when it seemed probable that the " Old League of Upper Germany " as it was called in the fifteenth century,[1] would extend itself so widely to the north by the addition of new cities as to grow into a power stretching from the Vosges to the Upper Danube, and perhaps including the western communes of Tirol. How different would European history have been had a league of republics covered the south-western Germanic lands, and had a like power arisen out of a strengthening and expansion of the league of Hanseatic cities in the north! *Dis aliter visum.* Things might have

[1] *Vetus Liga Alemanniae Superioris.*

been better than they have turned out, or they might have
been even worse, though it is hard to imagine anything worse
than the Thirty Years' War or than that war whose miseries
Europe has just been bearing.   Things do not always turn
out for the best, as some historical philosophers have vainly
preached: there have been many calamities redeemed by
no compensations.   But of Switzerland as she is now can
we say less or hope less than this, that a people which has
so learnt to love freedom in its truest sense, that has formed
such lofty traditions of patriotism and has cultivated through
them a pervading sense of civic duty,— that such a people
is as well armed against future dangers as any small people
can be?   To this people may fitly be applied, with the
change of one word only, the lines which Wordsworth, in
whose mind England and Switzerland were constantly associated as the two ancient homes of liberty, wrote of his own
country in her hour of gravest peril: —

> It is not to be thought of that the flood
> Of Switzer freedom, which to the open sea
> Of the world's praise, from dark antiquity
> Hath flowed, with pomp of waters unwithstood, . . .
> That this most famous stream in bogs and sands
> Should perish, and to evil and to good
> Be lost for ever: In our halls is hung
> Armoury of the invincible knights of old.

CANADA [1]

CHAPTER XXXIII

THE COUNTRY AND THE FRAME OF GOVERNMENT

THE study of popular government in Canada derives a peculiar interest from the fact that while the economic and social conditions of the country are generally similar to those of the United States, the political institutions have been framed upon English models, and the political habits, traditions, and usages have retained an English character. Thus it is that in Canada, better perhaps than in any other country, the working of the English system can be judged in its application to the facts of a new and swiftly growing country, thoroughly democratic in its ideas and its institutions. Let us begin by looking at those facts, for they determine the economic and social environment into which English institutions have been set down.

The Dominion of Canada is a country more than three thousand miles long from east to west, with a region, which at the meridian of 114° W. is about seven hundred miles broad from north to south. This region is interrupted to the north of Lakes Huron and Superior by a rocky and barren, and therefore almost uninhabited tract, which separates the fertile and populous districts of Ontario from those of the Prairie Provinces, Manitoba, Saskatchewan, and Alberta, lying farther west. Unless valuable minerals are discovered in many parts of this tract, as there have been in some, it may remain thinly peopled. The natural

[1] In order to prevent the first volume of this book from being much larger than the second it has been thought desirable to relegate the chapters on the United States to Volume II. and place in Volume I. the shorter chapters on Canada. The reader is, however, recommended to peruse first the account of democracy in the United States, as much of what is said regarding Canada will be better understood if the description of the United States, the economic and social conditions of which resemble those of Canada, while the political institutions are different, has been previously read.

resources of the Dominion, besides its still only partially explored mineral wealth, consist in vast areas of rich soil, in enormous forests, both in the eastern Provinces and in British Columbia and in the fisheries of the Maritime Provinces of Nova Scotia and New Brunswick, which give employment to a large and hardy population. There is coal in Nova Scotia and many parts of the West, with large deposits on the Pacific coast also; and the total quantity, estimated as second in the world only to that in the United States and Alaska, is more than sufficient to cause the development of manufactures on a large scale. Severe as are the winters on the Atlantic side of the Continent, the climate is everywhere healthy, favourable to physical and mental vigour, the death-rate low and the birth-rate high.

These conditions indicate the lines which economic development will follow. Agriculture is now and may long continue to be the chief source of livelihood, and forestry may provide employment for centuries if fires are checked and replanting is carried out on a large scale. Mining is now confined to comparatively few districts, but it, and the manufacturing industries also, aided by the utilization of the enormous volume of water power, cannot but increase. At present the bulk of the population are tillers of the soil, dwelling in rural areas or towns of moderate size; huge cities like those of Britain and the United States being comparatively few. Two only (Montreal and Toronto) out of a total population of about 8,000,000,[1] have more than 300,-000 inhabitants, and there are but five others whose population exceeds 50,000. Plenty of good land is still to be had at a moderate price, and the agricultural class lives in comfort as does also the less numerous class who produce goods for the home market. There is hardly any pauperism and need be none at all. No such opposition is raised to immigration as has been raised in Australia, so the population is likely to go on increasing for generations to come, especially in the western half of the country. The fact most important to note is that the land is almost entirely in the hands of small cultivating owners, an industrious and independent class. As great landed estates are unknown, so, too, great financial or commercial fortunes are comparatively

[1] In 1911 the population was 7,206,000.

few, those who have suddenly risen to wealth having mostly acquired it by an increase in the value of land, or of railroad properties, and by speculative land investments.

With the growth, however, of commerce and the development of the country generally the opportunities for accumulating wealth by business are now fast increasing as they did in the United States half a century ago. Meantime, one may note the absence in Canada of two factors powerful in the great countries of Western Europe and equally so in the United States. There are not many great capitalists, or great incorporated companies taking a hand in politics for their own interests and exciting suspicion by their secret influence. Neither has the element of working men, congregated in large centres of industry and organized in labour unions, yet found leaders of conspicuous capacity, nor acquired a voting power which, whether by votes or by strikes, can tell upon the action of governments and party organizations, constituting a force outside the regular political parties and, like the capitalists of France and America, using them for the furtherance of its own economic aims.

One feature which is conspicuous by its absence, alike in Great Britain, in the United States, and in Australia and New Zealand, is here of the first importance. It is the influence of Race and of Religion.

When Canada was ceded to Great Britain by France in 1763, the French-speaking inhabitants numbered 60,000. They have now grown to nearly two and a half millions, or about one-third of the whole population, and this by natural increase, the stock being very prolific, for there has been practically no immigration from France. The great majority of these French speakers dwell in the Province of Quebec, which was the region first settled, but a large number are also to be found in Eastern and Northern Ontario, in the Maritime Provinces and scattered out over the West. Of those in Quebec extremely few speak English. There they constitute a community retaining with its language its French manners and ideas, quite distinct from those of the British districts. This separation is mainly due to religion, for they are all Roman Catholics, deeply attached to their faith, and if no longer obedient yet still deferential, in secular as well as ecclesiastical matters, to

their bishops and priests.   Nowhere in the world did the
Roman priesthood during last century exert so great a power
in politics.

During the last twenty years the tide of immigrants to
Canada has flowed freely, chiefly from Scotland and from
the countries of Central and South-Eastern Europe.   There
have also come into the Western Provinces from the ad-
joining parts of the United States a great crowd of farmers
attracted by the cheapness of good land.   Nearly all of
these have been naturalized as Canadian citizens and are
rapidly blent with their Canadian neighbours.   Thus one
may say, omitting the most recent immigrants, that the
Canadian nation consists of two parts, nearly one-third
French speaking and Roman Catholic, two-thirds English
speaking and Protestant.[1]

The Constitution of Canada was prepared by a group of
colonial statesmen in 1864 and enacted in 1867, by a statute
of the British Parliament.   The scheme of government is
Federal, a form prescribed not merely by the diversities to
be found in a vast territory stretching westward from Nova
Scotia to the Pacific, but also by the aforesaid dual character of the population, one-third of which inhabits Quebec,
speaking French and following the Roman law established
there by France when her first settlers arrived, while in the
other provinces the common law of England prevails.   The
Federal system roughly resembles that of the United States,
framed seventy-eight years earlier, and that of Australia,
framed thirty-three years later, as respects the distribution
of powers between the Central or National and the Provincial Governments, each in the main independent of the other,
while the former has nevertheless, within its allotted sphere,
a direct authority over all citizens, with adequate means
for enforcing that authority.

As this federal form of government has little to do with
the subject that here concerns us, the actual working of
democratic institutions, it may suffice to call attention to

[1] Though very nearly all the French speakers are Catholics, by no
means all the Catholics are French speakers, for many of the German, Irish, Italian, and Polish immigrants are Catholics, so it might
be more exact to say that three-tenths are French speaking, and rather
more than one-third Catholics.   Conversions from either faith to the
other are uncommon, but the children of Catholics from the European
Continents often lapse from their faith, the Irish rarely.

three important points in which the National Government
has powers wider in Canada than in Australia or the United
States.

1. The legislative authority of the Dominion Government covers a larger field, and includes a power of disallowing acts of the Provincial Legislature.   This particular
power is, however, seldom used, and practically only where
such a Legislature is deemed to have exceeded the functions
assigned to it by the Constitution or to have violated any
fundamental principle of law and justice.

2. Judicial authority (except as respects minor local
courts) belongs solely to the Dominion Government.

3. All powers and functions of government not expressly
assigned either to the Dominion or to the Provinces respectively are deemed to belong to the Dominion, *i.e.* where
doubt arises the presumption is in its favour, whereas in
the United States and in Australia the presumption is in
favour of the States.

4. Amendments to the Constitution can be made not by
the people, but only by a Statute of the Imperial Parliament of the United Kingdom.   This follows from the fact
that the Constitution itself is a Statute of that Parliament.
But the provision is in reality no restriction of the powers
of the Dominion, for it is well understood that in such a
matter the British Parliament would take no action except
when satisfied that the Canadian people as a whole wished
it to do so, and were approving any request made by the
Dominion Parliament to that effect, just as the Act of 1867
was passed to give effect to what had been shown to be the
wishes of the Dominion itself.   This theoretic or technical
sovereignty of the British Parliament provides a more convenient method of altering the Constitution than the complicated machinery created for that purpose in the United
States and in Australia,[1] and is even more certain to
give to a dissident minority whatever consideration it
deserves.

The frame of the Dominion or National Government has
been constructed on the lines of the Cabinet or Parliamen-

[1] That machinery will be described in the chapters on Australia and
the United States respectively.   Other points in which the constitutional arrangements of Canada differ from those of the United States
will be noticed in Chapter XXXV.

tary system of Britain and all her self-governing colonies. Executive power is vested nominally in the Governor-General as representative of the British Crown; but is in fact exercised by a Cabinet or group of ministers, who hold office only so long as they can retain the support of a majority in the Dominion House of Commons. They are virtually a Committee of Parliament, and in it all of them sit. Thus the actual Executive is the creature of the House of Commons, possessing as against it only one power, that of appealing to the people by a dissolution of Parliament. If ministers do not dissolve they must resign, and if they dissolve and the election goes against them, they resign forthwith and a new Cabinet is formed. The relations of the Executive and Legislative Departments are thus far more intimate than in the United States, for the Ministry sit in the Legislature and are, just as in France and England, the leaders of its majority for the time being.

The Dominion Legislature consists of two Houses. The House of Commons numbers 235 members, elected on universal suffrage, woman suffrage having been in all the Provinces also, except three, recently adopted.[1] Its legal duration, subject to a prior dissolution by the Executive, is five years. The Senate consists of 96 persons nominated for life by the Governor-General, i.e. by the Ministry for the time being, as vacancies occur by death or resignation. A number of senators proportionate to population is assigned to each Province. Except in financial matters its functions are legally equal to those of the House, but it is in fact far less important, for though it revises and amends Bills, it seldom ventures to reject or seriously modify any measure sent up by the House of Commons. The latter is the real driving force, just as the House of Commons is in England and for the same reasons. The House controls finance; and since it has the making and unmaking of the Executive Ministries, is the centre of party strife. Contests between the two Houses arise only when one party comes into power after another party has had for a long time the appointment

[1] In the beginning of 1920 it had not been enacted in Nova Scotia, Quebec, and Prince Edward Island. Women are eligible for seats in the House of Commons, and are already members of one or two Provincial legislatures.

of senators, and effective opposition disappears after a few sessions, when vacancies filled by the new Ministry have changed the party balance.

The judges of the Supreme Court of the Dominion, and of the Supreme Courts in the provinces, as also of the County Courts, are appointed for life by the Executive (*i.e.* the Dominion Cabinet), and can as in Britain and Australia be removed from office only upon an address of both Houses of Parliament. They are taken from the Bar, and the salaries paid, though lower than in England, are higher than those which generally prevail in the United States. An appeal lies from the Supreme Court of Canada to the Judicial Committee of the Privy Council in England, of which a Canadian Justice of the Supreme Court is a member. There exists no veto upon the legislation of the Dominion Parliament except that which the Governor-General at the direction of the British Crown, or that Crown itself on the advice of the British Cabinet, might in point of strict law exercise, but does not in fact now exercise, although cases may be imagined in which its existence might be thought useful for the preservation of some interest common to the whole of the British Dominions or the fulfilment of some international obligation undertaken on their behalf. Neither does the Canadian Constitution contain any restrictions upon legislative power such as those imposed on Congress by the United States Constitution. The Dominion Parliament is limited only by the assignment of exclusive jurisdiction on certain specified subjects to the legislatures of the Provinces and by the fact that it cannot directly and by its own sole action alter the Constitution as set forth in the Act of 1867. Otherwise its powers are plenary, like those of the British Parliament, whose traditions it was desired to carry over into the New World.

While the Ministers and a very few of the higher officials change with the departure from power of one party and the accession to power of another, all the other posts in the Civil Service are held for life or " good behaviour," *i.e.* a man once appointed is not dismissed except for misconduct or proved incompetence. There is therefore no Spoils system in the United States sense of the term, a Civil Service

Commission having been recently created which fills up all posts. But in such higher appointments as are still left to the Executive, party affiliations and the influence of leading politicians count for much, so that it is not necessarily the best men who are selected. Civil servants having a secure tenure are not expected to work for their party, but they are not forbidden to do so, though if they do, and their party is defeated, they will probably be dismissed as offenders against propriety.

The Governments of the Nine Provinces (which correspond to the States in the Australian Commonwealth and in the U.S.A.) are also created, or rather re-created and remodelled by the Constitution of 1867, for most of them had existed before it was enacted.[1] They reproduce the system of Cabinet and Parliamentary Government provided for the Dominion, save in the fact that it is only the legislatures of Quebec and Nova Scotia that have two Chambers. The head of the Executive is the Lieutenant-Governor, who is appointed for a five years' term by the Governor-General, *i.e.* by the Dominion Cabinet for the time being, and is usually a member of the party to which the Cabinet belongs, and a leading politician of the Province. He does not, however, take any share in party politics,[2] but fills the place of a sort of local constitutional king, being advised by a ministry of six or seven members which has the support of the majority in the Legislature and is responsible to it. The system is, in miniature, that of the British Parliament and Cabinet. The Legislature is elected by universal suffrage for four years, subject to an earlier dissolution by the Cabinet. It has, under the Constitution Act of 1867, the power of amending its Provincial Constitution, subject to the rarely exercised power of disallowance vested in the Dominion Government. In the two Provinces which have retained Second Chambers filled by the appointment of the

[1] Manitoba, Saskatchewan, and Alberta have received their constitutions and Governments since 1867. Their territories were purchased by the Dominion Government from the Hudson Bay Company.

[2] Instances have occurred in which a Lieutenant-Governor took independent action in what was deemed to be the general public interest, the most recent being that in which (in Manitoba) a judicial enquiry was ordered into misdeeds alleged to have been committed by a Ministry. See as to this and the earlier case in Quebec the book of Mr. Justice Riddell on the Constitution of Canada, p. 108.

Executive as vacancies occur, few controversies have arisen, the Second Chamber generally complying with the wishes of the popular House.   No desire for the creation of a Second Chamber has been expressed in those provinces which do not possess one, perhaps because they take their notion of such a Chamber from the Dominion Senate, a body which, though not wanting in talent and experience, is weak because nominated: but the bicameral system has been, where it exists, of service in preventing jobs, and a Lieutenant-Governor of Ontario spoke to me of instances in which the existence of a revising body would have been useful in making it possible to reconsider and reverse an unfortunate decision taken by the Assembly.

This scheme of government seems at first sight less democratic than that of the United States, because the direct action of the people is not so frequently invoked, the people's share in the government being limited to the election of representatives to the legislature, Federal and Provincial. But the power of the people is in fact by and through that one function so complete that nothing more is wanted, and it is in one point ampler than in the United States, because the legislatures are restrained by no such limitations as both the Federal and the State Constitutions contain.   In choosing and instructing their representatives the citizens have all the means they need for giving effect to their will, for the representatives choose the Executive, and if the Executive and the Legislature differ, their differences can be promptly settled in appealing to the people by a dissolution of Parliament.   The Frame of Government which I have described in outline is accordingly highly democratic, and the experience of England in last century commended it as having proved both democratic and efficient.   It fixes responsibility upon representatives each of whom can be called to account by his constituents, and upon a small number of administrators each of whom can be watched, questioned, censured, and if need be expelled from office by the Legislature.   Given favourable economic and social conditions in the country where it is to be worked, it ought to give excellent results.

If any source of danger to peace and good government was discernible, it lay in the existence of two races which, though not hostile, were mutually jealous and showed no tendency to blend.

The Government of Canada has been worked, as in every other free country, by Party. That was contemplated when the Constitution was enacted, for parties had been in full swing for generations before 1867, and insurrections had occurred so late as 1837. In Canada as in England the parties run both the legislative and the administrative machinery, and are responsible to the people for the use they make of it. But before proceeding to examine how that machinery is actually worked it is well to look a little more closely at the conditions which Nature and History have here provided. They are eminently favourable, not only to the growth of population and of national wealth, but also to the orderly development of free self-governing institutions.

CHAPTER XXXIV

THIS land in which settlers from the two great races of Western Europe have been called to be fruitful and multiply and replenish the earth is a land where there is room for everybody for generations to come, and in which the ground is cumbered by few injustices to be redressed, no sense of ancient wrongs to rouse resentment, no slough of despondent misery out of which the worker finds it hard to emerge.

About three-fourths of the Canadian householders are farmers, nearly all of them owning their own farms, living in comfort, and all the more so because sobriety has become more general than it was thirty years ago. Not only are they well off, but nearly everybody is well off, the native part of the wage-earning population also being well remunerated and on good terms with the employers. It is only lately, and in places where there is a mass of recent immigrants, that labour troubles have created serious strife, and such grievances as the traveller hears of in the rural districts relate to the maintenance of a tariff on imports which raises the price of manufactured goods for the benefit of home producers and to the undue power which great railroads can exert in the districts they traverse, and, in some districts, to the action of great companies in controlling facilities for the transporting and disposal of crops. In Ontario and the Maritime Provinces as well as in the Western Provinces the schools are so abundant and excellent that there is practically no illiteracy except among the new arrivals from Europe. Every native English-speaking Canadian is educated, reads at least one newspaper, and as a rule takes an intelligent interest in public affairs, national and local. This is no less true of that large body of immigrants in the Prairie Provinces [1] which has come in from the United

[1] Manitoba, Saskatchewan, and Alberta.

States during the last thirty years, but not true of the recent immigrants from Eastern Europe. The people are assiduous churchgoers, and are, especially in the Scottish districts, much occupied with church affairs, but the pastors, although respected, do not generally exert political influence on their flocks. No rural population except that of Switzerland, is better qualified for the duties of citizenship and more ready to discharge them, though it ought perhaps to be added that there have been those who allow their willingness to be stimulated by the receipt of pecuniary inducements at elections, glossing over this lapse from civic virtue by the argument that they ought to be compensated for the time lost in going to the polling-place. This habit, not infrequent in Ontario, is quite as prevalent in the State of Ohio, on the other side of Lake Erie.

The class of workers in manufactures or mines is, as already observed, comparatively small, for there are few great industrial centres, and only four cities (Montreal, Toronto, Winnipeg, and Vancouver) with populations exceeding 120,000. So much of that class as speaks English or French is educated and takes an interest in politics, but it has not yet grown large enough to form in any one area, except, in Ontario and British Columbia, a working men's party in a Provincial Legislature. It is, moreover, less permeated by Communist or Syndicalist doctrines than is the same class in France and Australia. Here, as in the United States, the great strength of the two old parties which embrace men of all classes, has retarded the creation of a third party resting on a class basis. Except in the Maritime Provinces, the most recent immigrants perform a great part of the unskilled work of the country, and they furnish a soil more favourable to the propagation of the doctrines of any group of European extremists than does the native population. Till the Winnipeg strike of 1919, there had been few signs of antagonism between the wage-earners and the employers.

In the French-speaking districts of Quebec and of Eastern Ontario the conditions are altogether different. The inhabitants of these districts do not call themselves " French " but either simply " Canadians " or " French speakers," for they have little in common with modern France except their language and some traits of character. So far as they belong to France, it is to a France of the eighteenth, not of the twentieth century. Since the Revolution of 1789, and still more since the establishment of the present Republic in France, they have been but slightly affected by French political institutions or ideas; for though educated men read French books, the anti-clerical attitude of the Republicans who have governed France during the last forty years has been repellent. All through last century English thought and English ways told very little upon them; and that remarkable assimilative power which French culture possesses was shown in the fact that those Scotsmen or Englishmen who settled among them were almost always Gallicized in speech and religion. It is remarked to-day that few French speakers are to be found among the undergraduates of the leading non-Catholic Universities. Were the two elements to blend, they might possibly produce a new type of character, combining what is best in each, but of blending there is at present no sign. The difference of religion forbids it.

The birth-rate is so much higher among the French speakers than in the English districts that some of the former have hoped that Canada would end by being a French country, but the immigrants, if they come from the United States, speak English already, and if they come from Continental Europe learn English and not French. The probabilities therefore are that English will ultimately prevail and be the general tongue of the Dominion.

As compared with the British population of Ontario and the West, the standard of material well-being among these Quebec *habitants* is lower, because the land is poorer, the farms mostly smaller, the families larger, the people less energetic though equally industrious, and less well educated. But the greatest difference is seen in the power of the Roman Catholic clergy. The Church has large estates, with numerous and wealthy monastic establishments, and the people are nearly all fervent Catholics. The bishops used to rule through the priests, who were wont to direct their parishioners how to vote, and were generally obeyed, not only by the cultivators of the soil but by the wage-earners of the towns, till about thirty years ago. Even now they retain a real though much diminished power. Owing to the

rapid increase of the French-speaking population, which
would be still more rapid but for the high rate of infant
mortality, there has been a considerable migration from Quebec into Eastern Ontario as well as the Western Provinces.
Wherever the emigrant goes, the priest follows and retains
a certain influence, but it counts for more in the homogeneous
French-speaking masses of Quebec, the Provincial Government of which, though legally quite as democratic as that
of Manitoba or Alberta, is by no means the same in its
working.

Taking the native population of Canada to be as intelligent, educated, interested in self-government and qualified
for self-government as a traveller finds in any part of the
English-speaking world, we have next to enquire what are
the subjects which chiefly interest it, what are the issues by
which it, like all free peoples, is divided into political parties, and in what wise those parties conduct the affairs of
the nation.   As I am not writing a general account of Canada but concerned only with those phenomena which illustrate the working of democratic government, it is enough to
note in passing, without attempting to discuss, some topics
which, important as they are, do not belong to the sphere
of party controversy, such are the means of developing the
natural resources of the country, and its relation to Great
Britain and to the other Self-Governing Dominions.   External affairs, however, need a few words, for the fiscal relations of the Dominion to the United States have at times
become involved with differences of opinion between Pro-
tectionists and the advocates of Free Trade or of a low tariff,
and did in that way affect internal politics, the Protection-
ists declaring that the policy of their opponents would make
Canada dependent on her powerful neighbour to the south.
This ground of contention has tended to disappear as other
disputes with that neighbour have subsided.   In recent years
a series of treaties and commissions determining all boundary questions and providing methods of arbitration for the
adjustment of whatever controversies may arise over water
rights and transportation on railways along the borders of
Canada and the United States, have virtually removed causes
of quarrel, and hold out a promise of permanently good relations between the two great neighbour peoples.   The ar-

rangement made in 1817 by which no ships of war, other than two or three small vessels armed for police work, were to be placed on the Great Lakes, has been loyally observed, to the immeasureable benefit of both nations, for it has not only made forts and fleets superfluous, but has created an atmosphere of mutual confidence.

There were at one time persons in the United States who talked of the incorporation of Canada in their republic as a thing to be desired and worked for, and there were a few, though always only a few, Canadians who, looking upon this as a natural consequence of geographical conditions, held it to be inevitable. But during the present century such ideas have died out in Canada, and it is only a few belated and unthinking persons in the United States that still give expression to them. Those apprehensions of designs on the part of the United States for which there might have been grounds forty years ago, are now idle. The people of the United States have laid aside not only any thought of aggression but even that slightly patronizing air which formerly displeased the smaller nation. Sensible men in both countries recognize the many reasons which make it better for each nation that it should continue to develop itself in its own fashion, upon its own historic lines, in cordial friendship with the other. The United States feels itself large enough already: Canada does not wish to forgo that nationhood into which she has entered by the recognition accorded to her claims in the Peace Treaties of 1919.

In a country inhabited by two races of a different language and religion, it might be expected that these differences would form the basis of political parties. This might have happened in Canada, but for two causes. One is the Federal system of government which has permitted the French-speaking and Roman Catholic population to have their own way in that Province where they form the vast majority, and which similarly permits the inhabitants of English speech and Protestant faith who predominate in the other Provinces to legislate there according to their own views. The other cause may be found in the party system itself, which has associative as well as a disruptive power. On many questions which have nothing to do with race or religion English speakers are in agreement with French speakers, Protestants in agreement with Catholics, so that each political party is composed of both elements, neither of which could afford to offend and alienate the other. Sir Wilfrid Laurier, the distinguished leader whom the Liberal party lately lost, was a Catholic from Quebec, though too independent to be acceptable to the Catholic hierarchy. Yet he had the support not only of many Catholics in that Province but of Presbyterians and Methodists in Ontario and the west, while the chiefs of the Conservatives have frequently been helped by Catholic votes. When controversies, sometimes acute, have arisen over religious teaching in State Schools in Provinces where there is a considerable Catholic minority,[1] there has been a disposition to settle them by compromises, for the leading statesmen on both sides, feeling the danger of raising a racial issue between the French-speaking and the British elements in the population, do their best to smooth matters down, neither side wishing to commit their party as a whole because each would by such a course alienate some of its supporters. A like tendency to division between the two elements of the population has occasionally been revealed when questions arose involving the relations of Canada to Great Britain. This happened also with the use of the French language in schools placed in districts with a considerable French-speaking element. Though opinion comes near to unanimity in desiring to maintain a political connection obviously beneficial to both elements, the French-speaking population is less zealously ready to bear its share in responsibilities common to the British dominions as a whole, so at the outbreak of the Great War of 1914–18 the opposition to a proposed general levy of men to serve in that war found a wider support in that population than among the English-speaking citizens. The controversy, however, though it affected politics for the time being, passed away, and similar circumstances are not likely to recur.

Another subject which has been constantly before men's minds during the last twenty years has never, as it has in England, been taken up by either of the established political parties, because each has feared to lose at least as much as

[1] Especially in Ontario and Manitoba. In Quebec the Roman hierarchy get their own way.

it could gain by committing itself to a policy. It is that of the regulation or prohibition of the sale of intoxicants. Party leaders have been shy of touching this live wire, because it cuts across the lines of party division in the Provinces, so the agitation for prohibitory legislation, now enacted everywhere except in Quebec, was, as in the United States, left to independent organizations.[1] The question that has since 1867 been the most permanently controversial is that of a Protective tariff, a question argued less on general principles than with a view to the direct pecuniary interests of manufacturers on the one hand and agricultural consumers on the other. The struggle is not between the advocates of Protection and those of tariff for revenue only, but turns on the merits of a lower or higher scale of import duties.

Since 1867 — and for our present purpose we need go no further back — the questions which have had the most constant interest for the bulk of the nation are, as is natural in a prosperous and rapidly growing community, those which belong to the sphere of commercial and industrial progress, the development of the material resources of the country by rendering aid to agriculture, by the regulation of mining, by constructing public works and opening up lines of railway and canal communication — matters scarcely falling within the lines by which party opinion is divided, for the policy of *laissez faire* has few adherents in a country which finds in governmental action or financial support to private enterprises the quickest means of carrying out every promising project. So when party conflicts arise over these matters, it is not the principle that is contested — no Minister would expose himself to the reproach of backwardness — but the plan advocated by the Government or the Opposition as the case may be. The task of each party is to persuade the people that in this instance its plan promises quicker and larger results, and that it is fitter to be trusted with the work. Thus it happens that general political principles, such as usually figure in party platforms, count for little in politics, though ancient habit requires

[1] The sale of alcoholic liquors (except for medical and scientific purposes) and for export has been practically forbidden, in slightly different forms, in all the Provinces save Quebec.

them to be invoked. Each party tries to adapt itself from time to time to whatever practical issue may arise. Opportunism is inevitable, and the charge of inconsistency, though incessantly bandied to and fro, is lightly regarded. The tendency to an adaptive flexibility is increased by the duty —indeed the necessity — of tactfully handling the racial and religious feelings of the voters. Thus politics is apt to become a series of compromises, and the bitterness with which elections seem to be fought is softened by the fact that there is no sentiment of class hostility involved. The rich and the less rich — for one can hardly talk of the poor — the farmers, merchants, manufacturers, shopkeepers, professional men, have been found in both parties, and if the country be taken as a whole, in tolerably equal proportions. No Labour party has arisen except among the industrial workers of Montreal, Toronto, Winnipeg, and Vancouver, and among the organized unions of the miners on the Pacific coast. But though the feelings of antagonism which most powerfully affect men's minds are sedulously kept in the background, though most of the topics which during the last few decades formed the staple of controversy have been of transient import, not involving large general principles, the fact remains that parties have carried on a ceaseless strife with a surprising keenness of feeling. The historical causes of this lie far back in the past, behind 1867, and only one of them need be referred to — a religious aversion which, though not always avowed, intensifies party spirit among the more extreme Protestants as well as the more ardent Catholics. There is still in Ontario an Orange party, well organized in its Lodges, which rejoices to celebrate with triumphant processions and speeches, on the shores of the Great Lakes, the anniversary of a victory gained more than two centuries ago by one of the two parties that were then struggling for mastery in an island, distracted then as now, that lies three thousand miles away beyond the Ocean.

In Canada the motive of personal advantage which stimulates the activity of many party workers in the United States is hardly felt, for the places to be won are too few to enter into the mind of the average private citizen.

Neither is an attachment to doctrines essential, for here, as among the English-speaking peoples generally, the impulse to combat and to associations for the purposes of combat in politics is so strong that it can dispense with doctrines. Party seems to exist for its own sake. In Canada ideas are not needed to make parties, for these can live by heredity and, like the Guelfs and Ghibellines of mediaeval Italy, by memories of past combats. The pugnacity of a virile race is kept alive by the two unending sets of battles which are kept going, one in the House of Commons at Ottawa, the other in every Provincial Legislature. Men grow up from boyhood identifying themselves with their party and regarding its fortunes as their own. Attachment to leaders of such striking gifts and long careers, as were Sir John Macdonald and Sir Wilfrid Laurier, created a personal loyalty which exposed a man to reproach as a deserter when he voted against his party. And besides all this, there was that sort of sporting interest which belongs to a struggle between the Ins and Outs.

This vehemence of zeal I have described was, however, not usually carried into Provincial and much less into municipal elections, which latter have not generally been fought on party lines, though of course a candidate who happens to be popular with his party is likely to attract their votes. Neither does party feeling, except in a few localities, introduce bitterness into social life. As in England and the United States, it can co-exist with personal good feeling between the opposing armies. The same kind of sentiment which makes the undergraduates of Oxford and Cambridge cheer the rival oarsmen who have just vanquished their own crew in a boat race, and which requires the defeated candidate for the Presidency of the United States to telegraph his congratulations to his successful competitor, mitigates party strife. This happy tendency, quite compatible with violent talk and reckless imputations at election time, has helped to produce, and has been itself strengthened by, the excellent institution of the Canadian Clubs. About the beginning of the century a club was founded at Hamilton, Ontario, intended to foster both Dominion patriotism and local patriotism, and to promote the growth of an enlightened public opinion by bringing together men of both parties or of no party to listen to addresses on all sorts of non-partisan topics at lunch or dinner. Finding favour, the idea spread fast and far, till within a few years similar clubs had sprung up in nearly all the cities of the Dominion. They have been of great service in accustoming men of opposite parties to know one another personally and work together for common civic or national aims, and are now, especially in the English-speaking cities, a valuable factor in Canadian life, giving to eminent visitors from Europe and the United States opportunities· of bringing their views and counsels before Canadians of all classes, while in some places also filling a function similar to that of those non-partisan associations of business men in the cities of the United States which have there work for the betterment of social conditions and municipal reform.

Part of what has been said applies rather to the recent past than to the present, for the years since 1914 have seen many changes. The first of these was a schism in the Liberal party, arising over the question of compulsory war service, which led to a coalition of a section of that party with the Conservatives then in power. This combination may be transitory, and is less significant than the still more recent emergence of a small Labour party in some industrial areas, such as Montreal, Toronto, Winnipeg and the mining districts of British Columbia, and of a Farmers' party, which in the Province of Ontario [1] suddenly found itself after an election the largest of the various groups in the Provincial legislature, and formed a Ministry there. The example of the independent action which the landowning farmers had been taking, outside the old parties, in the North-Western States of America, did something to rouse Canadian farmers to a like assertion of their own special interests, inadequately represented in the legislature. But something may also be attributed to a general loosening of party ties and loss of confidence in the successive party Ministries, and indeed in the politicians generally who had been at the head of affairs in the Dominion and in the Provinces during the last fifteen or twenty years. Of this more hereafter.

Party organization is looser than in the United States and scarcely so tight as it has grown to be in England: nor is the

[1] The " Grain Growers of the West Association," lately formed in the Prairie Provinces, and now prospering there is another sign of agricultural discontent.

nomination of candidates that supremely important matter which it long ago became in the United States, for there is no such octopus of a party machine extending its tentacles over the country and practically controlling the action of most voters. A man gets accepted as candidate much as happens in England, often because he is of some local note, sometimes because, though not a resident, he is recommended by persons of influence in the party; and if once elected is, if assiduous and loyal, generally continued as the local party standard-bearer. Although, therefore the right of the constituency to determine its candidate is taken as a matter of course, the methods of choice are as fluid and informal as they have usually been in Britain. There is an increasing tendency to prefer local men as candidates. Provincial elections excite less interest, except when it is desired to punish a discredited Ministry, than do those to the Dominion House of Commons, and though both, speaking generally, are fought on the same national party lines, there are those who think it well to vote for candidates of one party in a Provincial and those of another in a Dominion election in order that the former may feel itself more closely watched. Neither in the Provinces nor in the Dominion does a party victory carry with it a distribution of " good things " among the minor politicians. To win an election is of course a gain to the leading politicians on the look out for office and to those few underlings who expect sometime or other to receive favours at their hands, but these places are trifling in number compared to those that have to be fought for as spoils of victory in the United States. In Canada, therefore, one hears little of Rings, and the Boss, though he exists both in and out of the legislatures, is nothing more than the figure, familiar in many countries, of the politician who brings to the business of intrigue more of the serpent's wisdom than of the dove's innocence.

When the citizen comes to the polls as a voter, by what motives is his vote determined?

In English-speaking districts, primarily by his party allegiance, and to some extent by his ecclesiastical sympathies, which in some districts are markedly anti-Roman. In French-speaking districts, primarily by the influence of the priesthood; yet that influence does not always prevail, for it may be overridden by attachment to a French-speaking national, or even local, leader who maintains an independent attitude. Secondarily by his own material interests, whether they take the form of desiring the imposition or the reduction of protective import duties, or that of seeking grants of public money for some local purpose, or of urging the construction of a railroad calculated to benefit his neighbourhood. This class of considerations has been often strong enough to override not only religious but even party loyalty, and is likely to grow stronger as party loyalty declines. Seldom, however, does it affect all the voters in any given locality. Thus the result of an election used to be somewhat more predictable in Canada than in the United States or in England, because party loyalty was, generally speaking, a more important factor.

CHAPTER XXXV

WORKING OF THE GOVERNMENT

FROM this study of the average citizen and the sentiments that move him when he comes to deliver his will on public affairs, we may pass to the machinery by which that will is brought to bear on the government of the country. His first duty is to elect representatives, so to elections a few sentences may be devoted.

These are fewer than in the United States because no administrative officers are chosen at the polls, all, both in the Dominion and in the Provinces, being appointed by the Executive Ministry. Elections are believed to be honestly conducted so far as the presiding officials are concerned, but personation and repeating occasionally occur, perhaps even ballot stuffing, for in Ontario a Government was not long ago supposed to have fallen because its electoral misdeeds had shocked the conscience of the best citizens. Neither are there any such riots as used to be frequent in England in former days. Each party allows the meetings of the other to be held peaceably, satisfied with having discharged its own heavy artillery of vituperation. Treating is no longer common, the consumption of intoxicants having been restrained by law, and will probably decline with the increased size of constituencies. Bribery, however, is not rare. The laws enacted on lines found effective in England failed to restrain these malpractices, usually managed by underlings, and apparently by both parties alike. Happening to hear a politician complain bitterly of the heavy expenditure by the opposite party which had caused the defeat of his own, I enquired why petitions had not been more largely presented by the losing side, and was answered that things might have come out which were better left in darkness. Each side had bribed because it believed the other to be bribing, and the wealthier party got the best of it; for money counts here as in most countries, and campaign funds are thought indispensable.[1]

From the electors we pass to the legislators. Those who sit in the Dominion House come chiefly from the professional and commercial classes, many of whom have a private income making them independent of their salaries, with a fair sprinkling of agriculturists, rarely from the wage-earning class. The percentage of lawyers is decidedly smaller than in Congress, and rather lower than in the British House of Commons. In the Provincial Chambers there is a larger proportion of lawyers of the second or third rank, the rest mostly farmers, and the average level of ability and education is somewhat lower than at Ottawa. No law or custom requires a member to reside in the place he represents, a fortunate adherence to British custom, for it opens to talent a wider door; but though some men of mark from the cities sit for constituencies with which they have no tie of family or residence, the majority, especially in the Provincial Legislatures, reside in their constituencies. The tendency to retain the same member from one election to another helps to increase the number of those persons who possess some experience. There are very few rich men, not because such persons would be distrusted by the electors, but because they prefer to attend to their business enterprises, finding it almost as easy to exert political influence on legislation from without as within. Membership in the Dominion Parliament has some little social value, but no more than that which attaches to any conspicuous success in commerce. In a country which opens up great possibilities to the man of business capacity, politics as a career does not greatly attract a man too scrupulous to use his political position for gainful purposes, unless of course his oratorical talents are such as to bring him at once to the front and to keep him there. It is not surprising, therefore, that the average of ability in the Federal Parliament should be, as most Canadians declare, rather lower to-day than it was thirty or forty years ago, in the days of Macdonald, Mackenzie, and Edward Blake. Nevertheless the presence of

[1] It was alleged at a general election not many years ago that large contributions to party funds had been made by some great manufacturing firms.

some men of eminent ability occasionally raises the debates
to a high level.   The House of Commons need not fear a
comparison either with Congress or with the Parliament of
Australia.   Proceedings are orderly: obstruction is seldom
resorted to; only in exciting times has there been any marked
personal acrimony.   That kindly *bonhomie* which is characteristic of Canadians generally maintains itself even in the
political arena.

The payment of members is inevitable in a country where
there is practically no leisured class, and where most members coming from long distances to live in a city of only
90,000 people, which is not a centre of commerce, must sacrifice their business to their political duties.   It has not
produced a class of professional politicians.   The salary is
$2500 (£500) for a session exceeding thirty days, subject
to a deduction of $15 a day for each day on which attend-
ance is not given, a sum not large enough to draw a man into
a parliamentary career, though it may sharpen his eagerness to retain his seat.   A feature in which Canada stands
almost alone is the recognition of the leadership of the Opposition as a sort of public office, service in which is thought
fit to be remunerated by a salary of $7000 (£1400) a year,
the Speakers of the Senate and the House having each $4000,
in addition to their allowance as Members of Parliament.

The rules, based on English precedents, which regulate
procedure on private bills have limited the field for " lobbying," rendering it less general and pernicious than in the
United States.   There is nevertheless a good deal of jobbery and log-rolling in the Canadian Legislatures.   It occurs
frequently in connection with the granting of public money
to localities, such grants being the means whereby a member
commends himself to his constituents, while at the same time
committing himself to a support of the Ministry which has
conferred the favour on him and on them.   Though trans-
actions of this kind have lowered the standard of honour
and the sense of public duty, they have not led to the grosser
forms of political corruption, for these are as rare as in the
United States Congress, while the Provincial Legislatures
are probably purer than those of most American States,
though the average virtue of members varies so much that
it is hard to make any general statement.   None sinks so

low as do the Assemblies of New York or Pennsylvania, but the atmosphere of two or three is unwholesome; and nowhere can absolute soundness be found. So far as one can ascertain, the level of honour in them and in the Parliament at Ottawa is below that exacted by public opinion from members of the Australian and New Zealand Legislatures. Probably the temptations are greater, especially in the Provincial Legislatures, largely occupied with local matters involving pecuniary interests, and the proceedings in which receive comparatively little attention from the general public.

From legislators in general we may proceed to those who have risen out of the crowd to be party leaders and Ministers. In Canada, as in England, political life is practically a parliamentary career which culminates in the Cabinet. There is little distinction or influence to be won in any other political field, though of course the heads of great banks or railroads, sometimes also those of great universities, may exercise quite as potent an influence. A man must begin by entering a legislative body and work his way up by proving his quality there. Whoever shows unusual ability is, as in England, marked out for office and for place, so long as he can hold his seat, whereas in the United States a man may be summoned from the Bar or business to some exalted post and return to the Bar or business after four years with no prospect of further public service. It may, however, happen that an office requiring special knowledge or experience is given to some one not in Parliament, and in that case a seat will be found for him or he will receive, as soon as a vacancy occurs, a place in the Senate carrying with it the prospect of office, so he seldom falls for long out of the running. Though eloquence and the tactful handling of men are, as by all Parliamentary Governments, valued more highly than administrative capacity, there is no lack of the latter quality. Such important departments as finance, justice, agriculture, and fisheries are usually in competent hands.

Describing these things by way of comparisons, which is the best way available, one may say that in every Canadian Cabinet there are two or three men equal to the average of a Cabinet in London or Washington, although the range of choice is naturally smaller in a smaller population. In the composition of a Ministry regard must be had not only to talent but also to the necessity for representing different parts of a vast area, both because this pleases the outlying Provinces, and because the national administration, being also the supreme council of the party in power, must be duly informed as to local political feeling as well as local economic conditions.

The methods followed in legislation have been generally similar to those of the British Parliament, and here as there speaking has become plain and businesslike, with little rhetoric. At Ottawa, as at Westminster, the never-ending battle of the Ins and Outs has gone on, the Ministry proposing measures and the Opposition resisting them, the Ministry taking steps and making appointments which the Opposition condemn as blunders or jobs. When there are no large issues of policy to divide the two parties, there are always questions of grants or subsidies or other administrative matters to furnish grounds for attack and recrimination. Much time is thus lost, but the process is inevitable where office is the prize contended for, and where every mistake brought home to the Government weakens its hold on the country and raises the hopes of the Opposition. It is moreover a necessary process, for if there were no fear of criticism and resistance who can tell how many more mistakes might be made and jobs perpetrated with impunity? Canada, like Great Britain, imposes no constitutional restrictions on the power of Parliament except those few contained in the Act of 1867, so the immense power possessed by an Administration backed by a majority would be abused if the right to interrogate and attack the Executive did not provide safeguards against the abuse of power equivalent to, though different from, those which the scheme of Checks and Balances provides in the United States. Criticism is wholesome for Ministers, and gives a certain sense of security to the people, yet it is not a full security, any more than are the checks and balances. Although there exist in the Canadian Parliament and in the Provincial Legislatures rules, modelled on English precedents, regulating procedure in the case of those bills, which have a local or personal object, these rules are less effective than in England, because not supported by so strong a force of long habit and watched by so vigilant an opinion. Many occasions arise for secret bargaining over bills as well as grants, many ways in which public interests may be sacrificed to projects promising private gain.

Government is in Canada more concerned with matters affecting the development of the country than Europeans can realize. The dominance of material interests has brought into the field great corporate enterprises, such as lumber (timber) and mining and machine-making and fishery companies, and above all the railway companies. The great railway systems have been few but powerful, indeed all the more powerful because few. There has been much " trading " between them and prominent politicians, for they need legislation, and in return for it they can influence votes at elections. An organization which has no politics except its own profits is formidable, and as an eminent Canadian has said, " Capital ends by getting its way." Some philosophic observers and some men of radical views have been alarmed. But the Canadian farmer is so eager for the extension of railroad facilities, and the man of business sees so clear a gain in the rapid development of the country's resources that there had been, down to 1914, comparatively little of that angry hostility to railroad corporations which had stirred the Western United States during the last thirty or forty years. At present, however, the tide of public opinion has begun to run more strongly than formerly against " Big Business." [1]

These conditions, and especially this ardour, not altogether selfish, of every community to expand and to make the most of its resources faster than its neighbours, have made every district and town and village eager to get something for itself. When the country began, about thirty years ago, to be settled more rapidly and thickly than before, roads were wanted, and bridges, and in some places harbours or improvements in rivers, and everywhere railroads, for the proximity of a line opens up a district and makes the fortune of a town. As in each locality there was little or no capital even for bridge or road building, resort was

[1] These lines describe things as they were before 1914. The taking over by the Dominion Government during the War, and the recent financial collapse of some important lines have so altered the situation that one must not venture to speak of the future.

had, and in some instances properly enough, to the public purse. The public purse once reached, and those ministers who held it finding no surer way of getting local votes than by obliging local applicants, it became the aim of every place and every member to dip as deep as possible into the National treasury. The habit was a demoralizing one all round. It intensified the spirit of localism which is as marked a feature in Canadian politics as it is in the United States, and for the same reasons. It lowered the standard of political thinking among the statesmen; it turned the political interest of the citizens away from the larger aspects of civic duty. These are phenomena which, though their beginnings are intelligible, surprise one in communities now so active and so prosperous as to be well able to tax themselves for many purposes on which grants are lavished by the Dominion Government, grants often needless, for they are given only " to bring money into the town," and apt to be wastefully administered. But the habit persists, as it is found persisting in New Zealand also.

What has been said of the Dominion House of Commons applies generally, allowing for their much smaller scale, to the Provincial Legislatures. They are divided upon the lines of the National parties, and upon these lines elections are chiefly fought, though with less heat than is shown in Federal contests, and with more frequent changes in the balance of party strength. The wide powers allotted to them by the Constitution, the only check upon which (save as regards education) lies in the power of disallowing their statutes reserved to the Dominion Government, are sometimes not wisely used. Cases have occurred in which legislation has virtually extinguished private property without compensation, a thing forbidden to a State Legislature in the United States, and the Courts have held that such a law, however objectionable, is within their legal competence. Whether it furnishes ground for the exercise of the Dominion disallowance has been doubted: but in a recent instance the propriety of that exercise has been affirmed by the Federal Government.[1] The methods and rules of pro-

[1] See as to this interesting point, Mr. Justice Riddell's *Lectures on the Constitution of Canada*, pp. 98 and 112 and notes, and also an article by Mr. Murray Clark, K.C., in the *Canadian Bankers' Magazine* for Jan. 1919.

cedure of these Provincial legislatures reproduce generally
the practice of Westminster and of Ottawa. In them also
the salutary principle that the public money can be voted
only at the instance of the Executive holds good.[1] Authority is concentrated in the Legislature and Ministry, instead
of being scattered among a number of directly elected officials; full accounts of expenditure are presented; members
can interrogate Ministers regarding every item.

There are few Standing Committees, usually eight only;
nor are there many private bills, circumstances which explain the slight demand hitherto made in Canada for those
institutions which have won so much favour in many States
of the American Union, viz. the Popular Initiative in legislation, and the submission to a Referendum, or popular vote,
of acts passed by the State Legislature. The chief sources
of that demand are explained in the chapters relating to
the United States, where it is shown that State legislatures
have lost the confidence of the people because they pass many
private acts for the benefit of the selfish interests of the
rich, and omit to pass some acts desired by large sections
of the people, at the bidding in both sets of cases of powerful
rich men or companies. Hence the Referendum is applied
to kill the " bad bills " and to pass those " good bills " which
the legislature refuses to pass. In Canada this has happened to a much smaller extent, because the rules of procedure make it harder to play such tricks, because there is
no powerful party machine by whose irresponsible control
of a Legislature such bills can be put through, and because
the majority, *i.e.* the Ministerial party, if it should try to
oblige the " selfish interests " aforesaid, would have to bear
the hostile criticism of an alert party Opposition. Assuming the level of public virtue to be much the same among
the legislatures of the two countries there is this difference,
that in an American State Legislature it is not the business
of any one in particular to check and expose a jobbing bill,
whereas in Canada — though it does sometimes happen that
unscrupulous members of both parties agree to " put

[1] In these and other respects Professor Henry Jones Ford compares
the Provincial Legislatures with the State Legislatures in the United
States, to the advantage of the former (*North American Review*, No.
194 (1911)).

through " a job — the leaders of an Opposition have a constantly operating personal motive for detecting and denouncing the misdeeds of any Ministry which should become the tool of rapacious wealth. Apart, however, from private bills there are sundry ways in which the Money Power can pursue its ends by obtaining benefits from representatives or ministries, sometimes through legislation, sometimes through the disposal of contracts or concessions. Suspicion has been rife as to the influence which the owners or promoters of large business enterprises can put forth in these directions, and enough has been unearthed to justify suspicion. Most Canadians say that although these evils are not new they have grown with the growth of the country, but at the same time express the belief, or at least the hope, that the fuller attention recently given to them will lead to their extinction.

The whole of the higher judiciary in Canada acts under Federal authority, although the administration of justice is left to the Provincial governments. Both the judges of the Supreme Court of the Dominion and those of the Provincial Courts are appointed by the Dominion Executive, and are selected from the Bar, the police magistrates only being appointed by the Provincial Governments. Men who have made their mark in politics are, as in England, sometimes chosen, but this, if it sometimes places second-rate men where first-rate men should be, has not injured the impartiality of the Bench, for though a man may owe his appointment to political party influences he ceases to be a politician so soon as he takes his seat, having no promotion to work for, and knowing his post to be secure so long as he does his duty faithfully. English practice has also been followed in making appointments for life (subject to a power of removal on an address by both Houses of the Dominion Parliament), but the salaries assigned even to the High Court Bench, ranging from $7000 to $8000 (with $10,000 for the Chief Justice of the Dominion), though sufficient to secure men of learning and ability, do not always attract the leaders of the Bar. The Courts have, as sound principle requires wherever a legislature is restricted in its powers by the provisions of a constitution enacted by superior author-

ity,[1] the function of passing judgment on the constitutionality of statutes; but it is a function of less scope and less
difficulty than in the United States, because practically the
only questions that arise relate to the respective competence
of Federal Courts and Provincial Courts as defined in the
Canadian Constitution of 1867. Moreover, the final decision in such cases belongs to the Judicial Committee of the
Privy Council in England as the ultimate Court of appeal
in suits brought from the Dominion, or from the highest
Provincial Courts. No such complaints as have been made
in the United States regarding the cutting down of statutes
by judicial decisions are heard in Canada, and this may be
one reason why no one suggests popular election as a proper
mode of choosing judges.

The respect felt for the judiciary, contributes to that strict
enforcement of the criminal as well as to that impartial administration of the civil law which are honourable characteristics of Canada. Lynch law is all but unknown. The
only recent breaches of public order serious enough to rouse
alarm were those which occurred during the great strike at
Winnipeg in 1919, and they are attributed chiefly to the
presence of a mass of recent immigrants from the backward
parts of Eastern Europe. The disorders of mining camps,
once so common in the western United States, are not seen:
nor have bands of robbers infested even the wilder districts,
for the Dominion Government has maintained there a force
of mounted police whose efficiency has been the admiration
of all travellers, and the officers of which have been allowed
— without complaints from the inhabitants — to exercise
pretty wide semi-judicial as well as executive powers. Such
of the aboriginal Indian tribes as remain in the North-
West and in British Columbia have been on the whole hu-
manely and judiciously treated, with few occasions for the
employment of armed force, and with few or none of those
administrative abuses which the United States Government
found it during many years impossible to prevent or cure,
because the administrative posts were so frequently given,
by way of political patronage, to incompetent or untrust-

---

[1] This principle is, however, not followed in Switzerland nor indeed
fully recognized by most lawyers of the European Continent. See
Chapter XXVIII. p. 401, *ante.*

worthy men. Nothing has been more creditable to Canada than the maintenance of so high a standard of law and order over its vast territory. Here, as in Australia, the people are not jealous of executive authority, because Englishmen have been long accustomed to see it exercised under parliamentary supervision.

Of Local Government not much need be said, because it presents few features of special interest. National politics have fortunately not been allowed to enter into the elections of the local councils, in which the chief aim is to find the best men of the neighbourhood. The rural schools are honestly but rather too parsimoniously managed: the towns pay the teachers better and maintain a creditable level of instruction. As regards the smaller municipalities the same holds generally true. In the large cities the conditions are different, and approach those which afflict the great cities of the United States. Where there are large sums to be spent and to be raised by taxation, large contracts to be placed, large opportunities for land speculation offered by the making of city improvements, and where the bulk of the voters have no interest in economical administration, abuses must be expected. Though there is in a few large cities some jobbery, the only grave scandals have occurred in Montreal, where about ten years ago peculation on a great scale was brought home to the municipal authorities. Toronto has a tolerably good record: so have Winnipeg and Vancouver. The local party organization sometimes takes a hand in the election of councillors by putting forward men who have served it, but the voters do not follow slavishly, for their chief desire is to find honest and capable men. It will be remembered that there is not in Canada, not even in the cities, a powerful party machine for choosing candidates, and that there are no administrative officers directly elected by the people except, in many towns, the Mayor.

CHAPTER XXXVI

THE ACTION OF PUBLIC OPINION

In estimating the volume and force of public opinion in Canada as compared with European countries and the United States, one must remember that vast as the country is, its population has not yet reached nine millions, that there are only three or four cities large enough to contain a society of highly educated men who can give a lead in political thinking, and that only three or four universities have as yet risen to that front rank which is represented in Britain by nine or ten and in the United States by more than double that number. There is, moreover, a deep cleft which separates the French-speaking Roman Catholic element, most of it under ecclesiastical influences, from the other elements in the nation, so that on nearly all non-economic subjects divergences must be expected, for where fundamental ideas and habits of thought are concerned, the French mind and the British mind do not move on the same lines, even when both may arrive at similar practical conclusions. One cannot talk of a general opinion of the whole people as one can for most purposes in Great Britain, and could in Australia till the rise of the Labour party. As a set-off to this disadvantage there has been, until recently, little in the way of class opinion, the native Canadian wage-earners having been moved by much the same sentiments as the farmers and traders, neither of the two great parties any more than the other identified with the interests of the rich or of the poor, and neither seriously accused, whatever imputations may be launched during election campaigns, of being the permanent friend or tool of capitalists. Most of those questions of material development which fill so large a place in men's thoughts, find favour or arouse hostility as they affect one particular region of the country, so that upon only a few of them can any common or national view be looked for.

Comparing Canadian opinion with that of the country which most resembles it in economic conditions as well as in democratic sentiment, it is to be noted that whereas in the United States there is much discontent with the working of some institutions, such as the system of elections, the conduct of the Legislatures and the political machine, and the reforming spirit is evoked by a sense of faults which have to be cured, no similar discontent took shape till it found voice recently in the Farmers' movement in Canada. The legislative and administrative machinery had been working smoothly, if not always creditably, and such dissatisfaction as arose impugned not the machinery but the men who worked it. Scarcely any one proposed constitutional changes. The self-governing powers of the Dominion have so long been admitted by the Mother Country that most Canadians, welcoming the fuller recognition given, especially in the negotiation and signing of the Treaties of 1919 and 1920, to the right of their Government to be consulted in and express its views upon all matters affecting the policy of the British Empire as a whole, see no need for altering the present constitutional relations, loose and undefined as they are, of the different parts of that Empire. Such large issues as those of State interference with private enterprise, of the respective merits of State or private owned railroads, of subsidies to steamship lines, of the regulation of immigration, especially as regards Oriental races, are discussed not on grounds of general principle, but rather on the merits of any particular proposal made. Few people stop to think of the principles. What interests them is the concrete instance, and it would be deemed pedantic to suggest that an apparent immediate benefit should be foregone lest deviation from principle should set a dangerous precedent. The press is ably conducted, and exerts quite as much influence as in the United States, but the daily newspapers, even those who speak with authority for their party, have only a slender circulation outside their Provinces, so great are the distances which separate the populous towns. When any grave scandal is brought to light, either in an abuse of its patronage by the Dominion Government or in some unsavoury job committed by one of the Provincial administrations, there is an outcry in the press, and the people put a bad mark against the peccant Minister, perhaps even against the Cabinet of which he is a member, for the people are sound, and hate corruption in whatever form it appears. But they do not see how such things are to be prevented, even by the dismissal of the particular offender, for the fault lies in the men, not in the institutions; so they await the next elections as a means of giving effect to their displeasure, though with no confident hope that those whom the next elections instal in power will be better than their predecessors. Thus there had not arisen before 1914 what could be called any general Reforming movement with a definite programme. Public sentiment has, however, since then enforced one considerable reform, viz. the extension of the Civil Service laws to cover nearly all offices, and thereby virtually extinguish political patronage.

The people watch what goes on in the Parliament at Ottawa and in their Provincial Legislatures with as much attention as can perhaps be expected from busy men in a swiftly advancing country, and they show an abounding party spirit when election day arrives. The constant party struggle keeps their interest alive. But party spirit, so far from being a measure of the volume of political thinking, may even be a substitute for thinking. A foreign critic who asks, as some have done, why the spirit of reform may seem to have lagged, or flagged, in Canada may be reminded of three facts. One is that the evils which rouse the reformers to action, such as has been taken, have usually been flagrant, more destructive of true democracy than have been the faults of which Canadians complain. A second is that in Canada, where the population is small in proportion to the territory, that section of the citizens which is best educated and has leisure for watching and reflecting on the events of politics has been extremely small, scarcely to be found except in a very few urban centres; and a third is that these centres are widely removed from one another, with thinly peopled tracts interposed. Toronto and the towns to the west of it form one such centre, Ottawa and Montreal another. Quebec stands detached to the east; Winnipeg is far away to the North-West, Vancouver and Victoria still farther off on the shores of the Pacific. Most of these cities are of recent growth, and in each of them the number of persons qualified to form and guide opinion is not large. The public opinion they create is fragmentary; it wants that cohesion which is produced by a constant interchange of ideas between those who dwell near one another; it is with difficulty organized to form an effective force. Here, however, time must work for good. The volume of serious political thinking in Canada may be expected to increase steadily with the growth of the leisured class; with the development of the Universities, already gaining more hold on the country; with the increasing numbers and influence of the younger and progressive section of the western farmers, half of them, it is said, university graduates; with the presence of a larger number of men of a high type in the Legislatures; and with a sense among all thoughtful citizens that the problems, especially the social and economic problems, which confront them in our day require more exact and profound study than they have yet received.

Here we get down to bed-rock: here the question arises, Is it a fault characteristic of popular government that the problems referred to receive insufficient study, seeing that in such a government as Canada possesses every opportunity exists for the men the country needs to show their capacity and make their way into parliaments and ministries, and seeing also that the nation, not distracted by questions of foreign policy and having long ago settled all the constitutional controversies, is free to bend its mind upon domestic questions? Has Canada been behind other countries in dealing with social reforms, with labour controversies, with tariffs, with the systematic development of national resources?

I will try to answer this by observing that the most burning of social reforms, that of the sale of intoxicants, has been dealt with, because public opinion took hold of the matter and did not wait for party politicians to trifle with it, and that to the adjustment of labour disputes Canada has made one of the best contributions of recent years in an Act prescribing enquiry and delay when strikes are threatened. The tariff is being still fought over, but so it is in many States, and Canada is so far not behind any other English-speaking country. But it must be admitted that the right method of conserving and developing natural resources either has not yet been found or that it has not been properly put in practice, though no subject is more essential to the welfare of a new country. Here the problem is threefold. The aims generally sought have been (a) to provide the maximum of facilities for turning forests and minerals to the best account, and for the transportation of products; (b) to prevent the absorption by speculators, for their own gain, of these and other sources of natural wealth; (c) to secure for the nation, so far as can be done without checking individual enterprise, the so-called "unearned increment" or additional value which land, minerals, and water power acquire from the general growth of population and prosperity. The pursuit of these three aims raises difficult questions as to the principles which ought to be laid down, questions which demand the patient thought and wide knowledge of the ablest minds that a government can enlist for the purpose. The application of these principles to a series of concrete cases must be entrusted to men of practical gifts, with clear heads and business experience, and with proved integrity also, for temptations arise on every side. Neither the eloquence of a debater nor the arts of the political intriguer are in place. But the British parliamentary system as worked in the self-governing Dominions is not calculated to find the men most needed. The talents it brings to the front are of a different order, and if men of the gifts specially required are found in a ministry, this will generally happen by a lucky chance. Canadian politicians have not, any more than those of Australia and the United States, searched for such men, and taken pains to stock the public service with them. The principles to be adopted would of course require the approval of the legislature, but political pressure ought not to be allowed to disturb their systematic and consistent application. So long as these matters are left to the chances of rough and tumble parliamentary debate or to be settled by secret bargaining between ministers, members, and "the interests," there will be losses to the nation as well as ground for the suspicions to which politicians are now exposed.

As it is one of the most interesting features of the political system of Canada that in it institutions thoroughly English have been placed in a physical and economic environ-

ment altogether unlike that of England and almost identical
with that of the Northern United States, and as the political
phenomena of Canada and those of the United States illustrate one another in many points, it is worth while to summarize here the main points in which the institutions and
the practices of the latter country differ from those of the
no less democratic government of Canada.

The States of the American Union have wider powers
than those of the Canadian Provinces, for the Constitutions
of the Union and of the States impose restrictions on the
National and the State Legislatures, whereas in Canada
there are no such restrictions, except those which arise from
the division in the Federal Constitution of functions between the Dominion and the Provinces.

The President of the United States has a veto upon the
acts of Congress.   There is (in practice) no similar veto on
the acts of the Dominion Parliament.

The Senate is in the United States the more powerful of
the two Houses of the Legislature.   The Canadian Senate
exerts little power.

The State Governor has in nearly all of the States a veto
on the acts of his Legislature.   The Lieutenant-Governor of
a Province has no veto, and the power of disallowance vested
in the Dominion Government is exercised rarely and only
in very special cases.

In every American State the judges of the higher Courts
are either (in a very few States) appointed by the Governor
or elected by the Legislature, or else (in the great majority
of States) elected by the people.   In the Canadian Provinces
they are all appointed by the Dominion Government.

In each of the American States some administrative offices are filled by direct popular election.   In the Canadian
Provinces all such offices are filled by appointment, nominally by the Lieutenant-Governor, practically by the Provincial Ministry, and the only elections (besides the municipal) are those held for the choice of representatives.

In the United States all elective offices, National and
State, are held for a fixed term.   In Canada posts in the
civil service, except those very few whose occupants change
with a change of government, are held for life, subject to
dismissal for fault or incompetence.

In many States of the Union the people vote directly on projects of legislation by means of the Popular Initiative and the Popular Referendum on bills passed by the Legislature, and in some they may vote also for the dismissal or retention of officials, by the Popular Recall. In Canada the Constitutions do not provide for a direct voting by the people on such matters.

In the United States all Legislatures are elected for a fixed term, and cannot be dissolved before it expires. In Canada they may be dissolved by the Executive Ministry before the legal term expires.

In the United States the principle of the Division of Powers between the three Departments (Legislative, Executive, and Judicial) is recognized and to a large extent carried out. In Canada the Executive and Legislative are closely associated.

As a result of this difference, Responsibility is in Canada more concentrated and is more definitely fixed upon a small number of persons than it is in the United States. In Canada, both in the Dominion and in the Provinces, Power rests with and Responsibility attaches to the Cabinet. In the United States, Power and Responsibility are divided between the Executive (President or State Governor) and the Legislature.

In the United States Federal Government the Cabinet are merely the President's servants. In the States of the Union the Governor has no Cabinet and advisers such as the Lieutenant-Governor has in a Canadian Province.

In the United States no Federal official can sit in Congress, no State official in a State Legislature. In Canada Federal Ministers sit in the Dominion, and Provincial Ministers in the Provincial legislatures.

To these constitutional contrasts let us add three other differences of high significance in practice.

There is in Canada no party organization comparable, in strength and its wide extension over the whole field of politics, to that which exists in the party Machines of the United States.

The only Canadian elections fought on party lines are those to the Dominion Parliament and to the Provincial

Legislatures. Local government elections usually turn upon local issues or the personal merits of candidates.

Such influence, now greatly reduced by the creation of the Civil Service Commission, as the Canadian Executive possesses over the bestowal of posts in the public services applies only to appointment in the first instance. Officials are not dismissed on party grounds to make way for persons with party claims, *i.e.* there is no " Spoils System."

Viewed as a whole, the government of Canada, although nominally monarchical, is rather more democratic than that of the United States. No single man enjoys so much power as the President during his four years, for the Prime Minister of the Dominion is only the head of his Cabinet, and though, if exceptionally strong in character and in his hold over his majority in Parliament, he may exert greater power than does a President confronted by a hostile Congress, still he is inevitably influenced by his Cabinet and can seldom afford to break with it, or even with its more important members, while both he and they are liable to be dismissed at any moment by Parliament. The voters are in the United States more frequently summoned to act, but in Canada their power, when they do act at an election, is legally boundless, for their representatives are subject to no such restrictions as American Constitutions impose. Were there any revolutionary spirit abroad in Canada, desiring to carry sweeping changes by a sudden stroke, these could be carried swiftly by Parliamentary legislation.

In winding up this comparison let us pause to note another difference between the United States and Canada which has some historical interest. In the former there has been from early days an almost superstitious devotion to the idea of popular sovereignty, and at some moments enthusiasm for it has risen so high as to make every plan which invokes the direct action of the people act like a spell. In Canada the actual power of the people is just as effective, and the same praises of the people's wisdom are addressed to the people by every orator with a like air of conviction. But in Canada neither the idea in theory nor its application in the incessant exercise of voting power has possessed any special fascination. The Canadians have never, like their neighbours to the south, fallen under the influence of this or any other abstract idea. They are quite content to be free and equal, and masters of their fate, without talking about Liberty and Equality. Having complete control of their administrations through their legislatures, they are therewith content. Popular sovereignty receives here, as in every democracy, all the lip service it can desire. But it is not a self-assertive, obtrusive, gesticulative part of the national consciousness.

CHAPTER XXXVII

To say that a Government is democratic through and through is not to say that it is free from defects. Of those which appear in Canada, some may be set down to the newness of the country, and others either to the form of the institutions or to those faults in their working which spring from the permanent weaknesses of human nature.

Taken as a whole, the institutions are well constructed, being in the main such as long experience has approved in Britain. Canada has made the first attempt to apply the Parliamentary system to a Federation; Australia and South Africa have followed. The experiment has been successful, for the machinery has worked pretty smoothly. Though some say that the Provincial Governments, each in the pursuit of its local interests, try to encroach on the Dominion sphere, while others complain that ten Legislatures and Cabinets, each with its administrative staff, are too many for a population of less than eight and a half millions, yet it must be remembered how difficult it would be to govern from any single centre regions so far apart and so physically dissimilar as the Maritime Provinces, the East Central Provinces, the Western Prairie Provinces, and British Columbia beyond the barrier of the Rocky Mountains.

Upon the working of the institutions, however, both of the Dominion Government and of the Provincial Governments each in its own sphere, divers criticisms may be made which need to be enumerated.

(1) There has been bribery at elections, though extensions of the suffrage have latterly reduced it, and from time to time and in some districts, a recourse to election frauds. Few elections — so it is believed — would stand if either party pressed the law against its opponents. Large sums are spent in contests, illegally as well as legally; Government contractors and persons interested in tariff legislation

contributing to campaign funds, and until the days of Prohibition liquor flowed freely at the expense of candidates or their friends.

(2) How much corruption there is among legislators it is hard to discover, probably less than is alleged, but doubtless more than is ever proved. Members rarely sell their votes, though a good many may be influenced by the prospect of some advantage to themselves if they support a certain Bill or use their influence to secure an appointment or recommend a contract. Two or three Provincial Legislatures enjoy a permanently low reputation: in the others scandals are more sporadic, while the Dominion Parliament maintains a passably good level.

(3) Suspicion has from time to time attached to Ministers in the Dominion as well as in Provincial Cabinets. Charges have been brought of the abuse of official position for purposes of personal gain, which, though seldom established, have obtained sufficient credence to discredit the persons accused and weaken the Administrations of which they were members, the heads of which were thought too lenient in not cutting off those branches which were becoming unhealthy. Calumny has never assailed any Prime Minister. Sir John Macdonald was blamed and forced to resign for having received from a great railway company large contributions to party funds, alleged to have been given in return for benefits to be conferred on it, but he never took anything for himself, and grew no richer through office.

The position may be compared with that seen in the United States for some years after the Civil War, when scandals were frequent, though they were both more frequent and grosser in scale than they are now in Canada, and when public opinion, though shocked, was yet not greatly shocked, because familiarity was passing into an acquiescence in what seemed the inevitable. However, things slowly improved, and the public conscience became as sensitive as it is now in New Zealand and was in England from 1832 till 1914. So it may become in Canada when the pace of material growth slackens, when temptations are less insistent, and men cease to palliate the peccadilloes of those who are " developing the resources of the country."

(4) The power of large financial and commercial interests over legislation and administration has at times been so marked as to provoke a reaction; so public opinion now looks askance at the great Companies, and sometimes deals rather hardly with them.

(5) There is, especially in the Dominion Parliament, which has larger funds to handle, plenty of that form of jobbery which consists in allotting grants of public money to localities with a view to winning political support for the local member or for his party.[1]

(6) The intrusion of National party issues into Provincial Legislatures has resulted in lowering the quality of those bodies, because persons who would not be chosen by the voters on their merits are supported as " good party men," and because their colleagues of the same party are apt to stand by them when they attempt jobs, or are arraigned for jobs committed.

(7) There is, as in all democratic countries, lavish expenditure and waste. The insistence of members who want something for their friends or constituencies, and the multiplication of offices in order to confer favours,[2] are the unceasing foes of economy, while the prosperity of the country makes the people splendidly heedless.

(8) The permanent Civil Service, though not inefficient, and containing some few admirable scientific experts, has not risen to the level of modern requirements, because too little care was taken to secure high competence, and favour prevailed even where special capacity was needed, affecting promotions as well as appointments at entrance. There has not yet been time to test the working of the recently created Civil Service Commission.

(9) The career of politics does not draw to itself enough of the best talent of the nation. This defect is often remarked elsewhere, as in Australia, France, and the United States, but in the last-named country there are obstacles to be overcome which Canada does not present, viz. the power of the nominating party Machine, and the habit of choosing as representatives none but residents in the district. In

---

[1] This is called in the U.S.A. the " Pork Barrel." It is common in New Zealand also, and not infrequent in France.

[2] This is complained of in France also (see Chapter XX. *ante*).

Canada the attractive opportunities opened to ambition by other careers partly account for the phenomenon, the general causes of which all over the world will be discussed in a later Chapter (Part III.).

(10) That decline in the quality of members of which Canadians complain has helped to create, here as elsewhere, a certain want of dignity in the public life of a nation that has already risen to greatness. The imputations which party violence scatters loosely even against men of spotless character must not be taken too seriously: they do not exclude a large measure of good nature and kindly personal intercourse. But they lower the tone of politics, and affect the respect of the citizens for the men who direct the affairs of State, bringing those affairs down to the level of that type of business life in which a man's only motive is assumed to be the making of a good bargain for himself.

Against these criticisms, which have been stated as nearly as possible in the way I have heard them made in Canada, there are to be set certain main ends and purposes of government which democracy has in Canada attained.

Law and order are fully secured everywhere, even in the wildest parts of the West. There is no lynching, and there had been, till the Winnipeg strike of 1919, hardly any unlawful action in labour troubles, on the part either of strikers or of employers. Civil administration goes on smoothly in all the Provinces.

The permanent Civil Service of the Dominion is, taken as a whole, honest, fairly competent, and not given to bureaucratic ways.

The judiciary is able and respected. Criminal justice is dispensed promptly, efficiently, and impartially.

The secondary schools and the elementary schools in the towns are excellent, and particular care has been bestowed on the provision for scientific instruction in agriculture.

Legislation of a public nature is as a rule well considered and well drafted. The finances of the Dominion, apart from those grants to localities already referred to, have been managed with ability though not with economy. National credit stands high, and taxation is not oppressive, having regard to the capacity of the people to bear it. No abuses

have arisen comparable to those which Pension laws have
led to in the United States.

There are those who regard the prohibition of the sale
of intoxicants as an inroad upon individual liberty, however
great the benefit to the community.   Apart from that controversial matter, the citizen is nowhere, not even in Britain
and the United States, better guaranteed in the enjoyment
of his private civil rights.   The Executive interferes as little as possible with him.   Neither does public opinion.

A government may deserve to be credited not only with
the positive successes it has achieved, but with the negative
success of having escaped evils that have vexed other nations living under somewhat similar conditions.   A few of
these may be mentioned.

Demagogism is supposed to be a malady incident to democracies.   Canada has suffered from it less than any other
modern free country except Switzerland.   Some of her
statesmen have been not over-scrupulous, some have deserted
sound principles for the sake of scoring a temporary triumph, but few have played down to the people by lavish
promises or incitements to passion.

Strong as party spirit has been, party organization has
not grown to be, as in the United States, a secret power
bringing the legal government into subjection for its selfish
purposes.

Municipal administration, though in some cities extravagant, has been in most of them tolerably honest and efficient,
not perhaps as pure as in English, Scottish, or Australian
towns, but purer than in the cities of the United States, and
than in some at least of those of France.

The spirit of licence, a contempt of authority, a negligence
in enforcing the laws, have been so often dwelt upon as
characteristic of democracies that their absence from Canada is a thing of which she may well be proud.   To what
shall we ascribe the strength of the Executive, the efficiency
of the police, the strict application of criminal justice, the
habi⁺ of obedience to the law?   Partly no doubt to the
quality of the population, both French-speaking and English-
speaking; but largely also to British traditions.   The habit
was formed under governments that were in those days

monarchical in fact as well as in name, and it has persisted. Though it is often said that the law is strongest when the people feel it to be of their own making — and the maxim is true of Switzerland — there is also another aspect of the matter. The sentiment of deference to legal authority, planted deep in days when that authority was regarded with awe as having an almost sacred sanction, has lived on into a time when the awe and sacredness have departed, and rooted itself in the British self-governing Dominions. It was in England never a slavish sentiment, for the citizen looked to and valued the law as granting protection while it demanded obedience. This is not the only point in which the Common Law of England has resembled the law of Republican Rome. Both, while they enforced submission to duly constituted authority, gave a legal guarantee to the individual citizen for the defence of his personal rights against any form of State power, always associating Liberty with Law.

The student of Canadian affairs who compares what Canadians have accomplished in developing by their own energy the material resources of their magnificent country, creating in many districts a wealth and prosperity which amazes those who remember what seemed the stagnation of half a century ago, feels some disappointment when he surveys the field of politics. Struck by the advantages which popular government enjoys in a country whose people, exceptionally industrious, intelligent, and educated, have a vast area of fertile land at their disposal, and enjoy the comforts of life in far larger measure than do the inhabitants of war-wearied and impoverished Europe, he expects to find democratic government free from the evils that have impeded its path in the Old World. Here, where there are no memories of past wrongs, no dangers to be feared from foreign enemies, no lack of employment, no misery or other ground for class hatreds, ought there not to be honest and efficient administration, general confidence in the government and contentment with the course which public policy has followed? These things, however, he does not find. He does indeed find much to admire and to rejoice at, yet the people, proud as they are of their country, are dissatisfied with their legislatures and their ministries. There is an unmistakable *malaise,* a feeling that something is wrong, even among those who are not prepared to say where the cause lies.

We are apt to expect public as well as private virtue wherever the conditions of life are simple; and it would be a pity if this amiable presumption in favour of human nature were to vanish away. But do the facts warrant the presumption? A virgin soil just cleared of trees may be made to wave with wheat, but it may also cover itself with a luxuriant growth of weeds.

The difficulties due to the differences of race and religion in the population do not explain this discontent, for those differences have not corresponded with party divisions and have not prevented the growth of an ardent national patriotism in both races. When on festive occasions one hears the English-speaking Canadian singing " The Maple Leaf," and the French-speaking Canadian the softer and sweeter air " O Canada, mon pays, mes amours," one perceives they are both alike expressions of devotion to Canada, and of sanguine hopes for a happy future. Whatever political difficulties may arise in the Dominion Government from the necessity of keeping the two racial and religious elements in good humour do not arise in Provinces where one or other element is entirely preponderant. Administrative errors, financial waste, the rather low tone of public life in three or four Provinces, cannot be thus accounted for; and they are the same defects that are complained of in Dominion Government. May there not, however, be certain conditions incident to a new country which help to explain the dissatisfaction which seems to be felt by thoughtful Canadians?

The charge most frequently brought against Canadian statesmen is that of Opportunism. It is a word which may be used, with no dyslogistic implication, to describe the action of a statesman who finds himself obliged to postpone measures which he thinks more important to others which he thinks less important, because he can carry the latter and cannot carry the former. In politics one must use the flowing tide, one must turn to the best account a people's fluctuating moods. But the term is more frequently meant to impute to a politician the absence of convictions, or at any rate of any fixed policy based upon principle, a trimming of

the sails to catch every passing breeze so as to retain office
by making the most of whatever chance of support may come
from any quarter.   If this latter kind of Opportunism has
been frequent in Canada and has told unfavourably upon
its public life a reason is not far to seek.   Since 1867 the
large and permanent issues of policy, such as that of Protection against Free Trade, have been comparatively few, and
have sometimes been allowed to slumber; and in their absence the smaller but nearer issues by which votes are captured have occupied the field.   Such were questions relating
to public works, including that of transportation facilities,
particularly by the construction and financing of railways.
To a country of vast spaces like Canada canals and such
facilities are of supreme importance, but they are treated as
questions not so much of principle as of practical needs, involving the claims of different localities in which local wishes
have to be regarded.   There have been many occasions in
other ways also in which questions of material benefit to a
district, or a city, or a great undertaking, or a strong financial group came before ministries and legislatures.   As the
country grew, demands for assistance from public funds
went on growing, and those who planned enterprises for
their own gain had occasions for securing benevolent help,
or acquiescence, on the part of Government, whether Federal
or Provincial.   Administrations placed in the middle of this
struggle for favours demanded by the representatives of the
districts affected, used their opportunities to strengthen themselves in the country and make sure of seats that had been
doubtful, while now and then individual ministers as well
as members were not above turning to personal account the
knowledge or the influence they possessed.   In every country
a game played over material interests between ministers, constituencies and their representatives, railway companies and
private speculators is not only demoralizing to all concerned,
but interferes with the consideration of the great issues of
policy on a wise handling of which a nation's welfare depends.   Fiscal questions, labour questions, the assumption
by the State of such branches of industry as railroads or
mines and the principles it ought to follow in such work as
it undertakes — questions like these need wide vision, clear
insight, and a firmness that will resist political pressure and

adhere to the principles once laid down. These qualities have been wanting, and the people have begun to perceive the want. In the older countries of Europe there is a body of trained opinion, capable of criticizing and more or less even of controlling the action of Governments, and the upper ranks of the Civil Service are a reservoir of knowledge and experience upon which ministers can draw. Canadian ministries enjoy these advantages in slighter measure, and the element of educated opinion is dispersed over an enormous country in cities far from the Federal capital and far also from one another. That opinion has not been strong enough nor concentrated enough to keep legislators and administrators up to the mark in efficiency or in a sense of public duty.

This last-named function may seem incumbent not on the few but on the many, that is on the great mass of honest and sensible citizens. But how are they placed? The worthy hard-working farmer in Ontario or Alberta reads in his newspaper attacks on Ministerial jobs, but as the newspaper of the opposite party denies or explains away the facts, he does not know what to believe. The seat of his Provincial legislature is far off, and Ottawa still further. If some gross blunder or crying scandal is brought home he may punish the offending Ministry by voting against it when next he gets the chance, but the candidate for whom he votes may be no better than the member his vote rejects, and may support a Ministry of no whiter a hue.

In every country, whatever its form of government, where the rapid exploitation of natural resources drags administrators and legislators to an abnormal extent into the sphere of business, opportunities cannot but arise for bringing exceptional temptations to bear on those who have favours to dispense, and the atmosphere which surrounds the tempters and the tempted grows unhealthy. This has happened from time to time in England and in the United States also. Their experience warrants the hope that when normal conditions return, and the air has cleared, the temptations will be reduced and the larger issues of policy again become the chief occupations of legislatures. As the country fills up and the class that is enlightened and thoughtful grows large enough to make national opinion a more vigilantly effective force, the tone of public life may rise, as it rose in England after the middle of the eighteenth century and in the United States after 1880. There are already signs of a keener sensitiveness and a stronger reforming purpose in the general body of the citizens.

The political faults visible in new countries may be disappointing, but they are more curable than those of old countries, so historians note with a graver concern symptoms of decline in European peoples to which the world had looked as patterns of wisdom or honour. Yet these also may be due to the sudden advent of new conditions bringing dangers hitherto unsuspected, and these, too, may pass away as one generation succeeds another. A young country like Canada must be expected to have some of the weaknesses of adolescence as well as the splendid hopefulness and energy which make the strength of youth. The great thing after all by which popular government stands or falls must be the rightmindedness and intelligence of the people. These Canada has.

Striking the balance between what democracy has done for her and what it has failed to do, it must not be forgotten that the coexistence, not only in the Dominion as a whole but in several provinces, of two races differing in religion as well as in language, contained the menace of what might have become a real danger. Think of Ireland! Canada has so far avoided that danger by the elastic nature of her institutions and the patriotic prudence of her statesmen. To those who have been watching the wild and wayward excesses to which the passion of nationality has been running in Europe, this will seem no small achievement, no small witness to the wisdom of the Canadian people and the spirit of mutual consideration and good feeling which the practice of free self-government can form. As the other general lessons which a political philosopher may draw from the history of democracy in Canada have been already indicated, one only seems to need further enforcement. It is drawn from a comparison of the experience of the United States. The Canadian Constitution was an adaptation of the British Constitution to the circumstances of a new country in which a Federal and not a unitary government was needed. It reproduced, with variations, certain features of the United States Federal system which experience had approved, while seeking to avoid the defects that experience had disclosed. It followed in other points the parliamentary and Cabinet system of Britain; and — what was no less important — it carried over into Canada the habits and traditions by which that parliamentary system had thriven. Hardly anything in it is traceable to any abstract theory. The United States Constitution was also created partly on the ancient and honoured principles of the English Common Law, and partly on the lines of the self-governing institutions which had worked well in the North American Colonies before their separation from the Mother Country.[1] But both the Federal Constitution and those of the several States of the Union were also largely affected, if not in spirit yet in form, by abstract conceptions, especially by the dogmas of Popular Sovereignty and of the so-called " Separation of Powers." [2]   Experience has shown that those constitutional provisions in which the influence of these doctrines went furthest are those whose working has proved least satisfactory, both in the National and in the State Governments.[3]   Here, as elsewhere, history teaches that it is safer to build on the foundations of experience and tradition than upon abstract principles, not that the abstract principles can be ignored — far from it — but because it is seldom possible to predict what results they will give when applied under new conditions. Philosophy is no doubt the guide of life. But political philosophy is itself drawn from the observation of actual phenomena, and the precepts it gives are not equally and similarly applicable everywhere: if they are to succeed in practice they must be adjusted to the facts of each particular case.

This suggests the remark that the experience of Canada has been short. Only half a century has elapsed since the

[1] Visitors to Canada are apt to be misled by the external resemblances to the United States, in such things as the aspect of the streets, the hotels, the newspapers, the railway cars, the currency, into supposing the people to have been more affected by influences from their southern neighbours than is really the case. In character and in political habits there are marked differences.

[2] This subject will be more fully explained and discussed in the chapters on the United States.

[3] Such as frequent elections, short terms of office, the election of judges by the people, the relations of Congress to the President.

Federal system of the Dominion was set to work. Since then the country has been developing and population has been growing at an increasing rate of speed. Though immigration is not likely to change the beliefs and tendencies of the inhabitants, and though the proportions of the French-speaking and English-speaking elements appear likely to remain for some time the same as they now are, so too the preponderance of the rural population over the urban, of the agricultural over the manufacturing, though it will diminish with time, as it is already diminishing, will apparently remain because depending on the conditions Nature has created. Neither is there any present prospect that institutions which have gained the general approval of the people will be fundamentally changed. But as economic problems arise, threatening internal strife and as intellectual movements are propagated from one nation to another, new ideas inspire new political aspirations and find their expression in politics. This much may be said: Canada is well prepared by the character of her people, by their intelligence and their law-abiding habits, to face whatever problems the future may bring, finding remedies for such defects as have disclosed themselves in her government, and making her material prosperity the basis of a pacific and enlightened civilization.

END OF VOL. I

13829

PRINTED IN THE UNITED STATES OF AMERICA